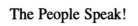

The People Speak!

Social History, Popular Culture, and Politics in Germany

Geoff Eley, Series Editor

*A History of Foreign Labor in Germany, 1880–1980: Seasonal Workers/
Forced Laborers/Guest Workers*
  Ulrich Herbert, translated by William Templer

*Reshaping the German Right: Radical Nationalism and Political Change
after Bismarck*
  Geoff Eley

*The Politics of the Body in Weimar Germany: Women's Reproductive Rights
and Duties*
  Cornelie Usborne

The Stigma of Names: Antisemitism in German Daily Life, 1812–1933
  Dietz Bering

*Forbidden Laughter: Popular Humor and the Limits of Repression in
Nineteenth-Century Prussia*
  Mary Lee Townsend

From Bundesrepublik *to* Deutschland: *German Politics after Unification*
  Michael G. Huelshoff, Andrei S. Markovits, and Simon Reich, editors

*The People Speak! Anti-Semitism and Emancipation in
Nineteenth-Century Bavaria*
  James F. Harris

The People Speak!

Anti-Semitism and Emancipation in Nineteenth-Century Bavaria

James F. Harris

Ann Arbor

THE UNIVERSITY OF MICHIGAN PRESS

Copyright © by the University of Michigan Press 1994
All rights reserved
Published in the United States of America by
The University of Michigan Press
Manufactured in the United States of America

1997 1996 1995 1994   4 3 2 1

A CIP catalogue record for this book is available from the British Library.

Library of Congress Cataloging-in-Publication Data

Harris, James F., 1940–
    The people speak! : anti-Semitism and emancipation in nineteenth–
century Bavaria / James F. Harris.
        p.   cm. — (Social history, popular culture, and politics in
Germany)
    Includes bibliographical references and index.
    ISBN 0-472-10437-3 (alk. paper)
    1. Antisemitism—Germany—History. 2. Jews—Germany—Bavaria—
Emancipation. 3. Jews—Germany—Bavaria—Public opinion.
4. Public opinion—Germany—Bavaria. 5. Bavaria (Germany)—Politics
and government—1777–1918. 6. National socialism. 7. Germany—
Ethnic relations.   I. Title.   II. Series.
DS146.G4H37   1993
305.892'4043—dc20   93-39955
                                                                           CIP

For
Catherine Ann Silvagni Harris

Acknowledgments

It is a pleasure to be able to thank all of the people and institutions that helped me in the research and writing of *The People Speak!* The University of Maryland, College Park, provided sabbatical time off, travel and research support, and assistance with the processing of the final manuscript. The National Endowment for the Humanities provided support for travel and research. In Munich the Bavarian Hauptstaatsarchiv, the Geheimes Hausarchiv, the Staatsarchiv Oberbayern, the Landtagsarchiv, the Staatsbibliothek, and the Staatsarchiv Würzburg were more than generous in providing access to holdings and advice. My thanks to all.

Numerous individuals provided important assistance. Two colleagues read the entire manuscript. James S. Cockburn made numerous stylistic suggestions and raised significant questions about the content. Marsha Rozenblit's queries and suggestions added to nearly every page and testify to her own expertise in modern Jewish History in Central Europe. I am indebted to Karl Schleunes of the University of North Carolina, Greensboro, who read and commented on the manuscript, especially for suggestions relating to chapters 2 and 3. Ms. Mary Ann Coyle, a graduate student, made many valuable suggestions for the manuscript. Professor John J. McCusker, formerly a colleague at Maryland and now Halsell Distinguished Professor of American History at Trinity University, San Antonio, Texas, gave excellent advice on the tables. Karl Stowasser, another colleague at Maryland, provided excellent assistance with the transcription and translation of several of the original documents. Antje Weger assisted with the tabulation of petitions and Ms. Susan Oetken and Ms. Darlene King helped in converting my obsolete disks into readable form. My sincere thanks to Joyce Harrison and the copyediting staff of the University of Michigan Press as well as to two anonymous readers who made excellent suggestions for improving the manuscript. I am indebted to all who contributed, but I alone am responsible for the final product.

Contents

Abbreviations

AAZ	*Augsburger Allgemeine Zeitung*
AfS	*Archiv für Sozialgeschichte*
AHR	*American Historical Review*
APZ	*Augsburger Postzeitung*
AT	*Augsburger Tagblatt*
AZdJ	*Allgemeine Zeitung des Judtenums*
BfdL	*Blätter für deutsche Landesgeschichte*
BLBo	*Bayerische Landbote*
BLBö	*Bayerische Landbötin*
BZ	*Bamberger Zeitung*
CEH	*Central European History*
DD	District Director
EBo	*Eilbote*
GHA	Geheimes Hausarchiv
GSR	*German Studies Review*
HbG	*Handbuch der bayerischen Geschichte*
H-pBkD	*Historisch-politische Blätter für das katholische Deutschland*
HStA	Hauptstaatsarchiv
HZ	*Historische Zeitschrift*
JFräLG	*Journal für fränkische Landesgeschichte*
JMH	*Journal of Modern History*
JSS	*Journal of Social Science*
KdA	Kammer der Abgeordneten
KdR	Kammer der Reichsräthe
L	*Lechbote*
LB	Lower Bavaria
LBIY	*Leo Baeck Institute Yearbook*
LFr	Lower Franconia
MF	Ministry of Finance
MFr	Middle Franconia and Mittelfranken

MFräZ	*Mittelfränkische Zeitung*
MInn	Ministry of the Interior
MJu	Ministry of Justice
MK	Ministry of Commerce
NB	Niederbayern
NFräZ	*Neue Fränkische Zeitung*
NN	*Neueste Nachrichten*
OB	Oberbayern
OFr	Oberfranken
OPf	Oberpfalz
Pal	Palatinate
Pf	Pfalz
RA	Regierungs Abgabe
RZ	*Regensburger Zeitung*
StAO	Staatsarchiv Oberbayern
StAW	Staatsarchiv Würzburg
Sw	Swabia and Schwaben
UB	Upper Bavaria
UF	Upper Franconia
UFr	Unterfranken
UP	Upper Palatinate
VBo	*Volksbote für den Bürger und Landmann*
VBö	*Volksbötin*
WStLBo	*Würzburger Stadt- und Landbote*
ZAA	*Zeitschrift für Agrarsoziologie und Agrargeschichte*
ZfbL	*Zeitschrift für bayerische Landesgeschichte*
ZGJD	*Zeitschrift für die Geschichte des Judens in Deutschland*

Chapter 1

Introduction

This book is a study of the effect of public opinion on state policy in the form of popular opposition to the Bavarian government's proposal in 1849 to make Jews equal to Christian Bavarians. To explicate the political issues, I study the bureaucratic context in which that decision was made and the communal context in which it was opposed. In this sense I describe and analyze the clash between the central state government and the local communities of Bavaria. Since the legislation directly affected Jews and since the opposition to Jewish emancipation was highly anti-Semitic, I begin with a description of the situation of Bavarian Jews and then analyze the attitudes, ideas, and organization of the opposition to emancipation. Because anti-Semitism, especially German anti-Semitism, is commonly perceived as leading to the Holocaust, I attempt to relate the anti-Semitism of the campaign against Jewish emancipation in 1849–50 to later stages in its history.

The focal point of the story occurred on 14 December 1849, when the lower house of the Bavarian Parliament, by a vote of ninety-one to forty, passed a bill for Jewish emancipation that mandated complete equality between Jews and Christians. Essentially the bill repealed a law of 1813 that defined and restricted Jewish life. King Maximilian II's ministries drafted and submitted the legislation to the lower house of Parliament, and his ministers, led by Freiherr Ludwig von der Pfordten, warmly and intelligently supported it. Most of the deputies voting for the bill were liberals or democrats, and the generally progressive newspaper press strongly endorsed their action. No other German state had initiated such far-reaching legislation on Jews. And it was not part of the legislation that had been quickly passed due to revolutionary pressure in 1848. Rather, it came after the defeat of the revolutionary forces in Baden in the summer of 1849 and after Bavaria rejected both the Basic Rights and the Constitution proposed by the German National Parliament meeting in Frankfurt am Main. The bill's passage in the lower house ended one of the longest parliamentary debates about Jews in nineteenth-century Germany.

News of passage of the bill for emancipation by the lower house came, as several petitions later noted, like a flash of lightning or a clap of thunder. At least it appeared so to many Christian Bavarians who could not believe that such action was possible. Reaction to the passage of the bill ranged from euphoria among Jews to anger and bitterness among broad elements of the Christian population. No sooner had the vote been taken than ardent opponents began to work to secure its demise in the upper house, basing their activity on the high level of popular antagonism toward the bill. A popular movement against emancipation, in this case against full equality of Jews with Christians, sprang up overnight and sent to the upper house hundreds of petitions requesting rejection. I discovered in the Bavarian State Archives 552 separate petitions from over 1,762 individual communities, which reveal why a very large part of the Bavarian population opposed Jewish emancipation. No other source for the study of popular attitudes toward Jews in Germany compares in size and content to these petitions. Although a number of motives emerge from analysis of their contents, anti-Semitism was the most important.

The overwhelming majority of the petitions were communal rather than personal in nature. Communities of all sizes and from all corners of Bavaria submitted petitions. Using local governmental reports from Lower Franconia, I describe in detail the communal role in the petition process in the region possessing the largest Jewish population in Bavaria. Study of this aspect sheds light on the roles of the central government and local communities in the campaign. On one level Maximilian II's administration supported the legislation and was not interested in seeing it die in an upper house catalyzed into opposition by the masses. But the communities perceived the central government as infringing on their communal rights.

The petition campaign culminated in a debate and vote for rejection in the upper house in February 1850. After defeat the government submitted a new proposal relating only to legal equality in the parliamentary session of 1851. But the most criticized and hated clauses of the 1813 law, those that restricted the admission of Jews to residency in communities and the accompanying restrictions on their right to marry, remained unchanged until 1861. The defeat in 1850 made the government more reluctant to push for complete change, despite the attempt it had made in 1849, while parliamentary and journalistic forces continued and even increased their support for repeal. The circumstances of the 1861 law show that the government's motivation behind its submission of new legislation for partial repeal of the residency restrictions was again closely linked to larger political events. Bavarian Jews were not fully emancipated until after the unification of Germany in 1870.

Remarkably, most of the story outlined above is unknown to the historical community. Only the debates in parliament have attracted any attention at all, and most analysts have treated them out of the wider context. Stefan Schwarz, the author of the standard history of the legal status of Jews in Bavaria, did not use the governmental files in Unterfranken, the petitions in the central archives in Munich, or several of the governmental and personal files relating to Jewish emancipation.[1] Schwarz therefore had great difficulty understanding the overall development of legislation for Jewish emancipation. And the most recent treatment of the debates by Karl-Thomas Remlein has progressed no further.[2]

Intent on explaining the growth of anti-Semitism in the first half of the nineteenth century, Elonore Sterling also found it difficult to deal with the parliamentary bill of 1849, because it was so pro-Jewish. The apparent paradox affected her understanding of the files of provincial reports on opinion relating to Jews, and she concluded, inaccurately, that the government, after investigating the campaign, had concluded that it had been fabricated. She did not know of the local reports in Lower Franconia, made no use of the press, and did not find the petitions—her statement that they did not exist has been allowed to stand for more than three decades.[3] In the old but standard history of Jewish struggle for emancipation in Bavaria, Dr. Adolf Eckstein devoted barely a paragraph to the bill, noting only its rejection by the upper house.[4]

Until very recently the entire history of the Jews in Bavaria has been relegated to passing references and footnotes, has been "marginalized" in the strict sense of that term. The best examples may be drawn from the most basic reference work on Bavarian history, the *Handbuch der bayerischen Geschichte*, vol. 4[1-2], *Das neue Bayern 1800–1970* (Munich, 1974), edited by Max Spindler. In these comprehensive volumes, Jews merit no separate treatment. While it may be argued that there were few Jews at any point in Bavarian history, it would seem hard to argue that they are not important to our understanding of the larger society. For the nineteenth century, the references are few and scattered—the comments on the 1813 Edict may be taken as representative. Thus E. Weis notes only that the law of 1813 gave Jews "freedom of belief" and, through grant of residency, at least an "improvement in their legal position"; W. Zorn refers to the 1813 law as the "emancipation law" that succeeded in drawing Jews out of their "special legal position" but denied them complete citizen and commercial equality until 1861, "when they could finally run inns and breweries."[5] There was far more to it than that.

Much of the best new research in Bavarian Jewish history stems from projects supervised by historians at regional universities in Bavaria. The best examples are the publication of a richly illustrated guide to an exhibition of Jewish history in Bavaria and an accompanying set of essays.[6] However, most of these projects, which probe the rich holdings of the Bavarian archives, date from only the last decade, for the most part from the last five years.

No one has studied the role of the newspaper press in the campaign against Jewish emancipation. The holdings are rich but unused. And here, too, anomalies occur. For example, one could argue that there would have been no campaign against Jewish emancipation without Ernst Zander, the editor of the *Volksbote,* and that the campaign's success was one of his own great personal triumphs. But these activities find no place in a published dissertation on Zander.[7]

Most of the following chapters document the emergence of a mass movement in Bavaria devoted to defeat of Jewish emancipation. In organization and tactics it was political, despite the fact that political parties in the modern sense were in their infancy in Germany and nonexistent in much of Bavaria. But the petition campaign was not a unique phenomenon, coming as it did on the heels of similar activity in 1848 by democrats and in early 1849 by conservatives. As part of a broader dissatisfaction with the democratic revolution of 1848, irritation with the government and lower house exerted pressure on popular sentiment alongside fear of and hostility toward Jews.

Several new theses emerge from the story of this episode in Jewish emancipation and of the opposition to it. Most importantly, "modern" anti-Semitism existed at the time of the 1848 revolutions in organized, political form and not merely as scattered riots in small towns in Baden or as wildcat speeches by one or two members of the Frankfurt Parliament. There was no anti-Semitic political party, but then there were no political parties as such until several years later. The overwhelming majority of historians date the emergence of "modern" anti-Semitism from the 1870s at the earliest. The term *anti-Semitism* was not used in the 1850s, appearing for the first time a generation later. Only a very few, among them Sterling, Reinhard Rürup, and Paul Lawrence Rose,[8] take exception to this periodization, and then only in a limited way. The emergence of modern anti-Semitism must be dated much earlier in the nineteenth century than historians currently accept.

In addition, the campaign of 1849–50 against Jewish emancipation shows that anti-Semitic ideas permeated the Catholic population of Bavaria, making it difficult to continue to hold the view that Catholics in Germany and Bavaria lacked the strong anti-Semitic tradition of Protestants in Prussia and the north. The existence of popular anti-Semitism in midcentury also forces us to look backward to examine the linkages between the treatment of Jews in the eighteenth and nineteenth centuries rather than to continue to try to understand the attitude toward Jews in the nineteenth century by reference to the Nazis and the Holocaust of the twentieth century.

The failure of Jewish emancipation in 1849–50 and the success of its opponents, not all of them anti-Semites, were part of the emergence of democratic political activity. Peasants and artisans, clergy and teachers, and mayors and aristocrats thought of Jewish emancipation as part of the damaging legislation of the revolution, as yet another consequence of the "March events" of 1848. Use of petitions to oppose Jewish emancipation was not an original tactic politically; similar forces had organized in a similar way only months earlier to defeat the Basic Rights and the Frankfurt Constitution. The great difference between the two movements lies in the ironic fact that King Maximilian's government strongly opposed the Basic Rights and Constitution but equally strongly supported the emancipation of the Jews. Thus, to oppose emancipation, conservatives had to oppose a conservative government. Based on their success in using popular force to counter what they perceived as a tilt to the left in early 1849, some conservatives saw democratic methods as useful tools for their own purposes later in the same year.

It was (and is) startling that the petition campaign against emancipation was democratically organized. Anti-Semitic conservatives and others on the right laughed at liberal and democratic criticism of the organizing activities of Catholic political organizations, newspapers, and even local priests because those criticizing had used exactly the same methods the year before for their own very different goals. Thus, democratic forms were used for nondemocratic purposes in 1849–50 in ways that very strongly suggest comparison to the *Bund der Landwirte* in the 1890s and national socialism in the 1920s. The use of democracy against itself, a key element of later fascist practice, may be found in action in Bavaria in 1849–50. Moreover, the campaign took place in a relatively open political atmosphere. Restrictions on the press and on political organizations emerged just as the debate over Jewish emancipation began in the upper house.

Finally, the events of 1848–51 show that the Bavarian central state administration and especially its bureaucratic and political leaders, Freiherr Ludwig von der Pfordten and his fellow minsters, led the way in promoting emancipation. This was a major departure from previous policy, and both the government's actions and von der Pfordten's motivations are difficult to unravel. Even though the 1849 bill failed, it must be remembered that the attempt was in pursuit of complete equality, something that most German states did not secure until 1867 or later. The support by the state, the parliament, and the press was not merely pragmatic and halfhearted. Those favoring emancipation spoke strongly and cogently on behalf of Jews, Jewry, and equality. One of the ways to understand the relation between a state and the larger society it governs is to study the way it treats its minorities, and the process of emancipation in Bavaria from 1813 to 1871 tells us a great deal about both the Bavarian state and its society.

Several aspects of the story and analyses that follow involve the problem

of modernity. Many historians, especially modernization theorists, assume a
basic, internal logic to the modern world. To them "modern" anti-Semitism
is an oxymoron meriting the term *paradox*. Modernization theorists explain
this phenomenon by arguing the incompleteness of the modernizing process
at any particular time. Students of anti-Semitism either see race as providing
the "modern" element in that ideology, or, as Rürup and Thomas Nipperdey
do, focus on anti-Semitism as a by-product of "modern" politics or as a
reaction to "modern" economic developments.[9] Confronted by the existence
of contradictions within the modern, as, for example, in the emergence of
antidemocratic forms from within democracy itself, historical figures and
historians react in varying ways. One response has been to deny any instability in the modern, that is, to reject whatever threatens one's own view of a
proper stability.[10] While both left and right accept the opportunity presented
by the instability in the modern, the center prefers the solidity of a closed
system. In the following chapters, I will attempt to demonstrate how it
happened that an antirevolutionary conservative state championed Jewish
equality with Christians, while most people, expressing their will democratically, successfully opposed the same effort with the help of a handful of
aristocrats, journalists, and communal leaders.

NOTES

1. Stefan Schwarz, *Die Juden in Bayern im Wandel der Zeiten* (Munich and
Vienna, 1963), 283.
2. See Karl-Thomas Remlein, "Der Bayerische Landtag und die Judenemanzipation nach der Revolution," in H.-H. Brandt, ed., *Zwischen Schutzherrschaft und
Emanzipation: Studien zur Geschichte der mainfränkischen Juden im 19. Jahrhundert.*
Mainfränkische Studien, vol. 39 (Würzburg, 1987), 139–208.
3. Sterling, *Judenhass: Die Anfänge des politischen Antisemitismus in Deutschland (1815–1850)* (Frankfurt am Main, 1969), 215 n. 134; originally published as *Er
ist wie Du: Aus der Frühgeschichte des Antisemitismus in Deutschland (1815– 1850)*
(Munich, 1956); Remlein, "Landtag," 177, repeats Sterling's speculation that they
were burnt in World War II.
4. Dr. Adolf Eckstein, *Der Kampf der Juden um ihre Emanzipation in Bayern*
(Fürth im Bayern, 1905).
5. For Weis, see "Die Reformen in Staat, Verwaltung und Gesellschaft unter
Montgelas (1799–1817)" in Spindler, ed., *HbG*, 4[1]: 51; for Zorn, see "Die Sozialentwicklung der Nichtagrarischen Welt (1806–1970)" *HbG*, 4[2]: 868.
6. Manfred Treml, Joseph Kirmeier, and Evamaria Brockhoff, eds., *Geschichte
und Kultur der Juden in Bayern* (Munich, 1988) and Bernward Deneke et al., eds.,
Siehe der Stein schreit aus der Mauer: Geschichte und Kultur der Juden in Bayern
(Nuremberg, 1989). And see the many works cited in ch. 2.

7. Elmar Roeder, *Der Konservative Journalist Ernst Zander und die politischen Kämpfe seines "Volksboten"* (Munich, 1971); Zander also does not appear in Remlein, "Landtag."

8. Paul Lawrence Rose, *Revolutionary Antisemitism in Germany: From Kant to Wagner* (Princeton, N.J.,1990), goes too far in asserting that all revolutionaries were anti-Semitic but establishes that many were. See my review in *AHR* 97, no. 2 (April, 1992): 571–72.

9. Discussed at more length in ch. 8.

10. Jane Caplan, "Postmodernism, Poststructuralism, and Deconstruction: Notes for Historians," in *CEH* 226, nos. 3–4 (Sept.-Dec. 1989): 269–270; for a broader consideration, see Steven Laurence Kaplan, "Long-Run Lamentations: Braudel on France," *JMH* 63, no. 2 (June 1991): 341–61. The same is true of such phenomena as "popular" conservatism, bureaucratic reform, and right-wing support for a free press and the right of petition.

Chapter 2

Jewish Life and Christian Social Engineering

Thomas Nipperdey's *German History* opens with the statement "At the beginning was Napoleon."[1] What was true for Germany as a whole was even
more accurate for Bavaria and her Jews. After all, Bavaria more than doubled
in size as an ally of Napoleon, managing to retain and even add to her
enlarged status in the settlement of 1815. Prussia did not gain nearly so much
territory or population proportionately as Bavaria did at the Congress of
Vienna. But the differences separating the two states went well beyond mere
size and rate of territorial growth. While Hohenzollern rule was firmly in
place in Prussia, Bavaria changed dynasty in 1799 when Elector Karl Theodor died and his cousin Maximilian Joseph of the branch house of Pfalz-
Zweibrücken succeeded to the throne.[2] Rather than weakness, this change
not only brought to the throne a more dynamic monarch, Elector Maximilian
Joseph, who became Maximilian I in 1806, but far more importantly it
brought into his service the brilliant and powerful Maximilian Joseph Freiherr
(after 1809, Graf) Montgelas.[3] As foreign minister from 1799 to 1817, as
minister of finance from 1803 to 1806 and 1809 to 1817, and as minister of
the interior from 1806 to 1817, Montgelas wielded vast influence over the
Bavarian state. His achievement was to produce a "modern" Bavaria charac-
terized by its compact, mostly contiguous territory, a centralized state structure, the secularization of ecclesiastical landownership, and a liberal constitution.

At the very beginning of his tenure in office in 1799, Montgelas faced
a crisis in the form of threats from Austria and France to the scattered
Wittelsbach holdings. Like other south German states, but unlike Prussia,
Bavaria was able to profit from a close relationship to expansionist Napoleonic France. After a roller-coaster ride from 1800 to 1815 in which Bavarian
holdings changed radically in relation to French fortunes, Bavaria emerged
from the Congress of Vienna with both a substantial increase in land and a

larger population in a much more compact kingdom. Gone were holdings in the Tyrol, in Austria, and, save for the Pfalz, in the Rhineland; in their place Bavaria received numerous pieces of Franconia, Swabia, and the Upper Palatinate. The enlarged state was also much more diverse religiously (more Protestant) and economically (more crafts and commerce in urban settings), and Montgelas tied them together with reforms from above.

Reform did not come as a consequence of expansion. Montgelas had already proposed reform of the state, bureaucracy, and society well before the crises and successes of 1800 to 1815.[4] Bavaria, unlike Prussia, had not experienced governmental enlightenment and the establishment of an absolutist state in the eighteenth century. Montgelas saw reform as the necessary antidote to obscurantism, backwardness, corruption, and inefficiency. At a time when Baron vom Stein and others in Prussia railed at the weaknesses and faults of centralized absolutism, Montgelas and his compatriots were introducing just such a "modern" absolutist structure in Bavaria. This explains why Stein's reforms sought to return control to local governments in Prussia at exactly the same time that Montgelas systematically subordinated similar communities to the state in Bavaria. It also explains why local self-government became a part of the liberal program in Prussia, while in Bavaria local communities resented the loss of power to the "reforming" state and generally supported one or another part of the political right.[5]

In Bavaria, centralization meant the expropriation of ecclesiastical, that is, Catholic, lands, and it stripped communities of rights often dating to the middle ages in the name of "constitutional" modernization. This structure was constitutional because many of the early reforms came through and with the Constitution of 1808, which, although decreed and providing for no parliament, was nonetheless a constitution.[6] Additionally, these reforms gave more rights to Protestants and Jews, present in larger numbers as the result of the acquisition of new lands. The capstone of Montgelas's creation was the Constitution of 1818, although it came a year after his dismissal. Hardly democratic, the parliament provided for in this constitution nevertheless represented all classes and castes in Bavaria except Jews and committed the king to a budget approved by parliament.

But what was welcome progress to many Protestants, Jews, bureaucrats, large cities, and merchants was anathema to small communities, Catholics, the church, and former feudal lords. These groups, broadly speaking, later constituted the two sides in the fight over Jewish emancipation. Enemies of the Montgelas reforms, led by the Crown Prince Ludwig, after 1825 Ludwig I, forced Montgelas out of office in 1817 during the wave of conservative reaction following the end of the Congress of Vienna. It is noteworthy and ironic that while momentum secured a promised constitution and parliament in Bavaria, a similar promise lay dormant in Prussia until 1848.

Yet the conservative reaction of the post-1815 era, while strong enough in Bavaria to topple Montgelas, never really reversed any substantial part of his package of reforms other than to return some communal rights through the *Gemeindeedikt* of 1818. The post-Montgelas order was best represented by King Ludwig, who came to epitomize a "stand-pat" policy. Embedded in the midst of the Montgelas reforms was the Jew Law of 1813, which also seemed to promise further progressive modifications but which did not change at all until 1851 and was substantively weakened only in 1861. That law and the Jews it defined are central to this study.

Jewish Life in Christian Bavaria

The rapid growth of the Jewish population in Bavaria coincided not only with the Napoleonic wars but with the rise of a modernizing, centralized state. Bavaria became a kingdom in 1806, the year of the demise of the Holy Roman Empire. Under King Maximilian I, Bavaria faced the problem of incorporating extensive new lands containing diverse populations into a new state in a reformist period. The "Old Bavarian" provinces of Oberbayern and Niederbayern were now joined by parts of what became the three Franconian provinces, the Oberpfalz, Schwaben, and the Pfalz. The newly acquired territories contained far more Protestants and Jews than did the old, causing Bavaria's Jewish population, which numbered about 3,000 in 1800, to grow to roughly 30,000 in 1813 and to over 53,000 in 1818 (table 2.1).[7] (See map 1.) Excluding Austria, Bavaria emerged in 1815 as the second largest German state after Prussia. With the exception of the Bavarian Pfalz and other minor border changes, it is the same state today.[8]

The Wittelsbachs, the ruling dynasty in Bavaria, had deliberately and systematically excluded Jews from their domains before the expansion during the Napoleonic era. There were, however, a few exceptions, the largest of which was the city of Munich. In 1816 more than 70 percent of all Bavarians east of the Rhine were Catholic. Nearly all Bavarian Jews, as well as Protestants, lived in the newer provinces of Unterfranken, Mittelfranken, Oberfranken, and Schwaben.[9] The Pfalz, which lay west of the Rhine, is not considered here because it was qualitatively so different from the other provinces in both its legal and governmental structures, which were strongly influenced by French control under the revolution and Napoleon. Under French law, Jews in the Pfalz were legally free and were not part of the emancipation process.[10] This study, therefore, focuses on what historians frequently call "Bavaria east of the Rhine," which will be referred to here simply as "Bavaria."

At just over 31,000 square miles, Bavaria was about the size of South Carolina and one-third the size of Prussia. Although in 1848 very few Jews

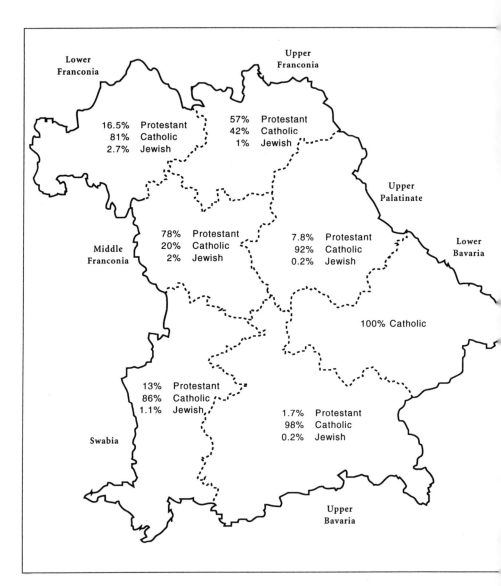

Map 1. Bavaria East of the Rhine, Religious Affiliations.
(Data from the 1852 census; see table 2.6.)

lived in the older provinces, they had lived there in larger numbers in the middle ages. Pogroms and persecutions occurred in areas that were or became part of Bavaria in 1147, 1288–89, and 1348–49. In 1348–49 the Jewish quarter of Würzburg, the capital of Lower Franconia, was razed and became the city marketplace.[11] Jews were readmitted to Würzburg only in 1803. In the centuries following the fourteenth-century pogroms, Christian princes and cities forced Jews to leave many areas of central Europe, and Bavaria was no exception. But Jews were not forced to leave all areas in Bavaria, and it is important to be clear about where they lived as well as how.

Because of the residence restrictions on Jews, nearly all statistical descriptions of Bavarian Jewry must be used cautiously. Among the most common stereotypes in the modern era is the perception of Jews as primarily city dwellers whether by choice or under duress. In 1840 a larger percentage of Jews lived in cities than did Christians, although the difference was not great, about 14 percent of Jews as compared to 11 percent of the total population. More unusual was the large number of Jews living in small, rural communities. But change occurred quickly in the nineteenth century in Bavaria, and by 1871 nearly one-third of all Jews lived in cities in contrast to just under one-sixth of all Christians.[12] Like any statistic, these figures are only averages that conceal the fact that in 1840 only 6 Jews lived in Nuremberg, 97 in Augsburg, 425 in Würzburg, 2 in Nördlingen, and none in Kitzingen. The statistics do not explain why the Jewish community in Fürth

TABLE 2.1.   Changes in the Jewish Population of Bavaria from 1818 to 1900

Province	1818[a]	1852[b]	1871[b]	1880[c]	1900[a]
Upper Bavaria	489	1,218	3,033	4,343	9,076
Lower Bavaria	5	10	111	134	294
Palatinate	10,470	15,606	12,466	11,998	10,108
Upper Palatinate	991	910	1,221	1,522	1,472
Upper Franconia	6,296	5,431	4,045	4,148	3,322
Middle Franconia	11,816	10,659	10,830	11,689	13,111
Lower Franconia	16,637	15,834	14,573	15,256	13,641
Swabia	6,514	6,365	4,369	4,436	3,904
Bavaria	53,208	56,033	50,648	53,526	54,928
% of Total population	1.46	1.23	1.04	1.01	0.89

[a]Data from Rudolf Wassermann, "Die Entwicklung der jüdischen Bevölkerung in Bayern im 19. Jahrhundert," *Zeitschrift für Demographie und Statistik der Juden* 1, no. 11 (Nov. 1905): 12. Apparently drawn from Bavarian government statistics.

[b]Data from Dr. Hermann Engelbert, *Statistik des Judenthums im Deutschen Reiche ausschliesslich Preussens und in der Schweiz* (Frankfurt am Main, 1875), 10, based on statistics collected earlier from the Bavarian Royal Statistical Bureau; see ibid., p. iv.

[c]Data from Friedrich Bosse, *Die Verbreitung der Juden im Deutschen Reiche auf Grundlage der Volkszählung vom 1. Dezember 1880* (Berlin, 1885), 66–82.

numbered 2,535 in 1840, while less than half as many lived in Munich, the capital of Bavaria and a city almost five times larger than Fürth.[13] Only better knowledge of exclusionary policies makes these anomalies understandable.

It is a mistake to think of exclusion of Jews as unique to cities. The fact that nearly 90 percent of all Bavarian Jews lived in cities and towns of less than two thousand population, and often in communities considerably smaller than that, conceals the related fact that in most of the communities of Bavaria there were no Jews at all. Of course, when one pauses to consider how few Jews there were in Bavaria (and Germany), it cannot be surprising that they were not spread equally across all communities. There were so few in relation to the total population that any form of concentration at all would have made it impossible for each of Bavaria's over eight thousand communities to have had even one Jewish resident. The question then is not whether Jews concentrated in certain areas or communities but rather in which and why. At least three separate forces were at work to produce this pattern: exclusion, inclusion, and concentration.

Exclusion, the easiest policy to describe and to understand, was the most commonly used. In the late Middle Ages various central European cities and states decided to deny Jews the right to reside within their jurisdiction.[14] Many Jews left Bavaria and Germany and moved eastward into what was then a more congenial environment. Some stayed behind but moved to areas that would accept them, and over the years a number were readmitted to some of the areas from which they had earlier been banished. But it was much harder for "foreign," non-Bavarian, Jews to gain admittance into Bavaria, which limited the available pool for Jewish population increase. Coupled with restrictions on the movement of Jews within Bavaria, the practice of exclusion made it difficult for a substantial number of Jewish urban communities, for example, Nuremberg, to grow quickly in the early nineteenth century. Many villages also excluded Jews, a practice permitted by law until 1861. Exclusion was a policy simultaneously but not uniformly employed at communal, city, and state levels.

Equally important and more fascinating is the fact that some areas not only accepted but even encouraged Jewish residency. However, tempting as it may be, one cannot conclude from this that those municipalities or feudal entities that admitted Jews were altruistic or even friendly to them. Such motivations cannot, of course, be excluded, but recent work in Unterfranken and Oberfranken show that the primary motivations were the traditional ones of either greed or need.

The most complete evidence is found in Lower Franconia in the years from 1800 to 1816, the era preceding the establishment of modern Bavaria. What was originally called the Lower Main Circle (*Untermain Kreis*) and only later the governmental district (*Regierungsbezirk*) of Lower Franconia, was pieced together out of the large *Hochstift* of Würzburg, an ecclesiastical principality, and a large number of smaller feudal holdings. The secular-religious division of centuries of earlier land rule is important because church lands regularly excluded Jews and feudal areas nearly as regularly accepted them.[15] For example, Würzburg, the capital of Lower Franconia, and earlier of the ecclesiastical lands, only readmitted Jews to residence in 1803, when that city permitted Moses Hirsch of Gaukönigshofen to reside there. Until then Jews had lived nearby in Heidingsfeld, which boasted close to 600 Jews in 1805, but the Jewish community there dwindled rapidly thereafter as many Jews moved to the bigger city. Even the rabbi moved to Würzburg in 1814, and by 1828 some 218 Jews lived there.[16]

The motives for excluding Jews from towns or cities were either religious or economic or both, but the reasons for accepting them were nearly always economic. Recent research shows a striking pattern of acceptance in Lower Franconia by either feudal lords or communal councils based on a hope that each could profit from having resident Jews. Much the same has been asserted for Oberfranken, albeit without the statistical base available for Unterfranken.[17] Nobles admitted Jews with the clear intention of taxing them at a much higher rate than other residents. Moreover, poor nobles made a practice of renting their empty castles to Jews at high rents.[18] One Jew, choosing a family name to comply with a law of 1808, decided on "Schloss" because he had lived in one so long.[19] Market towns (Märkte) tended to exclude Jews because they regarded them as providing too much competition for local Christian shopkeepers and tradesmen, while smaller towns saw Jews as an economic stimulus and were as willing as nobles to tax them.[20]

Finally, concentration occurred because Jews wished to live with other Jews for religious, ethnic, and cultural reasons. Religion played a major role in this respect, because it was difficult for solitary Jewish families to acquire kosher meat, provide religious education for children, and enjoy all the support a congregation could offer. Moreover, as we will see in connection with the regulative legislation of 1813, the government encouraged Jews to concentrate by denying small Jewish communities the right to have teachers, rabbis, and synagogues. Religion was not the only reason for Jews to want to live together. Housing was always a problem, and it was economically more feasible for two (or more) families to share one house than for one to live alone.[21] Also, Christians regularly excluded Jews from the larger community's social life. There was no possibility of intermarriage and no significant social interaction.[22] With few exceptions, Jews had no part in decision making in the larger community.[23] If a Jew wished to be part of a community, and most did, he had to seek to join an established Jewish community.

All the forces acting to concentrate Jews also existed in the larger Christian society. Bavaria was highly segregated along religious lines,

Catholics and Protestants largely living only with their coreligionists. As map 1 shows, Lower Bavaria stood out in this regard at the provincial level, but Upper Bavaria and the Upper Palatinate were not far behind. At the district, city, and communal levels, the same pattern of religious concentration could be found in the new provinces with larger numbers of Protestants, even in Middle Franconia, where Protestants outnumbered Catholics. Catholic-Protestant conflict had abated since the seventeenth century, but living patterns changed very slowly. With few exceptions, Bavarians still led a closed, insular, and very parochial life in 1849–50.

In combination, these factors concentrated the Jewish population in a limited number of communities. Little can be said in this regard about Niederbayern, because so few Jews lived there throughout this period, but this pattern held true for Oberbayern and the Oberpfalz. As late as 1852 only 1,252 Jews, amounting to little more than 1 percent of the city's population, lived in Munich. Together with the Jewish community in Au, a suburb of Munich soon to be annexed, they accounted for all but a tiny handful of the Jews in Upper Bavaria.[24] Similarly, in the whole province of Oberpfalz there were fewer Jews (915) than in the city of Munich, and they, too, were found in only a handful of communities.[25] All three forces, exclusion, inclusion, and concentration, were present in Old Bavaria, exclusion dominating the other two factors.

The situation in the three Franconian provinces and Swabia was quite different. Far more Jews lived in these four provinces. In Franconia in general, with variation from district to district, Jews inhabited numerous small communities, while in Swabia they were found in fewer, but larger, communities.[26] Data on Oberfranken show 47 Jewish communities in 1852,[27] but only 34 of them numbered seven or more families. About 3,500 Jews lived in these communities, averaging about 18 percent of their combined population, a minority that comprised less than 2 percent of the total provincial population. The concentration of Jews in a few communities is obvious, and in several cases it is impressive: in Demmelsdorf, 50 percent of the population was Jewish, and in Altenkunstadt and Zeckendorf, Jews comprised 45 percent and 44 percent respectively.[28]

Unterfranken provides the best view of Jewish residence, in part because it possessed the largest Jewish population in Bavaria, but also because its Jewish past has been the focus of recent historical work. By 1813 there were already 146 separate Jewish communities in Lower Franconia.[29] That number grew, partly as a result of territorial additions in 1815. By 1835 there were 215 Jewish communities, averaging over seventeen families per community.[30] In 1813, when they accounted for 4 percent of the population, Jews in Unterfranken resided in all but one district (Prölsdorf) and were geographically balanced between 70 communities in the more prosperous south and

76 in the poorer north. Just over 80 percent of all Jews lived in communities with fewer than one thousand people, and only twelve of the thirty-one cities in which governmental offices were located had a Jewish community.[31]

What at first appears to be a pattern of even distribution of Jewish residence in Unterfranken changes under closer analysis. Of the 146 communities in which Jews lived before 1813, only 29 lay under direct ecclesiastical jurisdiction, while 82 were under the rule of secular lords. But the communities in the ecclesiastical domains, though smaller and fewer, were far more wealthy, and those in the areas owned by the nobility were poorer and more numerous. Most of the poorer Jewish communities lay in the northern part of the province, and the wealthier were more frequently found in the south.[32] At this level of analysis, we begin to see that concentration must be thought of in economic as well as numerical terms.

Fortunately, we are able to discuss Jewish occupations and relative prosperity in Lower Franconia at a level of detail not possible for individual communities in other provinces. This allows us to generalize about Unterfranken, but only to suggest the possible similarity of other provinces. Gisela Krug's data on occupation are worth reproducing here and appear in table 2.2. They show very clearly that most Jews in Unterfranken were not rich and that direct commerical dealings in currency were very limited. Trade and commerce, at least for Jews, meant the buying and selling of cattle and livestock, trade of all kinds, brokerage, dealing in petty goods, peddling, slaughtering, and a few other crafts; additionally, some Jews were religious employees of the congregations. Most noticeable in this list is the relative absence of crafts, the total absence of farming or ownership of agricultural land, and the presence of so many traders, dealers, and brokers of all kinds. Analysis of Gaukönigshofen, also in Unterfranken, reveals almost exactly the same picture.[33] The explanation for this pattern lies in the traditional legal exclusion of Jews from both crafts and agricultural landownership and usage. Unable to earn a living in the "normal" ways, Jews turned to the areas in this economy either not barred to them or open at a reasonable price, and that meant some form of small-scale dealing or trade.

The enormous number of cattle dealers is among the best-known aspects of German-Jewish occupational life in the nineteenth and twentieth centuries. It is mute proof of the existence of a market economy in agricultural produce and parallel evidence of the economic utility of Jews. Not only did Jews deal in cattle, buying and selling in town and village, but they served as a source of cash and credit—they bought from peasants in cash and sold to them on credit. Cut off from agricultural land by law but needing it to feed and pasture the cattle they bought for resale, many Jews entered into contracts with peasants in which the latter would maintain a cow bought by a dealer in return for a portion of the cow when it was finally sold.[34] At issue here, and applicable to all occupations in some sense, is that Jews played a small but significant and needed role in the economic life of Bavaria. State tax records for 1803 provided the basis for Krug's description of the wealth of 1,000 of the 2,344 Jewish households in Unterfranken. Though the sample is neither complete nor random, it is a major source of information and allows analysis of more than just a village or two. The average value of the 1,000 households was 1,292 Gulden (hereafter fl followed by the sum), but in 50 communities the average was under fl 1,000, and in 25 under fl 500. Nearly 80 percent of all capital was possessed by Jewish communities in the south, highlighting the comment made earlier about the relative poverty of those in the north of Unterfranken. One third of these 1,000 Jewish households were located in land ruled by nobles, but they accounted for only 13 percent of all Jewish wealth. Among the occupations noted above, the cattle dealers (avg. assets = fl 1,403), goods dealers (fl 1,606), cloth dealers (fl 2,195), wine dealers (fl 6,040) and jewelers (fl 6,040) were the most prosperous. But there was only 1 jeweler and 170 cloth dealers. In contrast rabbis earned fl 600, cantors fl 66, and teachers a mere fl 55.[35] By way of comparison, in 1825 the lowest class of the Bavarian population, mostly peasants, earned between fl 100 and fl 149 yearly. The importance of any wealth is what it will buy, and in Lower Franconia before 1813, a Jew needed fl 1,000 to receive a *Schutzbrief*, literally a letter of protection granting the right of legal residency. Few Jewish households could pay the fee.[36]

TABLE 2.2.   Occupations of Jews in Unterfranken in 1813

Occupation	Number	Percentage
Court Jews	1	0.0
Money lenders	10	0.4
Cattle dealers	650	27.7
Dealers (unspecified)	504	21.5
Brokers	360	15.4
Dealers in small items	73	3.1
Traders (unspecified)	340	13.4
Butchers	124	5.3
Craftsmen, excluding butchers	20	.7
Religious employees (3 rabbis)	52	2.2
Poor (supported by the community)	210	9.0
Total	2,344	98.7

Source: Gisela Krug, "Die Juden in Mainfranken zu Beginn des 19. Jahrhunderts: Statistischer Untersuchungen zu ihrer sozialen und wirtschaftlichen Situation," in Harm-Hinrich Brandt, ed., *Zwischen Schutzherrschaft und Emanzipation: Studien zur Geschichte der mainfränkischen Juden im 19. Jahrhundert,* Mainfränkische Studien, vol. 39 (Würzburg, 1987), 66ff.

The specific data in Krug's table have been condensed into her own larger categories and translated; the total percentage does not equal 100 due to rounding.

As with wealth, our picture of household size in Unterfranken is limited to the data about the 1,000 Jewish families drawn from the 1803 records. Of the 1,000 *Schutzjuden* in Unterfranken, 823 were married men, 97 were widows, 75 were either single or widowed men, and 5 were orphans. There were 4,551 Jews in these households, giving an average family size of 4.5, the largest families normally those with the most wealth. Most startling is the proportion of dependent children over 20 years of age, 16.7 percent, and over 30, 1.7 percent. This is easily explained by restrictions on marriage. In all, 156 women and 242 men between the ages of 20 and 60 years of age, most between 20 and 40, did not have their own household and appear in statistical lists as dependent children.[37]

By all accounts Jewish religious life was traditional but not very sophisticated. The nearest Yeshiva was in Fürth in Mittelfranken, but it was in decline in the early nineteenth century and closed in 1827.[38] Rabbis in Bavaria were often educated at this Yeshiva, but there were few rabbis. In most communities, religious leadership was exercised by the chair or president of the religious community in lieu of rabbi, cantor, or teacher. Rabbis were so poorly paid that they often had to pursue other occupations: that was true, for example, of Seligman bar Bamberger before he became Rabbi of Würzburg.[39]

Except in a few large Jewish communities, such as Fürth, synagogues in Bavaria were small and nearly indistinguishable from other buildings. Only small architectural touches set them off from the surrounding structures. Normally the synagogue and ritual bath were located near the houses of members of the Jewish community, but ghettos did not really exist. In Oberfranken 23 of 25 synagogues had been founded between 1700 and 1851, but the oldest dated only to 1626.[40] In Unterfranken there were 130 synagogues by 1835, but only nine rabbis.[41]

In 1813 Jews in Bavaria lived predominantly in small communities in the new provinces, in numbers that were often sizeable percentages of the total population. Almost all were engaged in some form of business, even if only at the level of peddling, and were served by a minimal number of rabbis and synagogues. In that year the king decided to grant Bavarian Jews a constitution "in keeping with the welfare of the state."[42]

Progress? The 1813 Jew Decree

In the later years of the eighteenth century in German central Europe, "enlightened" leaders of state and society took an intense interest in Jews and Judaism. Moved by the desire to rationalize and strengthen the state, a wide variety of public figures addressed the role of Jews in somewhat the same fashion as they did the need for schools, improved law codes, and better roads. Many wanted to "improve" or "better" the Jews themselves. As used by the reformers, *improvement* varied in meaning, but most reformers focused on moving Jews out of peddling and into what they perceived as productive occupations, such as farming and crafts, simultaneously raising their moral standards and cultural values to a Christian-German level through secular education. In Prussia this was best stated by Christian Konrad Wilhelm von Dohm in 1781, in *On the Civic Improvement of the Jews;* in Bavaria by Johann Christoph von Aretin in 1803, in *History of the Jews in Bavaria.* Aretin requested a "Juden Edikt" with "forceful regulations against Jews who did not wish to be improved."[43]

The progress of Jewish emancipation in Bavaria, that is, the process of repealing or otherwise modifying some or all earlier legal restrictions on Jews, was part of a common development in Europe and particularly central Europe. The first significant breakthrough occurred in the 1780s in Austria as part of the enlightened reforms of Joseph II.[44] The French Revolution provided an even stronger stimulus to emancipation because it asserted universal human values rather than special legislation for Jews.[45] Moreover, territory added to France—for example, the land west of the Rhine, including what became in 1816 the Bavarian Pfalz—enjoyed the benefits of French revolutionary legislation. Napoleon later reduced the full equality of Jews in Alsace by a decree, the *Decret Infame* of 1808.[46] It was therefore normal for German states to engage in reforms of laws relating to Jews in the decade before the Congress of Vienna in 1815.

Prussia acted first, in 1808, by redefining the role of citizenship in cities to include all who qualified, without regard to religion. Despite some modifications, this provided many, though not all, Jews in Prussia with substantial benefits.[47] In 1812 Prussia added a more comprehensive Jew Law that made Jews generally free in economic and occupational spheres, but Prussia continued to exclude them from state service.[48] In 1813 Bavaria issued a decree defining Jewish life in general, following several earlier decrees affecting Jews in specific ways. Most importantly, the 1813 decree granted Jews a form of state citizenship largely in economic pursuits, but, like Prussia, Bavaria remained silent about political rights. And even the occupational benefits were less complete in Bavaria than in Prussia. Success in achieving emancipation from the most significant political and demographic restrictions only occurred in Bavaria in 1861, in Baden in 1862, in Württemberg in 1861 and 1864, and in Prussia in 1867, although a group of smaller states, including Brunswick, Hessen-Darmstadt, Hessen-Homburg, Nassau, Oldenburg, Saxony, Saxe-Weimar, and Waldeck, provided general emancipation in 1848.[49] Uniform and full equality came to most German Jews only with the establishment of the North German Confederation in 1867 and its extension to the south in 1870–71.

As described above, Prussia had already centralized its bureaucratic institutions in the late seventeenth and eighteenth centuries, and in the Reform Era it had modified that structure to eliminate weaknesses. In contrast, between 1800 and 1815 Bavaria introduced centralization and applied it to Jews as well as to Christians. Thus Bavaria's reforms were more consciously a form of constructive engineering and less one of judicious pruning and adjustment. Though both shared a good deal of common ground, the Bavarian government was more optimistic about the future benefits of such action than was true in Prussia. As we will see, Bavaria came to link further emancipatory measures for Jews to proof that the earlier steps had achieved their goals.

Beginning with a decree issued by Kurfürst Maximilian IV Josef in 1801, Bavaria enacted a series of laws and edicts, culminating in the *Juden Edikt* of 1813.[50] In many ways the 1813 law only compiled and regularized these earlier laws. But parts of the Edict were new, including especially the fateful paragraphs on residence. Since further legislation came only in 1851, the 1813 Edict ended the reforms for Jews and marked the beginning of a new era in which Bavarians, mostly Jews, simultaneously accepted and worked to modify or repeal part or all of this law. That the clauses of the 1813 Edict most hated by Jews were not altered until 1861 and that the last of the law was not repealed until 1871 should give some idea of its durability.

Both its longevity and its influence on Jews, negative and positive, are good reasons to examine the 1813 law more closely. The text in translation may be found in appendix A. It is clearly the single most important law relating to Bavarian Jews before the Nazi epoch. Referred to variously as the Jew Law, the Jew Decree, the Emancipation Law, and the Matriculation Law, the 1813 Edict has been seen as both emancipating and damaging Bavarian Jewry. Because some of its provisions were a significant advance over the past, it is seen by some historians as emancipatory;[51] since it did not provide full emancipation and even introduced new regulations of a distinctly hostile character, it is seen by others as merely another "special" law for Jews.[52]

What strikes one on first reading the Edict of 1813 is its comprehensive nature. In thirty-four separate articles, it dealt with all major areas of Jewish life in Bavaria. The first article defined eligibility for Jewish citizenship as belonging only to Jews legally resident in Bavaria. This was reiterated in article 11, which excluded all foreign, non-Bavarian Jews; in article 17, which stated that Bavarian Jews could not employ foreign Jews; and in article 27, which specified that rabbis must be Bavarian subjects. The intent to limit strictly the further immigration of Jews is clear, although we do not really know to what extent the latter was a problem; we have little good data on how many Jews were migrating into Bavaria before 1813. After that date few did.

"Bureaucratic red tape" characterizes many of the thirty-four articles, most of which stemmed logically from the grant of partial citizenship in article 1. If a Jew wished to become a legal resident, he had to prove his identity at his local police office, adopt a last name if that had not yet been done,[53] and notify the office of any changes in his status. The law directed the "police" to record all of these actions. By *police* the law meant a newly-emerging structure that gave the central state a presence on the local level through what was soon called a *Landgericht* (district office) headed by a *Landrichter* (district director). Although the German terms seem to indicate a judicial office and though the offices possessed some judicial powers, in practice their function was largely executive.[54]

Only two articles, 21 and 22, addressed the question of Jewish communal structure, first dissolving any and all existing Jewish corporations, then forbidding separate Jewish communities. By *community* the law meant a municipality of any size. Jews normally organized religious "communities," *Kirchengemeinde*, or congregations, but these were merely organizations to attend to Jewish religious needs and not civil structures. According to the new law, Jews, except for those Jews engaging in forbidden or restricted occupations or businesses, were to participate in the local municipality as Christians did. Lest the qualification be unclear, the clause further stated that Jews conducting normal business in agriculture would enjoy the full rights of local citizens, even with respect to communal properties. The 1813 law required that Jews live in the secular state, which meant the community. They could retain Jewish communities only in the narrow sense of a religious congregation.

Clearly these paragraphs had mostly secular rather than religious issues in mind. It is not as clear that, through the new law, the central state invaded the rights of the local secular community by telling them that they must grant Jews residency under defined circumstances. But the local communities considered themselves partially separate from the state and did not wish to admit Jews. Constructing a central state at the expense of communal rights and powers was typical of the reforming effort.

In theory the law gave Jews the right of citizenship in communities if they supported themselves economically in an approved manner. But the right to share in communal goods, to say nothing of the right to reside there in the first place, were among the most jealously guarded prerogatives of the communities. Because the law did not spell out how to administer the principle it enunciated, and because a Communal Edict of 1818 gave back to the communities the right to deny residence to anyone, the Jewish "right" to reside equitably in Bavarian communities remained largely theoretical. The communities saw the Jew Law of 1813 as an infringement of their rights that was dictated by the central state in Munich and did their best to frustrate it.

In educational and religious fields, the Edict clearly tried to "improve" the situation of the Jews. Articles 32–34 stated that Jewish children must attend Christian schools exactly as Christians did, except for religious instruction, and even permitted Jews to found their own schools if the teacher were paid at least fl 300 annually and the curriculum was the same as in Christian establishments. Jews desiring religious higher education first had to complete their public education, and rabbis had to be fluent in German and generally educated in a scholarly way (art. 27). These two-faced clauses required Jews to be secularized as much as possible while simultaneously granting them the right to practice their religion. In practice this meant that Jews sent their children to secular schools when they could not afford the privilege of having their own, and that rabbis were frequently examined by Christian officials on their knowledge of secular philosophy and Christian theology. Naturally, many refused to be examined,[55] leading to a shortage of approved rabbis and a rise in the number of those who were unapproved.

Like education, much of the 1813 Edict was internally contradictory. Article 23 granted complete freedom of worship, but it qualified that gift in later clauses, requiring that fifty families be resident in a given district in an area with a police office (*Landgericht*) in order for the Jews living there to have a synagogue and rabbi. That restriction denied the majority of Jewish communities in Bavaria the use of a synagogue however small. The puzzling requirement of the presence of a police office is explained by the attitude toward rabbis found in articles 25 through 30. These paragraphs required rabbis to be Bavarian Jews, to be fluent in German, to bear no blemish of usury or bankruptcy, to take an oath to the law, and not to intervene in civil or communal affairs on pain of arrest or fine. Article 28, requiring the oath, added that the rabbi "will teach or say nothing against [the laws of the state], will, if he learns of something contrary to them, faithfully report it to the authorities, and will refrain from any connections whatsoever with foreign powers." This phrasing reflects a perception of rabbis as, at the least, potentially powerful and seditious, presumably justifying the existence of a police office where a rabbi resided.

The negative attitude toward Jews in general differed little from that expressed toward rabbis. Articles 12–14 defined the state's policy on the right of Jews to marry and reproduce. Put simply, the Bavarian state in 1813 did not wish Jews to "be fruitful and multiply; fill the earth and subdue it!"[56] Article 12 stated the state's desire in no uncertain terms: "The number of Jewish families in communities where they presently reside ought, as a rule, not be increased, but should, on the contrary, be gradually diminished if it is too large." In the next article it is apparent that "too large" meant "in excess of the [number]" resident in 1813. And article 14 makes it clear that permission to marry would be granted only if the new family did not exceed the quota of 1813 and if the Jew in question pursued an approved occupation. Limitations on the right to marry, when coupled with restrictions on immigration, were intended to lower the number of Jews in Bavaria, and the Edict stated it openly.

But, and this too is part of the contradictory nature of the document, exceptions could be made. The prerequisites for granting an exception appear in article 13, which would allow residence if a Jew wanted to establish a factory or large "wholesale" business, if he adopted a normal craft and obtained a master's title, or if he purchased sufficient tillable land to support his family from it alone. In other words, Jews would be allowed to reside if they were valuable to approved areas of the economy.

Many of these restrictive articles, even those dealing with the economy, bring to mind the intent and practice of immigration laws. That appears out of place here because most Jews had resided in these towns and villages for generations. But Jews and Protestants were relatively new to the enlarged Wittelsbach state and had been acquired before they had been assimilated. The state did not see the Jews of Franconia, for example, as Bavarian Jews and hence included these clauses in the Jew Law of 1813.

A major new aspect of the 1813 law is located in the determination of "approved" commercial and economic pursuits. Though the state had formerly allowed Jews to engage actively in occupations like moneylending, peddling, various forms of brokering, and other pursuits that were seen as "damaging," it now intended to stop those practices. In this context articles 14 and 15 are of crucial importance. Article 14 prohibited Jews practicing *Schacherhandel* from marrying, "even if the number of accepted families would not thereby be increased." Article 15 granted Jews admission to all crafts and livelihoods, most of which had formerly been forbidden them, "in order to divert the Jews from their former inadequate as well as generally harmful occupations." It stated, moreover, that *Schacherhandel* was to be abolished as quickly as possible.

Few modern works on economics mention *Schacherhandel* or the related words *Kramhandel, Nothandel* and *Hausierhandel*. Only the last term is specific—it means peddling, going from house to house with one's wares. *Schacherhandel* was not a unique term, but it was the word that most directly attempted to define business practices considered "damaging" and commonly identified with Jews. It included any business popularly associated with shabby practices, sharp dealing, and immorality—usury was the common example but by no means the only one. In Bavaria all peddlers were considered to be *Schacher* by definition because haggling and dealing in used goods were such common aspects of their work. The term often implied that Jews succeeded in their dealings with Christians because they cheated and employed similar immoral means. Article 20 therefore forbade the practice of peddling and the vaguer *Nothandel* and *Schacherhandel*, denying Jews who pursued such businesses the right of residence and marriage.

The Edict consciously strove to move Jews away from all forms of *Schacherhandel* and into "normal" and "German" occupations, such as farming and the crafts. By doing so the state was attempting to make Jews more "productive" in an acceptable and moral fashion.[57] To the extent that the state considered the economic aspect at all, it considered Jewish engagement in peddling and usury to be damaging to the economy and to the people involved. In the context of the early nineteenth century, the Jews happened to be engaged, albeit frequently at the bottom, in businesses that would shortly and impressively outproduce the older occupations of farming and handwork. These businesses, or business practices, were seen as threats to a way of life. The Edict was not so much an economic document as it was a moral and social one. There was a definite tension inherent in the action of the reformers to use a more modern state to more efficiently protect and maintain much of the older and more unproductive economy. Though willing to modernize agriculture and the crafts, they were less eager to favor free commerce and the building of factories. Jews, earlier forced into occupations that were becoming successful and sometimes a force for change in the nineteenth century, were now to be forced back into the occupations that had earlier been forbidden them. The Edict was an exercise in social engineering, the product of a modernizing, centralizing, secular state, but one that existed in a largely nonmodern society.

Applied to most Jews, the Edict was economically retrogressive. Whether it was successful in terms of its goals for Jews can only be determined by examining its effect on Bavarian Jewry in later years.

Attitudes toward Jews

Attempts to evaluate the 1813 law in terms of its specific provisions—for example, its concern with the number of Jews engaged in peddling and its desire to curb, if not actually eliminate, that business—is useful but misses the vital point of the law: its concern with the role of Jews as citizens. A rereading of article 1 serves to emphasize that Jews were being granted citizenship in Bavaria and would no longer be considered foreign. That this citizenship was distinctly "second class" should not obscure this vital aspect. The 1813 law intended to improve Jews whether they liked it or not, because they were subsequently to share many of the rights of citizens.

As long as Jews had still been considered foreigners, it was irrelevant whether they lived and acted like Christians and Germans. Now that Jews were to be Bavarian subjects, even if they did not enjoy all of the rights of Christians, they had to become "Bavarian." This was the frame of mind in which the General Commissioner of the Pegnitzkreis (later, Mittelfranken), Baron von Lochner, wrote to the Ministry of the Interior in 1810 requesting a reform of Jewish education so that "Jewish youths lose the uniqueness of their life-style, that the one-sided nature of their behaviour be gradually deleted and that they become more responsive to the morals and customs of the Christian inhabitants."[58] In the treatment of almost all aspects of the question of "equality" as citizens, which constitutes the subject matter of the following chapters, the desire for Jews to become more like Germans and Christians to become full Bavarians is constant among a major segment of Bavarian Christian opinion.

In one sense, then, the 1813 law was a "bargain" the government proposed to the Jews. If Jews became German socially and occupationally, they could become Bavarians. If they did not, if, for example, they insisted on continuing to practice *Schacherhandel,* then they were specifically excluded from participating "as citizens," although they could "reside" where they already were living. At the level of reproduction, this bargain was even more general: marriage and continuation of the family became partially dependent on Jews fulfilling the unwritten "agreement" and moving into crafts and agriculture. Religion was not mentioned directly.

Jews understood this "bargain" and reacted to it in at least two distinct ways. Their first response was to attempt to take advantage of what the law offered, and they did so in large numbers in the ensuing thirty-five years. Thus they established numerous associations to encourage Jews to move into crafts and trades. But Jews also understood the "bargain" as promising them in return full citizenship and full acceptance in the future. Some historians argue that Jews understood the bargain, saw in it the hope of acquiring equality, and eagerly pursued assimilation and emancipation. This was a process by which many Jews in Germany consciously changed and, through their leadership, urged other Jews to do likewise.[59]

An article in the Bavarian Jewish journal *Die Synagoge* in 1839 entitled "How We as Jews have to Conduct Ourselves in the State" clearly and eloquently made the case for this bargain. Probably on Ludwig I's birthday, the anonymous author called upon Jews to willingly obey all laws, to seriously work for the state's well-being, to love all fellow citizens, and to strive constantly to make themselves more worthy of civil equality while holding fast to Judaism. It was especially important to the author that Jews obey laws that "have our good at heart," that "lift us out of the depths into which we had sunk in the past centuries"; to disobey such laws would be madness. Referring to Jews by their occupations, the writer chose as examples farming, crafts, art, science, and teaching, making no mention of business of any type. Bitter and hateful actions against Jews should, he argued, be endured and resisted only in legal ways. Insisting that he was not blind to the exclusion of Jews from some rights of citizens merely because they were Jews, he argued that such deprivation called for more and greater attempts at improvement, the reward for which was certain. If Jews would give up ignoble business and avoid any irregular craft, if they would strive to raise their talents and morals, then, "oh be certain, the goal will not be unfulfilled, the prejudice extinguished." His was an optimistic vision, especially so when one recalls that the laws he called on Jews to willingly obey were largely those contained in the Jew Law of 1813.[60]

Improvement is frequently taken to mean "modernization," a term with many meanings. As used here it is intended only to convey the idea that progress meant a shift away from older forms of Jewish life. In religion modernization meant the emergence of Reform Judaism. In economics it meant a shift into crafts and agriculture and away from peddling, but also into larger and more respectable commercial ventures. Professionally it meant a move into such socially approved and respected positions as medicine, law, and education. Socially it meant joining a wide range of bourgeois clubs, joining Christian organizations where possible, or if excluded, creating imitations. In politics it meant joining political clubs and, remarkably soon, standing for office. Some of these changes occurred only in the years after 1850, if they can be said to have ever genuinely taken place.

One historian asserts that Jews succeeded so well in changing that they "transformed" themselves into a modern subculture far in advance of the rest of German society.[61] But that did not happen everywhere at the same time. Progress was slower in Bavaria than elsewhere, partly because the 1813 law was harsher than similar legislation in other German states.[62] Individual Jews, especially converts, gained acceptance before Jews as a group, but not very many Jews found genuine acceptance "as Jews" in the first half of the nineteenth century.[63] There is the larger question of whether this bargain ultimately succeeded (discussed in part in ch. 8). But the relevant issue here is whether, as a result of the Edict, the condition of Jews improved in the years between 1813 and 1849.

Four years after the Congress of Vienna brought the Napoleonic wars to an end and one year after the newly enlarged Bavaria created a parliament in 1818, a series of anti-Jewish riots broke out. The riots of 1819 were and are regarded as among the last of an older tradition of anti-Judaism rather than as the herald of things to come.[64] They were both indicators of popular sentiment toward Jews and symptomatic of broader societal discontents that would play a major role in 1849, and they began in Bavaria.

The year 1819 is well known to students of European history as the year in which, following the murder of the counterrevolutionary writer August von Kotzebue by the radical student Karl Sand, Prince Clemens von Metternich of Austria convinced the German Confederation to institute repression of much political activity in what came to be known as the Carlsbad Decrees.[65] Directed against what Metternich perceived as the spread of revolution rather than an isolated terrorist murder, the resulting structure of press control and political restriction lasted until 1848. A contributing factor, according to nineteenth-century historian Heinrich von Treitschke,[66] was a series of riots that began in Würzburg and spread to other cities in Bavaria and to Baden, Hessen, Hamburg, and even Denmark. In Heidelberg some professors and students protected the Jews, but in almost all other cases, including Bavaria, that task fell to the state. The riots were clearly anti-Semitic, wholly illegal, and usually urban in setting.[67]

Until a generation ago, few historians had investigated these riots, and they disagreed on why they erupted. In *History of the Jews*, Russian historian Simon Dubnov wrote that fear of revolution and demagoguery took the "line of least resistance, and proceeded against the Jews."[68] This view appears far too simplistic and lacks significant evidence. In 1950 Elonore Sterling provided the first accurate and detailed description of the riots, arguing that they were a consequence of the economic aftermath of the Napoleonic wars, when craftsmen found it hard to compete with the sudden influx of cheap goods and lashed out against Jews, who they perceived as partially responsible because they were engaged in the import trades.[69] However, Jacob Katz denies Sterling's argument, holding that the rioters only felt anti-Jewish animosity, an animosity fueled by a spate of publications in the 1815–18 years. Moreover, the rioters did not attack other sectors of society and were most numerous in cities where municipal citizenship for Jews was still an open issue. The riots began, he believes, because "Jews had been permitted to live in places where they had hitherto been forbidden and to enter occupations previously closed to them."[70] Crown Prince Ludwig of Bavaria (later Ludwig I) thought much the same. He wrote to his sister, Empress Karoline Auguste of Austria, on 7 September 1819: "These upsets in Würzburg make me sad and I do not condone them, but if our government had not allowed Jewish residents in Würzburg in 1804 . . . there would be no problem. We are punished sooner or later for mistaken regulations."[71] The actual outbreak of the riots was apparently triggered by the new Bavarian parliament's discussion of article 16 of the 1815 *Bundesakt* (federal act) that appeared to enjoin religious freedom on member states, making it, as Rürup has noted, more than merely a Bavarian governmental issue.[72]

All analysts agree that the riots were an expression of popular sentiment rather than of government or elite attitudes. But the use of violence tells us very little about the "attitudes" toward Jews either of the elite or of the people in general. A good deal of printed literature appeared on the topic of Jewish emancipation in the years between 1813 and 1822, much of it anti-Semitic.[73]

After an initial delay, the state suppressed the disturbances, and everyone seemed to deplore the violence of the rioters. However, the fact of the riots makes it hard to assume that Jews were being accepted, even if only gradually, into Bavarian society. There are many aspects of the 1819 riots that remain inexplicable. Explanations of the riots in Würzburg in northern Bavaria, do not explain the outbreak of similar riots in very different places like Hamburg and even Kopenhagen. The spontaneity of the riots in Bavaria testifies to a popular source of the discontent, but not to its breadth or depth. We know that the rioters were a relatively small number, but we cannot assume that nonparticipants disagreed with their more active fellows. As we learn more about the anti-Jewish riots of 1819 and later years, including those of 1830 and 1848,[74] it becomes clearer that a common element was the popular belief that governments favored Jews. Those who perceived Jews as an economic, religious or political enemy concluded that their state not only had abandoned them to the Jews but had protected those Jews as well.[75] This was a widespread view in 1849 (as the analysis in chapters 5 and 6 will show). States did protect Jews in 1819, even if often late and reluctantly, and that may have contributed to the negative image of Jews in the popular mind.

Recent work on assimilation holds that, with very few exceptions, Jews were not accepted into Bavarian society but were tolerated and allowed to exist in their own separate communities.[76] In some cases even that did not happen, because communities charged Jews more for school, fined them for working in their own yards on Sundays, and forced them to sign the "List of Citizens" last. In Gaukönigshofen the election of the first Jew to a communal office occurred only in 1864. The author of a study of that town concludes that only after 1871 could one speak accurately of a single community in the village—until then there were two, Christian and Jewish. There was no intermarriage, and the only town association that had a Jew on its board was funded by a Jew for both Christians and Jews.[77] This picture of a Christian society reluctantly and incompletely tolerating Jews who lived among them in small and intimate communities is found throughout central and eastern Europe in those years.

Religious reasons for disliking Jews were common among all but a small number of Bavarians: Jews had ceased to be the "chosen" people when they had rejected Christ.[78] As late as 1862 a guide to sermon preparation stated that Jewry was the most fanatical enemy of Christianity.[79] Despite the disappearance of traditional obscurantist practices, the older view of Jews lived on in many ways. Ritual murder trials, for example, declined and disappeared in the last quarter of the sixteenth century, but the imagery and mythology of ritual murder survived into the modern age, as can be seen on rare occasions in the petitions formulated in 1849–50 against Jewish emancipation.[80] Despite popular attitudes toward Jews, attitudes that showed resistance to change, Jews were much more willing to take advantage of opportunities offered to them to improve their lives, and the results are evident in the condition of Jewry at midcentury.

The Condition of Bavarian Jewry in 1849

Anyone who reads the Jew Edict of 1813 in the context of the conditions of Jewish life at the time will naturally see changes in Jewish life in the years after 1813 as a reflection of that law. But the Jew Edict was not the only force affecting Jews in Bavaria. The strength and changing nature of the economy, the emergence of political life and a constitutional state, and the vision of a better life elsewhere coupled with increasingly modern means of travel also played a role in altering Jewish living conditions.

In the light of article 12 of the 1813 Edict, restricting marriage and Jewish population growth, it makes sense to begin an examination of the changes between 1813 and 1849 with some discussion of demographic alterations in the Jewish population of Bavaria. See table 2.3 for more detailed data on Jewish population increase during these years. In two provinces, Lower Bavaria and the Upper Palatinate, Jewish population showed remarkable stability over the entire era, and excepting only the city of Munich, the same can be said of Upper Bavaria. The Jews in Swabia increased substantially, by 60 percent, while in Middle Franconia they decreased in number by nearly 20 percent. In Upper Franconia Jewish population declined very slightly (-3.6 percent), as it did in Lower Franconia (-4.5 percent), while in the Palatinate Jews steadily increased (+ 48.7 percent). Until 1848 the Jewish population of Bavaria slowly increased in whole numbers but declined as a percentage of the general population, which grew by a quarter in the same period.[81]

In comparison to the total population, by 1849 Bavarian Jewry exhibited strong signs of decline. Data from 1852 and after (see table 2.1) show the decline accelerating. Contemporaries and modern statistical analysts have attributed this decline to a higher rate of emigration by Bavarian Jews than either other Jews in Germany or other Bavarians.[82] Rich but scattered data from parts of Württemberg and Bavaria drawn largely from the years after 1849–50 demonstrate that the first wave of Jewish emigration overseas started in Bavaria, caused an absolute decline in the Bavarian Jewish population by 1871, and brought about a fall in the "natural" Jewish growth rate. Data from 1856–58 show that Jews from Lower Franconia and Swabia constituted about 6 and 10 percent, respectively, of the total Bavarian emigration to the United States and 9 and 5 percent, respectively, of the emigration to other German states.[83]

A study of two Bavarian districts, Kissingen in Lower Franconia and

Germersheim in the Palatinate, argues that Jews emigrated because of the 1813 law. The figures for the rural district of Kissingen were not compiled by the state but rather by the two district rabbis, Doctors Adler and Lippmann, evidently in 1854, as the basis for a petition drive to support amelioration of the Jewish condition there. Describing the situation, Jacob Toury writes that "the plight of Bavarian Jews—whether predominantly tradesmen, peddlers, as in the Palatinate, or artisans and farmers, as in the Kissingen district—drove many to emigration."[84] The reason usually given by departing Jews was "no acceptance," in the sense of either residence or admission to a craft. Some rabbis and teachers left because communities weakened by emigration could no longer support them. A large number (Toury suggests one-half) did not appear on the residency lists at all, and he concludes that they must have lived in Bavaria "underground," that is, without being entered in the *Matrikel,* or Jew Roll. This meant, quite simply, that the government "winked" at illegal residence in some cases. Of those who left, six single Jews emigrated for every married emigrant. While some of the women may have been betrothed, Toury argues that the very high proportion of single men indicates frustration brought on by economic and marital consequences of the law of 1813.[85]

But we can see the effects of the 1813 law most clearly not in numbers of Jews but in the occupations they pursued. See table 2.4 for data on the occupations of Bavarian Jews by province for 1848 and compare it with

TABLE 2.3.   The Jewish Population of Bavaria by Province in 1818–1848

Province	1818[a]	1822[b]	1826[b]	1829[b]	1832[b]	1840[a]	1848[b]
Upper Bavaria	489	498	702	853	922	1,528	663
Lower Bavaria	5	12	4	12	9	15	0
Swabia	6,514	4,226	4,538	4,914	4,767	6,891	6,764
Upper Palatinate	991	742	716	732	728	1,061	774
Middle Franconia	11,816	14,191	14,706	14,617	14,528	11,377	11,451
Upper Franconia	6,286	6,246	6,602	6,672	6,666	6,568	6,017
Lower Franconia	16,637	17,017	17,301	17,769	17,914	16,451	16,255
Paltinate	10,470	10,470	12,998	13,927	14,473	15,396	15,574
Total	53,208	53,402	57,567	59,496	60,007	59,287	57,498
Total minus Palatinate	42,738	42,932	44,569	45,569	45,534	43,891	41,924

[a]Data from Rudolf Wassermann, "Die Entwicklung der jüdischen Bevölkerung in Bayern im 19. Jahrhundert," *Zeitschrift für Demographie und Statistik der Juden,* 1, no. 11 (Nov. 1905): 12. The total of the column for 1840 is incorrectly given in the original as 59,288.

[b]Data from *Verhandlungen, Kammer der Abgeordneten,* 1850, Beilage Band 3, Beilage 59, pp. 6–7. The original manuscript table is in the Bayerische Hauptstaatsarchiv, Kammer der Reichsräte, 2656. A printed version is in Stefan Schwarz, *Die Juden in Bayern im Wandel der Zeiten* (Munich and Vienna, 1963), 349–50; Schwarz evidently used the data as it appeared in the *Verhandlungen* and replicated its errors, which are numerous, so great care should be used.

tables 2.5 (a comparison of occupations of Jews in 1822 and 1848) and 2.6 (occupations of all Bavarians in 1852).

Such a comparison reveals a substantial increase in the number of Jews involved in agriculture and an even more impressive leap in the number listed as craftsmen. Over the same period, the number of Jews involved in peddling declined steeply. See table 2.7 for the change in peddling between 1822 and 1848 for those provinces reporting data. Other reports in the Ministry of Commerce confirm the data in table 2.7—Jews were gradually abandoning peddling. The effect of the 1813 law is most apparent in this latter data, because it provides reports on the specific Jews in each area who were peddling in 1848. Not only were there few Jewish peddlers, but their average age was extremely high. Clearly the state had successfully limited the addi-

TABLE 2.4.   The Occupations of Jews in 1848 (in number of heads of family)

	Wholesale (1)	Crafts (2)	Independent Agriculture (3)	Petty Shop-keeping (4)	Cattle Dealing (5)	Approved Schacherhandel (6)	Religious Employees (7)	Other (8)
Upper Bavaria	49	48	6	—	—	—	6	46
Lower Bavaria[a]	—	—	—	—	—	—	—	—
Palatinate[b]	—	636	80	(cols. 4–6 = 2,126)			—	340
Upper Palatinate	39	35	2	34	—	21	7	2
Upper Franconia	198	417	135	117	81	78	56	247
Middle Franconia	607	523	189	284	166	233	95	335
Lower Franconia	347	1,004	453	307	454	348	147	475
Swabia	366	346	139	93	53	122	61	294
Bavaria	1,606	3,009	1,004	835	754	802	372	1,739
% of Total Occupations	13	24	8	7	6	6	3	14

Source: Data from *Verhandlungen, Kammer der Abgeordneten*, 1850, Beilage Band 3, Beilage 59, pp. 6–7. See table 2.3 n.b.

Note: Percentages were calculated using $N = 12,369$, which is the number of Jewish families in the original manuscript table, and which agrees with the total in table 2.5.

Columns providing the number of families in the Matrikel, over the Matrikel, not in the Matrikel, a total of these three, and the total number of people ("Seelen"), also appeared in the mss. table.

[a]No data was submitted for Lower Bavaria, which had only fifteen resident Jews.

[b]No data was submitted from the Palatinate for either wholesale trade or religious employees; this probably resulted from a different mode of collecting data, because there were surely religious employees and highly probably some wholesalers.

[c]If the gross figures of 2,126 for cols. 4–6 for the Palatinate is added to the totals for these same cols. and a new percent calculated for these three columns as a whole, the result is 36 percent instead of 19 percent.

tion of new Jewish peddlers, and those who remained had, naturally, aged between 1813 and 1848.[86]

In Lower Franconia, where Krug found no Jews involved in agriculture in the pre-1813 years, 453 were reported in 1848. And in Unterfranken, where there had been a handful of Jewish craftsmen before the Edict, the state reported over a thousand in 1848. The same was true in all other provinces with the exception of Niederbayern, which had no resident Jews in 1848.[87]

Despite these remarkable occupational changes within the Jewish population, the contrast between it and surrounding Christian inhabitants, as presented in table 2.6, is dramatic. Eight times as many Christians as Jews worked the land in 1848. Unfortunately, trade, industry, and the crafts were lumped together in the 1852 census data, and although this mass is broken down into journeymen, apprentices, servants, clerks, and homeowners, it is not presented in ways that allow us to separate out trade and the crafts.[88] But

TABLE 2.5.   The Occupation of Jews in Bavaria in 1822 and 1848

	1822			1848			
	No. of Families	Agri-culture	Craft	Trade	No. of Families	Agri-culture	Craft	Trade
Upper Bavaria	89	1	—	88	152	6	48	49
Lower Bavaria	1	—	—	1	0	0	0	0
Swabia	855	107	92	(313)	1,474	139	346	634 (122)
Upper Palatinate	120	4	1	(56)	151	2	35	94 (21)
Middle Franconia	2,784	88	27	(562)	2,562	189	523	1,290 (233)
Upper Franconia	1,398	26	39	(486)	1,313	135	417	474 (233)
Lower Franconia	3,416	26	11	(1,188)	3,535	453	1,004	1,456 (348)
Palatinate	2,000	0	17	—	3,182	80	636	2,126
Bavaria:	10,663	252	187	2,694	12,369	1,004	3,009	6,123
% of total occupations		2.4	1.8	25.3		8.1	24.3	50

Source: Data from *Verhandlungen, Kammer der Abgeordneten*, 1850, Beilage Band 3, Beilage 59, pp. 6–7. See table 2.3 n.b.

Note: Occupations not shown in this table include religious employees, professionals, and so forth, whose numbers were small. Figures in parentheses are peddlers. In the column for trade for 1822, only Upper and Lower Bavaria gave totals for all types of trade.

In the columns for trade, data on the number of *Hausierer*, peddlers, was inserted, and all Jews engaged in trade in 1822 in Swabia, Upper Palatinate, Middle Franconia, Upper Franconia, and Lower Franconia were listed as peddlers. In 1848 this was no longer the case: in Swabia only 122 of 634 were peddlers; in Upper Palatinate, 21 of 94; in Middle Franconia, 233 of 1,290; in Upper Franconia, 233 of 474; and in Lower Franconia, 348 of 1,456. No data was given for the Palatinate in 1822, but in 1848 an insert stated that "a great part" of the 2,126 engaged in trade were peddlers.

all Bavarians engaged in the crafts and trade, including Jews, account for only 23 percent of the total in 1852. If wholesaling, petty shopkeeping, cattle dealing, and peddling are combined (table 2.4), Jews total 49 percent, not including any part of the 14 percent in miscellaneous occupations. In other words, the percentage of Jews in "commerce" was probably, at a minimum, three times that of Christians. To this we must add two other correctives to get a more accurate view of the comparative occupational structure of Jews and Christians: we must allow for those Christians in agriculture and crafts who also pursued trade, and we must do the same for the Jews.

Many Jewish craftsmen and farmers moved into their occupations largely, if not entirely, as a means of using the provisions of the 1813 law to obtain a place in the *Matrikel*. In one case a wealthy Jew qualified as a sieve-maker to gain residence in a particular town, but he never practiced his craft.[89] In one area of the Pfalz, some twenty-five Jewish families were said to "own land" but to "leave its cultivation to tenant farmers" while they pursued "their craft or commerce," which was their main source of livelihood.[90] Many Jews engaged in mixed occupations, frequently combining agriculture and trade or trade and a craft.[91] In the debate over the emancipa-

TABLE 2.6.   Occupations of All Bavarians by Province in 1852 (in number of heads of families)

	Agriculture	Agriculture[a] and Trade	Trade[b] and Crafts	Independent[c]
Upper Bavaria	88,646	12,860	42,866	22,111
Lower Bavaria	84,455	10,861	19,706	6,765
Palatinate	86,642	13,695	27,391	5,959
Upper Palatinate	74,548	13,279	21,215	7,221
Upper Franconia	78,129	14,325	32,758	6,982
Middle Franconia	66,507	12,991	34,801	10,801
Lower Franconia	89,275	18,190	20,082	6,123
Swabia	88,758	19,358	27,962	9,091
Bavaria	656,960	115,559	226,781	75,053
% of total occupations	66[d]	12	23	7

Source: "Bevölkerung des Königreichs Bayern nach Alter und Geschlecht, Familien verhältnissen, Religionsbekenntnissen, Erwerbsarten und Standen, dann Zahl und Bestimmung der Gebäude, auf Grund der Aufnahme vom Dezember 1852." Bound with *Beiträge zur Statistik des Königreichs Bayern* (Munich, 1850), table 14, 198ff. Due to numerous printing errors, especially transposition of 3 and 5, great care is needed in using this table.

[a]Agriculture and trade was a single entry in the census composed of those who were engaged simultaneously in agriculture as well as in a trade or craft—often termed *by-employment*.

[b]This was a single entry in the census.

[c]Included physicians, artists, scholars, men of independent means, pensioned officials, and the educated.

[d]$N = 996,505$—the total number of families in Bavaria.

tion bill, many speakers and publicists pointed to this mixed occupational structure among Jews, especially in the crafts. In Gaukönigshofen, Hirsch Schloss tried to have his son accepted as a *Gerber* or "tanner" to acquire residency. This became a very complex process that lasted from 1817 to 1823 and necessitated hiring and boarding a Christian master to train his son, making appeals to higher state levels (eventually to Munich), and finally agreeing to waive (for a fee) the need of a *Wanderjahre*, a year of journeying. Even though the village lacked a tanner, the local Christian tradesmen opposed a Jewish tanner; the other tanners in the district, all of whom were Christian, were hostile. The central government in Munich was far more inclined to grant Schloss the right than was the local community, and Schloss was willing to spend a lot of time and money on securing this qualification for his son. Schloss's desire for his son to become a tanner was clearly great, but it also had personal economic implications, because he himself enjoyed a substantial business in rawhides. Reviewing the effect of the Edict in pushing or attracting Jews into crafts and agriculture, Michel concludes that the result in Gaukönigshofen was only a cosmetic change. As late as 1871, practically speaking, all Jews there still made their living from trade.[92]

Between 1813 and 1849 Jews in Bavaria consciously and deliberately acted in an organized fashion to encourage their fellows to enter the crafts and agriculture. With this goal, Jews formed a number of organizations in a variety of communities. The statutes of one of them, the Support Association for Jewish Trainees in Agriculture and the Crafts in Bavaria, give us an insight into their operation. Issued in 1841, these statutes accompanied the refounding of an association originally established in 1826 and reorganized in 1830 as the Association for the Well-Being of Jews in Bavaria. This association was situated in Munich, whose rabbi, H. Aub, sat on its board, but any Bavarian Jew was eligible to receive its support. Its main goal was to encourage and support Jewish involvement in crafts and agriculture in

TABLE 2.7. Decline in the Number of Jewish Peddlers in Bavaria from 1822 to 1848

	1822	1848	% Change
Swabia	313	122	−61
Upper Palatinate	56	21	−62
Middle Franconia	562	233	−58
Upper Franconia ˙	486	78	−84
Lower Franconia	1,188	348	−71
Total	2,605	802	−69

Source: Data from *Verhandlungen, Kammer der Abgeordneten*, 1850, Beilage Band 3, Beilage 59, pp. 6–7. See table 2.3 n.b.
Note: Upper and Lower Bavaria did not provide data on peddlers, and the Palatinate lumped peddlers together with other commercial pursuits.

Bavaria, but its secondary purpose was more specific: to provide accident benefits to local members. The association was financed by monthly contributions from members and spent money largely on apprenticeship fees or—where there were none, for example, in agriculture—on clothes. Even by twentieth-century standards it seems to have been well-organized.[93]

A series of provisos found in the preamble and again in the body of the statutes throws light on the occupations of Bavarian Jews. The association stipulated that expenditures would not be limited to the heaviest manual labor to the exclusion of the most common pursuits, but that it would also not support luxury crafts. And though all were eligible in theory, only those who could prove identity and need and find an apprentice or trainee position in a local area "under the eyes of the executive committee" would be supported. Clearly the association was trying to walk a delicate line between supporting crafts that could easily become commercial shops and encouraging Jews to become involved only in "stoop labor" with no real future. While Jews did not wish to act so as to inspire critics to accuse them of promoting capitalism, they also had no interest in financing completely outmoded forms of work. It would seem that earlier experience had demonstrated that some Jews who were not really needy applied for support for ventures that were outside the occupational areas defined in the statutes.[94]

The first half of the nineteenth century in Bavaria was a period of slow, but steady, economic change, in which the economic worth of agriculture and crafts fell while commerce and industry rose. Jews, who were already heavily involved in areas enjoying economic growth, peddling excepted, were encouraged by both Christians and many Jews to enter economic fields of either low growth or decline—for personal, social, or political reasons. Torn by conflicting motives, some Jews, perhaps a good number, attempted to do both. In Prussia, where there was no law like that of 1813, the percentage of Jews in agriculture and crafts declined between 1843 and 1861, while that in trade and commerce increased.[95] Data for Arnsberg in Westphalia for 1818 and 1824 likewise show a rapid increase of Jews in commerce, including crafts, but no change in agriculture.[96]

But the Jewish economic experience in Bavaria was not at all unusual. Christian Bavarians lived in the same economy and experienced the same economic forces, albeit free of the peculiar pressure exerted on Jews. Christians, too, began to move out of agriculture and crafts and into trade, even when it ran counter to an ideology that increasingly identified the commercial world as a "Jewish" world. This movement is clear from the census of 1852 as shown in the agriculture and trade columns in table 2.6. Those who put together this demographic material obviously considered it important to show that many Bavarians who pursued agriculture also engaged in a form of trade or a craft. These totals, which, of course, included a few Jews, reflect an agricultural population in which nearly one-fifth also engaged in crafts or trade to make a living.

Even more interesting are data that show that many Christians were engaged in pursuits often contemporaneously identifed as "Jewish" and as being at the lower end of the status scale: peddling and begging. See tables 2.8 and 2.9 for data on violations of the laws on peddling and begging in the years 1847/48 to 1849/50.

Since the data in table 2.4 lists only 802 Jewish peddlers in all of Bavaria and none in Upper and Lower Bavaria, it seems that Jews were only a small percentage of all peddlers. And since only "violations" of the peddling laws are listed in table 2.8, it is almost certain that the actual number of peddlers was much larger and therefore the proportion of Jewish peddlers much smaller. Much the same is true of begging, but the totals are higher. Not only was the older stereotype of Jews as peddlers and beggars gradually becoming factually false, but the large number of Christian beggars contributed to the agitation against Jews because some argued that Jewish business practices had caused these Christians to take up the "beggar's staff."[97]

Jews were becoming more "Bavarian" and "German" in linguistic and cultural as well as economic ways. Yiddish had largely died out by the early nineteenth century in Bavaria, but Judeo-German (a Jewish dialect of German using Hebrew characters) replaced it for a time in the course of transition to German. In the nineteenth century, German became the spoken language of Jews in Bavaria, especially for business and the law. In 1800 in Zeilitzheim, all boys had Jewish names, but by 1860 only German names were in vogue.[98] Jewish journals appeared in German, as did many printed sermons. We have already seen that religious texts for school use were in German by the 1830s. Acculturation, as distinct from assimilation, was strongly underway by midcentury.

If progress was made in the years 1813–48, it was largely in the form of Jewish acculturation within a society that, formally at least, did not accept them. In this world the explosion of the revolution of 1848 seemed to be the signal for the final breakthrough into legal and political assimilation. The March revolutions of 1848 in most of the German states succeeded quickly and with little bloodshed. Within a few weeks most German states possessed press freedom, the right to found political clubs, and parliaments based on a vastly expanded suffrage. The states began to write new constitutions, most of which included religious freedom and emancipation of the Jews. Jews were admitted to the voting lists, to political clubs, and to candidacy for parliaments at almost all levels and in almost all states—including Bavaria. Much of this happened without the passage of specific legislation for Jews.[99]

Almost overnight, Jews in Bavaria ceased to be excluded from political life. The best evidence of this is the Bavarian law passed in the summer of

1848 giving all, including Jews, the right to be candidates for the lower house of Parliament. In the next election two Jews secured seats and sat as regular voting members of the house that discussed their further emancipation in late 1849.[100] The same development occurred in political clubs and in the National Parliament in Frankfurt. Men like Johann Jacoby, Gabriel Riesser, Moritz Veit, and Ludwig Bamberger, to name only a few, led Jews into German political life. The revolution signaled what Toury has called the entrance of Jews into citizenship.[101]

TABLE 2.8.   Violations of Police Regulations Concerning Peddling by Year and Province

	UB	LB	P	UP	UFr	MFr	LFr	Sw	Bavaria
1847/48	517	119	65	315	188	199	138	420	1,961
1848/49	388	186	49	614	142	198	129	282	1,988
1849/50	514	257	61	741	254	395	292	483	2,997
Total	1,419	562	175	1,670	584	792	559	1,185	6,946

Source: See table 2.9.

Note: UB (Upper Bavaria), LB (Lower Bavaria), P (Palatinate), UP (Upper Palatinate), UFr (Upper Franconia), MFr (Middle Franconia), LFr (Lower Franconia), Sw (Swabia).

TABLE 2.9   Violations of Police Regulations Concerning Begging by Province and Gender

	UB	LB	P	UP	1847/48 UFr	MFr	LFr	Sw	Bavaria
Men	2,510	2,105	4,054	1,608	1,688	2,059	1,257	2,226	17,507
Women	1,836	1,081	2,904	1,832	1,008	862	430	1,463	11,416
Children	454	486	2,649	556	847	419	250	226	5,887
Total	4,800	3,672	9,607	3,996	3,543	3,340	1,937	3,915	34,810
					1848/49				
Men	3,217	1,539	3,731	1,101	1,313	2,276	1,234	2,359	16,770
Women	2,076	615	2,478	743	820	584	317	715	8,348
Children	1,036	253	2,382	154	682	219	225	120	5,071
Total	6,329	2,407	8,591	1,998	2,815	3,079	1,776	3,194	30,189
					1849/50				
Men	3,135	1,198	4,460	1,095	1,078	1,400	1,500	2,293	16,159
Women	3,101	741	3,037	930	795	725	363	994	10,686
Children	805	351	2,631	171	580	385	282	162	5,367
Total	7,041	2,290	10,128	2,196	2,453	2,510	2,145	3,449	32,212

Source: Data from "Leistungen der Sicherheits-Wachen in den Jahren 1847/48 bis 1849/50 im Königreiche Bayern," in *Beiträge zur Statistik des Königreichs Bayern* (Munich, 1850 [sic]), 46–47.

Note: Abbreviations: same as table 2.8.

But it also meant the entrance of Jews onto the political stage alongside men like Otto von Bismarck and Robert Mohl. The former had made his maiden political speech in the Prussian United Landtag of 1847, in forceful opposition to Jewish equality in a "Christian" state.[102] Mohl, a liberal professor of law, said essentially the same in the Frankfurt Parliament, attacking Jews as a negative element in the new body politic and arguing for their exclusion. But Mohl was alone in his hostility, and nearly all of his fellow deputies, liberal and conservative, supported equality—his proposal had no chance of success.[103]

If Jews were startled to find opponents among the liberals in the St. Paul's Church in Frankfurt, the site of the Parliament, they must have been less surprised to read about attacks by peasants on Jews in Baden, Württemberg, and Bavaria. In addition to protests against taxes, feudal obligations, and rents, German peasants and townspeople protested against Jews, sometimes plundering their homes and frequently pressing them for renunciation of debts.[104] This was part of a larger process in which the same crowds also attacked nobles and burned deeds to land that they held, plundered state rent collection offices, and violated forest laws by stealing wood and poaching. In a petition of 1848 for agricultural reform, the author, a Bavarian, requested the abolition of feudal dues, the right to take wood from the state forest, and protection against the rural Jews.[105]

Little has been written about the extent and significance of violence, particularly spontaneous rural violence, in the early weeks of the 1848 revolution, and the anti-Jewish "excesses" of those weeks have suffered the same fate. Among the reasons for this relative neglect is the difficulty of "placing" such actions in the broader "political" framework of the revolution and is a consequence of frequent depiction of rural spontaneous violence as politically primitive or even as entirely apolitical. In part this stemmed from concern with political ideas and parties, which led to an initial overemphasis on the role of parliaments and their elite membership.[106] Later studies of political parties sought out local sources but concentrated on organization, something notably lacking in most rural outbursts.[107] Since the violence was temporary, limited to a few weeks in spring 1848, and since it did not seem to influence the decisions made in Berlin, Munich, and other capitals, it has usually been accorded minimal attention.

Influenced by the work of George Rude and Eric Hobsbawm elsewhere in Europe, some analysts have broadened the scope of what they mean by *political* to include even simple riots.[108] Manfred Gailus has argued cogently for reconsidering such rural actions in 1848 both as more pervasive than previously thought and, more importantly, as political events. He argues further that the direct action of aroused compatriots was deliberate, directed to specific goals that, while frequently economically self-serving, attacked structure rather than individuals, and that discriminated among objects of their anger in a considered fashion. He asserts that, even if they were often naive and limited goals, rural activists were politically organized, despite their use of such primitive methods as setting fire to estates and rent offices.[109]

But Gailus includes only a single reference to attacks on Jews, one taken from a text describing a violent episode. By explicating the violence in general, but not that directed against Jews, he conveys the, probably unintended, impression that anti-Jewish actions were either rare or nonpolitical or both.[110] This is all the more surprising in light of additional recent research showing that anti-Jewish or anti-Semitic violence, especially rural, was also far more common than previously thought.[111] One historian states that Jewish houses, businesses, and warehouses were destroyed or plundered in more than 180 areas,[112] and another describes a wide variety of such activities in many parts of Germany.[113] A new local study of Hessen shows a level of violence directed against Jews that is frankly surprising in view of the descriptions in most historical narratives.[114]

The newest picture of the spring of 1848 is of a rural society that, compared to 1830 and 1819, engaged in more rather than less violent activity of a political character. If we are to call illegal, direct action against landowners or rent officials "political," we ought to use the same term to describe similar actions against Jews. The problem is not paradoxical but arises where historians define antifeudal and anticapitalist direct action as "democratic," or imply it to be such, while hesitating to do the same for anti-Semitic actions.[115] Inclusion of anti-Semitic riots in such descriptions make the "politically active" rural populations appear far more conservative than democratic. If so, we must recognize that a base of discontent with "modern" government and with Jews already existed at the beginning of the revolution. It takes little imagination to ask how such people would regard the "revolution" in 1849, a revolution that by then had proposed more government and a more modern economy as well as equality for Jews.

If we accept the argument of Nipperdey and Rürup that anti-Semitism became modern when it became political and that it directed its energies against Jews as representatives of the liberal world,[116] then modern anti-Semitism began at least in 1848. Misperceptions of conservative governments as liberal by simple rural activists indicates the confusing nature of an era in flux. In many ways popular rural conservatives perceived the state as forcing them into a modern, political world by mandating a free press, elections, and parliaments that in turn produced legislation infringing on their rural communal rights. The common response, so noticeable in the petitions discussed below, was to threaten to act directly for their own good both politically and violently.

Like Mohl's attack on Jews in parliament, violence against Jews in the Bavarian countryside found little support elsewhere and was suppressed by the government. Perhaps some of this activity was the last gasp of the premodern world, an anachronism in revolutionary and postrevolutionary Germany.[117] Far fewer incidences of violence against Jews occurred in the second half of the century.[118] But neither violence nor the older policy of exclusion were serious issues for Jews after the events of March 1848. There were only two questions: would the changes made lead to complete civil equality, and would such equality mean acceptance? In Bavaria emancipation received a powerful boost from the revolution and led in 1849 to a bill for complete equality of Christians and Jews. The episode provides us with a unique opportunity to describe in rich detail the depth and quality of popular attitudes toward Jews.

NOTES

1. Nipperday, *Deutsche Geschichte, 1800–1866: Bürgerwelt und starker Staat* (Munich, 1983), 1.

2. This despite Austrian designs on Bavaria; see James J. Sheehan, *German History: 1770–1866* (Oxford, 1989), 261ff. and E. Weis, "Die Begründung des modernen bayerischen Staates unter König Max I (1799–1825)," *HbG* 4¹: 3–86.

3. To avoid confusion among Max Josephs, the following will refer to Montgelas only by his last name. For Montgelas, see Eberhard Weis, *Montgelas, 1759–1799: Zwischen Revolution und Reform* (Munich, 1971).

4. Actually, anticipating the dynastic change, Montgelas prepared by correctly guessing the eventual successor and then formulating his ideas for reform as early as 1796; Weis, "Begründung," *HbG*, 4¹: 7ff.

5. Sheehan, *German History*, 291ff.; Mack Walker, *German Home Towns: Community, State, and General Estate 1648–1871* (Ithaca and London, 1971), 21ff., 185–216, 284ff.; and esp. the depiction of Stein in Hans-Ulrich Wehler, *Deutsche Gesellschaftsgeschichte*, vol. 2, *Von der Reformära bis zur industriellen und politischen 'Deutschen Doppelrevolution,' 1815–1845/49* (Munich, 1987), 303–4.

6. E. R. Huber, ed., *Dokumente zur deutschen Verfassungsgeschichte*, vol. 1: *Deutsche Verfassungsdokumente 1803–1850* (Stuttgart, 1961), 1:141 describes, but does not print the text.

7. Rudolf Wassermann, "Die Entwicklung der jüdischen Bevölkerung in Bayern im 19. Jahrhundert," *Zeitschrift für Demographie und Statisitik der Juden* 1, no. 11 (Nov. 1905): 11.

8. Hans Fehn, "Das Land Bayern und seine Bevölkerung seit 1800," *HbG*, 4², 647–707.

9. Ibid., 685. Manfred Treml, "Von der 'Judenmission' zur 'Bürgerlichen Verbesserung': Zur Vorgeschichte und Frühphase der Judenemanzipation in Bayern," in Treml, et al.; *Geschichte*, 256, states that the new areas contained 96.5 percent of all Jews, 81.3 percent in Franconia and 15.2 percent in Swabia.

10. However, in some ways the Pfalz did play a role; e.g., deputies from the Pfalz sat in the Landtag and voted, almost unanimously, for Jewish emancipation. Where relevant the Pfalz will be considered. In several ways the Pfalz was similar to Alsace; see Paula Hyman, *The Emancipation of the Jews of Alsace: Acculturation and Tradition in the Nineteenth Century* (New Haven, 1991), and Vicki Caron, *Between France and Germany: The Jews of Alsace-Lorraine, 1871–1918* (Stanford, Calif., 1988), 75–76, 118–35.

11. Hermann Hoffmann, "Die Würzburger Judenverfolgungen von 1349" *Mainfränkisches Jahrbuch für Geschichte und Kunst* 5 (1953): 91.Also see Wilhelm Volkert, "Die Juden in Fürstentum Pfalz-Neuberg," *ZfbL* 26³ (1963): 601–5.

12. Wassermann, "Entwicklung," 12. In 1880 in Prussia, 80.8 percent of Jews lived in cities and comprised 3.1 percent of the total population, while in Bavaria urban Jews were only 2.07 percent of the total; see Friedrich Bosse, *Die Verbreitung der Juden im Deutschen Reiche auf Grundlage der Volkszählung vom 1. Dezember 1880* (Berlin, 1885), 68–82. It is difficult to credit Werner Cahnman's assertion that Jews "were not peasants of a different ethnicity. They were urbanites transmitted into rural folk," who, he adds, moved back to the cities later in the nineteenth century. See his "Village and Small-Town Jews in Germany: A Typological Study," *LBIY* 19 (London, 1974): 107–30. Also see Steven M. Lowenstein, "The Rural Community and the Urbanization of German Jewry," *CEH*, 13, no. 3 (Sept. 1980): 218–36. For Unterfranken see Remlein, "Landtag," 150.

13. Ibid., 13.

14. See Gisela Krug, "Die Juden in Mainfranken zu Beginn des 19. Jahrhunderts: Statistische Untersuchungen zu ihrer sozialen und wirtschaftlichen Situation," in Brandt, *Zwischen Schutzherrschaft*, 32ff.

15. Ibid., 57–58, 61–62, 63, 65.

16. Christoph Daxelmüller, "Jüdisches Alltagsleben im 19. und 20. Jahhundert am Beispiel Unterfrankens," in Treml et al., *Geschichte*, 288.

17. See Ulrike Krzywinski, "Jüdische Landgemeinden in Oberfranken (1800–1942): Ergebnisse des DFG-Projektes 'Judendörfer in Oberfranken,'" in Treml et al., *Geschichte*, 219. Also see Klaus Guth et al., eds., *Jüdische Landgemeinden in Oberfranken (1800–1942): Ein historisch-topographisches Handbuch*, vol. 1 (Bamberg, 1988).

18. Krug, "Juden," 32–33; William Zvi Tannenbaum, "From Community to Citizenship: The Jews of Rural Franconia, 1801–1862," Ph.D. diss., Stanford University, June 1989, 158.

19. See Thomas Michel, *Die Juden im Gaukönigshofen/Unterfranken (1550–1942)* (Wiesbaden, 1988), 172–73.

20. Krug, "Juden," 65. Statistically this showed up in the form of the presence of Jews in poor small towns, but not in more prosperous *Märkte*.

21. Overcrowded housing, even in rural areas, was frequent. See Steven M. Lowenstein, "Jewish Residential Concentration in Post-Emancipation Germany," *LBIY* 28 (1983): 472, citing a case in Fellheim, Bavaria, in which two houses held fourteen Jewish families each.

22. Michel, *Gaukönigshofen*, 246ff.; Daxelmüller, "Alltagsleben," 291, 294,

296. Krzywinski, "Landgemeinden," 222, writes: "In daily life together in the countryside, Jewish fellow citizens were regarded first as German, were esteemed as neighbors, and, in the various associations and in the political community, were viewed as active, engaged members." Even if she is referring to a later time period, this is hard to believe. The classic study is Jacob Katz, *Out of the Ghetto: The Social Background of Jewish Emancipation 1770–1870* (Cambridge, 1973).

23. The exceptions are what are interesting. See Jacob Toury, "Types of Jewish Municipal Rights in German Townships: The Problem of Local Emancipation," *LBIY* 22 (1977), 55–80.

24. Hendrikje Kilian, "Die Anfänge der Emanzipation am Beispiel der Münchener jüdischen Gemeinde," in Treml et al., *Geschichte,* 267.

25. See discussion in chap. 5.

26. See Falk Wiesemann, "Rabbiner und jüdische Lehrer in Bayern während der ersten Hälfte des 19. Jahrhunderts. Staat-Reform-Orthodoxie," in Treml et al., *Geschichte,* 278.

27. Krzywinski, "Landgemeinden," 219.

28. Guth, *Landgemeinde,* 393.

29. Krug, "Juden," 43.

30. Wiesemann, "Rabbiner," 278.

31. Krug, "Juden," 47, 49, 50. Unless otherwise noted, the material that follows is derived from this excellent study. Krug's sources were the tax records for 1803, a survey of the Landesregierung for 1810, the census of 1813, and numerous other local archival records; see "Juden," 25, for her description of her sources.

32. Ibid., 57–65.

33. Michel, *Gaukönigshofen,* 172ff.

34. Krug, "Juden," 69–70; for a sample cow contract, see Deneke et al., *Siehe der Stein,* 199.

35. Ibid., 72–87. For an excellent study of poor Jews, see Ernst Schubert, *Arme Leute: Bettler und Gauner im Franken des 18. Jahrhunderts* (Neustadt an der Aisch, 1983), 151–78, "Arme und missachtete Menschen: Die Landjuden."

36. Treml, "Judenmission," 256, cites von Soden, *Der baierische Landtag vom Jahre 1819* (Nürnberg, 1821), 107, that the law only oppressed the poor Jews. Zorn, "Die wirtschaftliche Struktur Bayerns um 1820," in Dieter Albrecht, et al., eds., *Festschrift für Max Spindler* (Munich, 1969): 627–29, cites material from 1825 that placed 115,300 families in the lowest class of the population by income earning between fl 100 and fl 149 per year and another 100,000 earning between fl 100 and fl 199 per year. Tannenbaum, "Citizenship," 299 n. 1, writes that the 1813 Edict ended the practice of selling *Schutzbriefe* by granting Jews a form of citizenship.

37. Ibid., 107–15.

38. Gerhard Renda, "Fürth, das 'bayerische Jerusalem,'" in Treml et al., *Geschichte,* 225–36. Michel, *Gaukönigshofen,* 212, describes the community as strongly orthodox.

39. Daxelmüller, "Alltagsleben," 290; Wiesemann, "Rabbiner," 278; Berthold Strauss, *The Rosenbaums of Zell: A Study of a Family* (London, 1962), 14–17.

40. Krzywinski, "Landgemeinden," 220–21.

41. Wiesemann, "Rabbiner," 278; Daxelmüller, "Alltagsleben," 288, notes the astonishingly large number of synagogues in villages and, in "Fränkische Dorfsynagogen," *Volkskunst. Zeitschrift für volkstümliche Sachkultur* 4 (Nov. 1981): 234–41, describes them.

42. The quotation is from the Jew Law; see app. A.

43. This is best described in David Sorkin's *The Transformation of German Jewry, 1780–1840* (New York, 1987), which has very complete notes and sources. Also see Manfred Treml, "Judenmission," passim, and Horst Möller, "Aufklärung, Judenemanzipation und Staat," in *Jahrbuch des Instituts für deutsche Geschichte*, vol. 3, *Deutsche Aufklärung und Judenemanzipation* (Tel Aviv, 1980), 119–53. Dohm's work appeared in Berlin and Stettin in 1781; Aretin's in Landshut in 1803. The best short discussion of Dohm in English is by Klaus Epstein in *The Genesis of German Conservatism* (Princeton, N.J., 1966), 220–29.

44. William O. McCagg, Jr., *A History of Habsburg Jews, 1670–1918* (Bloomington, Ind., 1989), 28ff., and Jacob Katz, *From Prejudice to Destruction: Anti-Semitism 1700–1933* (Cambridge, Mass., 1980), 223ff.

45. Arthur Hertzberg, *The French Enlightenment and the Jews* (New York and London, 1968), 314–68, on the revolution; Georges Weill, "French Jewish Historiography: 1789–1870," in Frances Malino and Bernard Wasserstein, eds., *The Jews in Modern France* (Hanover and London, 1985), 313–27; and Franz Kobler, *Napoleon and the Jews* (New York, 1976).

46. See Toury, "Types," 74–75 and Hyman, *Alsace.*

47. Rürup, *Emanzipation und Antisemitismus: Studien zur "Judenfrage" der bürgerlichen Gesellschaft* (Göttingen, 1975), 20; also Reinhard Koselleck, *Preussen zwischen Reform und Revolution: Allgemeines Landrecht, Verwaltung und soziale Bewegung von 1791 bis 1848* (1967; reprint, Stuttgart, 1975,), 59–61.

48. Toury, "Types," figure on p. 57; Rürup, *"Emanzipation,"* 29.

49. Huber, *Dokumente*, 141–247, esp. the notes.

50. For a good brief description, see Treml, "Judenmission," 252ff. The source of most of the reforms was Montgelas; see Eberhard Weis, *Montgelas*, 136–37. In his memoirs, Montgelas describes Jews in a very progressive fashion that is very similar to Dohm; see Georg Laubmann and Michael Doberl, eds., *Denkwürdigkeiten des Grafen Maximilian Joseph v. Montgelas über die innere Staatsverwaltung Bayerns (1799–1817)* (Munich, 1908), 138–42, in French. For a good idea of similar action elsewhere in Germany, see Helmut Berding, "Judenemanzipation im Rheinbund" in E. Weis, ed., with Elisabeth Müller-Luckner, *Reformen im rheinbündischen Deutschland* (Munich, 1984), 269–86.

51. Treml, "Judenmission," 252, sees the law as a document of enlightened state absolutism but recognizes its negative aspects.

52. Jacob Katz, *Prejudice*, 2.

53. Adopting a surname had been required by a law of 1808, but some Jews had not done so.

54. See E. Weis, "Reformen," 55ff. and notes.

55. Wiesemann, "Rabbiner," 278–79, 284. See also the material in Claudia Prestel, *Jüdisches Schul- und Erziehungswesen in Bayern 1804–1933* (Göttingen,

1989), 229ff., although most of her data is from the later nineteenth and early twentieth centuries.

56. Genesis, 1: 28.

57. See Joan Campbell, *Joy in Work, German Work: The National Debate, 1800–1945* (Princeton, N.J., 1989), esp. chs. 1 and 3.

58. Renda, "Fürth," 235, citing StA Nürnberg, Regierung von Mittelfranken, KdI, Abgabe 1900.

59. Sorkin, *Transformation,* passim. See his notes and bibliography for other works on the same subject, esp. most of the works of Jacob Katz. Evidence of the Jewish attempt to take advantage of what was offered in the early years may be found in Laubmann and Doeberl, *Denkwürdigkeiten,* 142 where Montgelas writes that "every time a Jewish family received the right to settle there was a complaint [by Christians] and in the last years of my administration of the Interior Ministry this burdened our work." Montgelas left office in 1817.

60. *Die Synagoge: Eine jüdisch-religiöse Zeitschrift; zur Belehrung und Erbauung für Israeliten,* jg. 2, heft 1 (Munich, 1839), edited by Dr. L. Adler, who probably wrote this piece, because the style and content are similar to his later writings.

61. Ibid., 107ff.

62. Treml, "Judenmission," 255–56; for the Jewish critique of the law, see Dr. A. Eckstein, *Kampf,* passim.

63. See Treml, "Judenmission," 260.

64. Thus Nipperdey, *Geschichte,* 249–50.

65. Nipperdey, *Geschichte,* 279ff., provides a good, brief description; for the flavor of an older version, see Heinrich von Treitschke, *Deutsche Geschichte im Neunzehnten Jahrhundert,* 5 vols. (Leipzig, 1927), 2:519ff.

66. Treitschke, *Geschichte,* 2:528ff.

67. See Jacob Katz, *Prejudice,* 92–104, and his "The Hep-Hep Riots in Germany in 1819: The Historical Background," *Zion* 38 (1973): 62-115, in Hebrew. The term *anti-Semite* was not yet in use.

68. Simon Dubnov, *History of the Jews,* vol. 5, *From the Congress of Vienna to the Emergence of Hitler,* trans. Moshe Spiegel (S. Brunswick, New York, and London, 1973) 27–30, who also wrote, inaccurately, that the authorities banished Jews as a result.

69. Sterling, "Anti-Jewish Riots in Germany in 1819: A Displacement of Social Protest," *Historica Judaica* 12 (Oct. 1950), 105–42.

70. Katz, *Prejudice,* 100, 102.

71. Cited in Max Domarus, *Bürgermeister Behr: Ein Kämpfer für den Rechtsstaat* (Würzburg, 1971), 96.

72. Rürup, *Emanzipation,* 21–22, who writes that the Hep-Hep Riots (as they were commonly called) raised the issue of the peoples' wrath," a Damocles' sword hanging over the emancipation question. Schwarz, *Juden,* 216, notes that incidents also occurred in 1820 and 1821 in Würzburg.

73. See Katz, *Prejudice,* 74–104; Selma Stern-Taeubler, "Der Literarische Kampf um die Emanzipation in den Jahren 1816–1820 und seine ideologischen und

soziologischen Voraussetzungen," *Hebrew Union College Annual* 23, part 2 (1950–51): 171–96; KTAV reprint, New York, 1968); Heinz Bender, *Der Kampf um die Judenemanzipation in Deutschland im Spiegel der Flugschriften 1815–1820* (Jena, 1939); brief abstracts of many of these may be found in Deneke et al., *Siehe der Stein*, 307–14. Also see Dubnov, *History*, 5:25.

74. See n. 105 and below.

75. Rainer Erb and Werner Bergmann, *Die Nachtseite der Judenemanzipation: Der Widerstand gegen die Integration der Juden in Deutschland 1780–1860* (Berlin, 1989), 218ff.

76. Thus Daxelmüller, "Alltagsleben," 291ff., and *Jüdische Kultur in Franken* (Würzburg,1988), 181ff. R. Po-Chia Hsia *The Myth of Ritual Murder: Jews and Magic in Reformation Germany* (New Haven and London, 1988), 208–9, discusses what he terms the preservation of these "memories of host desecration and child murders in collective folk memory."

77. Michel, *Gaukönigshofen*, 239–40, 242–43, 246ff.

78. Walter Zwi Bacharach, "Das Bild des Juden in katholischen Predigten des 19. Jahrhunderts," in Treml et al., *Geschichte*, 315–16.

79. Simon Knoll, *Predigten auf alle Sonn- und Festtage des katholischen Kirchenjahres für Stadt und Land*, vol. 1 (Schaffhausen, 1862), 128ff.

80. Hsia, *Ritual Murder*, 203ff., dates the beginning of the decline in the use of the ritual murder myth in the last quarter of the sixteenth century; the Fettmilch uprising of 1614 demonstrates that it took some time to completely disappear. Also Daxelmüller, *Kultur*, 182, and Karl Mistele, "Volkskundliche Aspekte traditioneller Judenfeindschaft," in Treml et al., *Geschichte*, 321–26, who argues that the medieval view of Jews persisted in areas without Jews.

81. Wassermann, "Entwicklung," 11.

82. Dr. Hermann Engelbert, *Statistik des Judenthums in Deutchen Reiche ausschliesslich Preussens und in der Schweiz* (Frankfurt am Main, 1875), 10, and Wassermann, "Entwicklung," 11 and see the debates in 1849 discussed below. Usiel 0. Schmelz, "Die demographische Entwicklung der Juden in Deutschland von der Mitte des 19. Jahrhunderts bis 1933," *Zeitschrift für Bevölkerungswissenschaft* 8, no. 1 (1982): 48ff.

83. Avraham Barkai, "German-Jewish Migrations in the Nineteenth Century, 1830–1910," *LBIY* 30 (1985): 301, 306–8, 310, 317; also he notes, p. 313, the concern of contemporary Jews about the size of this out-migration. If his figures are accurate for Bavaria as a whole, Jews left Bavaria at a rate between four and six times the rate for the total population.

84. Jacob Toury, "Jewish Manual Labor and Emigration: Records from some Bavarian Districts (1830–1857)," *LBIY* 14 (1971): 45, 51.

85. Ibid., 58–60. He also, p. 55, describes the typical emigrant in Kissingen as "professional" (by which he must mean "skilled") and the most active and hardworking manual laborers. Barkai, "The German Jews at the Start of Industrialization: Structural Change and Mobility 1835–1860," in W. E. Mosse, Arnold Paucker, and Reinhard Rürup, eds., *Revolution and Evolution: 1848 in German-Jewish History*

(Tübingen, 1981), 127–28, 135, agrees that most came from the rural areas and small towns but sees them as relatively poor.

86. BHStA, Munich, Ministry of Commerce, files 8679 and 8680, Hausierhandel der Juden, 1849–56 and 1857–69, respectively.

87. This is probably an error, because there had been a few Jews in Niederbayern earlier as well as a few years later.

88. "Bevölkerung des Königreichs Bayern nach Alter und Geschlecht, Familienverhältnissen, Religionsbekenntnissen, Erwerbsarten und Ständen, dann Zahl und Bestimmung der Gebäude, auf Grund der Aufnahme vom Dezember 1852," bound with *Beiträge zur Statistik des Königreichs Bavern* (Munich, 1850), 198ff.

89. Werner Cahnmann, "Jews," 120.

90. Toury, "Emigration," 47.

91. Monika Richarz, ed., *Jüdisches Leben in Deutschland: Selbstzeugnisse zur Sozialgeschichte 1780–1871* (New York, 1976), 32ff., and "Emancipation and Continuity: German Jews in the Rural Economy," in W. E. Mosse et al., *Revolution,* 95–115.

92. Michel, *Gaukönigshofen,* 172–73, 189–91.

93. *Statuten des Unterstützungs-Vereins für israelitische Ackerbau- und Handwerks-Lehrlinge in Bayern* (Munich, 1841), 3–25. One example of its modernity must suffice here: whenever the cash on hand exceeded fl 100, up to 50 was to be placed in some other interest-bearing instrument. Daxelmüller, *Kultur,* 76–77, implies that Prussia led the way in this regard with a Society for the Spread of Crafts and Agriculture among the Jews in the Prussian State founded in 1813; he also notes similar organizations in Coburg, Fürth, Würzburg, and Nürnberg.

94. In *Statuten,* see esp. pp. 3, 5 (art. 1), 7 (arts. 6–7).

95. Barkai, "Jews at Start," 131.

96. Arno Herzig, *Judentum und Emanzipation in Westfalen* (Münster, 1973), 67.

97. In Ingeborg Weber-Kellermann, *Landleben im 19. Jahrhundert* (Munich, 1987), 337, see the illustration of a begging family singing in an inn. See the discussion of the debates, the newspaper stories, and the petitions in chs. 3–6 below. Beggary was a major problem in France, too; see Eugen Weber, *Peasants into Frenchmen: The Modernization of Rural France, 1870–1914* (Stanford, Calif., 1976), 62–66.

98. Tannenbaum, "Citizenship," 48–49, 137–39, 142–43, 187–88.

99. See the essays in W. E. Mosse et al., *Revolution,* esp. Rürup's essay "The European Revolutions of 1848 and Jewish Emancipation," 1–53, and Mosse's "The Revolution of 1848: Jewish Emancipation in Germany and its Limits," 389–401. Also, Jacob Toury, "Die Revolution von 1848 als innerjüdischer Wendepunkte," in H. Liebeschütz and Arnold Paucker, eds., *Das Judentum in der deutschen Umwelt 1800–1850: Studien zur Frühgeschichte der Emanzipation* (Tübingen, 1977), 359–76.

100. Eckstein, *Kampf,* 101–2, citing a letter from Dr. Morgenstern to various Jewish communities, 27 Mar. 1849, calling for the establishment of committees.

101. Jacob Toury, "Der Eintritt der Juden ins deutsche Bürgertum," in Liebeschütz and Paucker, *Das Judentum,* 139–242. The Jews elected were Dr. Fischel Arnheim

of Hof and Dr. David Morgenstern of Nuremberg, both from areas with few Jews. See also Toury, *Der Eintritt der Juden ins Deutsche Bürgertum: Eine Dokumentation* (Tel Aviv, 1972), vii, for his concern that *Bürgertum* mean "citizenry," not economic status.

102. Otto von Bismarck, *Die Gesammelte Werke*, Bd. 10, *Fürst Bismarcks gesammelte Reden* (Berlin, 1894), 1:21ff.

103. Erich Angermann, *Robert von Mohl, 1799–1875: Leben und Werk eines altliberalen Staatsgelehrten* (Neuwied, 1962), 82–83, writes that Mohl's claim to be free of the older Jew hatred was, based on his own letters, simply false.

104. Eckstein, *Kampf,* 89–90, notes that in small towns like Burgkundstadt the motto was "Gegen Junker und Juden."

105. Erb and Bergmann, *Nachtseite,* 251–61, write that the anti-Jewish excesses in the 1848 revolution have been understated. Günther Franz, "Die agrarische Bewegung im Jahr 1848," 7 (1959): 176–92, contains the best descriptions and the worst interpretations; see esp. 179, 182, 184, 190–92. Also see Toury, "Wendepunkte," 365.

106. Veit Valentin, *Geschichte der deutschen Revolution von 1848–49* (Berlin, 1930–31; reprint, Aalen, 1968).

107. Joachim Paschen, *Demokratische Vereine und Preussischer Staat: Entwicklung und Unterdrückung der demokratischen Bewegung während der Revolution von 1848/49* (Munich and Vienna, 1977).

108. Among others, George Rude, *The Crowd in the French Revolution* (Oxford, 1959), and *The Crowd in History* (New York, 1964); Eric Hobsbawm, *Captain Swing* (New York, 1968), and *Primitive Rebels: Studies in Archaic Forms of Social Movement in the Nineteenth and Twentieth Centuries* (Manchester, 1971).

109. Manfred Gailus, "Zur Politisierung der Landbevölkerung in der Märzbewegung von 1848," in Peter Steinbach, ed., *Probleme politischer Partizipation im Modernisierungsprozess* (Stuttgart, 1982), 103ff., 107, 110.

110. Ibid., 94.

111. Günther Franz, "Agrarische Bewegung," *passim,* but this has been discounted because of his leanings toward Nazism. Dieter Langewiesche, "Die deutsche Revolution," *AfS* 21 (1981): 459–87.

112. Helmut Berding, *Moderne Anti-Semitismus in Deutschland* (Frankfurt am Main, 1986), 74; Erb and Bergmann, *Nachtseite,* 257, n. 128.

113. Erb and Bergmann, *Nachtseite,* 251–61.

114. Preissler, *Frühantisemitismus in der Freien Stadt Frankfurt und im Grossherzogtum Hessen (1810 bis 1860)* (Heidelberg, 1989), esp. 354ff.

115. For such usage, see Hermann-Josef Rupieper, "Die Sozialstruktur der Trägerschichten der Revolution von 1848/49 am Beispiel Sachsen," in H. Kaelble et al., eds., *Probleme der Modernisierung in Deutschland: Sozialhistorische Studien zum 19. und 20. Jahrhundert* (Opladen, 1978), 80–109; Gailus "Politisierung"; Rainer Wirtz, "Die Begriffsverwirrung der Bauern im Odenwald 1848: Odenwälder 'Excesse' und die Sinsheimer 'republikanische Schilderhebung,'" in Detlev Püls, ed., *Wahrnehmungsformen und Protestverhalten: Studien zur Lage der Unterschichten im 18. und 19. Jahrhundert* (Frankfurt am Main, 1979), 81–104.

116. Discussed in ch. 8 in more depth.

117. Nipperdey, *Geschichte,* 251.

118. Monika Richarz, "Emancipation and Continuity: German Jews in the Rural Economy," in W. E. Mosse et al., *Revolution,* 100.

Chapter 3

The Legislative Road
to Emancipation

Although the Reform Era in Germany ended with the Congress of Vienna in 1815, some smaller states followed through with earlier plans to establish parliaments. In 1818 and 1819 Bavaria, Baden, and Württemberg adopted constitutions providing for elected parliaments. The Bavarian Parliament dates from May 1818 and, until altered by changes made in the revolution of 1848, was a *Stände-Versammlung,* an assembly elected by estates or corporate groups. Of its two houses, the upper, the *Reichsräthe,* contained hereditary adult members of the royal family, heads of imperial noble houses, officials of the Catholic and Protestant churches, and a few royal officials and appointees. The lower house was drawn from estate owners, academicians, clerics, representatives of the cities and market towns, and those landowners who were not estate owners.[1] Its suffrage was too restrictive to merit the label "democratic," but the Bavarian Parliament was representative and possessed power to approve or deny all forms of legislation. The Bavarian Constitution predated the existence of any similar institution in either Austria or Prussia by a full generation.

The beginning of Bavarian parliamentary life did not mean a new era of reform from below. It was the opening of an era of conservative inaction by a monarchy led, after 1825, by the conservative Ludwig I, working with an upper house of an even stronger conservative bent and with a lower house containing only the germs of later liberal political strength. Over the years and especially after the revolutionary year 1830, the balance in the lower house shifted to the left, producing stalemates on many issues in which the monarchy and its conservative ministers—such as Carl von Abel (1788–1859)—backed by the upper house, confronted an increasingly critical and liberal lower house.[2] This general picture of legislative development is exactly reflected by the failure of repeated attempts to change the Jew Law of 1813. Change came for Jews and other Bavarians only in 1848, but ironically

51

it came as much from above as from below. The evolution of the struggle between conservatives and liberals over reform of the 1813 law clarifies the overall developments of 1848–49.

Hope: Attempts at Legislative Change, 1813–48

Despite the restricted suffrage and conservative structure of the Bavarian Parliament established by the Constitution of 1818, the existence of a public forum for debate about state law introduced representative government to Bavaria. Communities directed their complaints and requests to parliament as well as to the king and his ministers. In the first parliament in 1819, discussion turned to Jews because some communities submitted petitions complaining about Jewish peddlers and tradesmen.[3] A committee chaired by von Schmitt supported fifteen different suggestions for how to more tightly restrict Jewish peddling. Among four proposals accepted was one, passed 54 to 34, that called for an assembly of enlightened Jews to discuss how Jewry in Bavaria might better assimilate. The most significant piece of legislation on Jews was a proposal, passed 86 to 2, that the government draft a revision of the laws of 1813 relating to Jewish settlement, education, residence based on type of occupation, and all conditions of citizenship and submit it to the next legislative session.[4] It appeared to advocate reform favorable to Jews.

But the 1819 debates portray representatives agreeing almost unanimously that Jewish peddling was evil, harmful, and a symptom of Jewish unwillingness to assimilate in Christian Bavaria. Joseph Ritter von Utzschneider, burgomaster of Munich, proposed some of the legislation and stated at one point that "as long as the name 'Jew' exists these men will form a state within the state and be damaging to us." One deputy suggested making Jews equal to Christians as soon as possible but simultaneously agreed to tougher laws on Jewish peddling. Another deputy noted that the complaints about Jewish peddling came from sellers who would be helped by laws restricting peddling at the cost of consumers. The deputy's analysis of the advantages of competition for the consumer appear very modern, but the same deputy also called for Jews to assimilate by eating and drinking as Christians did, by holding religious services on Sunday, by marrying Christians, and by using German rather than Hebrew. He urged the state to regulate Jewish schools and to prevent encroachment on Christian churches. Most of the deputies who spoke favored tougher laws on peddling and criticized Jews and Jewish business. They divided into those who felt Jews would not change and those who felt that Jews could acculturate and should be assimilated if they became "Christian" in all but theology.[5]

The revisions that Parliament requested for the 1813 law were not a consequence of Jewish pressure for a vote for revision in their favor, as is implied in one of the few studies of Jews in this period, but rather manifestations of a desire to toughen the 1813 law.[6] Only this interpretation makes understandable the acceptance by the upper house and the agreement by the monarchy to submit such legislation. But the state did not submit legislation on the 1813 law, probably out of concern that raising the issue might open the door to easing rather than toughening the law.

During the reigns of Max I. Josef and Ludwig I—that is, until 1848—the Bavarian government chose not to submit any draft revision of the 1813 law to Parliament. In 1825 the king's council (*Staatsrat*) agreed on much tougher language regarding communal control of residence and marriage, wording that specifically justified the exclusion of special groups. Jews were not mentioned, but that was not necessary.[7] In the following two years, the government added regulations insisting more strictly that all Jews be educated according to general scholarly principles, which meant less study in traditional Yeshivas heavily oriented to Talmud and more in secular subjects, such as German, Latin and Greek, history, geography, natural sciences, philosophy, and literature. Some Jews called for exactly the same educational reforms at the same time.[8]

From 1825 to 1848 King Ludwig I dominated the Bavarian government. Historians have interpreted his rule as conservative, and his negative attitude toward Jews has been noted in his response to the 1819 riots.[9] Originally more moderate, Ludwig turned to the right following the revolutionary upheavals of 1830, while Parliament became more oppositional. Failing to secure support on a number of major issues, Ludwig turned decisively toward an even more conservative position.[10] In addition to other actions, the lower house requested the king to submit a draft for revision of the 1813 law that would alleviate the worst of the law's legal disabilities for Jews. Initiative for this request came from several deputies from the Pfalz and from petitions from several Jewish communities, among them that of Fürth. Too much should not be made of this, because the first version of the bill asked for equality only in law and on condition that religious Jews renounce the Talmud and change the Sabbath to Sunday! Much of the debate focused on the Sabbath clause. It was eventually cut, demonstrating the growing numbers of the reformist faction. Nevertheless, an amendment for lifting the restriction on residence failed, as did one to permit Jews entry into all schools.[11] The upper house modified the proposal slightly, accepted it, and passed it on to the king, albeit with the comment that "revision" (not repeal) of the 1813 law was all that could be expected. The king received the suggestion but did not act on it.[12]

Despite its drawbacks, this was progress. The 1831 Parliament was the first to ask for revision in favor of Jews, spelling out what it wanted in terms of equal status of Jews before the law. It should not surprise us that the majority of the deputies were not in favor of full equality. Several deputies defended Jews against the implied accusation that their religion served as an obstacle to equal citizenship, generally praised the changes taking place among Jews (i.e., the move into "German" occupations), and even argued that the Talmud did not pose a problem for Christians.[13] All of this had been said earlier in print, but not yet in Parliament.

Because Ludwig did not act on the request of the 1831 legislature, many of the same parliamentary leaders introduced a new resolution in 1834 for the "improvement of the civil condition of the Jews." Hoping, perhaps, to build on the sentiment expressed in 1831 and probably both misinterpreting and overestimating it, Dr. Schultz suggested repeal or revision of the clauses on residence and marriage in the 1813 Edict. Now, however, faced with the more radical request to allow Jews to live where they chose and to increase their numbers, the committee resolved not to permit Jews full citizenship, agreeing to accept revision only so long as it "was compatible with the interests of state and community," and adding that no revision should apply to Jews involved in *Nothandel*.[14]

This bill was wholly new and vastly different from the one debated in 1831. Even the earlier legislature had rejected an amendment that proposed revision of the residence restrictions. Reacting cautiously, the committee requested information on public opinion toward such revision. The state secured a negative report on the issue from regional officials, largely from the Oberpfalz. In the end both Parliament and the government did nothing in 1834.

Apart from unprofitable discussion of the possible establishment of a Jewish consistory to deal with the internal religious administration of Judaism in Bavaria, the 1834 debates introduced more than a decade of inaction. In 1845, however, Jews took the initiative by petitioning Parliament to request that the king submit legislation for full equality for Jews. In their petitions, Jews argued that they performed equal duties and should have equal rights. Specifically, they took issue with the exclusion of Jews from state service, especially from the judicial system. Ludwig I's directives to his ministers to either exclude Jews from branches of the state service or restrict them to lower and unimportant offices indicate that the monarch and his regime were in fact strongly hostile to Jews.[15]

Faced with the deadly combination of governmental hostility and a decade of parliamentary apathy, Jews cautiously petitioned Parliament to reintroduce reform.[16] One leader of the petition for change was Dr. Lazarus Adler, rabbi in Kissingen. In early 1846 Adler published a pamphlet clearly designed for maximum polemical impact, titled *The Civil Position of the Jews in Bavaria: A Memorandum Respectfully Submitted to the High Cham-*

ber of Deputies. In this petition, Adler argued that Jews deserved equality or at least repeal of legal restrictions, because Jews were loyal and hardworking citizens whose religion was no barrier to full support for the state. What made his polemic unusual in Bavaria was his argument that Jews were only restricted because of their religion—if Jews converted to Christianity, they instantly became citizens free of restrictions. From this beginning, Adler shifted his focus to Christianity, asking whether the restrictions placed on Jews were really Christian? Was it Christian to ask Jews to lower their numbers as the 1813 law intended? He even asked what it meant to be "Christian" if two Christian churches, Catholic and Protestant, called each other "unchristian." Clearly Adler was addressing the liberal deputies in the lower house of Parliament rather than the king or the conservatives.[17]

The Jewish initiative stimulated the relevant parliamentary committee, headed by von Gumppenberg, to report to the lower house a three-part proposal requesting the king to submit, to the next session, draft legislation for the repeal of laws restricting the Jews in the area of civil rights and legal process; to submit a "fundamental and modern revision of the Edict [of 1813]"; and, until then, to more moderately administer the paragraphs on residence and marriage and on trade in agricultural products.[18] The spirited and lengthy debate that ensued resulted in the passage of the first clause unchanged (by a vote of 92 to 30), the revision of the second to include protection of Christians (117 to 5), and the passage of the third unchanged (65 to 57). The upper house eliminated the third and most contentious clause on residence and sent the first two on to the king's council, which reported only that it would take the requests into "mature consideration." Nothing happened, and in 1847 Parliament renewed its requests. In November the Ministry of the Interior finally responded to the liberal pressure and, for the first time, began the bureaucratic process of putting together a bill for revision of the 1813 law.[19]

Ministerial agreement to revision and reform in 1847 constituted the major turning point in the history of the Jew Law of 1813. Had the revolution of 1848 not intervened in a few months, some form of liberal legislation would have been submitted and accepted. The debates in Parliament in 1846–47 mark the end of a development that began with the law of 1813, and the successful passage of legislation requesting revision marks the beginning of a new era in which Jews would, to use Toury's phrase, enter into citizenry.[20]

But embedded in the 1846 debates was the beginning of another development—the organization and enunciation of principles of popular political opposition to Jewish emancipation. Unlike any earlier legislative session except that of 1819, when Jewish peddling was the issue, the 1846 session awakened the opposition to the realization that they could no longer control Parliament or depend on the king and his ministers. By opposing emancipation, they simultaneously turned backward and forward: backward to religion, by claiming that Bavaria was a Christian state and that Jews could not be equal to Christians unless they were Christian; and forward to the newly emerging principle of democracy, the "will of the people" being found in petitions against emancipation.

Among those who voted for the committee's proposals in 1846 was Dekan (Dean) Götz, an early supporter of the bill. Götz made clear at once that he was only for revision, not for unconditional emancipation. His speech reminds us that the committee had proposed no more than revision. Götz stated the basis for his opposition—Bavaria was a Christian state.[21] This was a new principle not found in the 1813 Jew Law. If accepted, it meant that only conversion to Christianity could entitle a non-Christian to become a Bavarian. The issue was not how many Jews had become shoemakers or farmers as the 1813 law had urged them to do, but whether they could ever be considered equal to Christians if they were not Christian.

The speeches in favor of emancipation, especially those that spoke of the "success" of the 1813 law, suddenly appear secondary. There were two debates in 1846. The first was over the proposals for reform, especially in the general law code. The second was over full equality, especially in the area of residence rights. Some opponents of these proposals argued that the clauses changing residence and marriage status implied full emancipation. Speeches on revision versus equality were entangled in a way that is not easy to unravel. At least seven major speakers opposed full emancipation while stating their support for revision. The overwhelming support for reform, as evidenced by the votes on the first two clauses for legal equality and revision of the 1813 law, concealed a deeper division over full equality, which surfaced in the split on the third clause on residence. Many of the deputies supporting reform of the law code did so because they saw the 1813 Edict as having succeeded in its mission to turn backward Jews into modern Germans; they did not agree that Jews could or should be fully equal to Christians.

After many hours of a debate that featured all the old anti-Jewish arguments and continued into a special evening session after 5 P.M., Professor Dr. Ignaz von Döllinger rose to speak.[22] A respected academic and church historian, Döllinger had not yet gained the stature he would later enjoy, but his speech was the most intelligent and fascinating of the debate. Döllinger's speech had several levels. Regarding the committee proposals, he noted general agreement on the principle of revision and reform, an agreement disturbed only by disagreement over what kind and how much. He proposed an amendment to the second clause that would more directly "protect" the Christian population, especially the rural elements, from the economic danger of Jews. He opposed only those laws that either did not protect Christians or were used solely to hurt Jews. This introduced a new view of the 1813 law as a series of fences separating Jews from Christians, with the intention of guarding the latter from the former.

Döllinger's interpretation was problematic. It betrayed his origins in Franconia, origins to which the scholar gave voice when he recalled a Franconian saying from his boyhood: "One is lost if a Jew sees you at the window." The 1813 law had set out to force Jews to enter Christian society at the economic and communal level. But the professor argued that the question was whether changing the laws, especially through emancipation and equality, would change Jews' attitudes. He referred those who thought it would do so to societies where the laws had already been changed. He rejected the models of England, Belgium, and Holland as invalid on various grounds, but he thought that France provided a useful example because it had enough Jews and because French Jews had been emancipated for fifty-five years. (Since the Napoleonic Decree of 1808, restricting Jews, lasted until 1818, Döllinger should have said that Jews had been fully free for twenty-eight years.) He pointed out that few Jews in the area most affected by the Napoleonic revisions, Alsace, owned agricultural land and that those who did bought it for resale in smaller parcels. He added that, in 1818, the Jewish Central Consistory in France had instructed Jews to turn to agriculture, but they had not done so. All Jews in Alsace, he asserted, were still as they had been in 1789—committed to trade only. Usury still dominated Jewish business, he stated, and five-sixths of all court verdicts were against Jews, though they comprised only about 5 percent of the population. We know today that Döllinger's portrayal of life in Alsace and Lorraine was inaccurate, but no one challenged it then.[23]

The most intriguing part of Döllinger's speech was his claim that full emancipation would damage Judaism by encouraging Jews to become more Christian. In developing this point at length and with sensitivity, Döllinger demonstrated a reasonable knowledge of Orthodox and Reform tendencies in contemporary Judaism. He took the issue of the Sabbath as an example, arguing that some Jews had indicated that they would change their day of worship to Sunday. If they would do that, he asked, would they treat the other commandments differently? In an eerie foreshadowing of his later problems with the Catholic church, Döllinger also asked whether it was good for the state to intervene to supervise the training of rabbis. "A major tendency of modern government, at least in Germany, as we all know, is that [one wants to] govern too much, to intervene in everything, to be guardian to everything, to do everything oneself."[24]

Döllinger's speech represented a highly intellectual and even profound attack on emancipation and on Jews. Nothing substantial separated his position on a Christian state from that of Götz. And his economic analysis of

Jews did not differ in any serious way from that of representative Pfäffinger. Unlike Adler, Döllinger argued that no progress was possible if Jews held on to their Talmudic-rabbinical tradition. Could he have hoped that Jews would choose not to reform religiously and would opt against the process of emancipation?

By the end of the debates, it was clear that some revision of the 1813 law was imminent, though it would stop far short of equality. Speaking for the government, the royal ministerial advisor, von Zenetti, agreed with the need for revision and announced that the Ministry of the Interior was working on the problem. His only comments were that the 1813 law had been incorrectly derided as damaging to Jews when it had done much for them, improving conditions and opening up new opportunities. Yet the government thought the results of the law were discordant with its expectations, because Jews had used the new occupations in crafts and agriculture to become resident and then had returned as quickly as possible to business. Even the restrictions on numbers had not worked, von Zenetti argued; there were more Jewish families in 1846 than there had been in 1813.[25] Assuming that von Zenetti's remarks reflected government thinking, changes were about to occur in the 1813 law.

The committee chair, Freiherr von Gumppenberg, as floor manager of the bill in the house, was last to speak in the 1846 debate. He directed his comments mainly to Döllinger, emphasizing that the legislation before the house was not a bill for emancipation but a request that within three years' time the government submit a bill for the improvement of the conditions of the Jews. If those present were still alive, they would be present—a charming nineteenth-century view of politics—and could modify the bill as they saw fit. The president then took the final vote, the key parts of the bill passed overwhelmingly, and von Gumppenberg could relax—reform was on the way. Ironically, revolution arrived first.

Promise: The Emergence of a Bill for Full Emancipation

One of the great surprises of 1849 was that the government bill finally submitted to Parliament was not reformist but for nothing less than full equality of Jews with Christians. Its origin highlights the impact of the year of revolution in 1848. From late 1847 to late 1848 the state ministries spent a great deal of time and effort preparing legislation intended only to revise, or update, the law of 1813. Then, probably in late 1848, it discarded all this work and introduced a bill for full equality for Jews. The process tells us a great deal not only about the regime and the bureaucracy but about how the revolution precipitated a rethinking of governmental policies.

The first stage in this development was the gathering of information set in motion by directives dated 25 October and 17 November 1847 from the Ministry of the Interior for Church and Schools and the parallel Ministry of the Interior, respectively.[26] The records show a clear division of labor: the Ministry for Church and Schools took responsibility for those parts of the 1813 law relating only to religion or religious institutions, clauses 23 to 34; the larger ministry dealt with the secular role of Jews in society, clauses 1 to 22.

The obligation to collect this information descended on the shoulders of the governor of the province of Oberbayern, who promptly delegated the work to the police office and the city magistrate of Munich. A more specific directive of 13 December stated that the request for information was *sehr dringend* (very urgent) and requested a reply within four weeks. On 11 February 1848 the police office of Munich submitted a lengthy report in three parts on the clauses relating to religion, based largely on a report submitted by the leaders of the local Jewish community, especially Rabbi Hirsch Aub.[27]

Although they took a firm position against special laws, Aub and his colleagues were happy and thankful to be asked to suggest ways to revise the law in a modern fashion. Before making specific requests, they asked for the recognition of the Jewish religion as a church (*Kirchengesellschaft*), the establishment of a consistory (*Oberkirchenbehörde*) to administer Jewish religious affairs, and the establishment of university departments devoted to Jewish theology within the Bavarian universities. These requests derived from the discussions of the late 1830s, and the authors noted those origins. The new departments for Jewish religious studies were to combine traditional Talmudic studies and modern scholarship; the cost, they argued, would be paid by the state.[28]

The subsequent commentary on clauses 23 to 34 of the 1813 law assumed that some articles would become moot if Judaism became a state religion. Criticism of what remained was direct and forceful. Special laws, as in article 30 of the 1813 law restricting rabbis to ecclesiastical duties, brought opprobrium to Jews and should be eliminated. There was no need for the negative language about rabbis' loyalty (art. 27). It was hard and unreasonable only to allow synagogues in areas with fifty Jewish families (art. 24). And rabbis should be included together with Christian school inspectors (arts. 32 and 33). Finally, and perhaps most indicative of the increase in Jewish self-confidence, was the request that because Hebraic, Talmudic, and rabbinic studies were difficult, specialized, and best begun at an early age, high schools located in cities ought to offer interested students courses in this field taught by local qualified rabbis (a revision of art. 34). This demand demonstrates that the Jewish community was not trying to avoid Talmud and rabbinics. These suggestions became irrelevant, because the state decided to ask for equality rather than revision and piecemeal repeal.

The documents accompanying Aub's commentary, a table giving a statistical breakdown of the Jewish community in Munich and Aub's treatise on the Jewish oath, are not as significant as the commentary on the 1813 law. The numbers given in the table describe a community far smaller than that reported in the census figures, listing 662 Jews in Munich compared to the census estimate of over 1,000.[29] Aub's essay, submitted on 17 January 1848, was a straightforward argument for the abolition of the old Jewish oath and a request for recognition of a formula used by and acceptable to Jews. It was based on religious texts, French practice, changes introduced in other German states, especially Austria, and arguments found in the German-Jewish newspaper, the *Allgemeine Zeitung des Judentums*. The essay was well-written, but like all attempts at revision of laws restricting Jews, it soon became obsolete.

It took the provincial governor until 9 April to put together a report with his recommendations. That document, sent to the Ministry of Church and Schools, not only accepted almost everything suggested by Aub and his fellows but even used their phraseology, sometimes verbatim. It disagreed only with the request for the addition of Jewish teachers to Christian schools. It stated that the position taken by the administration of the Jewish community in Munich and by its rabbi (Aub) was "intelligible, proper, and reasonable." The governor disagreed with the request for Jewish teachers in Christian schools because the "great majority of Christian parents would absolutely never entrust their children to a Jewish teacher." His report supported the establishment of a Jewish consistory.[30]

Eventually the Ministry for Church and Schools drew up a draft bill incorporating the points suggested from below.[31] Like the provincial governor of Upper Bavaria, the ministry recommended the establishment of a Jewish consistory based on the recognition of Judaism as a religion more or less on a par with Christian churches. The "israelitische Kirchenrath" of Bavaria would deal with rituals and rabbinics, would supervise theological instruction, would be commissioned and supported by the state, and would consist of three religious and two lay members. The bill proposed allowing establishment of synagogues in areas where only twenty (not fifty) families lived in a two-hour travel radius, and it specified varying pay scales for rabbis based on the number of families in an area. It also specified the election of religious communal officials and permitted a "German" school for Jews if taught by a qualified teacher. The penultimate article appears almost as an afterthought, stating simply that the bill repealed clauses 23 to 34 of the 1813 law.

If this law had been passed as it stood, without any change in clauses 1 to 22 on secular life, it would have constituted a major step forward for Jews in Bavaria. If there had been no reference to clauses 1 to 22, it probably would have passed easily. That probability forces us to direct our attention to the other directive of late 1847, which requested information on clauses 1 to 22 of the *Juden Edikt*. Gathering information on these clauses proved much more difficult than investigating the other clauses, because social, communal and political issues were more important to Bavarians than Jewish religious practice or theology. Almost all the actors involved in the process felt that Jews could and should do as they wished in religious ritual and worship and even in the education of their own children. Religion and education were not major issues in 1848–49, but communal and state matters were.

On the religious clauses of the 1813 law, the government had consulted only the Jewish religious community and the university for input. But regarding clauses 1 to 22, the governor of Upper Bavaria queried a series of district directors on the sentiment in their jurisdictions. This query took far longer to implement than the earlier consultations and was still in process at the lower levels when revolution erupted in March 1848. In the midst of a revolution, the Ministry of Church and Schools was writing its final report, and the Ministry of the Interior was still gathering information on popular opinion on Jews. This was time-consuming because instead of merely inquiring whether and to what extent the 1813 law should be changed, the directive of 13 December 1847 sought to investigate complaints against Jews, to inquire which restrictions on Jews could be eased, and to determine whether and to what extent Jewish emigration had resulted from the 1813 law over the previous five years. Under the circumstances of the revolution, it was impossible to do this quickly.

The fascinating exchange of official correspondence that ensued throws more light on the problems of a bureaucracy during a revolution than on the Jew Law of 1813. At the height of revolutionary activity in March and April, the state ministry repeatedly demanded a report from the governor of Upper Bavaria. The governor passed the demand on to the city magistrate of Munich, who was responsible for data collection because almost all Jews in the province lived in the capitol city. Unable to comply because of "recent events," the magistrate either asked for more time or did not respond, leading the governor to defend his subordinate to the ministry. On 29 April the magistrate finally sent in his report. Not surprisingly, the governor, probably Bernhard Freiherr von Godin, did not submit his covering report until 4 July.[32]

The governor's report is astonishing. Even more strongly than in the report on religious issues, the governor of Upper Bavaria recommended the full repeal of clauses 1 to 22 of the Edict and the introduction of complete equality of Israelites with Christians. The governor noted the size of the Jewish community, acknowledging that four families had emigrated in the previous five years. He noted Jewish involvement in normal trade and the absence of Jewish peddlers. Finally, he included a summary of the reports on the emancipation issue from the thirty-eight governmental districts in the province. Because the governor noted that only seven districts (including Dachau) favored full emancipation,[33] while eight opposed it and twelve favored partial emancipation, one must ask how he could conclude by recommending full emancipation?

The governor's recommendation is partly explained by his additional statement that most districts, including the twelve advocating only revision of the 1813 law, favored abolition of the residency requirement, the most important of the clauses. There is no way to substantiate this claim from the reports in the file, but if the governor was correct, his conclusion was reasonable. Moreover, the governor's review of the past history of Jewish emancipation shows his personal support for emancipation. He volunteered the opinion that Jewish emancipation would undoubtedly be discussed and agreed on in the Frankfurt Parliament, noting that the Bavarian Parliament had recently abolished any discrimination based on religion for both active and passive voting.[34] In his mind the emancipation issue had already been decided in Bavaria.

The governor argued for residential equality on the ground that if Jews were subject to the same obligations of citizenship as Christians, they should enjoy equal privileges and rights. The standing laws of the state would suffice for control of immigrating Jews just as they did for Christians. He saw no problem in the number of Jews in an area, especially because the current law was not enforced. Reforms in the area of landholding and feudal dues would render moot the restrictions on Jewish land purchases. The governor thought Bavaria should make the political and communal rights of Jews equal to those of Christians, as other states had done, as Frankfurt would do, and as Bavaria itself had done in its electoral law.

Recognizing the existence of complaints about Jews, the governor noted that hatred for Jews was limited almost entirely to the commercial field. He argued that the reason for the economic presence of Jews in rural areas was the economic weakness of the peasants, a situation that would not be changed by denying emancipation and restricting Jewish trade. Improvement in the condition of peasants would come by raising the moral and ethical level of all classes of people and ensuring legal freedom to everyone. In the governor's opinion, "Jews, against whom the hate of the people has directed itself, are probably only found where an unregulated, bad economy rules." By the middle of the summer of 1848, relying on reports from the oldest and most conservative parts of Bavaria, albeit reported by a liberal governor based on data from Munich, the bureaucracy had recommended full emancipation.

The qualitative leap from bureaucratic fact-finding as a necessary prerequisite to modifying the Jew Law of 1813 to the decision to push for full equality mirrors the changes that occurred in Bavaria's government in general in 1847 and 1848. The conservative minister von Abel resigned in 1847, forcing Ludwig to appoint moderate ministers. In March 1848 Ludwig I abdicated in favor of his more moderate son Maximilian. And sentiment in the lower house shifted substantially to the liberal side throughout the first half of 1848. Regardless of changes in popular sentiment, difficult to accurately measure, we can sharply delineate the change in the role of state government during these months. For a variety of reasons, some personal, some the result of pressure and fear, the administration took the initiative in a radical new solution to the Jewish question. Whether the monarchy's attitude had also changed is less clear.

Hesitation: Maximilian II

Despite the label of urgency attached to the gathering of information in the winter and spring of 1848, the administration did not submit a bill to Parliament until May 1849. One reason for the delay was the time it took for the two ministries of the interior to agree on a common draft bill, probably with the added complication of the new involvement of the Ministry of Justice.[35] But there was an even more important complicating and delaying factor—the leadership of King Maximilian II.

Largely overlooked by historians more interested in his arrogant and individualistic predecessor, Ludwig I, or in his even more unusual and peculiar successor, Ludwig II, the prosaic Maximilian II became king at the end of March 1848. His father and son interested themselves in art, but Maximilian favored scholarship. And his father and son treated government as a necessary evil, but Maximilian took it seriously and put in long hours on state matters of all kinds. His personal life was without blemish. He was married to the daughter of the king of Prussia, and he was genuinely interested in the common people of his country.[36] Better known for his desire for Bavaria to play a strong role in German unification, Maximilian did not assume a clearly defined role in domestic political and social policy. At first described as a moderate and even liberal monarch with modern views, perhaps because of his necessary role in the 1848 era, more recent scholarship has tended to paint him as conservative, though not reactionary.[37]

The immediate cause of Maximilian's elevation to the throne was not only the revolution but a scandal connected to the very visible Lola Montez. By 1847 citizens and ministers in Bavaria considered Ludwig either too strongly influenced by Lola or bewitched by the former foreign dancer. At a critical point, Karl von Abel, a staunch conservative and longtime minister under Ludwig, resigned together with three other ministers as a gambit intended to force Ludwig to mend his ways. Offended, Ludwig accepted the resignations and appointed liberals as replacements. These men began to prepare liberal legislation a year in advance of the reforms advocated in the revolution.[38] The Lola Montez affair helps explain Ludwig's decision to abdicate in March 1848. He clearly felt pressured and deserted by his people and ministers alike. It also helps explain the relatively sudden openness of Ludwig's ministers to Jewish emancipation in 1847.

Maximilian II became king of Bavaria in the first month of revolution and had to accommodate himself and his regime to it for several months. On 4 June 1848 the Parliament passed a series of laws securing, among other things, ministerial responsibility, a new and liberal electoral law, freedom of the press, the abolition of most feudal obligations, and a reform of the legal system.[39] In large part these laws satisfied the demands made in March 1848 by citizens' groups and fulfilled promises made by Ludwig I on 6 March prior to his abdication. Jewish emancipation was not among those demands, but Ludwig had promised improvement in the condition of the Jews. The laws of 4 June helped Jews because they were applicable to all state citizens, including Jews.[40]

Elections to Parliament were held in this climate in late 1848, producing a liberal, democratic lower house. The new minister of the interior, the liberal Gustav Freiherr von Lerchenfeld, promptly suggested Jewish emancipation, among other legislation, as the best and safest way to secure Jews as supporters of the state. Given this advice, King Maximilian hesitated. Throughout his reign he was famous for demanding as much information as possible, a proclivity that put great pressure on the entire bureaucratic structure. Before deciding, Maximilian quickly sought input from the former conservative minister Karl von Abel, Professor of Law Karl Friedrich Dollmann, and Maximilian's former tutor, the famous philosopher and Berlin professor Friedrich Wilhelm von Schelling. All were outside the governmental bureaucracy, and the king's reliance on them testifies to his desire to get advice other than that offered by his ministers.

In his letter to Schelling, Maximilian described von Lerchenfeld's argument that emancipation would make Jews supporters of the state, adding, "I am myself not clear on this point." He needed advice in a hurry because, as he added in a postscript, his ministers wanted to use the draft law in the elections just beginning. Werner Cahnman suggests that the draft law was that of 29 May 1849, which clearly and unequivocally supported Jewish equality with Christians, but no draft is in the files, and it may have been a different wording. Schelling's reply to the king was for a long time unknown, but Cahnman discovered it in Maximilian's papers in Munich.[41]

Schelling wrote in reply that Jews were nomads by nature, not given to life within a state and especially not within a German state. Experience had taught him that it was impossible to exclude such hostile elements forcefully, since they would find a crack through which to enter. Exclusionary methods had to be abandoned, and in this sense he saw no objection to article one—the article providing Jews with equality. One could even hope, Schelling thought, that equality would encourage conversion of Jews to Christianity. As they became equal members of the state organism, they would be chained even closer to the state. They would also soon realize that the state was incompatible with the Jewish religion. Initially emancipation would result in the overpopulation of the universities by Jewish lecturers, but the government still had the power to control pushy Jews, and he anticipated that all Christians, given the rising mistrust of the people, would seek to blunt the encroachment and pushiness of the Jews.

In a personal letter to Maximilian written the next day, Schelling added that if emancipation did occur, the king should consider establishing a Jewish religious faculty. He even recommended some of his former students for positions in such a body. November 1848 had seen a substantial move to the right in most parts of Germany, and Schelling made very clear that he, too, had no use for anarchy and agitation, which could only be controlled if one took a strong and uncompromising position. In this regard he praised the prince of Prussia, the later William I, who had been sent to England because of his antirevolutionary stand in March 1848.[42] The burden of Schelling's advice was to accept emancipation as inevitable but fraught with danger because of the nature of the Jew. While supporting emancipation, Schelling hoped that "the Jew" as Jew would fade away. One could support emancipation in 1849–50 and still be anti-Judaic and perhaps even anti-Semitic.

Dollmann recommended against full emancipation because the great majority of the Christian population opposed it. In his opinion, very common at the time, Jews could not be state officials because they could not be given authority over Christians. He proposed a gradual process of "improvement" in the legal position of Jews in a variety of areas. The conservative von Abel, supported full emancipation on pragmatic grounds similar to those of Schelling but without the latter's scholarly justification, and he advised controls on usury and commercial chicanery that would apply to Christians and Jews alike.[43] Taken as a whole, the advice given to Maximilian inclined toward emancipation but was not enthusiastically supportive.

Despite the urgency of Maximilian's request for information in late 1848, the state took no action in the new year of 1849 except for the ministries' exchange of drafts of the law.[44] There is no convincing evidence that the government used the promise of a law for Jewish emancipation in the electioneering of 1848. The state ministers had much to concern them. A new, more democratic, Parliament was elected in November 1848 and took office in January 1849. The minister of the interior changed twice, in December 1848 and in March 1849, interrupting continuity in the office that held direct jurisdiction over the legislation. In addition, the government was under the intense popular pressure of a petition campaign concerning acceptance of the *Grundrechte* (Basic Rights) and the Constitution of the Frankfurt Parliament.[45] It did not help that the democratic lower house and the conservative upper house took opposing positions. During these weeks the king decided to reject both the *Grundrechte* and the Frankfurt Constitution, knowing that this would antagonize large segments of the populace. Thus the government moved slowly for several quite substantial reasons apart from hesitation over the legislation for Jewish emancipation.

All extant drafts of the bill for emancipation of Jews dating from April 1849 show the same basic structure—two or three very simple articles stating that Jews were now equal to Christians. But the earliest version grounded equality in both the Bavarian Constitution and the Basic Law of the Reich, a phrase quickly dropped because of the king's announcement on 23 April that he recognized neither the Basic Rights nor the Constitution produced by the Frankfurt Parliament. At about this point, the Ministry of Justice advised adding the term *staatsbürgerliche* (state citizenship) to go along with the terms *politische* and *bürgerliche* (communal citizenship).[46]

Maximilian's rejection of the Frankfurt Constitution was a major political decision that raised the possibility of a second revolution. At the time of the rejection, the Bavarian Parliament was not in session, having adjourned on 8 March, and it did not reconvene until 16 May. Moreover, Maximilian appointed a new minister of justice, Karl Joseph Freiherr von Kleinschrod, on 5 March; a new minister of finances, Joseph von Aschenbrenner, on 7 March; a new minister of the interior, Georg Friedrich von Forster, on 8 March; a new minister of the interior for church and schools, Friedrich von Ringelmann, on 16 March; and a new minister of foreign and royal affairs—who also held the portfolio for trade and public works—Ludwig Freiherr von der Pfordten, on 18 April. On 20 May the king requested military aid from Prussia to suppress uprisings in the revolutionary Pfalz, and two days later he suspended the local parliament there. On 29 May the *Staatsrat* met in this climate and agreed to submit a bill for Jewish emancipation to Parliament, a decision that can only be understood in the context of the events from March to May.[47]

It fell to the minister of the interior for church and schools, von Ringelmann, to suggest submission of a bill for Jewish emancipation in May 1849. He did so in a strong report to the king dated 24 May, reporting on the discussion of that day in the ministerial council. He began by stating that full Jewish emancipation was an article of the belief of the day. Other states had already granted emancipation, and article 146 of the Frankfurt Constitution guaranteed it. Emancipation was now law in the twenty-nine states that had accepted the Constitution. In Bavaria, Jews could now sit in the Parliament, and he asked how they could logically be denied lesser posts? Up to this point his reasoning was standard. Then he added that Jews had been the strongest agitators for the Frankfurt Constitution because they would have won emancipation through it, and that therefore, because it had been rejected, "one must seek to calm them." More generally he argued that the ministers must submit laws that would calm the parties occupying the center of the political spectrum, that is, those who supported reform and the Constitution and who would be angry at its rejection. A bill for Jewish emancipation was one way to do that. He had, he wrote, talked with the presidents of both houses of Parliament, and they agreed on how "*necessary*" it was in the next session of Parliament to introduce as many laws as possible that would win the support of "public opinion." He closed with a request that the draft law for Jewish emancipation be submitted to the next sitting of the *Staatsrat*.[48]

Maximilian and his advisors recognized that many Bavarians would be angry at their rejection of the Frankfurt Constitution and of a new, national German state. They were not sure how radical the popular response might be. Among a variety of available options that could be used to pacify those hurt feelings and frustrated hopes was the offer of reformist legislation. The government apparently favored legislation that would appeal to the center and moderate left. Jewish emancipation seemed made-to-order.

Foreign policy also played a role in the decision to propose Jewish emancipation, although not an obviously important one. In the files of the *Staatsrat*, dated 24 May 1849, is an unsigned note addressed to the royal ministerial council. The author noted that he had made a similar argument on a similar draft law for Jewish emancipation a year earlier, a fact that excludes von der Pfordten, then a Saxon minister, from the list of possible authors. The note reads that Bavaria would lead the way in comparison to the other German states: "Where is there a German state that has fully emancipated the Jews? To my knowledge, as this draft does it, nowhere."[49] It is tempting to see this as a royal note, both because of the use of the first person and because of the interest in German affairs. The argument was that Jewish emancipation would make Bavaria appear more liberal, and that by taking the lead in this aspect of reform, Bavaria might win points as a leader in Germany.

On 29 May the *Staatsrat* met to decide whether to submit the bill to Parliament. As a sign of things to come, all the state ministries supported the legislation, often forcefully and intelligently. In addition to the king's concern that the bill might encounter difficulties, only minister of justice Freiherr von Kleinschrod warned about possible upsets in Franconia over the end of restrictions on citizenship, expressed fear of possible cheating of peasants (by Jews) in the future, and cautioned about the possible "sensational" effect of ending residency controls on Jews. But he, too, agreed that one could not refuse lesser privileges to those who had already been granted greater rights. Privy Councillor von Roth submitted a position paper on Jewish emancipation to the *Staatsrat*, arguing in much the same vein as had von Ringelmann. Noting that the Bavarian populace had split into activists who would like Jewish emancipation and a "silent" majority who would either oppose it or be indifferent, he advised submission.[50] The *Staatsrat* unanimously approved submission of the bill.

Before submission of the bill, Maximilian II publicly declared Bavaria's nonrecognition of the Frankfurt National Parliament, and therefore also of its Constitution, on 5 June 1849. Five days later he dissolved the Bavarian Parliament and called for new elections. To make sense of what happened in late 1848 and early 1849, one must balance the state's palpable and real fear of popular resentment against the government for its rejection of the Frankfurt Constitution with the recognition that Max II disliked the new constitution more than he feared the people. Consequently, full equality for Jews, which Max II's government had originally seen as a useful political device for improving the national standing of the monarchy and ministry with public opinion, became in spring 1849 an equally political tool to draw attention away from the same state's choice of a counter-revolutionary stance.

Maximilian's government did not discard the emancipation legislation but submitted it unaltered to the new Parliament. Explanation for the decision to continue governmental support for the bill, which had been promised in May before its "necessity" declined substantially with the failure of the revolution in May and June 1849 and before the new July elections in Bavaria had produced a less liberal Parliament, must be located in ministerial support for Jewish emancipation throughout the summer and fall of 1849. Although Max II's personal involvement appears to have ceased in summer 1849, ministerial support for the bill remained strong. In the period during which all this occurred, no one knew what would happen once the committees of the lower house received the bill.

Fulfillment: The Lower House Passes a Bill for Emancipation

In October 1849 two committees of the Bavarian Lower House considered the draft bill for Jewish emancipation that had been forwarded by the *Staatsrat*. The committees, especially the third, under the leadership of Scharpff, took their job seriously. In his report to the whole house, Scharpff provided a relatively lengthy history of the restrictions to which Jews had been subjected between 1551 and 1813. In October the committee asked the minister of the interior for information on Jews. They specifically wished to know the number of Jewish families, what occupations they pursued, how many families were engaged in peddling, and what changes had taken place since 1813. The committee worked particularly hard because of the strident opposition to emancipation by one of its members, Dr. Anton Ruland. On 17 October Ruland proposed an alternate bill that retained the 1813 law but allowed for a few improvements. When the committee draft passed 11 to 5 in a joint session of the two committees on 24 November, all amendments, including Ruland's, failed.[51] But the struggle was just beginning.

Parliamentary committees worked in relative anonymity, shielded from the glare of public scrutiny by the nature of this initial stage of the legislative process. But whether private or public, the level of opposition to emancipation, viewed as a function of the numbers voting for and against the draft, did not vary even by a single percentage point between the committees (68.8 percent for) and the whole house (69.5 percent for). Most of the arguments later used by both sides in the full assembly first saw the light of day in the committee rooms, but only some of those debates are available to historians. The debates in the lower house, which began on 10 December, lasted five full days and gave thirty-five speakers, all but a few of whom were members of the Parliament, the opportunity to air their feelings on the subject. The debates and the ensuing 91 to 40 vote for passage triggered extensive press coverage and massive popular reaction. Because this was the longest and most public discussion of Jews and Judaism in nineteenth-century Bavaria, if not in Europe, it is astonishing that there is virtually no reference to it in the historical literature.[52]

Despite the expression of some rather unthinking and very vulgar anti-Semitism, the intellectual and substantive content of the discussion in Parliament was relatively high. The give-and-take was almost solemn, more so perhaps because of the direct and obvious governmental support for the bill. From beginning to end of the consideration by the lower house, the government genuinely defended its draft. And, although pressure had eased because of the defeat of revolutionaries in June and the election of a less democratic and more liberal-conservative set of representatives in July, the ministers backed the bill to the hilt. The government may have been playing for popular support in May, but it supported the bill in December when the political need for it no longer existed. One can only conclude that the ministers genuinely believed in this legislation and were not acting solely out of self-serving pragmatism. Their convictions emerge even more clearly in the debates.

The hard core group challenging the draft legislation included Dr. Anton Ruland (1809–74), Johann Nepomuk Sepp (1816–1909), Joseph Franz von Allioli (1793–1873), and Professor Ignaz von Döllinger (1799–1890). All were Catholics, Ruland was a priest, and all but Sepp were trained in theology. Sepp was a historian and a prolific writer. All were academicians with ties to higher education, and two were noble. In contrast, the government's leading spokespersons were Ludwig Freiherr von der Pfordten (1811–80), Friedrich von Ringelmann (1803–70), Gustav Freiherr von Lerchenfeld (1806–66) and Friedrich Adam Justus Graf von Hegnenberg-Dux (1816–72). Von der Pfordten was foreign minister and minister of trade and public works, and on 22 December he became the first chair of the ministerial council, or prime minister. Von Ringelmann was minister of the interior for church and educational affairs. Lerchenfeld had served as both foreign minister and minister of the interior in 1848. Von Hegnenberg-Dux was first president of the lower house and later became a minister. All were noble, and three possessed higher titles of nobility. All the challengers were conservative; the government defenders were moderate conservative, liberal, or progressive, but not democratic or radical. It was a unique confrontation.

Because the government introduced the emancipation legislation, its opponents, mostly conservative, were in the novel position of challenging the state and attacking Jews rather than defending the state and Christianity against challenges from Jews and liberals. In consequence, although traditional arguments against Jews and their emancipation abounded in the criticism of the bill, they played a secondary role.

Most of those who seriously criticized emancipation in the debates, and some who defended it, saw Jews as foreign in religion, culture, nature, and even occupation. Dr. Anton Ruland asserted that Jews were still foreigners after living in Bavaria for a thousand years. Sepp argued that Jews were not assimilable as Jews but could become German by ceasing to be Jews. He even asked, rhetorically, how Jews could form a single nation with Germans if they could not eat with them. Döllinger, too, saw Jews as unassimilable in general: they were still a scattered people in isolation from others and must be made into Germans. Allioli maintained that the intimate connection between politics and religion in Jewry made it impossible for a Bavarian Jew to stop being a Jew, even if he renounced the Talmud. Deputy Wolfsteiner agreed, stating that religion came first for Jews, hence they would not cooperate with other religions even if granted equality.[53] These arguments differed fundamentally from those of 1846 and earlier, which in most respects echoed the thinking of the writers of the 1813 law—that Jews could and should become German. Allioli and Wolfsteiner argued that due to the Jewish religion such a development was impossible.

Most opposition speakers also agreed that Jewish religious beliefs and teachings on trade and commerce made the Jews more prone to business than other peoples, more cohesive and insular, and much more willing to be unethical in business practices with Christians while moral with fellow Jews.[54] Among the oldest and most common criticisms of Jews was the argument that Jewish religious laws applied a double standard of ethical behavior to Jews. The opposition speakers repeated the age-old assertion that Jews were free to charge Gentiles with usurious interest that they did not apply to Jews. This reasoning appeared, explicitly or implicitly, in every major speech by the bill's opponents, in conjunction with a low estimation of Jewish moral character in general. In his first speech against the bill, Ruland stated that ancient history showed that the Jewish character was evil, harsh, disloyal, and ungrateful, and that modern history taught that Jews were avaricious, presumptuous, cowardly, and cruel. Sepp noted that Jews used their "overpowering" mental abilities only to obtain gold and to enslave and oppress others, citing as proof Egypt under the pharaohs, Spain before the expulsion in 1492, and Poland and Russia in modern times; he located contemporary Germany midway between the Polish and Spanish extremes. Dr. Mayr viewed Jews as sly and deceptive, by nature avoiding muscular work and tending to the easier and more profitable commercial life. Allioli agreed that Jews were in commerce because they "liked it." Dr. Koller noted that character was the issue and that Jews could and should emancipate themselves—by changing their characteristics.[55]

Closely tied to the charges that Jews were foreign and immoral was the fear of Jewish economic domination. If this bill were made law, Dr. Mayr stated, Jews would buy up land, become residents, and in a short time seize control of all business.[56] Allioli used a statistical table produced by the Ministry of the Interior to show that Jews were still predominantly in business,[57] adding the claim that most Jewish artisans were too. More important, Allioli claimed that Jews wanted to control Christians. Later in the debates, responding to the countercharge that so few Jews (60,000 out of 4.5 million) could hardly be a threat, Sepp argued that Jewish power was concentrated because of their unity—they actually had the advantage over Christians because they were a "people-within-a-people." The prestigious educator Döllinger emphasized this fear of the economic power of Jews, illustrating his point as he had in 1846, with two familiar Franconian folk-sayings.[58]

Defenders said little about the obvious point of Jewish religious difference, although Freiherr von Lerchenfeld sarcastically asked how long it had been since Catholics and Protestants had regarded each other as evil. Almost all the bill's proponents who spoke on this issue considered Jews no more pernicious than Christians. The social and religious past of Judaism was not the issue. Von der Pfordten put it bluntly when he said that the bill was emancipating not the old Judaism but the new, reformed Judaism. Moreover, if Jews were different, the cause, according to Freiherr von Harold, lay in past exclusionary and repressive measures by Christians. Specific charges about Jewish religious law and theory were hard for most defenders to answer, especially facing an array of academics whose field was either theology or church history. Eventually, one of the two Jewish deputies, Dr. Arnheim, took the floor to clarify the role of the Talmud in Judaism, explaining that not all Jews accepted a single interpretation of it. But Arnheim refused to play a greater role in the debates, because he might be seen to have a vested interested in the outcome. Rabbi Hirsch Aub of Munich helped defend the Talmud through an essay, which the president of the assembly read aloud to the house.[59]

Denigration of Jewish character and morals did not go unanswered in the 1849 debates. Supporters of Jewish emancipation often conceded that Jews were immoral, asserting only that emancipation would cause them to improve. But von der Pfordten praised the strong family life of Jews and their thrift and clean living, and he also noted that, unlike Christians, Jews neither drank nor gambled. Von Hegnenberg-Dux, the president of the assembly, similarly pointed out that Jews did not have a monopoly over usury. Scharpff, too, commented that even Christian priests and monks could be regicides. Stating a general principle, von Ringelmann argued that existing laws would deal with usurers as usurers, not as Jews.[60]

Most speakers opposing emancipation argued that because of Jewish "talent" for business, simple Bavarian peasants were unable to compete and faced economic ruin. In response a whole series of supporters ridiculed the fear that over four million Bavarians felt toward fewer than 60,000 Jews of all genders and ages. If four million Christians could not compete with sixty thousand Jews, von Harold opined, that said little for the intelligence and abilities of the Christians. Von Ringelmann did not believe so few genuinely threatened so many, but he could not approve the wisdom of passing laws to protect the incompetent in the marketplace. Von Lerchenfeld ironically pointed out—rather sharply, judging by the minutes—that Jews were in business because earlier special laws had excluded them from farming for a thousand years.[61]

In addition to these largely standard arguments on both sides of the question of Jewish emancipation, the debates produced charges that centered on the relation of Jews to the state. The first argument held that Bavaria was a Christian state and could not admit Jews to equality without changing the state from Christian to secular. The second held that Jews were both naturally rebellious and historically involved in revolutionary activity, especially during the recent revolution. Both attackers and defenders seemed wary of these issues, and for the most part only a few of the leading speakers on each side developed these arguments or counterarguments in depth.

This conflict dominated the debates over the judiciary. Several deputies took issue with the bill because it would make it possible for Jews to serve as judges with authority over Christians. Breitenbach introduced an amendment to eliminate this aspect of the law, implying that he would support the bill only with that proviso. Though some other examples of the problems of Jewish equality in a Christian state arose—including Sepp's provocative, but ludicrous, question whether Christians would have to observe the Sabbath on Saturday instead of Sunday—they were generally insignificant by comparison to the judicial area. As for the overall question of the Christianity of the Bavarian state, most opposition deputies probably agreed with Schmid that Christianity was a cement holding the state together. Döllinger, however, was willing to allow Jews to hold office, even as judges and university professors, on the ground that the Christian state was secular in its public function.[62] His modern and subtle reasoning was lost on most opponents, and opposition to Jewish judges became a major issue in the petition movement.

Government supporters appeared hesitant to reply to the potentially damaging question of the Christian nature of the Bavarian state. Ironically, no supporter of emancipation had the courage to agree with Döllinger, an opponent, that the state was not Christian in its public functions. To avoid taking a stand, several deputies simply asserted that the state would not cease to be Christian because Jews could be judges and officials. A related argument held that Jews were so few in number that the state was Christian because 99 percent of its inhabitants were Christian.[63] As for Jewish judges, supporters of emancipation argued that since Jews were already serving in higher capacities, for example, as deputies and as lay judges on juries, it was illogical not to extend this right to include similar offices at lower levels. Von der Pfordten made this argument forcefully, stating that whether or not those rights should have been given earlier was now irrelevant.[64] The best reply that the opposition could give was Sepp's comment that the earlier decision to allow Jews to vote and be candidates for Parliament had been reached "too quickly."[65]

One speech on the Christian state stood out as much for its frankness and lucidity as for its delivery by the man who became Bavaria's first prime minister within a week of the debates—Freiherr Ludwig von der Pfordten. As the seventh speaker in the first session following two major attacks by Ruland and Sepp, von der Pfordten established the government's case. Much of his message focused on the practical. Drawing on two and a half years of experience as a judge in the province with the largest number of Jews and protective laws, Lower Franconia, he argued that the law did not in practice protect Christians, partly because many did not wish to be protected. Christians needing loans from Jews themselves circumvented the laws. But he agreed that the position of judges was special and that most Bavarians would not endure Jewish judges. He noted that, as a practical matter, there would be few Jewish judges because there were few Jews and even fewer Jewish lawyers. He also candidly reminded the deputies that the government considered more than scholarly qualities in appointing judges. The government would not, for example, appoint a Catholic judge in a Protestant area or vice versa. He doubted that the government would appoint a Jew to an old Bavarian district where few or no Jews lived. Such candor demonstrates how far von der Pfordten was prepared to go to ensure passage of this legislation.[66]

Von der Pfordten took an important role in steering the bill through the lower house. Unfortunately historians have not paid sufficient attention to him or to his views on Jews.[67] His friendly relations and correspondence with Berthold Auerbach demonstrate that he counted some Jews among his acquaintances, but this says little about his relations with Jews in general.[68] Queried about his political principles and program for Bavaria by Maximilian in 1849 before his appointment, von der Pfordten described himself as a progressive and realistic conservative. He referred, for example, to the *Grundrechte* (the Basic Rights) as the *Grundunrechte* (basic nonrights), which, he sadly thought, were not to be prevented. Though willing to admit the need for an upper house in which nobles would retain some power, von der Pfordten foresaw that it would have to be vastly curtailed because any attempt to retain its current power would "only nourish the revolution."[69]

Von der Pfordten's progressive conservatism should not obscure his mistrust of revolution. In a series of essays on topics set for him by Maximilian, von der Pfordten consistently expressed moderate conservative ideas. In one of the essays, "What Remains in the Current Epoch?" dated January 1850, von der Pfordten blamed the upset of the previous years on the Enlightenment, which had undermined Christianity. It was still unclear, he wrote, what would happen with the new sects in Christianity and in Judaism. Jews talked of building sects and of emancipation, he commented, but many practical difficulties existed, among them the introduction of Jewish emancipation. He felt that the concordat with the Papacy gave Bavaria a firm foundation against further disintegration. He went on to note that a republic was not a serious option, because too many people opposed it. In point after point, von der Pfordten described change as to be expected, but he advocated furthering change in a conservative way. Because so many conservatives perceived Jews as revolutionaries, it is surprising that the moderately conservative von der Pfordten supported emancipation. But he argued that the people were no longer a "docile mass" and that all state policies must be acceptable and in the interest of the commonweal. Von der Pfordten maintained that a strong monarchy would be seen as more permanent if it were based on popular support.[70]

During the *Vormärz*, it became common to portray Jews as liberals because some Jews expressed vocal support for political change and progress.[71] The events of 1848 led many observers to use the term *revolutionary* to describe Jews, because many Jews supported the revolution in one form or another. Opponents of Jewish emancipation attacked the bill by employing the common view of Jews as revolutionaries or opponents of the government. Sepp described the "Hebrew people" as possessing a ferment of disquiet, and he opposed emancipating them because it was exactly the emancipated, educated Jews who were revolutionaries. Pointing to Johann Jacoby, the famous Jewish democrat from Königsberg, Sepp asserted that Jews were revolutionary by nature.[72]

Supporters of emancipation did not deny Jewish involvement in revolutionary parties and movements. Some, evading the issue of revolution, described Jews as law-abiding, loyal to the state and to their neighbors. Only two speakers responded directly to Sepp's accusation. Von der Pfordten admitted some truth to the assertion that Jews were "natural" revolutionaries. He explained that it was natural, for example, that a young Jew of twenty-five, fresh from the university, who encountered a repressive and exclusionary state, would choose to attack it. Just as *Schacherjuden* used money to open doors, the educated Jew used revolution. But von der Pfordten asserted that these talented Jews, if emancipated, would become as conservative as Christians, supporting "Order and Quiet," on the ground that he who has possessions protects them. This was a conservative argument in keeping with von der Pfordten's political philosophy. So, too, the president of the assembly, von Hegnenberg-Dux, described emancipation as politically intelligent. Jews had naturally rebelled because they had been under so many restrictions. From this he drew the lesson that, if the state removed the restrictions, Jews would become law-abiding because they would own property, and anyone who owned property was conservative.[73]

Taken as a whole and judging by the responses of the deputies in all the speeches, the attacks on Jews do not appear to have been much more than preaching to the converted. The most telling arguments against emancipation were not anti-Semitic in nature. There were three main areas of concern to the deputies: public opinion, communal rights, and the nature of the economy. The first two were the most important aspects of the entire debate.

Long before a barrage of petitions in late December 1849 and January 1850 documented the tremendous surge of public opposition to emancipation, Parliament was aware of the state of popular opinion and concerned with how to treat it. Not a single speaker from either side disputed the claim that most people in Bavaria opposed full emancipation. Several opponents distinguished, perceptively, between public opinion, which opposed emancipation, and press opinion, which favored it. Ruland argued strongly and at length that Bavarians opposed the draft law. He closed with an appeal to vote against, which would irritate the press, "who will revile you," but would please the greater part of the people.[74]

In one form or another, the other major opposition leaders echoed Ruland's point. But all exhibited some care in what they said, because most of them were political and religious conservatives who had opposed the powerful influence of public opinion in 1848. Some clearly felt that after bowing to the "general will of the people" so much in 1848, it was only fair to be consistent and, because the people opposed the proposition, not to emancipate the Jews in 1849.[75] Döllinger, too, reminded the liberal and democratic supporters of the bill that the will of the majority, in this case Christians, was their principle, but that they were now violating this by making laws only for the minority, the Jews.[76] Granted that most Bavarians opposed full emancipation, the opposition argued that its supporters were inconsistent in opposing the will of the majority.

Ironically, the supporters of the law—most of them democrats and liberals, together with some moderate, progressive conservatives—recognized and admitted that public opinion did not support them. Even though 1849 was unlike 1848 and the political tide was running in a conservative direction, supporters of the bill were still liberal enough to be reluctant to challenge public opinion directly, though they were simultaneously uninterested in surrendering to it. The very first speaker cautioned his colleagues not to be "misled by the so-called public opinion of your electoral districts into doing something that [your] hearts do not support." Von der Pfordten also recognized the "dissension" in the country, but he stated that the government must do what was best, even if that was contrary to public opinion. He argued that in the future, in 1870 or 1880, the people would agree. His was a standard conservative position often used by the opponents of Jewish emancipation earlier in 1848 and 1849. Both sides had reversed their positions of the previous years on the meaning and use of public opinion.

Von Lerchenfeld admitted that the deputies should "consider" public opinion and that it should "influence" the final judgment, but he implied that one need not blindly and mechanically follow it. Scharpff, too, admitted the popular opposition but noted that the men now using it had opposed public opinion on other issues. The last speaker, von Ringelmann, reminded his listeners that the government originally had pursued Jewish emancipation in response to the popular pressure of March 1848 and had remained "true to our given word."[77] This was disingenuous: von Ringelmann knew that the decision by the ministers in April and May 1849 to push for full emancipation was a ploy to disarm the irritation of people angry at the rejection of the Frankfurt Constitution.

Only von Hegnenberg-Dux, in a speech made after the end of debate, knowing that no opposition leader could respond, met the issue of public opinion head on. Though not denying that the people opposed the bill, von Hegnenberg-Dux took issue with the overused concept of "the people." He was convinced that the *Volk,* at least the great mass of it, understood as little about emancipation as they did about the German National Constitution. The issue was religious fanaticism, not religion itself. What fifteen-year old, he asked, had not imbibed the tradition that every Jew was a usurer, a cheat? Under these conditions it would be difficult to accept emancipation directly. As for the importance of the majority, he pointed to majority opposition to public schools and support for the lottery to show that majority opinion could be wrong. The misfortune of the era was that they had lost one of the two pillars supporting the state, the religious conscience, without having obtained the second, the legal conscience. Irrespective of its effect, his speech stands as the most candid legislative response to the reality of public opposition to emancipation and also as a telling analysis of the role of public opinion in a democracy.[78]

Questioning which side public opinion favored also raised practical issues. Dr. Mayr, for reform but against full emancipation, stated that he had received from his electoral district many letters against unconditional emancipation. The attitudes of his constituents reflected their experiences, he said, and that was hard to criticize. Sepp put the issue more directly when he asked how many of his colleagues had been advised to vote for emancipation by their constituents and how many had the courage to inform their voters of their support for the bill. Two representatives, Dr. Jäger and Freiherr von Lerchenfeld, noted that public opinion could be influenced by the deputies— by passing the bill.[79]

Uncertainty about the consequences of contradicting public opinion by granting full emancipation underlay the entire debate. Sepp raised the issue on the first day, arguing that because Jews had been helped in the past by the emperor, the bishops, and the princes, the people had had to protect themselves through pogroms (*Verfolgungen*). The proposed law, he contended, sold out the German people to the Jews, and it, too, would encourage direct popular action. He had heard the phrase himself: "If you emancipate them, you must hunt them all from the country or kill them dead." In Franconia, he added, the people said there would be a new pogrom, which he wanted to avoid. Schmid expressed similar sentiments in more modern terms, wishing for no law that might reignite revolution. Only von Lerchenfeld, at the conclusion of his speech, took notice of these threats, commenting first that he had never thought to see such "agitation." He concluded, quite astonishingly, that if the opposition insisted on fearing Jews so much, they really had only two choices: to deport them or to kill them. The alternative to such fear was to join him in voting for emancipation.[80]

The people were also at the center of the debate over the role of the community in the emancipation of the Jews. Here, as in the discussion of the meaning of public opinion, several representatives argued forcefully that while ostensibly the legislation introduced by the government affected only the 60,000 Jews, in reality it affected the entire population of Bavaria, four and a half million strong. Three issues were involved: the material effect on the community, decision-making jurisdiction over communal prerogatives, and the relation of the community to the state. All these issues existed independently of the Jews, but the bill for emancipation brought them to the surface.

Bavaria was a country of some 8,000 communities. Most were small, numbering their population in the hundreds. In 1849 the bulk of Bavaria's population lived in these small communities, but they were beginning to decline under modern economic pressures and urban growth. Many of these communities had existed for hundreds of years, and the great majority possessed laws relating to internal structures and daily life that owed little or nothing to the state. One of the most important powers retained by communities after their incorporation in the state was the right of residence. The Edict of 1813 had modified this right, and the 1818 law on communities had returned that power. But the proposed emancipation would take it away, at least as far as Jewish residency was concerned. The fight was over whether the community or the state should decide if a Jew was allowed to live in a given area.

Nearly all the deputies who spoke against emancipation mentioned the community, but none did so in depth or at great length. Representatives, even those who opposed Jewish emancipation, did not come from small communities and were probably not attuned to these issues. In two lengthy speeches against emancipation and Jews, Sepp referred only indirectly to the communal situation when he noted that one could not give rights to Jews without taking some away from others. Döllinger, too, supported the autonomy of the community only in passing. Ruland, Allioli, and Wolfsteiner argued in various ways that the local community, rather than the state, should decide the issue, largely on the explicit or implicit grounds that a majority in each community was more important to the people than a majority in the Parliament or in Bavaria as a whole. Ruland even urged that local residence should be granted only after a positive vote of three-fifths, rather than the normal majority, of the local citizenry. Wolfsteiner added that because Jews were more accepted where they lived and disliked where they traded, the communities should decide where they should live.[81] While the autonomy of the community was a serious issue in its own right, opponents of Jewish emancipation undoubtedly also used it against Jews.

The broad base of support for the autonomy of the community can be seen in the process of the proposed amendments to the emancipation bill. Of ten amendments offered by deputies, seven proposed retention of the communities' "absolute veto" (as the right to decide residence was commonly called): five came from deputies who made it quite clear that if their amendments were accepted, they would vote for the rest of the bill;[82] two added other nonessential restrictions to the request for the absolute veto.[83] Two other amendments asked for restrictions in other areas to serve as guarantees against expected problems produced by emancipation.[84] And two deputies spoke for amendments to retain the absolute veto.[85] Sepp's amendment to retain most of the 1813 Edict was the only one rejected without discussion.[86] Because deputies wishing to oppose proposed amendments were asked to rise—that is, to reject discussion of a colleague's proposal publicly—the overwhelming defeat of Sepp's alternative must be seen as a firm rejection of any significant return to the policies of 1813.

That leaders of the antiemancipation group showed a relative lack of interest in communal rights indicates that they did not want these amendments to succeed and increase the likelihood that a modified emancipation bill would then be easily and surely passed. At least some of those supporting amendments retaining the absolute veto in some form, like Boos, Breitenbach, and Forndran, saw and spoke to the larger issue of the relationship between the community and the state.[87] In the final voting, after all amendments had been defeated, four of their authors (Paur, Forndran, Pitzner, and Hirschberger) voted for full emancipation. Boos, too, despite his desire for the absolute veto, joined the majority. The desire for communal autonomy (not necessarily just on Jewish issues) expressed by several deputies, some of whom later supported the bill, was not lost on the government.

Supporters of the bill and representatives of the government, in several important cases the same men, clearly recognized the danger posed by a wider discussion of communal rights in the specific debates over Jewish emancipation. Only one speaker, Dr. Bayer, linked the community to "national" issues, noting that while communal autonomy was important, so too was the autonomy of the German people who had given their word on freedom and equality[88]—the reference was to the Frankfurt Constitution, by this time a dead letter. Government representatives approached the issue in quite a different way. Von der Pfordten laid down the ministerial position.[89] As on other issues, von der Pfordten demonstrated a practical, pragmatic approach to the problem. While supporting the right and need for Jews to be free of residence restrictions, not least because of their cruel impact on family formation, he asserted that the government was not proposing that Jews immediately spread through the country, especially to areas where they had never lived. Not all communities possessed the veto, von der Pfordten noted, and the government recognized Jewish faults as well as virtues. Nevertheless, the government did not feel that a special law was necessary. On this point he made himself as clear as he had on the issue of judicial appointment: if the deputies trusted government officials to follow the will of the community, there would be no need for such amendments. Von Lerchenfeld agreed, arguing that if a community opposed Jews, none would move there.[90] Von Ringelmann did not expand on von der Pfordten's arguments, but at the very end of his speech, he added that if the Fink amendment passed, the government, because of the need for votes, would not oppose the amended bill.[91] This was not a retreat but a sign that the government was not entirely certain of its votes on the amendments and would do all it could to achieve passage of an emancipation bill.

The strongest pressure for unconditional acceptance of the bill and against the theory of the centrality of the community came from the house leadership. Both positions were elaborated only at the end of the debate, when there was no possibility of reply. The second president of the lower house, Weis, unconditionally supported the government's bill and argued against any modifications on the grounds that the bill was just and politically necessary. It has been said that communities are the foundation of the state, he commented, but they exist within the state and not by themselves.[92] The first president, von Hegnenberg-Dux, was even more direct. The autonomy of the community was important to him, but the state must be *Lebensfähig* (viable), and if the community reverted to a "republic" in a medieval sense, there would be no viable state. He asked the deputies if they were willing, in the interests of the autonomy of the community, to expand that autonomy to include the communal election of the teacher and the priest as well as the exclusion of the Jews?[93] The extent to which the doubt in von Hegneberg-Dux's mind on this point reflected general sentiment is uncertain, but only one unimportant amendment passed.

King Maximilian II played no direct role in any of the debates in the lower house. To assume that he personally supported the bill because all his ministers did is not justified by the evidence. But Bavarian history since 1799 and Montgelas's rise to power demonstrates the powerful role of leading bureaucrats—even, or perhaps especially, progressives like Montgelas and, despite his lesser stature, von der Pfordten. It makes more sense, especially in light of the role of the Wittelsbach family in the approaching *Reichsräthe* decision in 1850, to see Max II as allowing his ministers their way on Jewish emancipation—a luxury made possible by the obvious collapse of the revolution. We must not see these men as liberals or democrats because they supported equality for Jews, but rather as the progressive conservatives and moderate liberals they were.

On the final vote, the bill for complete Jewish equality with Christians passed 91 to 40 and needed only the agreement of the *Reichsräthe* before the king could sign it into law. From the beginning the government intended the shift from a reform bill to one for full equality as, in part, a means of influencing left-wing public opinion. The bill did produce a stunning impact on public opinion, but it did so on the right, not the left.

NOTES

1. Huber, *Dokumente,* 1:141–56; for Baden, dated Aug. 22, 1818, see 1:157–69; for Württemberg, Sept. 25, 1819, see 1:171–200. Sheehan, *German History,* 411–17, is the best recent treatment in English; also see Weis, "Begründung," 74–84.

2. For Abel, see M. Spindler, "Die Regierungszeit Ludwigs I (1825–1848)," *HbG,* 4¹: 198–99, and "Die konservative Periode 1832–1847," *HbG* 4¹: 175–210, in general. Also H. Gollwitzer, *Ludwig I. von Bayern. Königtum im Vormärz. Eine politische Biographie* (Munich, 1986), *passim.*

3. See Bavaria, Landtag, *Kammer der Abgeordneten. Verhandlungen 1819–1917/ 18* (Munich, 1819 et seq.), 13 July 1819, Protokolle, bd. 14, 362–63, par. 18, entries a–n.

4. See ibid., bd. 6, 138ff., 11 Mai 1819.

5. The debates are in ibid., bd. 5, 137–257. For von Utzschneider's statement, see 226. Use of the 1819 volumes is difficult but may be improved by using *Vollständiges alphabetisches Reportorium über die Verhandlungen der Stände des Königreichs Bayerns im Jahre 1819* (Munich, 1821).

6. See Stefan Schwarz, *Juden,* 213–16. Schwarz does not cite the volume of debates (5) here and directly quotes as statements what were questions in the original. Schwarz treats the debate over peddling separately (195ff.) and does not connect the two.

7. Schwarz, *Juden,* 229–30.

8. Claudia Prestel, *Jüdisches,* 61ff.

9. Gollwitzer, *Ludwig I.,* 603–4, writes that as crown prince, Ludwig repeatedly voiced his hostility toward Jews. But Schwarz, *Juden,* 232 n. 72, cites Geh. Hausarchiv München K 79 L 3 no. 175, which is in Maximilian II's Nachlass, as containing a draft of a bill for full emancipation dated 1828; in connection with a comment by Ludwig in a letter to Schenck about the talents of an individual Jew in the same year, Schwarz speculates that Ludwig was the source for reform and his ministers the source of opposition to emancipation. The note to Schenck, his minister of the interior, was innocuous (see Max Spindler, ed., *Briefwechsel zwischen Ludwig I von Bayern und Eduard von Schenck, 1823–1841* (Munich, 1930), 59–60, dated Berchtesgaden, 14 Sept. 1828. Schwarz's mistaken speculation is explained in that the draft bill, though in the file cited by Schwarz, reads "1848" rather than "1828," understandably so since Maximilian only became king in 1848 and the rest of the file contains documents only from 1848 and later on Jewish emancipation.

10. Max Spindler, "Regierungszeit," 152ff., and W. Lempfrid, "Der bayerische Landtag 1831 und die öffentlichen Meinung," *ZfbLG* 24 (1961): 1–101. Ludwig wrote to Schenck on 6 May 1831 urging him to stand firm against the attacks in the lower house; see Spindler, *Briefwechsel,* 187.

11. *Verhandlungen,* bd. 22, 1831, 129th sitting, 5 Nov. 1831, 37–132.

12. Described in Schwarz, *Juden,* 234–39, with no explanation for Ludwig's actions despite the author's belief in the king's support for reform (see n. 9 above).

13. See the speeches by deputies Lösch, Lang, Weinmann, Freiherr von Closen, and Rudhart in *Verhandlungen,* n. 11 above.

14. Schwarz, *Juden,* 239–42, describes the 1831 legislation as "too optimistic." *Nothandel* meant trade in necessities but also connoted sharp business practices; see p. 24, above.

15. Dr. A. Eckstein, *Kampf,* 70ff.; Schwarz, *Juden,* 254.

16. Eckstein, *Kampf,* 78; the Fürth Jewish community feared the negative results of mass petitions, but twenty-six were submitted.

17. Dr. Lazarus Adler, *Die bürgerliche Stellung der Juden in Bayern: Ein Memorandum, der hohen Kammer der Abgeordneten eherbietigst vorgelegt* (Munich, 1846), 3–23, dated 20 Jan. 1846.

18. Schwarz, *Juden,* 259.

19. *Verhandlungen,* Beilagen bd. 7, 1846, Protokoll der Sitzung des 3. Ausschuss, 18 Apr., and *Verhandlungen der Kammer der Abgeordneten der Stände-Versammlung des Königreichs Bayern im Jahre 1845/46,* bd. 2, 345ff. and esp. bd. 11, 7 Mai 1846, 125–288; and Schwarz, *Juden,* 265ff. Also *Verhandlungen,* Beilagen-Band 7, 17 Apr. 1846, Beilage L (fifty), 71.

20. Jacob Toury, "Eintritt," 139–242. For "citizenry," see ch. 2, n. 101.

21. Verhandlungen, n. 15 above, bd. 11, 59th session, 7 Mai 1846, 125ff. All the speeches referred to are from this source.

22. For Döllinger's speech see ibid., 171–98. See also speeches of Pfäffinger (137–48), Schäzler (163–66), Vogel (240), and Schlund (250–51).

23. See Paula Hyman, *Alsace.*

24. Döllinger's speech in n. 22 above; Eckstein, *Kampf,* 82–83, saw Döllinger's speech as ruining the chances for emancipation.

25. Specious reasoning statistically; see table 2.3, esp. the decline from 1832 to 1848.

26. There were two ministries of the interior, one limited to matters affecting only churches and schools, the other responsible for everything else. Both directives were addressed to the government of Oberbayern and are in StOB, RA 2090, 33875. What follows is also from this file. Also see Eckstein, *Kampf,* 106.

27. StOB, RA 2090, 33875. Why the ministry chose Oberbayern as the province to investigate was never spelled out; indeed, other provinces may have been asked, although I found no evidence of this. No reason was given for seeking information at the lower level, other than the fact that the city of Munich had to report because no Jews lived elsewhere in that province.

28. Eckstein, *Kampf,* 92 n. 26, indicates that some Jews opposed a Jewish consistory. The prospect was attractive to Jews who found it hard to support private Jewish education in Bavaria; the authors noted the need to close the religious school in Fürth some years earlier.

29. Compare to table 2.1, which gives 663 for 1848, probably from this same source, but more than 1,200 for 1852.

30. StOB, RA 2090, 33875, Bericht zur k. Staats-Ministerium des Innern. Die Verhältnisse der israelitischen Glaubensgenossen betr., 74–85. Some of this material is paraphrased in Schwarz, *Juden,* 266ff.

31. Found in GHA, Nachlass Max II, 79/3/175, and dated only Munich, 1848. Schwarz, *Juden,* 271–72, paraphrases this document also, but he dates it, incorrectly,

from the year 1846. Since it followed the submissions of spring 1848, it probably dates from late spring or summer of that year.

32. StOB, RA 2090, 33875. Only drafts remain and the signature is illegible; Schärl, *Beamtenschaft*, 798–99, records that Bernhard Freiherr von Godin was forced to retire in October 1848 because of the disturbances of that month.

33. My count, based on the summary of the original reports, which is all that appears to remain in the files, is slightly different: eight for change, nine for no change, ten for modified change, and eleven did not respond.

34. This must refer to the decision of 4 June 1848 and indicates that this document must have been written between then and 4 July, when it was submitted. The governor's comment that a favorable result in Frankfurt would be helped by the presence there of a number of Jews does not appear to be meant in a derogatory sense.

35. The first dated document in the Ministry of Justice files is that of 3 Apr. 1849, but it refers internally to a decision of 26 Nov. 1848 that the Ministry of Justice produce a draft for the Ministry of Church and Schools. See BHStA, Ministry of Justice, 13389.

36. Hans Rall, "Die politische Entwicklung von 1848 bis zur Reichsgründung 1871," in *HBG* 4[1]: 249–50.

37. For the older view, see M. Doeberl. *Entwicklungsgeschichte Bayerns*, vol. 3, *Vom Regierungsantritt König Ludwigs I. bis zum Tode König Ludwigs II. Mit Einem Ausblick auf die Innere Entwicklung Bayerns unter dem Prinzregenten Luitpold*, ed. Max Spindler (Munich, 1931); for newer interpretations, see Horst Hesse, *Die sogenannte Sozialgesetzgebung Bayerns. Ende der sechziger Jahre des 19. Jahrhunderts. Ein Beitrag zur Strukturanalyse der bürgerlichen Gesellschaft* (Munich, 1971), and Leonhard Lenk, "Revolutionäre-Kommunistische Umtriebe im Königreich Bayern: Ein Beitrag zur Entwicklung von Staat und Gesellschaft 1848–1864," *ZfbL* 28[12] (1965): 555–622.

38. See Gollwitzer, *Ludwig I.*, 668ff. for the Lola affair, 708ff. for the events leading to resignation; Spindler, "Briefwechsel," 210ff.

39. H. Rall, "Politische Entwicklung," *HbG*, 4[1]: 230–31.

40. Eckstein, *Kampf*, 98ff., argues that sentiment was against the use of petitions requesting emancipation because the time was not right. Some hoped that the Frankfurt Parliament would solve the problem, and others favored requesting suspension of the special laws on Jews.

41. For Maximilian's letter to Schelling and for the replies to Maximilian's entreaties for advice, including Schelling's, see GHA, 79/3/175, in a file on Jewish emancipation. See also Werner J. Cahnman, "Friedrich Wilhelm Schelling über die Judenemanzipation," *ZfbLG* 37[2] (1974): 614–23. Alfred D. Low, *Jews in the Eyes of Germans: From the Enlightenment to Imperial Germany* (Philadelphia, Pa., 1979), 186, is a good example of the riskiness of predicting responses without the original: Low speculated that Schelling supported equality on the assumption that Maximilian was progressive and would not have requested advice from Schelling if he thought the answer would be negative. Low's "logic" must have been reinforced by the knowledge that Max did submit a bill for emancipation.

42. Cahnman, "Schelling," 614–15; also see Ludwig Trost and Friedrich Leist,

eds., *König Maximilian II von Bayern und Schelling: Briefwechsel* (Stuttgart, 1890), 160–61 for the king's original letter, dated 13 Nov. 1848.

43. See n. 41.

44. Most of this interoffice correspondence is in the files of the Ministry of Justice, BHStA, MJu, 13389, dated between 3 and 21 Apr.

45. Described in Rall, "Politische Entwicklung," 233ff.; all analysts misinterpret the volume and rhythm of the popular movement for and against both the Basic Rights and the Frankfurt Constitution. The petitions, over 1,100, submitted by communities all over Bavaria, between Dec. 1848 and May 1849, show two waves of agitation, one in winter, the other in late spring. In Landtags Archiv, Munich, Karton 867, III Ausschuss, J 3-A (Faszikeln 1–4), "Adressen für [und "gegen"] unbedingte Einführung der Reichs Verfassung und der Grundrechte," 13 Landtag, 1849. This is analyzed in James F. Harris, "Rethinking the Categories of the German Revolution of 1848: The Emergence of Popular Conservatism in Bavaria," *CEH* 25, no. 2 (1993): 123–48.

46. All drafts are in BHStA, MJu, 13389, without dates, but two copies of the same draft appear in GHA, Nachlass Max II, 79/3/175, and one of these is the one that Schwarz, *Juden*, 232 n. 72, mistakenly identified with 1828.

47. The King's actions are described in Rall, "Politische Entwicklung," 235; Schwarz, *Juden*, 279, expresses surprise at the quickness of the action on Jewish emancipation in May, but he also says nothing about the political situation. The great concern over the possible consequences of rejection of the constitution may be seen in the request for Prussian military help, but it was also evident in Bavaria proper, where the state bureaucracy and the army took steps to prevent an expected uprising; see my "Arms and the People: The Bürgerwehr of Lower Franconia in 1848 and 1849," in Larry Eugene Jones and Konrad Jarausch, eds., *In Search of a Liberal Germany: Studies in the History of German Liberalism from 1789 to the Present* (New York, Oxford, Munich, 1990), 133–60. Von der Pfordten received correspondence from Karl Freiherr von Welden, who was in Ansbach and Nuremberg in May, stating that there was no doubt that the nation wanted revolution; see letters of 9, 20, and 31 Mai from Ansbach and 13 Mai from Nürnberg in GHA, Nachlass v.d. Pfordten, 7, 144.

48. In GHA, Nachlass Max II, 79/3/175, because the report was addressed to the king.

49. BHStA, Staatsrat, 3384.

50. In detail in Schwarz, *Juden*, 280–81. Von Roth's *Motive* is in GHA, Nachlass Max II, 79/3/175, dated 29 May 1849. Eugen Franz, *Ludwig Freiherr von der Pfordten* (Munich, 1938), 168–69, reduces this complex situation to the misleading statement "He [von der Pfordten] had introduced the bill because the greater part of the liberal public and the entire left demanded it."

51. *Verhandlungen 1849. Kammer der Abgeordneten. Beilagen Band I*, Beilage 9, p. 116; Beilage 59, 1–4, dated 3 Dec. 1849 when it was accepted; pp. 8–9 for Ruland's argument and p. 10 for his bill. For Ruland, see Max Pauer, "Dr. Anton Ruland," *Mainfränkisches Jahrbuch für Geschichte und Kunst* 12 (1960): 305–11, for laudatory biographical details, but nothing on Jewish emancipation.

52. Schwarz, *Juden,* 283, gives it three short sentences, but the committee work receives a full paragraph. Karl-Thomas Remlein, "Landtag," 139–208, remedies this in part.

53. *Verh. Abg. K.,* 1849, vol. 2, Ruland, 38th sit., 10 Dec., 485–86, and 38 sit., 10 Dec., 499ff.; Sepp, 40th sit., 12 Dec., 554–61; Döllinger, 41st sit., 13 Dec., 572ff.; Allioli, 39th sit., 11 Dec., 519ff.; Wolfsteiner, 39th sit., 11 Dec., 528ff. For Sepp, see Dr. Johann Nepomuk Sepp (1816–1909). *Ein Bild seines Lebens nach seinen eigenen Aufzeichnungen. Xenium zum hundertsten Geburtstag (7 August 1916). 1 Teil. Von der Geburt bis zum Abschluss der öffentlichen Tätigkeit* (Regensburg, 1916), 127–28.

54. See J. Katz, *Prejudice,* for a good treatment of this tradition.

55. *Verh. Abg. K.,* 1849, vol. 2, Ruland, 10 Dec., 485–86; Sepp, 497–505; Mayr, 11 Dec., 513–14; Allioli, 11 Dec., 519 ff.; Koller, 12 Dec., 540–41; Döllinger, 13 Dec., 568–69.

56. Mayr, 11 Dec., 513.

57. See table 2.5.

58. Allioli, 12 Dec., 519ff.; Ruland, 10 Dec., 485ff.; Sepp, 12 Dec., 554–61; Döllinger, 13 Dec., 577–78.

59. Von Lerchenfeld, 13 Dec., pp. 587–92; von der Pfordten, 10 Dec., 505ff.; von Harold, 10 Dec., 492–93; Arnheim, 11 Dec., 523–24 and 13 Dec., 578; Aub, 13 Dec., 563. The reading of the Aub letter elicited a charge of favoritism, but the president responded that there was only one letter from Jews and so many from Christians (against) that he could not read them all.

60. Von der Pfordten, 10 Dec., 550ff.; von Hegnenberg-Dux, 14 Dec., 598ff.; Scharpff, 14 Dec., 602ff.; von Ringelmann, 11 Dec., 532ff.

61. Von Harold, 10 Dec., 492–93; Krichgessner, 11 Dec., 525ff.; von Ringelmann, 11 Dec., 532ff.; von Lerchenfeld, 13 Dec., 587ff.

62. Breitenbach, 13 Dec., 563; Sepp, 10 Dec., 499ff.; Schmid, 12 Dec., 535ff.; Döllinger, 13 Dec., 567–78. See J. Friedrich, *Ignaz von Döllinger: Sein Leben auf Grund seines schriftlichen Nachlasses,* 3 vols. (Munich, 1901), 3:38ff., 46ff. Friedrich presents him as for emancipation but against the bill only because of its effect on communities.

63. See especially von Lerchenfeld, 13 Dec., 587–92.

64. See especially von der Pfordten, 10 Dec., 508ff.; also von Ringelmann, 11 Dec., 532ff.

65. Sepp, 12 Dec., 574ff.

66. Von der Pfordten, 10 Dec., 505ff.

67. E. Franz's *Pfordten,* is the only biography. Pfordten's Nachlass, in GHA, Nachlässeversammlung, is very large, and such material may be buried in one or the other set of correspondence.

68. GHA, Nachlass von der Pfordten, 7, 109, Briefe; there are eight from Auerbach, between 1845 and 1847, and they begin "Mein lieber Freund."

69. GHA, Nachlass von der Pfordten, 25, 1, dated 1849 only, entitled "Points that Minister von der Pfordten ought to address." Pfordten was then a minister in the Saxon government. His reply, in partial draft form, undated, is also there. Gollwitzer,

Ludwig I., 592, notes that Ludwig removed von der Pfordten from his position at the University of Würzburg in 1841 and transferred him to a court in Aschaffenburg for expressing progressive ideas.

70. Gollwitzer, *Ludwig I.*, 125, "Arbeiten für Max II."

71. See, e.g., Max Seitz, "Die Februar- und Märzunruhen in München 1848," *Oberbayerisches Archiv für vaterländische Geschichte* 78 (1953): 1–104. GHA, Nachlass von der Pfordten, 603, depicts Ludwig as equating aggressive Protestantism with liberalism and Jewish emancipation with revolution.

72. Ruland, 10 Dec., 484–92; Fink, 10 Dec., 439–95; Döllinger, 13 Dec., 567–78; Sepp, 12 Dec., 554–61.

73. Von der Pfordten, 10 Dec., 510; von Hegnenberg-Dux, 14 Dec., 596–601.

74. Ruland, 10 Dec., 485, 490–91, though Jäger, 541–43, mentioned that he knew that many people were against the law from his reading of the newspaper; Also see Wolfsteiner, 11 Dec., 531; Schmid, 12 Dec., 535ff.

75. Hirschberger, 13 Dec., 553–54.

76. Döllinger, 14 Dec., 577.

77. Romnich, 10 Dec., 483–84. Von der Pfordten, 510–11; von Lerchenfeld, 13 Dec., 587–92; Scharpff, 14 Dec., 602–5; von Ringelmann, 14 Dec., 605ff.

78. Von Hegnenberg-Dux, 14 Dec., 600–601.

79. Mayr, 11 Dec., 513; Sepp, 12 Dec., 554ff.; Jäger, 13 Dec., 541–43; Lerchenfeld, 14 Dec., 587–92.

80. Sepp, 10 Dec., 497–505; Schmidt, 12 Dec., 535ff.; also Breitenbach, 12 Dec., 544; Hirschberger, 12 Dec., 553–54; von Lerchenfeld, 14 Dec., 591–92.

81. Döllinger, 13 Dec., 577; Ruland, 10 Dec., 490; Allioli, 11 Dec., 519ff.; Wolfsteiner, 11 Dec., 528–31.

82. See von Wenning, 549ff.; Hirschberger, 553–54; von Pitzner, 561–62; Finks, 562; Paur, 581.

83. Breitenbach, 12 Dec., 544; Heine, 551ff.

84. Thus Allioli, 12 Dec., 562, on commercial concession, and Forndran, 562, on a variety of guarantees.

85. Mayr, 11 Dec., 513; Boos, 12 Dec., 543–44.

86. Sepp, 12 Dec., 561.

87. Boos, 12 Dec., 543–44; Breitenbach, 12 Dec., 544; Forndran, 11 Dec., 514.

88. Bayer, 12 Dec., 537ff.

89. Von der Pfordten, 10 Dec., 508ff.

90. Von Lerchenfeld, 13 Dec., 591ff.

91. Von Ringelmann, 11 Dec., 534.

92. Weis, 13 Dec., 581–86.

93. Von Hegnenberg-Dux, 14 Dec., 598ff.

Chapter 4

The Struggle over Jewish
Emancipation in the Bavarian Press

Bavarians learned of the passage by the lower house of the bill for full Jewish equality with Christians through news reports in the press.[1] Many of the petitions sent to the upper house begin with the phrase "We have learned in the press."[2] Newspapers were the most important single vehicle of news dispersion. It cannot be surprising that the press also played a major role in forming popular attitudes toward Jews and the bill and stimulating people to act.

Unfortunately, practically nothing has been written about the role of the press in the struggle over Jewish emancipation in Bavaria in 1849–50. Although much has been written on the press in general, especially on the Catholic press, there is almost no mention of the press coverage of the debates in the lower house and the petition drive against the bill for Jewish emancipation, or of the press' direct role in the conflict. Yet the press was important, even critical, in the revolution of 1848 and in its participation in the struggle over Jewish emancipation.

Even before the first bloody clashes between crowds and the military erupted in Vienna and Berlin in mid-March 1848, the stirrings of revolutionary sentiment had eliminated the press censor. Legislation providing legal freedom from censorship quickly followed in nearly every German state, and this, coupled with heightened popular interest in events, led to increased circulation and the founding of a number of new papers by the end of 1848.[3] Old and new papers alike devoted much more space to political news and to editorializing than ever before. This substantially enhanced the role of newspapers as the most common vehicle for communication among individuals and groups in German society. By thus linking state and society, the newspaper press became the most powerful means for the people to influence the government and for the state to manipulate the people.[4]

In revolutionary 1848 the political newspaper press was a liberal, progressive, democratic, and even radical force.[5] But 1848 also stimulated the growth of a smaller conservative press and, in some areas, a politically active religious press.[6] In 1848 and 1849 the politically liberal and leftist press generally supported Jewish emancipation while the politically conservative and Catholic press usually opposed it, setting the stage for a confrontation and test of strength between these two camps over Jewish emancipation.[7] It is natural to ask which side, left or right, better reflected Bavarian public opinion? But it is also important to ask which political segments of the press demonstrated the more innovative approach either in their coverage of news or their attempt to influence the campaign for or against Jewish emancipation. Analysis of the role of the press provides telling insight into the campaign for Jewish emancipation and the development of political life in Bavaria.

The Newspaper Press and Bavarian Jewry in 1848–49

It is easy to exaggerate the ability of the press to influence public opinion in the post-1848 era. Contemporaries, from kings and ministers to journalists themselves, frequently equated the attitudes of the newspaper press with public opinion. No one questioned the existence and power of public opinion in the aftermath of March 1848. Thus King Maximilian II wrote his new minister of the interior, Graf von Reigersberg in 1855, at the height of the conservative 1850s, to remind him that governments could no longer ignore the power of public opinion. He had used the press to mold and direct public opinion as much as possible, the king wrote, and hoped his new minister would understand this position of the government. From the first days of his reign, Maximilian treated the press carefully, attempting to use it for his own purposes whenever possible.[8]

Such comments easily lead to the conclusion that the newspaper press was both large and powerful. But though there were more newspapers after 1848 than before, relative to its population Bavaria had very few newspapers. The most accurate list of newspapers is based on the postal service records, because the great majority of publications were sold by subscription and sent through the mail.[9] Only 154[10] papers together published 43,956 copies per issue in Bavaria, including the Pfalz, in only 48 cities or towns. There were fewer copies of newspapers than there were Jews. Many papers did not appear daily, so for a population of well over four million scattered among more than 8,000 separate communities, this meant less than one copy per day for every 102 Bavarians. By 1885 the number of papers in Bavaria had quadrupled, and circulation had increased proportionately, but in 1848 the numbers were still low.[11]

The distribution of newspaper publishers in Bavaria in 1848 highlights still further the real limitations on publication. Most of the newspapers were located in two of the eight provinces, Upper Bavaria and Swabia, and almost exclusively in the major city in each area, Munich and Augsburg. Twenty-eight papers with a circulation of 14,925 appeared in the capital, and twenty-three with a circulation of 14,625 were printed in Augsburg. Thus one-third of all papers and two-thirds of all circulation came from two of Bavaria's 8,000 municipalities. At the other extreme lay the province of Lower Bavaria, where nine newspapers in five cities enjoyed a total circulation of 811, or about 1.9 percent of the Bavarian total. Middle Franconia was the runner-up to Swabia and Upper Bavaria, boasting a total of twenty-one papers in seven cities, with a circulation of 4,609. The two biggest newspapers in Bavaria were the Augsburg publications, the *Augsburger Allgemeine Zeitung* (8,896 circulation) and the *Augsburg Abendzeitung* (3,102 circulation), which together accounted for over 27 percent of the total circulation in Bavaria.[12]

Such minute circulation statistics make it hard to describe the press as manipulating either the people or the government.[13] In addition one must consider that many, perhaps half, of the peasants were illiterate.[14] Cost must also be considered as a limiting factor for circulation. The average price of papers varied substantially by province, type, quality, and frequency of publication.[15] The *Neueste Nachrichten* in Munich was cheap at fl 2 per year for a daily, but the daily *Augsburger Allgemeine Zeitung* at fl 17 per year, and even papers a quarter of its cost, was too expensive for most Bavarians.[16] One of the few recent studies of small-town Bavaria argues that there was little political literature published in or for the rural areas, that most communication was oral, and that the political press did not reach the middle and lower levels of this population.[17]

Of the few newspapers produced in 1848 in Bavaria, most were nonpolitical. Only about a quarter of the papers are extant today, and they are largely the more significant, larger circulation, political papers. Probably one-third of the newspapers in Bavaria were nonpolitical and never mentioned Jewish emancipation. Among the remaining papers, the treatment of the emancipation bill varied widely. If the press wielded influence in 1849, it did so in ways other than through mass circulation of a common position on issues.[18]

Newspapers exerted influence on popular and governmental attitudes through their coverage and editorial positions. Most political newspaper editors contented themselves with merely describing the debates in the lower house of Parliament. A few editorialized for or against Jewish emancipation, most without extensive accompanying justification. The power of the press originated in the fact that the educated class largely accepted newspaper accounts and positions as reflective of informed opinion. A handful of papers, most of them on the political left, attempted to stimulate the "people" into some form of political action in 1848. The right-wing press did so in

1849–50. As was the case with public opinion in general, a major reversal in press opinion occurred between early 1848 and late 1849.

Though Bavarian newspapers did not request the emancipation of the Jews in March 1848, they generally supported the increasingly radical resolutions passed in the numerous political assemblies held in all parts of the state, some of which included Jewish emancipation in their demands.[19] But the famous Munich petition of 3 March did not include emancipation, even though Ludwig I's response to it on 6 March promised "improvement in the condition of Israelites."[20] The press generally accepted the idea of reform of the laws on Jews, but most papers saw no need to push for emancipation.[21]

Newspapers in general paid little attention to Jews or Jewry before the debates over the bill for emancipation began in December 1849. Most papers did not bother to report the government's first public announcement of emancipatory legislation in May 1849. Even the *Neueste Nachrichten* in Munich, which normally gave careful and complete coverage to the legislature, ignored the news of an emancipation bill. The *Bayerische Landbötin* and the *Volksbötin,* however, seized the opportunity to comment, perceptively, that all the legislation introduced in May was "leftist," merely camouflage for the government's rejection of the Frankfurt Constitution.[22]

Lack of press coverage did not result from any unusual attempt by the Bavarian government to restrict access to its deliberations. From at least as early as May until as late as November 1849, scarcity of news on the bill must have resulted from an editorial decision not to report these events. Presumably those decisions were based on assumptions about reader interest, the importance of the issue, and the cost of coverage. Papers that would later be vociferously involved on both sides were uniformly quiet, but the *Allgemeine Zeitung des Judentums* (*AZdJ*) reported events meticulously, establishing the availability of information. In a chronicle of the year 1848, the *AZdJ* listed the dates of all action affecting Jews, from anti-Semitic riots in rural areas to all the Bavarian government's public announcements. Its correspondents noted and commented on Maximilian II's speech from the throne in January 1849, in which he promised reform legislation for Jews; on the election of a Jew, Dr. Morgenstern, to the Parliament in February; and on von der Pfordten's opposition to the Basic Rights and his new bill for Jewish equality in May.[23]

The *AZdJ* greeted the May legislation pessimistically. When the king dissolved Parliament in June, it predicted that the newly proposed law would be dropped. Its correspondent commented that Jews were simply a "plaything" and asked which ministers would remain in office if the bill were reintroduced.[24] After the bill resurfaced, the *AZdJ* followed its progress in committee from 10 September to 19 November, albeit still cynically.[25] The prospects for passage of emancipation in the lower house appeared dubious to the *AZdJ*, and the paper thought Bavarian Jewry so steeped in hyperortho-doxy that it foresaw little Jewish support for the bill. One writer presciently expressed the fear that petitions would be generated by the ultramontanes and that agitation would become so great that the government and Parliament would gladly drop emancipation.[26] The *AZdJ* only became optimistic when the committees voted for the bill and sent it to the floor of the lower house. The former pessimists now predicted passage.[27] The cynicism of the *AZdJ* probably derived from its knowledge of previous Bavarian governmental opposition to Jewish emancipation. Presumably its optimism derived from a changed perception of the government as now sincerely supporting the bill.

The committees' vote in favor of the bill coincided with the first serious signs of interest in the bill's fate by Bavarian newspapers in general, and it seems to have come as a particular shock to those papers opposed to it. Just as Jews began to feel optimistic, the opposition, ominously, began to take interest. On the practical level, lack of coverage by most papers is under-standable given the fast pace of change in 1848. By comparison to monarchs like Ludwig I and the pre-March governments, the parliaments established or modified in 1848 appeared far more fascinating and were much more open to newspapers—one had only to sit in the visitor's gallery and take notes to find a story. While the Bavarian and Frankfurt parliaments were in session, major Bavarian papers tried to report on both. That meant covering three separate legislative chambers in two cities: the upper and lower houses in Bavaria and the plenary sessions in Frankfurt. But exciting and important debates and decisions could also be found in the Austrian Assembly, in the Prussian National Parliament, and in parliaments in most of the other states in Germany. Few papers were ready or able to field paid reporters, so they were content to rely on amateur, unpaid correspondents and lengthy excerpts copied directly from papers in the cities where the parliaments were located. In such a situation, it was easy to ignore committee work until something significant happened, which, in the case of Jewish emancipation, meant until passage by the combined committees on 24 November 1849.

Most newspapers gave their readers no description of the discussions in the committees, but almost all pointed out that committee passage now meant debate by the entire lower house of Parliament, beginning on 10 December.[28] Some, like the *Lechbote* and the *Bayerische Landbötin,* predicted that the debates would be "interesting" because of the existence of sharp differences of opinion.[29] These almost laconic comments were the first indications to the typical reader that a conflict was building. The *Mittelfränkische Zeitung* in Nuremberg added to its notice a statement that emancipation's "time had come," and the paper expressed hope, citing the *Augsburger Allgemeine Zeitung,* that Germany would not lag behind other states in freeing this oppressed people.[30]

Like the *Mittelfränkische Zeitung*, several papers indicated their support or opposition for Jewish emancipation. But before the lower house debates, only two papers, both democratic, troubled to editorialize in lead articles for Jewish emancipation, and none did so in opposition. An editorial was a lead article, usually with a title and sometimes signed, usually appearing on page one. But such articles were relatively rare. Even some dailies providing political news did not utilize this technique, and others did so sparingly. Many local papers never adopted the use of leads or editorials. Study of a substantial part of the Bavarian press in 1849 indicates that papers employing editorials were frequently left-wing, although a few on the right used the same technique. Editorializing was not only the most obvious way to try to mold opinion but nearly the only way.[31] Usually only the most important issues received editorial treatment, and Jewish emancipation soon fell into that category.

Die Volksbötin, a liberal-to-democratic paper in Munich, and one of the two papers that took an editorial position prior to the debates, supported the bill in a lead entitled "Something about the Jews." It was time, the unknown lead writer stated, to become civilized as far as Jews were concerned, to realize that many Jews had become successful and to recognize that though some Jews might still engage in "sharp" business practices, some Christians did too. Was it any wonder, the editorial asked, that Jews were not friendly to Christians after years of persecution? The writer concluded that the government law was good but noted the existence of opposition, especially from "our black brothers," Catholic priests, who were encouraging country folk to send petitions against it. Referring to this agitation as a "shameful act," the writer explained that no community would be forced to accept anyone, Jewish or Christian.[32]

The other paper to treat the Jewish issue was the radical *Neue Fränkishe Zeitung (NFräZ)* in Würzburg, which published a series of four lengthy front-page articles entitled "The Jewish Emancipation Question" in November, before the bill had been passed in committee.[33] The four-part article quite clearly favored emancipation, but its importance stems from its criticism of a long brochure described by the writer as making the rounds in the upper reaches of local society.[34] The language of the article was florid and self-righteous, and its author did not hesitate to condemn the aristocratic, bureaucratic, and ultramontane opponents of emancipation. But his main technique in attacking the offending brochure was to quote from it at length without commentary to show bias and inaccuracy that he apparently thought would be self-evident. The third installment of the article began with a long quotation from the brochure carried over from the previous edition with no word of caution or introduction to the reader. Treating the brochure in this fashion, the *NFräZ* inadvertently widened its circulation at no cost to its anonymous author.

The brochure that occasioned both articles in the *NFräZ* is one of very few printed antiemancipation brochures still extant today. Its lengthy title, "Judaism and the Emancipation of the Jews or Equality of the Same in all State-citizenship Rights with Christians in all Connections," was not unusual for Bavaria in 1849.[35] But the brochure was really two separate pieces. Pages 3 to 53 discussed the material referred to in the title, and pages 54 to 63 were a "Short Explanation" of a presentation by twenty-seven Jews of Unterfranken for improvement of the position of the Jews, largely in terms of revision of the 1813 Edict.[36] The brochure depicted the 1813 law as humane but misunderstood by Jews. This was one of the rare attempts by opponents of emancipation to defend the Edict, but the author's "proof" was laughable. Most of the brochure was an assertion that Jews were lazy, greedy, and cheaters because of their religion. It was a simple polemic and very poorly written.

But the writer who supported emancipation in the editorial in the *NFräZ* was not much better stylistically or very well informed factually. In response to the brochure's slurs on Jewish religious practices, the author said much the same about the Catholic Church on other issues. The writer "admitted" that Jews cheated and took advantage of Christians and would continue to do so as long as they were oppressed. The author expected the ultramontanes to do all in their power to prevent emancipation, and expressed bitter irritation with the Jews for not contributing to the proemancipation cause. Incensed at the tendency of some Old Conservative Jews (Orthodox?) to work with and depend on the ultramontanes, the article's final sentences spoke eloquently about what Jews had to fear from their supporters:

> But shame to those who, like an animal parasite, depend on their enemy, who want to learn nothing from history. Shame especially to those who today, in defense of their interests, ask whether freedom or slavery will be more profitable. . . . The free [Jews] stand on the democratic side and want freedom. May those who deal with the ultramontanes live again in dirty, stinking ghettos, at oath-taking stand on a pigshide [and] pay the same entry fee at the gates as for pigs, [for] they have no inclination and no merit for a more honorable position!

Only a week later the *NFräZ* published a two-part article, "Something More on the Jewish Emancipation Question," which was signed at the end "by a Jew."[37] This author responded to the same brochure largely correcting mistakes and deliberate errors relating to Judaism. The writer expressed confidence that the Enlightenment had corrected the old belief that Jews poisoned wells; maintained that the people would no longer allow themselves to be drawn into violence against Jews; and, in closing, voiced optimism that the brochure would not change public opinion, which supported emancipation. On the day before the debates began, 9 December, the *NFräZ* printed an article, "Father Ruland in the Bavarian Lower House," which concluded that the priest was an "evil-thinking falsifier of the truth."[38] Whatever the drawbacks of its writers, the democratic and apparently anticlerical *NFräZ* supported the bill unambiguously from the start.

Not all newspapers agreed with the *NFräZ*. Negative reaction to the committee's vote was not long in coming, and it derived almost exclusively from a small number of conservative Catholic papers like the *Lechbote,* the *Augsburger Postzeitung,*[39] and, especially, the *Volksbote für den Bürger und Landmann,* edited by Ernst Zander. Among all the editors of nineteenth-century political newspapers in Bavaria, Zander stands out as one of the most unusual, innovative, and powerful. He played a major role in the opposition to Jewish emancipation.

Zander was often accused, inaccurately, of Jewish birth, but he may well have been an illegitimate son of the Princess of Sohms-Braunfels. He was born in Mecklenburg as a Lutheran, converted to Catholicism in 1830, adopted the name Ernst (not his legal name), became a British citizen in 1830, married an Irish woman, and returned to Germany after trying his hand at journalism in England, Belgium, Portugal, France, and Austria. Enjoying an income on about the same level as a high government official, Zander was completely irresponsible financially and was always broke. When pressed, he showed talent at raising money from rich benefactors, but he was not above accepting press subsidies from the Bavarian and Austrian governments, and in 1848 he literally tried to blackmail Maximilian II's administration in an attempt to get money he felt was due him.

After a number of years in journalism in Bavaria, Zander founded the *Volksbote* on 1 April 1848. The paper quickly became the most influential pro-Catholic, conservative paper in Bavaria. There seems little doubt that Zander was responsible for the *Volksbote*'s success. Nearly all observers, then and now, credit Zander's achievement to a combination of hard work, brilliant insight into the mind of the common man, and an innovative and attractive journalistic style. But most were simultaneously repelled by Zander's willingness to use vicious and vulgar invective, his ultraconservative and zealous pro-Catholic stances, his suspiciously democratic appeal to the masses, and his unpredictability. In addition to being viciously anti-Semitic, Zander favored a liberal view of press freedom and German unity under Prussian leadership but opposed most other liberal reforms. In later years he attacked the growing south German opposition to the Prussian north, especially in 1866 and after. It is impossible to stereotype his politics as simplistically liberal or conservative.[40]

When he received news of the committees' passage of the bill for Jewish emancipation, Zander exploded. He questioned whether the deputies had voted as their constituents wished, noting that the chair of the committee, Scharpff, was from the Palatinate, where Jews were largely emancipated. He cited a letter to the deputies of the Eichstädt electoral district from their constituents that was antiemancipation and that stated the district was too. One fine day, the *Volksbote* noted on 9 December, we will wake up with a Mister Aaron or Schmul as minister of church and schools or named to a bishopric or parish. On the following day, the opening day of the debates, the *Volksbote* said the deputies acted as if they were representatives of the Jews and not of Bavarians.[41] The opening salvo had been fired, and no one who read the *Volksbote* could doubt its position.

Coverage of the Debates in the Lower House

Most newspapers thoroughly covered, although not entirely in an unbiased way, the nearly five full days of debates on Jewish emancipation in the Bavarian lower house. The intensity of the press response reflected an explosion of popular interest, which could be measured by the crowd in the visitors' gallery in Parliament.[42] Most papers arranged for a correspondent—in the case of Munich papers, usually the editor—to attend the sessions, take notes, and write summaries of the proceedings. Some reports were more thorough than others, indicating the degree of interest, the cost, or both. Papers unable to afford their own correspondent often reprinted reports from other papers.[43] Nearly every political newspaper in Bavaria covered the debates, affording their readers the unusual opportunity of reading descriptions of the longest set of debates on Jews in Bavarian history.

But not all newspaper readers received objective news with their subscriptions.[44] Editors often did not distinguish between factual news and editorializing, so most papers commented on the speakers and speeches at the same time that they reported on them. Moreover, the selection of speeches and speakers was often tendentious. Some, like the *Regensburger Zeitung*, made critical references to speakers opposing the bill and in many little ways revealed a proemancipation stance.[45] The *Bayerische Landbötin* in Munich provided its readers with very good coverage of the debates but could not resist criticizing Dr. Sepp, an opponent, as prone to mix truth with falsehood, the serious with the superfluous, and the insupportable with the provable.[46] The *Volksbötin* also gave lengthy coverage, but in addition to constant criticism of Sepp, it praised the government speakers for the bill, notably von Ringelmann and von der Pfordten.[47] The democratic *Gradaus mein deutsches*

Volk made no effort to conceal either its distaste for the "black brothers," Ruland, Sepp and company, or its gleeful surprise that the political right now had to oppose the government.[48] After its earlier editorials for emancipation, the *Neue Fränkische Zeitung* covered the debate with a mixture of reprints from other favorably inclined papers. It also ran short pieces, frequently accompanied by bad poetry written by Anselm Freiherr Gross von Trockau, who lambasted Catholic criticism of Jews. One of the paper's correspondents wrote that while he was listening to the debates it was like being in the middle of the Council of Constance, because opponents "dredged up" material about Jews from three thousand years of history.[49] Much of the newspaper rhetoric was not far behind the opponents in the dredging process.

Although papers supporting the emancipation bill outnumbered those in opposition, they did not outdo them in the use of biased rhetoric. The *Lechbote* in Augsburg combined brief, but reasonably objective, stories with two lead articles on 13 and 14 December that were extremely antagonistic. "The Jew is Still the Old Jew—Even when Emancipated" criticized emancipation, using material drawn directly from Ignaz von Döllinger's speech in the 1846 Parliament. The Jew was "eternally" the same, and safeguards against him were needed—as the situation in Alsace proved.[50] Essentially the same message appeared the next day under the milder heading "Concerning the Emancipation of the Jews," but this article was more direct and more hostile than that from the day before. The mass of the people saw Jews, it said, as exploiters, as vampires. Jewish economic success was based on slyness, cheating, lies, and usury. Jews were the irreconcilable enemies of Christians who had given them so much already. To give Jews more through emancipation, to give them control of public offices, would turn Bavaria into a wasteland. Jews had not changed over the past thousand years and would not in the next thousand. The *Lechbote*'s writer even quoted the Roman prefect Rutelius's comment that "if the Jews were not controlled by the weapons of Pompei and Titus, then the poison of their pestilence would spread and the conquered would become the conqueror." The writer claimed this comment appropriate to 1849 if the bonds on Jews were loosed.[51]

Both the *Lechbote* and the *Postzeitung* operated within the traditional limits of journalistic practice in Bavaria. And the response of Zander's *Volksbote* to the debates of 10–14 December, that is, up to the final vote, was also normal, even if it was far more critical and vulgar than any other paper. Its anti-Jewish bias pervaded every article and practically every paragraph. It criticized the logic of giving Jews more rights simply because some rights, such as the right to sit in Parliament and on juries, had already been granted. It labeled the earlier decisions "mistakes" and saw no sense in compounding such error.[52] It attacked the "red" papers, the *Gradaus* and *Volksbötin,* for supporting the bill and "reminded" them that their stance went against the wishes of the people. It added for good measure the claim that the Jews had not supported the government in 1848 but the Bavarian people had.[53] The *Volksbote* was offended that the Parliament was even seriously discussing full emancipation.[54]

The frustration evident in the *Volksbote*'s coverage of the parliamentary proceedings turned rapidly to anger upon passage of the bill on 14 December. There was not enough space in the paper's columns to contain Zander's pent-up irritation and fury with the deputies. His initial response was an article entitled "Disgraceful Proceedings in the House of Deputies," with the title in extra large, black type and introduced to the reader by a pointing hand—rare publishing techniques in 1849. Zander seized on the actual process of ending the debate to accuse the leadership, especially the president of the lower house, von Hegnenberg-Dux, of exhibiting outright favoritism and duplicity by cutting off debate when speakers, especially opponents, remained.[55] Zander's irritation was clear in another article in the same issue devoted to identifying those who voted for the bill. In addition to listing in a black-bordered box the names of those deputies who voted for the bill, the article singled out Tafel, Knollmüller, Boos, and Thinnes as responsible for passage. All four were Catholics. The first was a "red" from the Pfalz. The last had merely abstained because he had not been allowed to speak. Knollmüller and Boos were priests. Since a two-thirds majority (88) had been needed, the votes of these four Catholics, unlike all other Catholics in the assembly, provided the margin of success. Votes for and against by province, according to the *Volksbote,* are shown in table 4.1.

The Struggle over Emancipation

The *Volksbote* announced its strategy for overturning the action of the lower house in the same issue in which it described the passage of the bill, and it did so in a fashion that quickly defined the context of both its reaction to the decision and its preparations for the deliberations of the upper house.[56] The tone of the article is reminiscent of a forecaster warning of the end of the world, of a carnival barker, or of an officer rallying his troops for a last stand. Zander called on the citizens and peasants of all communities in Bavaria to bestir themselves to influence the upper house, which could still reject the bill. In apocalyptic tones, he called for petitions—unless the people preferred to bow before District Director Schmul. He urged all to pursue a proper, legal form of protest but to lose no time. He urged a particular list of demands: a two-thirds vote by communities on residence; exclusion of Jews from judgeships, tax and finance offices, and church positions; and the abolition and punishment of *Schacherhandel.* To facilitate submission of petitions, he volunteered the services of the *Volksbote* to receive and forward them, but he cautioned all community members to sign under the community seal to demonstrate the legitimacy of the signatures. From the start Zander's strategy was remarkably thorough.

In the sixty-three days between passage by the lower house and the beginning of the consideration of the bill in the upper house, hardly a day passed when the *Volksbote* did not publish an article or two against emancipation. Other opposition papers, like the *Lechbote* and *Augsburger Postzeitung*, devoted far less space to the issue, although they were no less opposed to the bill. One of the most acute articles on the role of Jews in economic life appeared in the *Augsburger Postzeitung* under the title "The Emancipation of the Jews from the Standpoint of State Economics." Familiar with socialist, especially Fourierist, criticisms of the power of big capital and Jews, the author described Judaism as a single large bank from which the little Jews could acquire money for investment; the little Jew found the deals, which the big Jew financed. To this writer, emancipation was another form of the struggle between free trade and protection, between north and south Germany. If we want uncontrolled freedom of business and crafts, the article concluded, then we should grant emancipation; if not, then we ought not give the Jews these rights.[57]

Supporters of emancipation were also relatively quiet, expecting, it seems, that the upper house would ratify the large majority in the lower house. Most supporters of emancipation were content to criticize the opposition to emancipation on moral grounds rather than on the basis of public opinion. Many proemancipation papers questioned the morality of the petitions cited by the *Volksbote* and others and questioned whether the petitions really represented the people. Only a few tried to organize popular support. Some attempted to influence the upper house by invoking royal support, by deriding the vulgarity and violent tone of some of the petitions, and by suggesting that the "antiquated" upper house justify its existence by voting for emancipation. But the *Volksbote,* unique in the extent of its coverage, its hostile tone, and new methods, succeeded beyond its wildest dreams.

Zander's *Volksbote* called for petitions against emancipation in every issue. On 18 December a letter to the *Volksbote* described the popular organization of citizens in Neuötting for a petition against emancipation and emphasized the eager support given by men who normally did not participate in such actions. Zander printed the letter and added his encouragement to other communities to organize petitions.[58] Every article on related aspects of the emancipation issue concluded with a call for petitions, often using raised type or the pointing hand to draw attention to the matter. On 21 December, a week to the day after passage of the bill, Zander began the daily publication of a running list of petitions received against emancipation. This regular section, titled "Petitions against Jewish Emancipation," appeared on either the first or second page of the *Volksbote* in large black type under the now ubiquitous pointing hand.[59] Each entry gave a number to each petition, added the number and names of the separate communities supporting it, and included excerpts, sometimes lengthy, from especially interesting petitions.[60] As the number of petitions and communities submitting them soared, interest in this section intensified. Most political papers in Bavaria cited the *Volkbote*'s totals, ensuring their distribution to every corner of the state.[61]

Zander was not a typical conservative, and he was not at all embarrassed about using a method largely associated with his democratic opponents in 1848. Indeed it was not his first use of it. He had encouraged petitions against the Basic Rights in the previous spring and had published a running list of opposing communities. Rather than complain about its fickle nature, Zander merely questioned whether what passed as public opinion was really an accurate reflection of it. He argued that in the earlier campaigns against the Basic Rights and the Frankfurt Constitution, the "real" people of Bavaria had not been heard. The majority of the lower house had supported the emancipation bill, but the *Volksbote* strenuously asserted that the deputies did not represent the people as a whole. Zander maintained that their decision interfered with the rights of the people.[62]

The irony of the situation was not lost on Zander. "Whoever wants a good chuckle," he wrote just before New Year's Day, "should survey the position of newspapers, big and small, on Jewish emancipation and compare it to the treatment last year of the Basic Rights, the laws for freedom of occupation, of movement, and of the right to subdivide property." Then, he wrote, all had trumpeted that the "people must express itself," must send addresses for the unconditional acceptance of this or that; why did not those trumpets bray forth now for emancipation? Because, Zander argued, they

TABLE 4.1.   Votes on Jewish Emancipation in the Lower House by Province

Province	For	Against
Upper Bavaria	10	11
Lower Bavaria	3	12
Upper Palatinate	6	7
Upper Franconia	14	0
Middle Franconia	14	1
Lower Franconia	17	1
Swabia	11	7
Palatinate	16	1
Bavaria	91	40

Source: Volksbote, no. 49, *Beilagen zum* . . . (Sun.), 16 December, 1, München, 15 December, provided this listing.

Note: According to the *Regensburger Zeitung*, no. 348, 17 December, 1, München, 14 December, eleven or twelve of those voting against were Catholic clerics, only two of whom voted for the bill.

knew the people did not want it. Responding to criticism of the *Volksbote*'s "agitation" against emancipation, Zander ridiculed the other papers' refusal to recognize petitions that frustrated their desires.[63] When a progressive paper asked when the "Mischief of the Addresses" would stop, Zander replied mockingly: "Really! To want to lessen the peoples' right to petition because they don't agree with the progressives!"[64] He defended the vulgarity and directness of some petitions in the same vein. If anyone wanted to know how the people really felt, he wrote, they would see through the form to the substance, and that would be better than if a lawyer had written the petition.

Papers supporting the bill for emancipation leveled three criticisms against the *Volksbote*'s petition campaign: that it was dangerous and perhaps could turn violent; that it was not numerically significant; and that opponents, Catholic priests especially, used improper methods for collecting signatures and in representing communities. Each of these criticisms received substantial play in the press and led the *Volksbote* to strike back with an accusation of its own that the government, through the Ministry of the Interior, pressured community officials not to support the petitions.

Much of the newspaper press criticized the *Volksbote* and the ultramontanes for using fanatical language and encouraging direct action. Comments abounded about Zander's writing style, which he deliberately adapted, often using dialect, to appeal to peasants and people in small towns. Zander's critics called his prose "cheeky,"[65] "insulting," "reckless," "wild fanaticism,"[66] and, frequently, "vulgar."[67] The *Würzburger Stadt- und Landbote* noted that the *Volksbote* deliberately excerpted from the sharpest, most threatening petitions, enjoying the freedom to be violent without doing so directly.[68]

Most newspapers opposed more than just the passionate tone of the articles in the *Volksbote* and its few allies. Many feared the results of such popular agitation. The *Neueste Nachrichten,* normally restrained and noncommittal, editorialized very strongly against the use of "any means" by a "certain party" to oppose emancipation. The paper argued that to "stir up" the country folk in this way, especially through use of the press, was a crime, and that those engaged in it should consider well the consequences. In that paper's opinion, those native Bavarians who shamelessly used vulgar means to criticize the lower house disfigured that parliament.[69] Although the phrase "any means" may appear vague, in December and January 1849–50 it no doubt implied violence.

In Würzburg the radical *Neue Fränkische Zeitung* wrote that the ultramontanes had "throw[n] all caution overboard" when they manipulated the "ignorant" masses in old Bavaria into participating in "anti-Jewish actions and riots." It identified three papers as leading the campaign, the *Postzeitung* in Augsburg, the *Volksbote* in Munich, and the *Bayerische Presse* in

Würzburg, adding that the editors, Ludwig Schönchen, Ernst Zander, and Moritz Brühl, were renegade Jews, "because Christians were too proud or honorable to do such things."[70] Some leftist supporters of Jewish emancipation were not above using slander and were themselves anti-Jewish.

Other papers, too, feared the results of the sentiments expressed in the petition campaign. The *Bayerische Landbötin* commented that the passions found in the petitions frequently exceeded the normal limits of legal civic life and that for these antiemancipationists the goal of the petitions was not as important as their form. One theme stood out in these petitions: that the government itself was undermining the welfare of its own people. One writer for the *Bayerische Landbötin* was troubled by references in some petitions to raised flails and scythes that "could be used on the Jews and, if necessary, also on a ministry that goes so far as to extend to the Jews the protection of the laws."[71]

Zander did not take such criticism of his and the *Volksbote*'s intemperate use of words seriously, especially not, he wrote, when other papers referred so frequently to Catholic priests and opponents of emancipation as the "Pfaffen," the "Schwarzen," and the "black brotherhood."[72] But from the beginning Zander spoke out firmly against violence. In the article of 18 December reporting the first spontaneous assembly of a village, Neuötting, to organize a petition against emancipation, he noted that the conclusion of the letter accompanying the petition had been even more "earnestly" written than the lines quoted and that the *Volksbote* would not print it. We seriously warn citizens and peasants, he added, to use only legal methods; the decision is up to the upper house, and one should only submit petitions.[73] Two days later, probably in response to the rash wording of additional petitions, he wrote an editorial strongly denouncing the use of force. All we need, he wrote, are legal means; whoever uses force surrenders his own rights by acting illegally. "Moreover it's truly no heroic deed to fall upon a defenseless Jew here or there, . . . only disgraceful." Urging use of petitions rather than mistreatment, he preached that "the Christian uses the law and the duty of self-preservation, he defends himself and his against damage, but he does not use violence."[74]

When some accused the *Volksbote* party, as it was frequently called,[75] of engaging in revolutionary activity, Zander again turned the table on his opponents. He gleefully noted on Christmas Day, "One cannot trust one's eyes," when seeing democratic papers prate about the damage that opposition to emancipation does to "legal order." Those who used to call for uprisings themselves blame us now for doing the same; they call us—the Pfaffen, the Philistines, the dumb peasants—a "revolutionary" party. Zander reminded his critics that the proper way for the people to express their views, the legal way, was through petitions. This might be uncomfortable for those supporting emancipation, but it was right.[76] Whenever Zander saw a challenge to the petition process, he defended the latter as the legal, proper way of protesting. Opponents of emancipation were not revolutionaries, he insisted, but democrats and leftists were. Similar comments, though lacking the verve and humor of the *Volksbote,* appeared in the *Lechbote* and *Augsburger Postzeitung.*[77]

Because it was inconsistent for democrats to attack the petition method, and because Zander made such tactics so embarrassing, most supporters of emancipation quickly shifted to criticizing the process used to organize the signing of the petitions, consequently questioning the meaning of the large number of signatures. Simply stated, many liberal newspapers claimed that those circulating the petitions, especially the clergy, took any signatures they could get in any way they could get them, including those of women and children.[78] The normal practice was that only male heads of families or households voted or signed such documents. Almost no women and children signed, but emancipation supporters used the accusation that they did to undercut the credibility of the petitions.

Some newspapers claimed that opponents of Jewish emancipation shamelessly manipulated the issues, for example, leading peasants to think that emancipation would mean celebrating Sunday on Saturday.[79] The *Volksbötin,* among the most critical of these purported methods, also argued that the conservative Catholic Pius Associations falsely presented their own petitions as representing the civic community.[80] Again, other than isolated incidents, there is no evidence in the petitions to support these charges, and there is much evidence to the contrary.

When the *Volksbötin* claimed that an address in Straubing had been circulated improperly, the local mayor and council denied it, stating that the petition had been circulated according to custom and with their permission, had accepted no signatures from wives and children, and was therefore accurate.[81] Only a small number of papers argued that community officials had misused their office to support opposition to emancipation. But accusations that mayors went from house to house seeking petitions and encouraged other mayors to do likewise surfaced in the press.[82] Although unusual in the context of earlier practice, such activity was hardly illegal. It testifies to the emergence of political activity at the grass roots level in this period. But the modern character of this tactic probably shocked traditional observers as much as its message did the supporters of emancipation.

Skepticism about the number of signatories stemmed in part from hostility to the process of petition circulation. The numbers themselves were hard to dispute, although some papers made an effort to do so. The *Volksbötin* doubted the authenticity of the signatures collected and seriously argued that not one-tenth of those signing knew what they were doing. Even fifty thousand signatures were only, it speciously argued, one-one hundredth of the population—the *Volksbötin* mistakenly confused heads of households with total population.[83]

Questions about the number of persons signing petitions against emancipation raised the related issue of how to evaluate those petitions that a mayor and his council, usually about five or six individuals, signed in the name of their community. The *Bamberger Zeitung,* noting in late January that in 261 communities the communal councils had signed in this fashion, concluded that the actual number of citizens represented must be considered much higher than only the number of written signatures.[84] Even the correspondent for the *Allgemeine Zeitung des Judentums* agreed with this analysis.[85] Early in the campaign the *Volksbote* raised the issue of the significance of the eighty-one signatures from Hirschau. The paper pointed out that this total was fully representative considering that the signatories were among the "most respectable" citizens of a city of 1,406 people and therefore constituted a substantial percentage of male heads of household (see app. C, no.3).[86]

As for petitions signed only by officials, Zander remarked that they signed for their communities.[87] He, like other editors, noted the position of the "official" *Neue Münchener Zeitung* on the petitions—that all must be treated equally. But, he added, the "rascalocracy" mocked them as "stupidity petitions" and ridiculed a few hundred thousand in a state of four to five million. As any schoolchild knew, he argued, that was confusing heads of household with total population, including women and children. Who, he scathingly asked, thought that in a community of 500, where only 10 officials signed, the remaining 490 were for emancipation? Could those with a fifth sense tell how many of the nonsigners were for? Why, he asked bluntly, were there no addresses for emancipation? Because other than a few Jews, he continued, no one wanted it. He noted that only two petitions favored emancipation, one from a rabbi in Munich, the other from a rabbi in Bamberg.[88]

As data on the petitions appeared in the *Volksbote,* observers began to produce statistical analyses of their origin. The single most obvious fact to emerge was that petitions were most numerous in the Old Bavarian areas, such as Upper and Lower Bavaria, where no Jews lived.[89] The *Würzburger Stadt- und Landbote* concluded that opposition came from areas where fear of an "unknown evil" ruled.[90] In its analysis of the vote on 14 December, the *Neueste Nachrichten* noted that 37 of the 40 parliamentary opponents represented areas with few or no Jews (11 from Oberbayern, 12 from Niederbayern, 7 from the Oberpfalz, and 7 from Schwaben).[91] Such commentaries were intended to cast doubt on the significance of petitions submitted only out of fear based on ignorance. Neither the *Lechbote* nor the *Volksbote* mentioned this analysis directly. But Zander took pains to emphasize that opposition to emancipation came from the entire country, and he carefully drew attention to opposition from Franconia, where most Jews resided. Both sides seemed to demonstrate that public opinion was only to be followed or cited when it agreed with one's position.

When the *Mainzer Journal* published a letter from Lower Franconia stating that the people hoped to lose a good part of "our Jews" to other areas as a result of the new law, Zander commented that this was why "so few petitions have been sent against emancipation from Unterfranken . . . (though there were still very many)."[92] His reasoning was that people in Lower Franconia also disliked Jews but felt that emancipation would be good for them if it encouraged Jews from their province to move elsewhere. One must balance Zander's explanation against the report by the *Bayerische Landbötin*, which noted that a real "excitement" over the endorsement of emancipation by the lower house could be seen only in Franconia. The report implied that all was calm in the south and that the southern citizens would honorably support the government and the upper house whatever its decision.[93] That analysis conflicts with the existence of several petitions from "Old Bavaria" that also threatened violence. In noting that nearly 1,500 communities had submitted petitions against emancipation, Zander commented that the *Volksbote* had received letters and reports from areas where Jews were heavily settled ("eingenistet," or nested, like a rat), all saying Christians needed emancipation from Jews.[94]

Zander challenged those who doubted the reality of opposition to emancipation to produce petitions supporting emancipation. The *Lechbote* had noted that in Augsburg an attempt to organize a petition in support of emancipation had been stillborn.[95] The oppositional *Postzeitung,* in a more sympathetic article than one might have expected, argued that the best proof that popular opinion did not agree with the vote in the lower house lay more in the small number of petitions favoring emancipation than in the large number against.[96] The *Mittelfränkische Zeitung* reported that the Synod of the Free Christian Communities in Nuremberg, a minority movement, supported emancipation, and the paper hoped this would produce more petitions in support,[97] but there is no petition from such a group in the archives. The *Neue Fränkische Zeitung* in Würzburg came closest to an adequate response, but it, too, failed to produce a serious popular address for emancipation. It merely published a protest against the local petition and a "declaration" for emancipation by the executive committees of the local March Association (36 members), the Workers' Educational Association (7), and the Gymnastic Association (6).[98] The declaration read in part: "To circulate an address for the emancipation of the Jews with good results would be easy for our organization; but to petition in this fashion is against our principles. We leave [the decision] simply to the sense of honor of the upper house to save the good name of Bavaria in [Europe]." The first part of this comment was, of course, sour grapes; the second either highly naive or disingenuous. It was a pitifully weak response.

Some opponents of emancipation argued that criticism of the petition campaign against emancipation had diminished the number of petitions and signatures of opponents. The *Lechbote* in Augsburg publicly criticized the heads of some guilds for removing a petition from circulation and returning it unsigned, frustrating their members' free expression of opinion.[99] But the biggest issue of the entire campaign was the claim that the government had actively discouraged petitioning against emancipation. The energetic actions of Hohe, the director of the chamber of the interior in Lower Franconia, provided the evidence for this charge.

Early in the campaign, Zander commented insightfully on the relation of state officials, largely the district directors, to the higher levels of the bureaucracy. In response to criticism of the *Volkbote*'s agitation against emancipation, Zander observed that many officials, hoping to "warm a chair at a higher level," used all their powers against petitions opposing emancipation, although many of them had earlier helped to organize petitions supporting the Basic Rights and the Frankfurt Constitution.[100] A week later the *Volksbote* printed a letter from the mayor of Regnitzgmunde in Upper Franconia stating that the people opposed emancipation there but feared what would happen to their officials if they submitted a petition. Zander replied that they should not worry, that the government could not punish them for petitioning, because it was their right to do so.[101] Zander was less than candid in giving this advice. He knew that state ministries could easily discipline officials for any reason.

In late January several mayors in Lower Franconia communicated to the *Volksbote* their irritation and concern about government pressure. The mayor of Kirchlauter in the rural district of Baunach reported that the district director had said he would "get" mayors who signed the addresses, because there was a royal order forbidding such a step without the approval of the district director.[102] Zander immediately expressed the hope that the ministry would reprimand Rückert, the district director involved, because no one at any level could interfere in the petition process, and ministers who did should be indicted. Petitioning was, Zander reiterated, a constitutional right. In the lower house, Sepp asked the government whether it was pressuring mayors. The minister of the interior, von Zwehl, quickly denied that charge, insisting that the directive of 15 December had been used only to prevent possible excesses stemming from the decision of the 14th.[103] But the government was clearly on the defensive.

On 6 February the *Volksbote* reported that on the day after von Zwehl's declaration, a district director in Lower Franconia had sent the following order to mayors in his district:

> Nr. 1555. One has informed us that in Grusshausen an address to the Reichsräthe concerning the political and citizen equality of Jews has circulated. The mayor must report immediately who organized the address, how many signatures it has, whether it has circulated in the surrounding area, and in general the more specific details.
>
> Hassfurt, 30 January 1850
> Royal District Director Scheuer (very urgent)

Zander saw this as "bureaucratic chicanery and oppression," not as "investigation." He wrote that ministers who did not appreciate criticism of bureaucrats should put their own house in order, and that if they were interfering with the petition process, they should reprimand themselves. If emancipation was a failure, they should drop it rather than interfere with legitimate activity by the communities. The *Volksbote* was curious whether the upper house knew what was happening, advising supporters that "one should not forget on what ground one stands and how the weather looks."[104]

Scheuer's letter to the communities in his district was no more than a reasonably faithful copy of a directive from the chamber of the interior in Würzburg requesting information. Surprisingly, that directive also had been leaked to the press, appearing in the *Bayerische Landbote* on 24 January.[105] But Zander, preferring his own sources, made no mention of that, perhaps because the outlook seemed increasingly favorable for the *Volksbote* rather than for emancipation.

The importance of the newspaper contretemps over the government's role in Lower Franconia in gathering detailed information lies more in illustrating Zander's paranoia and the role of the press than in describing the effect of the investigation on the petitioning. If the state discouraged the submission of petitions against a government-sponsored bill, it cannot be established through study of the newspaper coverage of the incident. Zander's fear of government influence had some basis both in fact and in a perception by common people that "information gathering" was more than met the eye (see chapters 5 and 6). The campaign struggle over Jewish emancipation apparently stimulated local officials to "leak" information to the press, which published it and pursued it using modern, investigative methods. Also, and importantly, this incident highlights again the substantial clash between the conservative press, which opposed emancipation, and the state, which had proposed it.

Not all coverage of Jewish emancipation between the passage of the bill through the lower house and the discussion in the upper house concerned the petition process. Such papers as the *Volksbote,* which fervently opposed emancipation, published materials likely to help their cause, and supporters of the bill acted in exactly the same fashion. As justification for its agitation against emancipation, the *Volksbote* sought any material that could be made to show disadvantages to Christians, direct or indirect, of the new legislation. As evidence of damage, the *Volksbote* pointed to the loss of communal assets. It cited a letter from Franconia stating that a local community of three hundred citizens had communal assets valued at fl 200,000 which, according to this bill, would soon be shared by Jews who had not contributed to them. That, the unknown letter writer argued, was not equitable to Christians. Where were the Jews' fields, forests, and meadows?[106] As for future indirect damage, the *Volksbote* began to publicize incidents involving Jews to prove their innate economic immorality, undue influence over Christians and judges, and hostility toward Christians. Some of these "news" reports were quite long, and somewhere in each article Zander shamelessly noted its relation to emancipation. Whether any or all of these incidents were real or accurately described is almost impossible to tell. One can only speculate on the effects of the technique, but it cannot have helped Jews or emancipation. No "news" about Jewish progress or achievements appeared in the *Volksbote.*[107]

Because many papers endorsed Jewish emancipation, even though they did not devote nearly as much space to it as Zander did in opposition, control of the press became an issue. Opponents of emancipation argued that Jews controlled public opinion, or at least its expression in newspapers. Already in December 1849, the *Volksbote* stated that the most radical papers were in Jewish hands and "manufactured" public opinion. The same theme was implicit in a lead article of 2 January entitled "Money Rules the World." A few days later, Zander "explained" that practically all Bavarian newspapers kept information on Jews from the people because these papers were edited by Jews, coedited by Jewish writers, or under Jewish influence. What these papers published passed as public opinion, Zander wrote, but it was all the product of Jewish fabrication. Likewise, the *Augsburger Postzeitung* speculated that Jews were behind the *Allgemeine Zeitung*'s coverage, asserted that most papers were written by Jews and demagogues, and referred to newspapers supporting emancipation as "Jew-papers." [108]

In the course of these two months of campaigning, the supporters of emancipation contributed little that was new. Except for coverage of Rabbi Aub's declaration that obedience to the Talmud was not required of Jews, signed by 40 of the 41 rabbis in Bavaria, almost nothing appeared.[109] Rabbi Aub's declaration was a response to accusations made about the Talmud by Sepp and others in the lower house in December. Stating that the Talmud was not religiously "binding" was a weak response because it implied that the criticisms of the Talmud were somehow accurate. The press did little to support Jewish emancipation, contrary to Zander's claim that Jews controlled it, and neither did the Jewish community. A correspondent from Bavaria to the *Allgemeine Zeitung des Judentums* complained bitterly that Jews did "Nothing, Nothing, Nothing" in response to all this—they trusted in the goodness of their cause.[110] Though this is true in general, there was at least one exception.

In the middle of the *Volksbote*'s campaign against the emancipation bill, Rabbi Dr. Lazare Adler of the resort city of Kissingen in Lower Franconia wrote an "Open Letter" to deputies "Ruland, Sepp, Allioli and Company," refuting the errors and exposing the "hate and passionate enmity" in their speeches in the lower house. It appeared in two lengthy parts in the *Neue Fränkische Zeitung* on 1 and 2 January and in the *Mittelfränkische Zeitung* on 12 and 13 January, [111] and it also appeared as a brochure, a common occurence then.[112] Later in the month, a Munich correspondent for the *Neue Fränkische Zeitung* reported that Adler's letter caused "a great stir."[113] Lost in the relative obscurity of this whole affair, Rabbi Adler's response was, if not unique in Germany, very nearly so in Bavaria, because it was much more than merely another defense against defamation.

Adler's essay should be seen on three different levels: as a careful refutation of errors about Jews and Judaism, as a hard-hitting criticism of hate and discrimination against Jews, and as a declaration that Jews did not fear men like Ruland, Sepp, and Allioli. The tone that permeated Adler's reply was new to Bavaria. He began by stating that his intention was to provide the public with the truth and to expose hate, at the same time denying a reverse passion. We Jews, he insisted, sympathize and feel compassion for you Christians. You are the stronger, Adler admitted, but future generations must know that oppressed Jews have the courage to expose their most powerful enemies through the weaponry of simple truth.

Adler spent much of the first installment of his letter on the issue of Christianity rather than Judaism, utilizing a very effective question and answer technique. Adler cited Matthew 7:12: "All that you want others to do to you, do you unto them; that is the law of the prophets." He then asked: "Is that correct? Yes or no? Answer no if you dare! If yes, then you are not Christian for how could Christians be so cruel and mean to Jews?" Using other Christian principles exemplified by relevant citations from the New Testament, Adler played this theme with sophistication for some time.[114] In the second installment, he turned to common errors and inaccuracies in the arguments of opponents, especially on the Jewish treatment of neighbors and strangers, emphasizing the positive aspects of Judaism that had been either perverted or ignored by their enemies. Adler derided the German desire to change Jews socially and economically as deceptive, because Jews were unable to reside in areas with farm land for sale or open positions in the crafts. He called the forces that used public opinion to restrict Jews inconsistent for not also supporting the peasantry and the "peoples' voice" on the issue of abolition of the *Zehnter* (a tax). Were they, he asked pointedly, only thinking of the Church, which benefited financially from that tax? He stated flatly that such critics of Judaism as Ruland, Sepp, and Allioli had never read the Talmud, because if they had they could not make such statements about it. But, he continued, all Christians had had the opportunity to read Jewish school books in German for thirty years: "Have your school inspectors found anything damaging to the state or morals there? Yes or no? If yes, you have violated your duty in not saying anything to the government; if no, you have got to admit it and stop lying. We have compassion for you," Adler concluded, "and do not hate you, but we do not fear you either. We believe in a Messiah who represents love in the world."

Zander could not refrain from responding to Adler's article, probably because it bothered him intensely.[115] He described Adler's arguments very vaguely, giving no examples, making no effort to present them accurately, and perverting and twisting the few he mentioned. Beginning by belittling the rabbi—"Adler von Kissingen he dubs himself"—Zander went on to state that Adler wanted to whitewash all Jews and falsely blacken the reputations of all Christians "who will not bow to Jewish rule." Referring to Adler's arguments as "fantasies," Zander magnanimously wrote, "We'll give him some crumbs, though, since he's written four pages, which seldom comes from a Jew and a well-educated one at that!" Reversing the facts, Zander declared that if Jews wanted to inject religion into the campaign, Christians would respond. As news coverage of Adler's article, Zander's treatment was worthless; as invective, it clearly revealed his ardent anti-Semitism.

Almost as soon as the lower house had passed the bill, newspapers began to report on rumors and speculation about its chances in the upper house. Correspondents and editors in general were not afraid to speculate, but papers opposing the bill did not do so, perhaps thinking that predictions of passage or rejection might undercut the petition movement. However, almost all papers supporting the bill followed rumors of its chances. In late December and early January, almost all reports predicted passage by the upper house.[116] Correspondents to the *Allgemeine Zeitung des Judentums* from Munich originally noted that the upper house, to demonstrate its independence of Jews and other progressives, was only too willing, according to the signs, to let the bill fail. But other correspondents to the same paper soon wrote that the upper house contained few opponents of emancipation.[117]

Newspapers speculated on everything. Count Rechberg, named floor manager of the bill in the upper house, fell ill, which delayed the day of consideration, and he had to be replaced. Several papers reported that the new floor manager, Count Montgelas, favored the bill; others more accurately reported that he opposed it.[118] The *Allgemeine Zeitung des Judentums* reported yet another rumor that the upper house wished to delay consideration until the constitutional clauses dealing with the communities had been revised,[119] and other papers agreed with a modified version of this analysis.[120] By late January newspapers generally recognized the success of the *Volksbote*'s program.[121] Just as the debates began, the *Bamberger Zeitung* reported a rumor that the government might withdraw the bill to avoid defeat.[122]

As the campaign against Jewish emancipation gained what appeared to be massive momentum, and as the day of reckoning in the upper house approached, journalistic supporters turned away from criticism of the petition process. Supporting the bill, the *Bamberger Zeitung* regarded the petition campaign as shameful but so powerful that the editor was reduced to hoping that the upper house would accept the law, undeterred by the opposition of public opinion.[123] The *Bayerische Landbote* also feared the effect of the petitions on the upper house, but it saw possible hope for the bill because the highest circles of society and government, unlike the common folk, recognized emancipation as a just request.[124]

Sensing defeat, several newspapers supporting emancipation attempted to transform the struggle from one between people and Parliament to one between the upper house and the royal ministries. The *Bayerische Landbötin* argued that "a few hundred" petitions would not kill the bill in the upper house; if the government made Jewish emancipation a "Cabinetfrage," with a change of cabinet as the price, the bill would pass. Rejection of the bill, the paper stated, would be damaging to Bavarian constitutional life, not just a blow to Jewish hopes: "May those who have to decide never forget this!"[125] The *Allgemeine Zeitung des Judentums* essentially agreed: if the ministers strongly favored the bill, the opposition in the upper house would be insignificant because the same nobles who opposed emancipation had said, on the amnesty issue, that they would follow the king because they were monarchists.[126] By the time the upper house began its deliberations, the liberal press had been reduced to hoping for success through either the power of the monarchy or the altruism of the princes. A few were openly cynical. The *Volksbötin,* for example, predicted failure, claiming that the upper house would vote emancipation down and why not? It was 1850; two years earlier it would have passed.[127]

There were a few indications from opponents that influence from the king and the press might make the upper house amenable to a compromise. A long article in the *Augsburger Postzeitung* addressed the issue of the "Mission" of the upper house on Jewish emancipation, concluding that all special laws against Jews should be abolished and that Jews should have equal civil rights. Calling for an end to the use of executive action against *Schacher,* it advocated restrictions on licenses to peddle and supported the movement of Jews into crafts, but it asked Jews to wait for further rights to be established through the constitutional process. It recognized the difficulty of the task faced by the upper house and noted the government's need to act due to its earlier and precipitous promise of improvement. But, it stated, the many petitions against emancipation compared to the few for indicated that the lower house was not supported by the majority of the people. Therefore the upper house should, at the cost of its popularity in the press, listen to the great majority of the people and act to secure peace by modifying or rejecting the bill.[128] Incapable of even such a meager compromise, Zander made no change in the *Volksbote*'s request for simple rejection.

Postmortem

The prestigious *Historisch-politische Blätter für das katholische Deutschland* printed a remarkable contemporary analysis of the journalistic success of the *Volksbote* and Ernst Zander, which helps explain the role of newspapers in issues concerning Jews in Bavaria in 1849–50.[129] The unknown author began with the premise that the press in general was in the hands of corrupt, ruined people speculating only in destruction, chaos, and revolution, who were at best ignorant swindlers and madmen, many of them Jews whose first principle was a bitter hatred of everything Christian. The real problem, however, was with the respectable people who read democratic papers to appear nonreactionary and criticized the right-wing press to show bipartisanship. Editors who "gave the devil no compliments" or "called [an] evil by its own name" were reviled by all. The creators of this radical public opinion were the political clubs that owed their origin to the French Revolution. The people were true to the king. The center of revolutionary propaganda was in the cities and succeeded because of the indolence and cowardliness of the "well disposed," who were the greatest obstacle to political and economic order.

But the author of this description of the press acknowledged an exception—the *Volksbote*. No paper had as much influence on the thinking of the people as Zander's paper. Zander was responsible for the numerous and strong petitions against the Frankfurt Constitution and Basic Rights, for the spread and increase in power of the Association for Constitutional Monarchy and Religious Freedom, and for the awakening of the people from their apathy. The author could not approve of Zander's methods, but the rest of the press was no better, and if it were left to the "well disposed," nothing would get done. In conclusion, the author expressed the hope that the *Volksbote* would inspire others to imitate it, for there was a need for papers that were not designed only for the richer and more educated reader. This editorial was written before the antiemancipation campaign in which the *Historisch-politische Blätter* also editorialized against emancipation, writing that sacrificing Christians to Jews was not equality.[130]

This essay is especially important because it documents Zander's success in his use of a new and radical style of journalism well in advance of later developments in the 1870s. Even if conservative papers did not rush to imitate the *Volksbote*, the prestigious *Historisch-politische Blätter* recognized and preached the value of its example. The journal criticized Zander's allies who were "too respectable" to use his techniques even in a modified fashion. The campaign against Jewish emancipation was journalistically innovative and politically successful.

Evaluating the role played by journalism in the campaign against Jewish emancipation in Bavaria depends a great deal on what questions one asks. Good news coverage of even relatively minor events began only with the lower house debates on 10 December 1849. Until then, the press ignored nearly all actions of the king, his ministries, and Parliament. After 10 December journalists covered the debates very well, but with the exception of some editorializing both for and against, that meant largely passive reportage of speeches. The petition campaign quickly became news and demanded coverage, but its most thorough treatment came from those few papers opposing emancipation. Liberal and democratic papers that had exulted in popular expressions of opinion in 1848 reacted to popular opposition to emancipation with silence, minimal coverage coupled with critical comments, or outright condemnation. Most were embarrassed by both the *Volksbote* and the positive response of many of their own readers to the call for petitions. Some were not entirely free of anti-Jewish bias, despite their endorsement of emancipation. The debates in the upper house received the same type of coverage followed by expressions of sympathy with the Jews, sadness for the political turn to the right, irritation with the upper house, and then silence. Jews were no longer news.[131]

In stark contrast to the very "normal" journalistic treatment by most of the political press a minority of papers opposed emancipation, and one, the *Volksbote*, did so creatively. Using a technique borrowed from the democrats and radicals and already tested successfully by conservatives in the campaign against the Basic Rights and Frankfurt Constitution in the spring of 1849, Zander stimulated those elements in the population who wanted to prevent Jewish emancipation into more intense action. The *Volksbote* did not create that opposition but encouraged it to express itself to stop the process of emancipation and provided a vehicle for that expression. Those clerics who opposed emancipation, largely Catholic priests in Catholic Bavaria, and those town mayors who were also opposed found in the *Volksbote* arguments to be used, a forum for expression of their views and encouragement, and practical advice on how to use a traditional method, the petition, to the best advantage. Not only did most of the political press, which more or less favored the bill, not counter this activity in any significant way, but it even gave the campaign more publicity and a certain measure of credence by reprinting quite regularly the number of petitions flooding into Munich. Zander's influence, as the *Historisch-politische Blätter* so aptly noted, was much greater than was reflected in the *Volksbote's* large circulation of about five thousand.

In retrospect it seems clear that both Ernst Zander and most of the rest of the journalistic world recognized what the government discovered at exactly the same time through the investigation set in motion by the ever-inquisitive Maximilian II. All knew that the overwhelming majority of the common people who had an opinion, quite a large number, opposed emancipation. Zander and his cohorts on the right trumpeted this "news" to all who would listen, while the liberal and democratic papers tried desperately to shift the discussion away from the popular will and toward reason and justice. But the reality was the same whether underlined, avoided, or silenced. Most Bavarians did not want to fully emancipate the Jews in 1849–50. In this respect, the role of the votes in the upper and lower houses became secondary. During the debates in the lower house, opponents of emancipation had asked what the deputies would do if they knew more directly what the people thought. Counterfactually, one must doubt that the bill would have received its bare two-thirds majority in the lower house if the vote had been held at the end rather than at the beginning of the petition campaign.

Zander's achievement should be measured not only by the influence he exerted on Bavarian public opinion and the *Reichsräthe* on the issue of Jewish emancipation but by the stimulus he provided to the press in general. The *Volksbote's* success stemmed not from government subsidy but from popular support in the form of a large and growing circulation in the face of combined ministerial and liberal opposition. Despite Zander's personal financial unreliability, the *Volksbote* sold large numbers of subscriptions and inspired petitions against Jewish emancipation. His journalistic methods were innovative and enjoyed the best form of flattery—imitation. The moderate conservative administration of von der Pfordten abhorred the *Volksbote* and its editor, but this was not only personal irritation at political opposition or disgust with Zander's vulgarity but concern at the power of an unbridled press. It is not surprising then that this same administration soon initiated new controls on the press and that the conservative Zander vehemently opposed such repression.

Zander's accomplishments in Bavaria paralleled the actions of men like Hermann Wagener, the creative but unruly editor of the conservative *Kreuzzeitung* in Prussia. Wagener's vulgar, popular conservatism also dissuaded many conservatives from working or associating with him. Thus Ernst Ludwig von Gerlach, the highly principled Prussian conservative who had recognized the need for and been instrumental in the founding of a conservative newspaper to counter the journalistic successes of the left, broke with Wagener in 1860 over questions involving principle and morality. Study of papers like the *Lechbote* and *Postzeitung* shows that Zander and Wagener were not isolated examples, even if few others lived up to their standards of innovation, vulgarity, and ability to irritate conservative elites. They were the advance guard of a freer and more modern, but not necessarily more liberal or more principled, press.[132]

The public sphere, to use Jürgen Habermas's term, changed profoundly in 1848 and 1849.[133] More members of the educated middle class acquired a share in governmental power through election to Parliament, by appointment to the bureaucracy, by joining a political organization, or by writing for a more politicized press. But these were only changes in degree when compared to the *Vormärz*. In March 1848 public opinion expressed itself so spontaneously and so broadly that it frightened governments into acquiescence. In the struggle over the Basic Rights and Constitution in 1849, both right and left showed signs of reverting to the direct action of the early days of the revolution. When the executive in Bavaria opted to work with the lower house and the press in pursuit of Jewish emancipation, it anticipated success, fearing only local expressions of dissatisfaction. The campaign against Jewish emancipation demonstrated a radical change in many people's view of public opinion. Not only Zander, but many people, including some at the communal level, recognized this change. Few on the right were as willing or as able as Zander to incorporate the new reality into their personal political life. Many on the left who had been willing to rely on popular forces when the people seemed bent on progress recoiled from a populace opposing change and the left, taking refuge in reason and education. The news in 1849–50 was that neither the government nor the press controlled the people. Whether the people did is yet another issue.

The power of the opposition press, especially of men like Zander, should not be exaggerated. Much of its success lay in accurately reflecting what the people thought and wanted. The best understanding of popular attitudes toward emancipation of Jews derives from analysis of the actual petitions.

NOTES

1. Press normally meant newspapers, but there were a few periodicals.
2. See ch. 5.

3. See my "The Authorship of Political Tracts in Post-1848 Germany," *German Studies Review* 10, no. 3 (Oct., 1987): 413–41; Fritz Pfundtner, *Die Münchener politische Presse im Revolutionsjahre 1848* (Würzburg-Aumühle, 1939), 21.

4. This is the theme of Elizabeth Noelle-Neumann's *Spiral of Silence: Public Opinion—Our Social Skin* (Chicago and London, 1984).

5. Heinz-Dietrich Fischer, *Handbuch der politischen Presse in Deutschland 1480–1980* (Düsseldorf, 1981), 186ff.

6. Ibid., 202ff.

7. See Reinhard Rürup, "Emancipation and Crisis. The 'Jewish Question' in Germany 1850–1890," *LBIY* 20 (1975): 19.

8. Leonhard Lenk, "Revolutionär-Kommunistische Umtriebe im Königreich Bayern: Ein Beitrag zur Entwicklung von Staat und Gesellschaft 1848–1864," *ZfbL* 28 1/2: 618–19, letter dated Munich, 24 Nov. 1855. Also H. Rall, "Politische Entwicklung," 231. Pfundtner, *Politische Presse,* 18–20, describes Maximilian's earliest attempts based on materials from the royal files.

9. Johann Brunner, "Die bayerische Postzeitungsliste von 1848" *ZfbL* 3 (1930): 481–85.

10. Brunner reached this total by counting three special Sunday extras of the same newspaper as separate papers. Pfundtner, *Politische Presse,* 21–22, estimated about 90 not counting nonpolitical papers; but he could only locate 47 and used only half of those.

11. Max Allaire, *Die Periodische Presse in Bayern: Eine statistische Untersuchung* (Zweibrücken, 1913), 25, table 1. See Hans Fehn, "Land Bayern," 680: in 1840 the population was 4,370,977; in 1871, 4,863,450.

12. My computation, based on Brunner's data; see n. 9 above.

13. This is true even if we admit that each paper had several readers; but some individuals subscribed to two or more papers.

14. W. Robert Lee, "Family and 'Modernisation': The Peasant Family and Social Change in Nineteenth-Century Bavaria," in Richard J. Evans and W. R. Lee, eds., *The German Family: Essays on the Social History of the Family in Nineteenth- and Twentieth-Century Germany,* (Totowa, N.J., 1981), 98. See also Rolf Engelsing, *Analphabetentum und Lektüre: Zur Sozialgeschichte des Lesens in Deutschland zwischen feudaler und industrieller Gesellschaft* (Stuttgart, 1973); Karl Schleunes, *Schooling and Society: The Politics of Education in Prussia and Bavaria 1750–1900* (Oxford, New York, and Munich, 1989), 83, 107.

15. The average for Niederbayern was fl 2.96, for Oberbayern, fl 4.2 per year. My computation is based on Brunner's data, see n. 9 above, 482–84. Using Pfundtner's data in *Politische Presse,* 96ff., the yearly average cost was fl 3.79.

16. See income levels in ch. 2.

17. Werner K. Blessing, "Allgemeine Volksbildung und politische Indoktrination im bayerischen Vormärz: Das Leitbild des Volksschullehrers als mentales Herrschaftsinstrument," *ZfbL* 37[2] (1974): 494–95.

18. Many of the papers no longer extant are the small weeklies, like the *Schwarzenburger Wochenblatt* from Marktbreit in Unterfranken. Of the twenty-five Bavarian weeklies in 1848, most were probably nonpolitical. Also, some of those no longer

available, like the *Deggendorfer Bote*, may have been weeklies. The twenty-three professional publications, ranging from the *Bienenzeitung* in Eickstadt to the *Medizinische Chirurgische Zeitung* in Munich, were most probably nonpolitical.

19. F. Welfauh, *Was erwartet das Volk, Was erwartet Deutschland von Bayerns Ständen?* (Munich, 1848), included Jewish emancipation as the 17th of 21 points, devoting to it a total of one sentence.

20. See M. Doeberl, *Entwicklungsgeschichte*, 3: 144–45, 175–76, 281.

21. Correspondents to the *AZdJ* were furious at the lack of activity by Jews; see no. 48, 26 Nov. 1849, 688, dated Munich, 19 Nov.; no. 50, 10 Dec., 712, aus Bayern, dated 1 Dec.

22. *Bayerische Landbötin* no. 87, 2 June, 518, dated Bayern, München, 30 Mai; *Die Volksbötin (VBö)*, no. 24, 31 Mai, 94ff., "Sitzung der bayerischen Volkskammer vom 30 Mai 1849."

23. The *AZdJ* was published in Leipzig and edited by Rabbi Dr. Ludwig Philippson of Magdeburg, but as the leading Jewish newspaper in Germany, it took intense interest in news affecting Jews everywhere. See *AZdJ*, no. 6, 5 Feb. 1849, 76–77, dated München, 22 Jan.; nos. 7 and 9, 12 and 26 Feb., 90, 113–114 on Morgenstern's election; no. 22, 29 May, 293, dated München, 17 May, on von der Pfordten.

24. *AZdJ*, no. 26, 25 June 1849, 353, dated München, 16 June and much the same on 3 Sept. in no. 36, 505–6, dated Aus Baiern, in Aug.

25. *AZdJ*, no. 39, 24 Sept., 550–51, dated München, 10 Sept.; no. 48, 26 Nov., 688, dated München, 19 Nov.

26. *AZdJ*, no. 50, 10 Dec., 712, dated Aus Baiern, 1 Dec.

27. *AZdJ*, no. 51, 17 Dec., 725, dated München, 25 Nov., and no. 52, 4 Dec., 741–42, dated Aus Baiern, 7 Dec.

28. *Würzburger Stadt- und Landbote (WSuLB)*, no. 285, 29 Nov., 1, dated "Tagesneuigkeiten," and no. 295, 11 Dec., same. Essentially, I used only papers with extant continuous runs. The *Augsburger Tagblatt*, no. 340, 11 Dec. 1849, p. 1770, dated 8 Dec., clearly described Scharff's report; the *Augsburger Postzeitung*, no. 158, Beilage, 11 Dec., dated München 9 Dec., did too.

29. *Lechbote*, no. 339, 10 Dec., 1312, dated München, 8 Dec. and *Bayerische Landbötin*, no. 243, 11 Dec., 1179, dated "Deutschland, Bayern, und München," 9 Dec.

30. *Mittelfränkische Zeitung (MFräZ)*, no. 340, 6 Dec., 1, dated München, 3 Dec.; on 10 Dec., no. 344, dated 7 Dec., it provided the text, without comment, of Ruland's proposed substitute bill.

31. For pamphlet publication, see Harris, "Authorship," passim. The *MFräZ*, no. 346, 12 Dec., dated 2 München, and 9 Dec. in datelined entries, supported the bill prior to the debates.

32. *VBö*, no. 186, 7 Dec., 1, dated "Etwas von den Juden!" The writer seems to have felt that communities would retain their veto rights, but with the draft as yet unamended, that was not the case. I know of no petitions written or submitted at this stage.

33. *NFräZ*, nos. 328, 329, 331, 332, dated 24–25, 27–28 Nov.

34. The reference is unmistakably to the brochure *Das Judenthum und die Emancipation der Juden oder Gleichstellung derselben in allen staatsbürgerlichen Rechten mit den Christen in Jeder Beziehung* (Würzburg, 1849); its author was given only as "Von M. in W." It seems fairly certain that this polemic was the same as that sent to the king in July of 1849 by P. A. Megner, a merchant in Würzburg. There is no notation by the king or indication of his attitude toward the brochure. The king filed it with other documents on emancipation, but he continued his plans for full emancipation. See GHA, Nachlass Maximillian II, no. 80/1/249b, P. A. Megner to Maximillian II, 20 July 1849. The document is ninety-two pages of handwritten manuscript. In an even earlier letter he seems to be referring to another, earlier piece on the Jews.

35. *Das Judenthum*, see n. 38.

36. Probably dating from 1846 or after.

37. *NFräZ*, no. 339, 340, 5 and 6 Dec.

38. *NFräZ*, no. 343, 9 Dec.

39. Dr. Ludwig Schönchen, editor of the *Augsburger Postzeitung*, chaired the local Pius Verein and was also a member of the Association for Constitutional Monarchy and Religious Freedom; see Anton Doeberl, "Die katholische Bewegung in Bayern in den Jahren 1848 und 1849" *Historisch-politische Blätter für das katholische Deutschland* 170, hefte 9:502; Karl Feistle, *Geschichte der Augsburger Postzeitung von 1838–1871: Ein Beitrag zur Geschichte der katholischen Presse* (Ph.D. Diss., University of Munich, 1951), 31ff.

40. As we will see below, even Zander's fiercest opponents recognized his power. All biographical material is from Elmar Roeder, *Zander*, esp. 1–11, 33, 40–44, 49–50, 53, 64, 68–69, 262–76. According to A. Doeberl, "Bewegung," 2:66, Zander called for establishing a Pius Verein as early as 11 Apr. 1848.

41. *Volksbote für den Bürger und Landmann* (hereafter *Volksbote* and *VB*), no. 288, 8 Dec., dated 1 Bayern München, 7 Dec.; no. 289, 9 Dec., dated München, 8 Dec.; no. 290, 11 Dec., dated 1 München, 10 Dec.

42. See, e.g., *MNN*, nos. 346–49, 12–15 Dec., 1, München, which described the galleries as "crowded," "thickly crowded," and, on the 14th, "overfilled." The *Lechbote* recognized the public interest, but no. 345, 16 Dec., dated München, 15 Dec. described the galleries as dominated by democrats and Jews. The *Augsburger Postzeitung*, no. 296, 14 Dec., dated Munich, 12 Dec., suggested throwing the "Jew boys" out of the galleries.

43. Thus the *Eilbote*, no. 100, 19 Dec. reprinted the report in the *Volksbote* of 15 Dec. about the actual vote and the *NFräZ*, no. 347, 13 Dec., 1, dated München, 10 Dec., reprinted the full description from the *Augsburger Abendzeitung*.

44. In this regard, on this issue the *MNN*, *BZ*, *NFräZ*, and *WüSLB* were almost entirely objective, even though they generally supported the bill.

45. *Regensburger Zeitung* (*RZ*), no. 343, 12 Dec., dated München, 10 Dec., described Representative Sepp as one of the biggest "Judenfresser" of the movement.

46. *BLBö*, no. 244, 12 Dec., 1, dated München, 10 Dec.

47. *VBö*, nos. 189–93, 11–15 Dec., in many separate articles.

48. *Gradaus mein deutsche Volk*, nos. 346–50, 11–15 Dec., usually datelined München.

49. *NFräZ*, nos. 347–52, 13–18 Dec.—a wide variety of articles.

50. *LB*, no. 342, 13 Dec., 1 df, "Der Jude bleibt der alte Jude—auch emancipirt"; reference to Alsace was common, see the earlier debates in ch. 3.

51. *LB*, no. 343, 14 Dec., Mz "Ueber die Emancipation der Juden." For Rutelius, see the excerpt from "De Reditu Suo" 1, 371–98, no. 542, in Menahem Stern, ed., *Greek and Latin Authors on Jews and Judaism*, vol. 2, *From Tacitus to Simplicius* (Jerusalem, 1980), 660–64; a poem from the early fifth century, it reads in part: "And would that Judaea had never been subdued by Pompey's wars and Titus' military power! The infection of this plague, though excised, still creeps abroad the more: and 'tis their own conquerors that a conquered race keeps down."

52. *VB*, no. 291, 12 Dec., 292, 13 Dec., 1.

53. *VB*, no. 293, 14 Dec., 1, München, 13 Dec.

54. *VB*, no. 290, 11 Dec., 1 München, 10 Dec.

55. *VB*, no. 295, 16 Dec., 1 München, 15 Dec. The *VB* did not appear on Monday (the 15th), when Ruland raised the issue of the cutoff in the House.

56. *VB*, no. 295, 16 Dec., 1, München, 15 Dec.

57. *Augsburger Postzeitung*, no. 171, Beilage, 28 Dec. 1849.

58. *VB*, no. 296, 18 Dec., 1–2, München, 17 Dec.

59. *VB*, no. 299, 21 Dec., 2.

60. See, e.g., *VB*, no. 302, 25 Dec., 1, citing the address from Feichten and Kirchweidach in the rural district of Burghausen: the excerpt stated that by voting for this bill, deputies identified themselves as betrayers of the people.

61. *Augsburger Postzeitung*, no. 6, 7 Jan. 1850, replicated Zander's numbers in block letters like the *Volksbote*, although in a smaller typeface.

62. *VB*, no. 300, 22 Dec., 1, München, 21 Dec.

63. *VB*, no. 306, 30 Dec., 1, München, 31 Dec.

64. *VB*, no. 1, 1 Jan. 1850, 2, München, 31 Dec.

65. *VBö*, no. 195, 18 Dec., 1, "Hört!"

66. *RZ*, no. 361, 31 Dec., 1, München, n.d., no. 8, 8 Jan., 1, München, n.d.

67. *NN*, no. 354, 20 Dec., 1, München, 18 Dec., "Über die Emanzipation der Israeliten."

68. *WSüLBo*, no. 307, 28 Dec., 1.

69. *NN*, no. 354, 20 Dec., 1, München, 18 Dec., "Über die Emanzipation der Isrealiten."

70. *NFräZ*, no. 356, 22 Dec., "Die Judenemanzipation und die Ultramontanen." It criticized their opponents' vulgarity.

71. *BLBö*, no. 258, 29 Dec., München, 26 Dec.

72. *VB*, no. 297, 19 Dec., 1, München, 18 Dec.

73. *VB*, no. 296, 18 Dec., 1, München, 17 Dec.

74. *VB*, no. 298, 20 Dec., 1, München, 19 Dec.

75. A loose term here, used to describe the opponents of emancipation, not just the ultramontanes or Catholics.

76. *VB*, no. 302, 25 Dec., 1, München, 24 Dec.

77. *LB*, no. 347, 18 Dec., Augsburg, 17 Dec.; *APZ*, 170 Beilage, 25 Dec., "Zur Abwehr," Aus Franken, 21 Dec., called Jews traitors.

78. *BLBö*, no. 18, 22 Jan., 1, München, 19 Jan., citing the *Nürnburger Korrespondent; VBö*, no. 196, 19 Dec., 1, Bayern, no. 198, 21 Dec., 790; no. 200, 23 Dec., 1, Bayern, no. 10, 11 Jan., 46.

79. *RZ*, no. 14, 14 Jan., 58, München, 11 Jan., the example was Hofheim.

80. *VBö*, no. 198, 21 Dec., 790, also citing the *AAZ* article questioning the opinion of the Central Association for Constitutional Monarchy und Religious Freedom as not synonymous with the inhabitants of Munich.

81. *VBö*, no. 10, 11 Jan., 46, but the paper doubted the letter's credibility.

82. *VBö*, no. 196, 19 Dec., 1, Bayern, accused the mayor of Deggendorf of circulating a petition without approval of the magistrates and of accepting the signatures of children. The *NFräZ*, no. 16, 16 Jan., 54–55, München, 9 Jan., claimed nearly the same for Euerdorf, where a note accompanying the petition told mayors to sign, to forward it to the upper house before the 12th, to spread it to other communities, and to use their seals.

83. *VBö*, no. 13, 15 Jan., "Ist der Bauer aufgerecht?"; *NFräZ*, no. 52, 21 Feb. 1850, "Die Juden Nichtemanzipation," similarly described the eighty-thousand signatures as not 1/50th of the population. Also see the *NFräZ*, no. 20, 20 Jan., "Die Würzburger Adresse gegen die Judenemanzipation."

84. *BZ*, no. 27, 27 Jan., 2, München, 24 Jan. See ch. 5 for data on the number signing for the community. The *APZ*, no. 19, 27 Jan. 1850, 49, "Mahnung in Sachen der Judenemanzipation," argued that if only a few Old Bavarian newspapers could elicit such a strong response, it must mean the people were behind them; so too the *Augsburger Tagblatt*, no. 16, 16 Jan. 1850, 77, dated Munich 12 Dec.

85. *AZdJ*, no. 5, 28 Jan., 55ff., München, 13 Jan. (Privat).

86. *VB*, no. 299, 21 Dec., 1, München, 20 Dec.

87. *VB*, no. 306, 30 Dec., 1 München, responding to the *Augsburger Abendzeitung*'s claim that the average number signing was small.

88. *VB*, no. 17, 19 Jan., 1, München, 18 Jan. In the end there were seven petitions for, but at this point, Zander may have been accurate.

89. *BLBö*, no. 33, *Ausserordentliche Beilage*, 30 Jan., 2 (164), München, 28 Jan.; *NFräZ*, no. 11, 11 Jan., 2 (38), München, 9 Jan., noting also that these were the most Catholic areas. See ch. 5.

90. *WSüLBo*, no. 27, 31 Jan., 2 (106).

91. *NN*, no. 353, 19 Dec. 1849, 1, München, 17 Dec.

92. *VB*, no. 32, 6 Feb., 2 (126).

93. *BLBö*, no. 259, 30 Dec., 1, München, 28 Dec. There were too few petitions threatening violence to find a pattern. See the discussion in ch. 5.

94. *VB*, no. 26, 30 Jan., 1, München, 29 Jan.

95. *LB*, no. 21, 21 Jan., 1, Augsburg, 20 Jan.; *VB*, no. 7, 8, Jan. 1850, noting that Volkhart, a friend of the popular deputy von Oettingen-Wallerstein, could only get twelve signatures for emancipation. The left was not immune to anti-Semitism. Paul Lawrence Rose argues that anti-Semitism was intrinsic to revolutionary thinking. See his *Anti-Semitism* and my critical review in *AHR* 97, no. 2 (Apr. 1992): 571–72.

96. BHStA, KdRR 2656, no. 10, *Beilage zur Augsburger Postzeitung*, 15 Jan., "Zur Mission der Reichsräthe Kammer für das Gesetz über Emancipation der Juden."

97. *NFräZ*, no. 28, 28 Jan., 1; it did not.

98. *NFräZ*, no. 20, 20 Jan., 1, "Die Würzburger Adresse gegen die Judenemanzipation"; two members of the Märzverein were also members of the educational and gymnastic associations.

99. *LB*, no. 6, 6 Jan., 1, in large type over the stories for that day. Also see no. 21, 21 Jan., 1, Augsburg, 20 Jan.

100. *VB*, no. 306, 30 Dec., 1, München, 29 Dec.

101. *VB*, no. 6, 6 Jan., 1, 5 Jan.

102. Zander said the actual expression was much coarser. See *VB*, no. 23, 26 Jan., 1, München, 25 Jan.

103. *VB*, no. 27, 31 Jan., 1, München, 30 Jan. reporting on the 57th sitting of the Lower House. Zander concluded hoping that the lower-level officials who exceeded their authority would be censored.

104. *VB*, no. 32, 6 Feb., 1, München, 5 Feb. Hohe's directive of 15 Jan. (BStW Prä 325) had been leaked to other papers earlier; see below.

105. *BLBö*, no. 26, 24 Jan., 126 (2), Würzburg, 19 Jan., from Werneck in Unterfranken. The *Würzburger Stadt- und Landbote*, no. 23, 26 Jan., 1, "Tagesneuigkeiten," carried it as news of Sepp's interpellation, and, 1–2, same no., gave the details of Wallerstein's interpellation that made no reference to names of officials or places. The alert *AZdJ* noted the circular from Werneck, dated 17 Jan., without comment, in no. 7, 11 Feb., 86ff., München, 4 Feb.

106. *VB*, no. 2, 2 Jan., 1, München; the technique of publishing letters was new but not unique. Was Zander capable of making up letters? Some read very well indeed.

107. *VB*, no. 8, 9 Jan., 1, München, 8 Jan. on Jews in Amberg speculating on success of the bill by buying up four or five of the best houses; no. 9, 10 Jan., 1, München, 9 Jan., asking how many Christians were ruined by Jews, etc.; no. 15, 17 Jan., 2, on the Jews' happiness in France having a Jew as minister of finance; no. 17, 19 Jan., 2, on Jews' power in Schwaben over Christians in a rural district; no. 26, 30 Jan., 2, München, 28 Jan. on so much Jewish trickery in Landsberg that it had impoverished the district and, in footnotes, a similar example from Franken; no. 27, 31 Jan., 1, München, 30 Jan., reporting an incident in Schwaben where a Jew defrauded a Christian (quite lengthy); and no. 41, 16 Feb., the day of the vote in the upper house, 2, München, 15 Feb., a long horror story of Jewish economic evil in Moosham in rural district Stadtamhof, Opf. But a correspondent to the *Augsburger Tagblatt*, no. 45, 14 Feb. 1850, responded to the *Lechbote*'s use of a recent case of thievery involving Jews by noting that one individual was not equivalent to the members of a religion and that several Christians had also been involved.

108. *VB*, no. 295, 16 Dec., 2, München, 15 Dec.; no. 5, 3 Jan., 1, München, 2 Jan.; no. 5, 5 Jan., 1, 4 Jan. The *Lechbote* did not venture so far, but did argue that the *Correspondent von und für Deutschen* favored emancipation because its editor, Dr. Ph. Feust, was a Jew. No. 4, 4 Jan., 4, Augsburg, 3 Jan. *APZ*, no. 299, 18 Dec. 1849, Munich, 16 Dec.; no. 25, 29 Jan. 1850, dated "Deutschland"; no. 26, Beilage, 7 Feb. 1850, "Und Wenn die Juden nicht emancipirt werden?"; no. 48, 25 Feb. 1850, Munich, 16 Feb.

109. *BLBö*, no. 27, 1 Feb., 110, München, 29 Jan.; *LB*, no. 32, 1 Feb., 1, and

Vom Lech, 31 Jan., responded that because one could not allow one to judge oneself, the declaration must be opposed; the *VB*, no. 30, 3 Feb., 1, München, 2 Feb., said essentially the same.

110. *AZdJ*, no. 7, 11 Feb., 86ff., 30 Jan.; Aub's declaration appeared in no. 8, 18 Feb., 98, München, 1 Feb. A young Jewish diarist, Adolph Kohn of Munich, tracked the events of 1848–51 very conscientiously, but he only noted a few events concerning Jews, such as the approval of the election of Dr. Morgenstern after a dispute—he attended the lower house sitting "which is so important for Jews"; when the emancipation law failed in the upper house he noted that the three royal princes had all voted against, including Karl, "der alte Hurenbalg"; see Norbert Conrads and Günter Richter, eds., *Denkwürdige Jahre 1848–1851* (Cologne and Vienna, 1978), 103, 184, 259, 264–65.

111. *NFräZ*, no. 1, 1 Jan., 1, and no. 2, 2 Jan., 1–2 "Offener Brief an die Herren Landtags-Abgeordneten Ruland, Sepp, Allioli und Konsorten," noting that the author was a Jew, Dr. Adler, in Kissingen, who wrote in Dec. 1849, before the vote for passage. *MFräZ*, nos. 12–13, 12–13 Jan., same title.

112. Harris, "Authorship," 417–20.

113. *NFräZ*, no. 29, 29 Jan., 2 (94), München, n.d.

114. Adler was not a novice; he had probably written on the role of the Jews in Bavaria in 1839, and he had published a petition as a brochure in 1846. See ch. 2, n. 60; ch. 3, n. 17.

115. *VB*, no. 26, 30 Jan., 2, München, 29 Jan.

116. *WSüLBo*, no. 3, 2 Jan., 10; *MFräZ*, no. 7, 7 Jan., 1, München, 4 Jan.

117. *AZdJ*, no. 1, 1 Jan., 3–5, Munich in Dec.; no. 5, 28 Jan., 55, München, 4 Jan.

118. *WSüLBo*, no. 16, 17 Jan., citing *Nürnberger C.; Bamberger Zeitung*, no. 26, 26 Jan., 2, München, 23 Jan., cited the appointment of Montgelas as proof that the rumor that the upper house would not treat the bill was false. For predictions that Montgelas would favor emancipation, see *Eilbote*, no. 12, 9 Feb., 72 (2), München, 31 Jan.; *WSüLBo*, no. 31, 5 Feb., 1; and the *BLBo*, no. 39, 5 Feb., 190 (2), München, 3 Feb. Among those predicting that Montgelas would reject the bill, see *RZ*, no. 43, 13 Feb., 1–2, München, 8 Feb.; *BLBo*, no. 48, 13 Feb., *Ausserordentliche Beilage*, 1, München, 11 Feb.; *BLBo*, no. 5, 5 Jan., 20 (3) München, 1 Jan.; *BZ*, no. 6, 6 Jan.

119. *AZdJ*, no. 6, 4 Feb., 69 (1), München, 23 Jan., and no. 9, 26 Feb., 113–114, München, 11 Feb.

120. *WSüLBo*, no. 1, 20 Jan. 1850; *RZ*, no. 43, 13 Feb. 1850, 1—2 (München), 8 Feb.

121. *RZ*, no. 43, 13 Feb. 1850, 1–2 (München), 8 Feb.

122. *BZ*, no. 49, 18 Feb., 1, München, 15 Feb.

123. *BZ*, no. 6, 6 Jan., "Über die Judenemanzipation in Bayern."

124. *BLBo*, no. 5, 5 Jan., 20 (3) München, 1 Jan. and no. 11, 11 Jan., 1, München, 9 Jan.

125. *BLBö*, no. 13, 16 Jan., 1, München, 13 Jan.

126. *AZdJ*, no. 5, 28 Jan., 55–56, München, 13 Jan.

127. *VBö*, no. 39, 14 Feb., 1, München, 13 Feb.; the *BZ*, no. 47, 16 Feb., 1, München, 14 Feb., said essentially the same.

128. BHStA, KdRR 2656, no. 10, Beilage to the *Augsburger Postzeitung*, 15 Jan. 1850, "Zur Mission der Reichsraths-Kammer für das Gesetz über Emancipation der Juden," by von der Donau in Jan.

129. *HPB*, Vol. 24, 1849, 2:1–39, "Die Zeitungspresse und das Volk." Except where noted, what follows is from this source. Also see Pfundtner, *Politische Presse*, 25–27, for a brief description.

130. *HPB*, Vol. 24, 1849, 2:827–28. Döllinger was uneasy about mixing religion and politics and told Jörg so in a letter of 6 Mar. 1849; this was a response to Jörg's letter of 20 Feb., in which he noted that the editor of the *Volksbote* had guaranteed that eighty thousand armed peasants were prepared to go to the city, presumably Munich, and, evidently, to shut down the revolution; in Victor Conzemius, "Ignaz von Döllinger und Edmund Jörg: Analyse einer Freundschaft und ihres Zerfalls," in Albrecht, *Festschrift*, 46-47.

131. See ch. 7.

132. See Helmut Diwald, ed., *Von der Revolution zum Norddeutschen Bund. Politik und Ideengut der preussischen Hochkonservativen 1848–1866. Aus dem Nachlass von Ernst Ludwig von Gerlach. Erster Teil: Tagebuch 1848–1866*, p. 417, entry for 20 July 1860 and 424ff. Also see *Zweiter Teil, Briefe, Denkschriften, Aufzeichnungen*, (both parts, Göttingen, 1970), p. 1137, no. 536, E. L. von Gerlach to Jacob von Gerlach, Magdeburg, 4 May 1863, where he complained of the reluctance of conservatives to use the press in any innovative way. "It is as if one went to war," he wrote, "but, disliking the smell of gunpowder, left it at home."

133. Jürgen Habermas, *The Structural Transformation of the Public Sphere. An Inquiry into a Category of Bourgeois Society*, trans. Thomas Burger (Cambridge, Mass., 1989), esp. 27, 82–85, 236–50.

Chapter 5

The People Speak!: The Petitions against Jewish Emancipation

The wave of petitions against the bill for Jewish emancipation was spontaneous, extremely broad-based, and genuine. Long believed lost or destroyed,[1] the petitions are a unique and rich source for the study of popular attitudes toward Jews, the Bavarian Parliament, and the state in general. Their largely anonymous authors addressed many different facets of Jewish emancipation, including the role of the lower house that passed the bill and of the administration that introduced it, and they offered their perceptions of Jews and their suggestions for a solution to the problem posed by the restricted status of Jews in the Bavarian state and civil society.

Because the unknown authors took pains to explain their reasons for opposition to Jewish emancipation, the petitions are far more important than solely for their utility in counting opponents and supporters. And because the petitions came, with only three exceptions, from communities (1,723) or organizations (28), they represent far more than 86,795 signatures. As expressions of communal sentiment, the petitions present an opportunity for ascertaining the extent to which they accurately reflected the sentiments of individuals in those communities.

The Petitions and the Communities

It is tempting to think of petitions as requests for specific favors, and in many cases, that was true.[2] But in the campaign against Jewish emancipation of 1849–50 and during the revolution in general, most people called their communications to the government addresses (*Adressen*), which carried another meaning. While many of the addresses made specific requests of the upper house of Parliament, the writers also used the medium to express their frustrations and to air their grievances. A large number of the communities addressing the *Reichsräthe* did so as a means of stating what they thought their rights were, how they were being violated, what they thought the upper house ought to do, and, in several cases, what they would do if it did not. On balance, the petitions were political documents submitted by irate citizens rather than supplicatory pleas from loyal subjects.

At the outset it is important to be clear about the context in which people organized the petitions against emancipation. It is impressive that so many separate actions occurred so quickly. In under two months 1,762 communities and organizations from Bavaria east of the Rhine learned of the decision of the lower house and reacted by organizing or agreeing to petitions. Normally these petitions consisted of several pages of text presenting the petitioners' requests or statements, the signatures of communal officials, the impression of the seal, and the signatures of the community members. Although the village scribe prepared many petitions in a fair hand, most were simple statements accompanied by such traditional phrases as "your most obedient and faithful servants." The overwhelming majority were written, distributed, signed, and submitted in late December 1849 and in January and early February 1850—41 percent in the last two weeks of December and 29 percent in the first two weeks of January.[3] (See table 5.1.)

Submission of so many petitions was a remarkable feat of political action, even more so considering that the midwinter weather conditions were very harsh that year in areas like the Bayerische Wald. Deciding what to say and how to say it to persuade the upper house to reverse the decision of the lower house required the active involvement of one or usually more individuals in the 552 separate petitions. But the number of participants expands greatly when we consider that in a large number of cases, the organizers either posted or read the petition aloud to the citizens after which those wishing to sign did so. Usually, the mayor (*Vorsteher*) and his councillors (*Bevollmächtigten*) witnessed or validated the signatures and affixed the communal seal to the document. In many cases the local priest signed for the parish (*Pfarrei*) and occasionally affixed the parish seal. Finally, each petition had to be sent to the upper house in Munich by post at a rate of 3 kreuzer per page. Over 62 percent of all communities attached the signatures of those communal citizens supporting the petition in addition to those of the mayor and his advisors, while 29 percent at least included either the signature of the mayor alone or of the mayor and councillors. In 179 of the communities (10 percent), the petitions stated that the mayor and officials signed "in the name of" a specific number of citizens, and in 144 communities (8 percent), they signed "in the name of the whole community." Over 92 percent of all participating communities acted "officially" by their own customary standards.

Only about every third community produced its own indigenous petition. The others acceded to a petition framed by another community. This process had already been used the previous year in the campaign for and against the Basic Rights and the Frankfurt Constitution and was probably much older, testifying to the cooperation and common action of neighboring communities. In some cases organizers copied by hand a petition formulated elsewhere, although this was relatively rare. In the city of Augsburg the local editor of the *Augsburger Post Zeitung* printed and distributed forms for signature under a common petition, but this method was unique to Augsburg. In a few cases—for example, in Regensburg in the Upper Palatinate—a petition appeared in the local newspaper. When newspapers elsewhere reprinted it, as happened in Passau in Lower Bavaria, some communitites there, thinking it a suitable statement of their attitudes, copied and used it. Most of this process was spontaneous and demonstrates a degree of political interest not often associated with rural Bavaria in the mid-nineteenth century. Such actions testify to the intensity of the popular concern with Jewish emancipation.[4]

By conservative estimate, nearly one-quarter of all communities in Bavaria east of the Rhine and somewhere between 10 and 20 percent of all adult male citizens or heads of families participated in the antiemancipation

TABLE 5.1. Origin and Type of Petitions Against Emancipation by Province in 1849–1850

Province	Total No.[a] Communities with Petitions	No. of[b] Actual Signatures	No. of People[c] Represented by Petitions "in Name of"	No. Sent[d] by Communi- ties with No Signatures	No. Sent[e] with Mayor's Signatures Only
Upper Bavaria	487	19,923	5,437	157	41
Lower Bavaria	265	13,062	5,604	54	4
Upper Palatinate	247	8,534	3,272	117	16
Upper Franconia	97	3,805	270	36	4
Middle Franconia	113	3,434	800	62	4
Lower Franconia	264	9,743	913	113	71
Swabia	250	8,819	1,956	107	52
Bavaria	1,723	67,320	18,252	646	192
Total unknown	30	1,101	122	18	2
Total	1,753	68,421[f]	18,374[g]	664	194

Source: Bayerische Hauptstaatsarchiv, Munich; Kammer der Reichsräthe, 2656–61; author's computation.

Note: Twenty-four petitions came from communities with no officials signing and no seal, probably representing a small part of the total citizenry. Additionally, twenty-eight petitions came from associations, such as political clubs or craft groups.

[a]Includes all communities that could be identified by province.

[b]Includes all signatures to all petitions, even those signed only by a mayor or the mayor and town councillors.

[c]This is the number of people stated as represented by these petitions, frequently named as citizens or heads of family, but without their signatures.

[d]In these cases the officials of the communities signed, but no lists of signatures of citizens were appended, and they were not represented by the "in name of" convention.

[e]These were still considered official.

[f]From 904 communities, or 75.7 signatures per community.

[g]From 185 communities, or 99.3 signatures per community.

campaign by signing a petition. This figure is low because it does not include an estimate of the number of people in the 144 communities that submitted petitions stating that the "entire" community opposed the bill but giving no numbers of citizens and containing no signatures.[5] Many communal officials noted that the signatures were of all of the local citizenry or all that could be reasonably collected in a short time in midwinter.[6] Others noted that they knew of "no one" in the area who supported the emancipation bill, although presumably they meant only Christian citizens.[7] There is no reason to doubt the veracity of the communal mayors and council members who attested to the validity of these petitions.

In comparison, the struggle over the Basic Rights and the Frankfurt Constitution in the first half of 1849 generated 1,150 petitions, of which 615 favored the documents and 535 opposed them. If we count the number of communities supporting each petition, as in the case of Jewish emancipation, we find the division in sentiment reversed: 1,573 communities opposed the constitution, and only 1,046 favored it. While the 1,150 petitions submitted in reaction to the debate over the Basic Rights and the Constitution outnumbered those adopted over Jewish emancipation, the time period involved was twice as long and involved two issues.

Political activity was far more common in rural Bavaria than most histories indicate. And almost all of Bavaria was rural. The campaign against Jewish emancipation followed the struggles over the Basic Rights and Constitution in early 1849 by only six months and the revolution by about a year. Jewish emancipation was only a part of the earlier developments and was never a major part. But correlation of rural opposition to Jewish emancipation in 1849–50 and antagonism to the Basic Rights and Constitution appears close. Of the 28 communities in the totally Catholic rural district of Landshut in Lower Bavaria that submitted petitions against the Basic Rights, 19 also opposed Jewish emancipation. More importantly, 21 other communities who had not bothered to oppose or support the Basic Rights found time to submit petitions against the bill for Jewish emancipation. The pattern found in Landshut seems to hold good for much of Old Bavaria. In the rural district of Eichstädt in Middle Franconia, where Catholics dominated (constituting 99 percent of the total population), 4 communities petitioned against the Basic Rights, but 31 did so against Jewish emancipation. And in the middle Franconian rural district of Kipfenberg, only 2 of 9 communities that opposed the Basic Rights petitioned against Jewish emancipation, but an additional 12 not heard from earlier joined their ranks in 1849–50.[8]

More detailed study of Lower Franconia provides a better view of the correlation between opponents and supporters of the Basic Rights and Constitution and those against Jewish emancipation. Of 20 communities from Lower Franconia who petitioned against the Basic rights and Constitution, 5 submitted petitions against Jewish emancipation. Of the 113 communities that submitted petitions in support of the Basic Rights and Constitution, 4 petitioned against Jewish emancipation: the small cities Ebern, Gemünden, and Lohr, and the rural community Pflochsbach in the rural district of Rothenfels. Although this is a small portion (3.5 percent), it raises the question how many on the left opposed Jewish emancipation. Though four is a small number, there were no petitions supporting Jewish emancipation in Lower Franconia.

As for democratic organizations, Langewiesche has shown that 283 political clubs, almost entirely democratic, existed in Lower Franconia in 1849.[9] Of those communities that boasted a democratic club, 22 (8 percent) submitted petitions against Jewish emancipation. Of the 113 communities in Lower Franconia petitioning for the Basic Rights and Constitution, 35 (31 percent) possessed democratic clubs. Evidently, communities and organizations could be mobilized by democrats for general political goals, but not for Jewish emancipation. Among those opposed to the Basic Rights, it was easier to produce petitions against Jewish emancipation, even in a period of increasing political apathy, than against the Basic Rights and Constitution. The state did not restrict the left more than the right; the state and the left pursued the same goal. Only the right complained of government interference. The left, showing strong signs of anticlericalism, accused the Catholic church of interfering.

Missing in the clash over Jewish emancipation was any significant percentage of the over one thousand communities supporting the Basic Rights and Constitution, both of which included statements of religious equality.[10] Only six petitions, three from individuals, one from a civic association, and two from communities with large Jewish populations, supported emancipation.[11] Petitioning was a demanding task and a far more direct form of political action than voting.[12] The state organized and paid the cost of elections, but submission of petitions demanded communal time, effort, and money, and even involved some risks. If one allows for the wintry conditions, the much shorter time period allotted emancipation than the Constitution, and unified governmental, parliamentary, and press support, it is astonishing that opponents of Jewish emancipation generated approximately as many petitions as were submitted in the struggle over the Basic Rights and Constitution.

Criticism of Parliament and the Revolution

Shock, disbelief, and anger at the lower house of the Bavarian Parliament appear more frequently than any other complaint in these petitions, and such criticisms usually appear in the first sentence. The petitions nearly universally voiced hostility to the action of a substantial majority of the peoples' representatives in Parliament. The petitioners held that the 91 to 40 vote of 14 December not only was wrong but did not represent the opinions of a majority of Christian Bavarians. Some petitioners tried to underplay the strength of the large majority in the lower house, as some journalists did, by describing it as "thin" or a "four-vote majority" and arguing that the constitution required a two-thirds majority (88 votes) for passage of changes in fundamental laws.[13] Others took exception to procedural issues, such as the cutoff of debate while opponents still wished to speak, the presence of unruly "Judenbuben" or "Jew boys" in the galleries, and even the "brevity" of the six-day debate.[14]

More than half of all petitions expressly stated their criticism of the Bavarian Parliament. Many (45 percent) denied that the Parliament genuinely represented the people on this issue. Some bitterly described the vote as a sellout (4 percent) or betrayal (3 percent). Many petitions claimed that "the people" were really against the bill but could only prove it by a petition.[15] Petitioners went to great lengths to obtain signatures and the approval of communal leaders to demonstrate the unrepresentative nature of the parliamentary majority that voted for Jewish emancipation. Some petitioners noted the discrepancy between the total number of Jews (approximately fifty-seven thousand) and Christians (approximately four and a half million) in Bavaria. They asked why their representatives had worked for the few rather than for the many, implying, where they did not actually state it, that all Christians either opposed emancipation or would be injured by it, and that it was unfair and undemocratic to work only for the few.[16] In various ways many petition writers assumed that a law that helped Jews would hurt Christians.[17]

Attempting to explain why a majority of the peoples' representatives had voted in support of Jewish emancipation, many petitioners described the bill as an integral part of the "revolution," by which they meant the reforms of the previous twenty months dating back to March 1848. The petitioners thought the emancipation bill, like some of those reforms, violated the rights of the Bavarian people.[18] For example, two communities in the Oberpfalz stated their loyalty to the 1818 Constitution, which had been seriously altered by such reforms as the electoral law of 4 June 1848 expanding the suffrage, eliminating the estate basis of Parliament, and allowing Jews to sit in the lower house.[19] In the same vein, several communities complained that the new legislation rescinded the guarantees made in the Jew Decree of 1813.[20] Community after community stated that this bill was yet another example of the "March events" of 1848 and of the legislation pushed by the left in both Bavaria and Germany. They identified a variety of specific enactments—such as the abolition of feudal land obligations and hunting rights, the grant of freedom of movement and of occupation for artisans and workers, and the right to subdivide estates—but they also spoke about Jewish emancipation generally as part of the Basic Rights and the Frankfurt Constitution.[21] Several commented that they had thought the defeat of the Frankfurt Constitution earlier in 1849 would mean an end to the storm of unwelcome changes, only to find that all would now be lost through Jewish emancipation. Many communities judged Jewish emancipation to be equally as important and damaging as the Basic Rights not only to their civic rights and privileges but, more importantly, to their possessions and material well-being.[22]

In addition to wrathfully expressing their indignation at the lower house, many communities tried to explain why their representatives had acted contrary to the interests of their constituents. Assuming that the law was not in the best interests of Christian Bavarians, several petition writers blamed the passage of the bill on either the inability or the unwillingness of the deputies to help the people. As petitions from Stepperg and Riedensheim expressed it, the simple rural people expected more from representatives of whom they had had a good opinion.[23] From Walpertskirchen in Oberbayern came the laconic comment that it was sad that peasants made better decisions than ministers or deputies.[24] The intelligent deputy who voted for emancipation could keep his "super-cleverness," one petition stated, for "we know what's what."[25] Communities in Eggenfelden in Niederbayern were shocked that representatives could be so blind.[26] Even simple country folk could see that the bill was a calamity.[27] Clearly the "representatives" had not investigated the real situation in the towns and cities.[28] Time and again the writers referred to the representatives' lack of sensitivity toward the people; "the iron stone of a representative!" exclaimed one.[29]

Hostility toward the Parliament ran very high, and the language used about Parliament rivaled that directed at Jews in bluntness and vulgarity. "Poisoned snakes' tongues" and "faithless liars"[30] were only two of the epithets used to describe the "so-called" men of the people[31] who had known that most people opposed emancipation but had voted for it anyway.[32] Seventeen separate petitions accused the representatives either of betraying the people or of outright treason,[33] and another twenty-one specified that the deputies had sold out, usually to the Jews.[34] Three even specified the price— 30 pieces of silver.[35] The Bavarian people had been either "sold out and betrayed" or "bought and won over."[36]

The irritation directed at Parliament seemed to promise future political action. One of the best indications of potential troubles was a group of petitions that singled out "their deputy" for criticism. A petition from Niederbayern summed up this sentiment well when it cautioned the representatives who had betrayed them that "the people stand behind you."[37] Petitioners told Baron Harold, district director and deputy of Tuntenhausen in RD Aibling, Oberbayern, that he would have gotten barely one vote if "we knew then what we know now." They made this position clear to other representatives in various ways. In Kirchlauter, RD Baunach, Unterfranken, the communal petition stated that their deputy, Kleindienst, had "acted against his mandate." One petition compared the well-known supporters of emancipation, deputies Lerchenfeld and Wallerstein, to Herod and Pilate.[38]

Not all responses limited future action to the legal process of petitioning. Though several communities, clearly fearful of state retaliation, emphasized their use of "proper" means,[39] others made it clear that they had lost faith in their representatives and the Parliament and must therefore "help themselves."[40] Sixty-five citizens of Degernbach, Oberbayern, signed a petition stating that if emancipation passed, only "coercion and force" would make them "obedient" to the state. Twenty-six communities in the rural districts of Dorfen and Haag, Oberbayern, supported a petition speculating that emancipation might create "tensions," which would not help Jews. Schnackenwerth, Unterfranken, suggested it could lead to "upset and violence." Niklausreuth, Oberbayern, asked whether it would cause a pogrom. And in Niederbayern a petition stated simply that sentiment was so strong that Jews had better watch out. Sentiment ranged from a "cooling" of love for the state, to predictions of *Judenverfolgungen* (pogroms) and statements that communities would defend themselves (against Jews) with weapons if necessary.[41] In Untersambach, Unterfranken, the author of the petition affirmed that Jewish emancipation was a new tool that the *Umsturzpartei* (party of subversion), would use to incite the people to a new revolution.[42] The government had ample reason to be cautious about the possible effects of emancipation on the populace—both on Jews and on the state.

In addition to these antiparliamentary sentiments, many Bavarians identified Jews as revolutionaries. Numerous petitions described emancipation as part of the program of the "left," of democrats, of Social Democrats, of the *Umsturzpartei,* of Communists, and of revolution.[43] Not a single petition described the political left as a force in the community. Bavarian communities in general exhibited a remarkably high degree of civic homogeneity. In the campaign over the Basic Rights and the Frankfurt Constitution in 1849, very few communities formulated petitions both for and against, although sentiment was relatively evenly divided.[44] Opinion in Bavaria differed on the issues, but among rather than within the communities.

Many of the petitions stated directly that Jews were leftists and revolutionaries. Some made this statement in terms of the recent revolution, stating that they had seen Jews "everywhere" in the revolution,[45] indeed that they had been in the forefront of revolutionary activity.[46] Others were far more generic, arguing, for example, that Jews were a "turbulent" people[47] that worked with the left.[48] To make changes, one petition noted, one needed "uprising," and the Jews knew how to generate that.[49] Revolutions cost money, another reasoned, and we know that the Jews work with the reddest revolutionaries.[50] Four communities in Stadtamhof near Regensburg asserted that Jews were not politically loyal.[51]

Loyalty was very much an issue. A constant refrain in the petitions was shock that those who had remained loyal in 1848 (for example, Christian peasants) were now to be hurt by Jewish emancipation, and those who had been unfaithful, the Jews (directly or indirectly), were to be rewarded.[52] Moreover, Jews were still a problem according to some communities, because they worked for the left. More than one writer with a good imagination accused Jews of using Jewish emancipation to stir up another revolt,[53] of opening a second doorway to revolution using emancipation,[54] and of using it merely as the excuse to establish a peoples' party.[55] Two petitions even saw Jews as creating a proletariat that would undermine the pillars of the state.[56]

Part of the source of Jewish influence, according to a handful of petitions, was Jewish association and power in the press. Where there is a democratic paper, there is a Jewish editor, stated a petition from Lower Bavaria—an area in which no Jews lived.[57] Other Lower Bavarians asserted that Jews were at the top of revolutionary activity and were the worst of the press.[58] Still others saw criticism of the "pernicious" daily press as equivalent to criticism of the Jews.[59] Some petitions attacked the amnesty bill, passed only days after the defeat of Jewish emancipation in February 1850, because it dropped charges against "red democrats and Jews," while loyal Bavarians had suffered defending the state and would suffer more as a result of Jewish emancipation.[60]

Although this intense hostility toward Parliament, the left, and even the ministers stemmed from opposition to Jewish emancipation, the petition campaign was symptomatic of much more. Considered part of the opposition to the events of March 1848, to the Basic Rights and Frankfurt Constitution, and to the left in general, the campaign was an additional index of the movement of Bavarian public opinion to the right in 1849. Ironically, it used many of the arguments used by democrats in 1848. A constant refrain found in many petitions was that opposition to emancipation was the will of the people, that representatives should be true to popular opinion, and that, if necessary, the people should act to help themselves. Although violence did not occur over emancipation, largely because the upper house ultimately rejected the law, the petitioners employed aggressive language in the name of the principle that the "voice of the people was the voice of God," a recurring motif in the petitions.[61] Had the next election occurred in early 1850, rather than in 1855, many of the ninety-one deputies who voted for emancipation might have had serious problems with reelection.

The obvious widespread anger at the political origin of the bill for Jewish emancipation and the perception of it as part of the political world of

1849–50 portray the participants in the petition campaign as politically alert, sophisticated, and involved. Not only was the campaign an opportunity for anti-Semites to let off steam, but it allowed many Bavarians to voice their disgust at the changes attempted by the revolution. Many petitioners were hostile toward Jews, and anti-Semitism played a role, one that is best seen in the context of the arguments against emancipation.

The Arguments Against Jewish Emancipation

The lower house was the single most frequent target of criticism in the petitions, and the strongest and most pervasive reason for opposition to emancipation lay in the petitioners' negative attitudes toward Jews. A very large portion of the criticism of the legislators' bill for emancipation was hostility toward Jews. It is difficult to clearly disentangle criticism of Parliament from that of Jews, but it is also hard to distinguish among the several types of anti-Jewish or anti-Semitic justification found in the critiques of the Jews. Almost all of the major discrete arguments against the bill for Jewish emancipation overlapped, even when presented separately. Economic complaints were so often rooted in beliefs about the Jewish religion and Jewish "character" that it is tempting to say that they were always entangled, an assumption that is highly problematic. What emerges is a picture of a complex conceptualization of Jews by not-so-simple country folk.

Many Christian Bavarians feared Jews. They disliked the Jewish religion, respected Jewish talents and success, and regarded Jews as unalterably different. But surrounding and permeating all these sentiments was genuine fear, especially of Jewish economic domination. Over half the petitions singled out "Jewish" business practices and even "Jewish" businesses as a reason to deny emancipation, to reject equality for Jews. Many expressed anger at the "pretty" theories of deputies who appeared to be ignorant of reality in the countryside. To persuade their readers, many gave examples, most very difficult to confirm or deny, of the damage done by Jews. Good Christian families, it was said repeatedly, had been "driven to the beggar's staff" by Jews.[62] The small number of Jews—40,427, or barely 1 percent of the population of Bavaria east of the Rhine—did not lessen fears in villages and towns. According to residents of Hirschau in the Oberpfalz, Jews were not to be feared less because they were few in number, since in Hirschau only one Jew was enough to damage the community. (see app. 3).[63] We describe Jews, the petition from the community of Feldkahl in Unterfranken read, not as we would like them to be but as they are.[64]

Though the petitions appear to be entirely genuine and reliable indexes of popular opinion in villages and towns, that does not mean that they present an accurate picture of the Jewish situation. Bavarian Jews were no worse (and no better?) than other Bavarians. Of primary importance are the attitudes, beliefs, and discourse about Jews found in the petitions, because these, too, were part of Bavarian reality.[65]

One problem in evaluating the content of the petitions is that many were written in a formulaic, almost ritualistic fashion, which assumed that their readers understood all that was said. These petitions represented the discourse, or language, of the local people. The petitions made many of the same points found in the parliamentary debates and contemporary press, but they did so in words, phrases, and anecdotes derived from the local inn or church rather than from a university-educated journalist, representative, professor, or priest. Though the most articulate citizens supposedly composed them in attempts to put popular feelings in reputable prose, they succeeded in only a few cases. The petitions were blunt, even threatening, and critical to the point of viciousness. Sometimes written in a good hand using grammatical German rather than local dialect, they still expressed the sentiments of the villagers. They were clear and unequivocally genuine expressions of popular attitudes.

Many petitions made abundantly clear their use of terms like *Schacher*. In Schwaben seventeen communities supported a petition that described Jews as "prowling" around the village like a tiger bent on murder; they know how to drive down the value of cattle and horses, the petition continued, and when they have done so, they go after the debtor.[66] Jews were only interested in money, according to a petition from sixteen communities in Oberfranken, and thus they had an advantage over Christians, who, the petition implied, valued other things.[67] In some rural communities, *Schacher* connoted the opposite of farming and crafts;[68] in others it meant disreputable petty trading, especially peddling, pursued without the fixed cost of a shop.[69] A petition in Oberbayern described Jews as "slyly" going from house to house trying to get each kreuzer by any means, inducing wives to cheat their husbands, children and servants to steal from their masters. There was, the petition read, no house utensil, no stolen article, that they would not accept for sale on commission.[70]

Most argued that dealing in and with money was the Jews' greatest talent and most feared weapon. In most of Bavaria, *money* meant more than merely coin and was nearly synonomous with debt, usury, and speculation.[71] The term for usury, *Wucher,* was used nearly as much as *Schacher,* and often the two went together. Trade, one petition writer argued, gave Jews control of metallic currency.[72] In turn, money made it possible to buy land for use in speculation.[73] Our land and shops, freed by the reforms of 1848 and 1849, will now become the focus of Jewish speculation, read a petition from seven communities in Upper Bavaria.[74] Jews stole houses, according to a petition from Unterfranken, by buying them with money earned selling coffee, tobacco, and clothes in sneaky ways.[75] Even more to be feared, according to many petitions from a variety of areas, was *Güterzertrummerung* or *Güter-theilung*, the breaking up of landholdings into smaller parcels for resale.[76] One petition asked rhetorically if the abolition of feudal dues that made land more open to such "breaking up" had been "designed" to make Christian children renters from Jewish landlords.[77]

None of these petitioners indicated that they thought Jews might want to own land for its own sake—that is, as an agriculturally productive source on which to live and labor—or that Jews might genuinely wish to live as artisans. Petitions uniformly regarded Jews as unwilling to pursue agriculture.[78] Those that owned or purchased land did so for other reasons than working it themselves. We see no Jew in his fields, one petition stated, because they do not work with their hands.[79] Burgkundstadt in Oberfranken reported that some Jews had been allowed to reside in excess of the number permitted by the 1813 law because they were in crafts, but that most had soon turned to *Schacher*. So, too, in Unterfranken, a petition stated that many Jews entered crafts, but only those that they could convert into *Schacher*.[80] Petitioners expressed irritation at the Jews' unwillingness to engage in traditional manual labor, quoting the Biblical injunction to "earn one's bread by the sweat of one's brow."[81] Some petitioners asked that Jews be emancipated only after they had taken up agriculture and crafts.[82] Underlying the economic criticism, however, was the often-stated belief that Jews were traders by nature, that they were, in a real sense, the opposite of Germans, who were naturally either farmers or artisans.[83]

Some petitions focused on intelligence or cleverness as the difference between Jews and Christians. A petition representing eighteen communities in RD Schwabmünchen (Schwaben) asked for protection for the less intelligent among the country folk from the intelligence and slyness of the Jews. Without protection, Jews would soon dominate trade; this explained how only 60,000 could control the millions of country people.[84] Thirty-three communities in RD Türkheim supported a petition that requested protection for the "less intelligent" country folk, noting that the latter had not progressed as much as Jews since 1551, and asking for a return to the laws of that year to control Jews.[85] In Unterfranken two communities signed a petition arguing that "city people" were better educated and able to deal with Jews. The same petition ridiculed "equality" because it was not found in nature. Some petitioners seriously argued that Jews were superior to Bavarians in areas like business but definitely not better morally.[86]

Religious feelings and beliefs played a powerful and complex role in the expression of opinion against Jewish emancipation. About 21 percent of all petitions used religious arguments to deny Jews emancipation or equality. Additionally, 3 percent requested the specific exclusion of Jews from any office with control over the Christian religion, and another 18 percent demanded exclusion of Jews from any state office and especially from judge-ships.[87] Although it is not always evident, because of vague wording and requests for exclusion that gave no explanation, the great majority of the requests for exclusion of Jews from offices justified such exclusion on the basis of the Jewish religion. There was a racial component here as elsewhere, but it played a minor role in this regard. About 40 percent of all petitions called for rejection on religious grounds of some sort, but the specific reasons given varied.

Surprisingly, no petitioners attempted to restrict the practice of Judaism as a religion, and only a relatively small number claimed that Judaism was flawed as a religion. Indeed, few petitions mentioned Judaism.[88] Use of the term *Jews,* in the plural and denoting a people, was much more common. A few petitions stated that Christians in a particular community had no problem with the Jewish religion but rather with Jews, even if the petition left no doubt that the reason they disliked or feared Jews derived from their religious heritage. Basic to our understanding of this thinking must be the recognition that theology played little or no role among the Bavarian people; daily life and misperceptions of it, past history, and traditional values counted most. A petition from the city of Amberg and four neighboring communities noted that Jews were born "haters" of Christians, but that "they" did not hate Jews and were not their enemies.[89] Residents of six communities in Kipfenburg in Mittelfranken recognized and accepted the Biblical injunction "Do unto others as you would have others do unto you," but they saw no reason to let "foreigners" rule them.[90] As Christians, these petitioners recognized that they should love their neighbor and even their enemy, but because they perceived Jews as unethical toward Christians, they refused to grant them equality and wished to exclude Jews from office.[91] Many Bavarians accepted the religious values of Christians and Jews in their respective religious orbits but rejected as impossible the equal coexistence of these two different religions in the same society.

The clearest statement about Jews in a religious context, one that can be found in about 10 percent of all petitions and over 20 percent of those dealing with religion, was that Jews hated Christians, that Jews were the enemies of Christians, and that Jews were the ones who were hostile. It varied a little from "sworn" to "born" enemies to the death, but the message was the same: Jews hate us.[92] Petitioners found proof of enmity to be self-evident in "Jewish" economic practices, which were uniformly judged to be injurious to Christians. In a few cases, petitions described Jews as Christ-killers,[93] or as the anti-Christ,[94] and ascribed the fate of the Jews to their refusal to accept Christ, citing Matthew 27:25, "His blood be on us and on our children."[95] Two petitions, one perhaps written by a cleric, detailed the "well-documented" murders of Christian children by Jews in the middle ages.[96] But all these "historical" proofs together were very few in number. For most petition writers it was sufficient to know that Jews hated them and were the enemy. Everybody but the members of Parliament knew why Jews were enemies.[97]

Some petitioners argued that the Jewish religion taught Jews to be anti-Christian and to cheat and exploit Gentiles whenever possible and by any means.[98] In RD Höchstadt, Schwaben, one petition was nearly a litany on this point: all know that Jews deceive Christians as a God-ordained act; all know that their children are taught to cheat Christians; all know that Jews will not recognize other beliefs.[99] A petition from Unterfranken claimed that home education in the Talmud was so "full of love" that Jewish children spoke about bowling with the heads of Christians.[100] Another spoke of God's directives to Jews to pray thrice daily for damage to Christians, finally asking how, in light of this, they could be equal to Christians?[101] From the rural district of Beilengreis in Mittelfranken came a petition labeling Jews worse than a pestilence but immediately claiming that the petitioners practiced no religious intolerance. They granted Jews their beliefs but saw Jews as evil because of their religion. It was implied that Judaism was fine for Jews so long as they were not part of Christian society. Jews were vampires who wanted the last drop of "our" blood, the petition continued, a claim that was not a phantom, the petitioners insisted, but historical fact.[102] Despite their frequent denials, the petitions attacking Jews on religious grounds made up in bitterness and intolerance what they lacked in numbers.

Embedded in the perception of Jewish hatred and enmity toward Christians was the argument in a substantial number of petitions that Bavaria was a Christian state in which Jews might live but could not hope to be equal citizens because they were not Christian.[103] Although not all petitions made the argument directly, the reasoning was usually that a Christian state meant "Christian" laws, values, and people. "To be Bavarian [was] to be Christian," according to one petition,[104] and another spoke of a "Christian Volk in a Christian state."[105] Six communities in Middle Franconia requested that if emancipation passed, they be permitted to "completely separate the Catholic church from the state."[106] We are not fanatics who are against all other religions, a petition representing 161 citizens of Traunstein in Oberbayern stated, but in a Christian state Jews should not decide about Christian matters.[107] This rationale may also be found in the 123 petitions requesting that Jews be excluded from state office, especially the judiciary, and in 17 additional petitions seeking to exclude Jews from any control over Church affairs. The latter is more understandable when one realizes that some petitioners genuinely feared the appointment of Jewish bishops and a switch from Sunday to Saturday as the day of worship as both the result and intent of Jewish emancipation.[108]

As was apparent in relation to religious issues, many Christian Bavarians viewed Jews as foreign. In over 20 percent of these documents, petitioners felt it necessary to insist that Jews were a foreign element, people, or nation. The Trade and Craft Association of Augsburg called Jews "oriental," and three communities in RD Königshofen, Unterfranken, referred to Jewish presence as "Asiatic cholera."[109] Some preferred the term *Handelsvolk* or *Schachervolk*, with *foreign* accompanying it.[110] And still others referred to Jews as a "Volk im Volk," a "people within a people."[111] But most petitions merely described Jews as different or separate and usually specified how, often using a formula possibly picked up from such newspapers as the *Volksbote* (or perhaps the *Volksbote* acquired it from the people). Thus petitions described Jews as foreign in "morals, customs, and religion";[112] as "different" in "religion, economy, customs, and morals";[113] as "separate" in "morals, speech and religion"; [114] as "foreign in morals, customs, and speech";[115] and as foreign in "blood, speech, and religion."[116] All sounded very much alike and, even when vague, made it quite clear that Jews were not Bavarians.

The petitions leave little doubt that a substantial gap separated Jewish and Christian Bavarians. A significant number of petitions stated flatly that Jews could never assimilate.[117] In language very much like that used in the religious sphere, one petition stated: we love the Jews as fellow humans, but they will never assimilate with us; to give them equality would be like putting a fox in a chicken coop.[118] If they live in a foreign land, one argued, it is not our fault; God commanded that they wander forever as atonement for killing Christ.[119] Probably imitating one of the speeches in the lower house, several petitions used the analogy of a householder who is asked or told to admit foreigners into his home. Christian love, a petition from Oberbayern stated, does not require me to bring a foreigner into my home.[120] Given this sentiment, the relative absence of requests that Jews either leave Bavaria or convert to Christianity is remarkable. There were very few cases of the former and no direct evidence of the latter. Only a few petitions echoed the *Volksbote* by "urging" Jews to emigrate,[121] but one community did take pride in helping a Jewish family emigrate.[122] Several communities protested against sending their own children to America or Hungary while simultaneously making it easier and more attractive for Jews to stay in Bavaria.[123]

Like most communities in Bavaria, the great majority of the communities submitting petitions were small, typically under 500 in population. See table 5.2 for a comparison of population in towns and villages to that of cities and market towns according to the census of 1852. Most Bavarian Jews, over 75 percent, lived in villages, small market towns, and small cities of fewer than 2,000 inhabitants. Jewish residence was not random and tended to be concentrated in specific communities. So, for example, of the 113

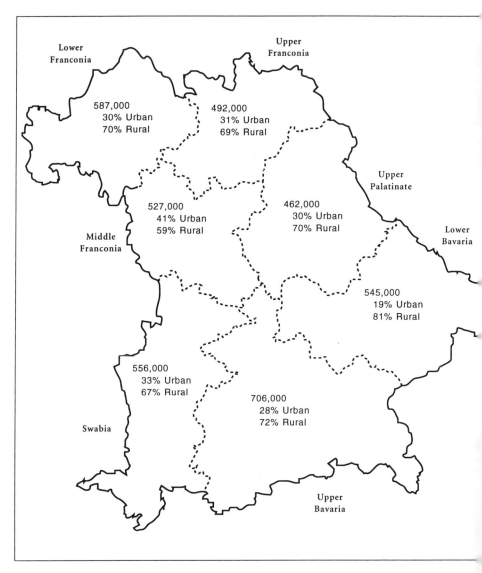

Map 2. Population of Bavaria by Province, Including the Percentage Urban and Rural by Province. (Data from the 1852 census; see table 2.6.)

largest cities and market towns in Bavaria, those with a population of over 2,000, only 45 contained resident Jews; and, of these, 11 contained a total of forty-two Jews of all ages and genders. It is possible to describe the eight Jews in Kronach as a community, but it is ludicrous to do so for the cities of Passau, Arzberg, and Staufen, each with one resident Jew. Living or residential patterns of Jewish settlement could not be random or natural—that is, they could not fluctuate as Jews wished based on such factors as costs and opportunity—because some areas, both cities and communities, deliberately excluded Jews. Consequently, Jews resided largely in smaller towns and cities. And in nearly every case they were present in numbers and percentages out of all proportion to their part of the population as a whole (1 percent).

If emancipation occurred, towns already possessing a large resident Jewish population could anticipate adding a sizable number of people to the communal citizenship rolls. This anticipation raised concern about Jews holding office in the villages, but more citizens worried about sharing their communal goods, literally *Gemeindevermögen*, with Jews.[124] A petition from Ebernburg in Unterfranken noted that their community had 100,000 Gulden in *Vermögen* and feared Jews would get access to it if they were emancipated.[125] Some petitions specified fear of loss of particular rights, such as the right to deadfall wood in common forests,[126] and some even feared loss or

TABLE 5.2. Urban[a] and Rural Population by Province in 1852[b]

| Province | Bavaria East of the Rhine | | | |
	Total Population	Independent Cities	Cities/Markets	Villages
Upper Bavaria	706,409	94,394 (13%)	107,097 (15%)	504,918 (72%)
Lower Bavaria	544,543	27,697 (5%)	77,758 (14%)	439,088 (81%)
Upper Palatinate	462,297	30,208 (6%)	109,613 (24%)	322,476 (70%)
Upper Franconia	492,424	41,967 (8%)	111,963 (23%)	338,494 (69%)
Middle Franconia	526,686	110,783 (21%)	105,036 (20%)	310,867 (59%)
Lower Franconia	587,172	38,996 (7%)	136,024 (23%)	412,152 (70%)
Swabia	555,828	71,847 (13%)	110,582 (20%)	373,399 (67%)
Bavaria	3,875,359	415,892 (11%)	758,073 (20%)	2,701,394 (70%)

Source: Data from the 1852 census; see source to table 2.6.

[a]Data were entered in the 1852 census based on the status of municipalities rather than on arbitrary numerical totals. Thus some independent cities, or cities of the first class, were smaller than some cities or markets of the second or third classes. Similarly, some smaller cities and markets were not as large in numbers as some rural communities. The term *village* is used to avoid confusion with the generic use of *community* and designates any community that was not accorded the status of independent city, city, or market. No "village" was over two thousand in population, but several market towns were significantly under that total. Thus in Bavaria in 1852, *rural* is a meaningful term, but *urban* implies more than the old, historical entities that made up many of the larger communities could deliver.

[b]Totals are for civil population only. The military population was 63,721.

dilution of Church assets.[127] A number argued, not always in a sophisticated manner, for the independence of the community, by which they meant the right to decide issues as a community without interference from the state.[128] Although they seldom elaborated on these issues in their petitions, they knew what they wanted. One hundred and forty separate petitions specifically asked for the retention of their traditional right of absolute veto, that is, admission only by a two-thirds vote of the community, over any potential resident, Jewish or not.[129] These requests, over 25 percent of all petitions, were made in addition to requests for rejection of the bill as a whole, and it is highly probable that many of the petitions that asked only for rejection also had the absolute veto firmly in mind. It was the most common and most desired single request made in the petition campaign, and though the petitioners did not always link the absolute veto to Jews desiring residence, the two went together.

A testimony to the spontaneity and individuality of the petition writers may be seen in a unique document submitted by 125 artisans and a few peasants from the city of Hirschau in the Oberpfalz (see app. 3).[130] In addition to irritation with the lower house, concern for the crafts, and a prediction that Jewish business would produce a proletariat, the author(s?) devoted a substantial amount of space to the effect of emancipation on the communal distribution of money through marriage. In Hirschau, the petition stated, money and "temporal possessions" changed through marriage in the form of dowries and inheritance. But because no marriages were possible between Jews and Christians, money obtained from Christians by Jews through exploitation could not be regained through customary "marriage rotation." The petition presents a picture of marriage as a social mechanism for the distribution of wealth, working to prevent large-scale accumulation by one family. It is unclear how accurate this description was either in Hirschau or elsewhere, but in a city of 1,483 with one resident Jew (Hirschau in 1852), it must have had little significance.[131]

Improvement Instead of Equality

Judging by the wording of many of the petitions, it is also entirely possible that, had the bill allowed for retention of the absolute veto, it would not have been so hotly opposed by so many communities. Several deputies had requested retention of the absolute veto during the debates in the lower house, but the government and the bill's supporters had rejected any such modification.[132] Although the petitioners faced a situation in which simple opposition to Jewish emancipation was both the most logical and the easiest position to take, fifty-six petitions addressed themselves to the question of permitting Jews improvements short of full equality. Many did not perceive any incompatibility between this stand and the request for the absolute veto and asked for both. Thus three communities in Traunstein in Oberbayern stated that they would be indifferent to emancipation if the bill would not make it possible for Jews to hold official positions. They were not intolerant, they said, and did not want to drive Jews out of Bavaria, but they could not accept equality.[133]

Conflict over how much should be allowed to Jews had its origins in the earliest days of the revolution, when Ludwig I promised "improvement" in the condition of Jews on 6 March 1848 and his son and successor Maximilian II reiterated that promise on 22 March, immediately after becoming king.[134] A large number of petitions showed a fine sensibility to the difference in meaning between *improvement* and *equality*,[135] as well as a genuine unwillingness to oppose the king's promise. The king's word must be upheld, several petitions stated, but that did not mean equality.[136] A few expressed loss of trust in a royal government that had replaced a promise for improvement with one for equality.[137] In a variety of ways, several petitions went to lengths to show that the March promises had not "implied" equality,[138] some reading like legal briefs in this regard.[139] Many petitions were vague on what they were willing to include under "improvement," and some were careful to state only that they did not oppose improvement, leaving open the degree to which they supported it.[140]

Part of the vagueness about improvements appears to have stemmed from the bill's emphasis on equality. Petitioners asked themselves what important rights they needed to protect themselves if equality became law. These rights emerge as a type of last-ditch defense, usually beginning with the absolute veto, but often including exclusion of Jews from offices, especially in the judiciary, and controls over *Schacherhandel.* Many of the petitions requesting these three rights unquestionably did so while simultaneously supporting *some* improvements. A number of those stating support for improvement also insisted on one or all of these rights.[141] Some of the petitions appear very peculiar. For example, one urged that Jews be given their freedom but not equality, implying that people could be free without being equal.[142]

Interestingly, some petitions reflect the influence of liberalism, especially in legal areas. Several petition writers stated their willingness to agree to equality in law, even though they also requested exclusion of Jews from offices and communal retention of the absolute veto on residency.[143] We are not opposed to progress, one petition read; the Jew is a man, too, and is also under the protection of the laws.[144] But the petitioners separated equal rights of the individual under the law—that is, the rights of the state citizen—from the rights of the individual as part of a community or Church. Thus, communities stated their readiness to support "just improvements,"[145] even emancipation, but not at the cost of the community,[146] the Church,[147] or, more simply, themselves (Christian Bavarians).[148]

For a few petitioners, the question raised by equality was whether Jews were, literally, equal to Christian Bavarians. A petition from Karlstadt in Unterfranken agreed with the principle "equal rights for equal duties" but argued that Jews had not had equal duties and that, even after hundreds of years in Bavaria, Jews were still foreign and therefore were not equal.[149] Bavarians in Niederbayern similarly argued that one could not make people who refused to share customs and morals, who would neither work nor eat with Christians, equal.[150] Another maintained that Jews were not badly treated, were under the law, and had not deserved equality,[151] presumably based on a perception of them as unethical and lazy.[152] One petition, totally ignorant of Bavarian laws controlling Jews religiously, "reasoned" that Jews would be "more than equal" under this law because they would have rights over Christian churches and schools.[153]

The existence of sentiment supporting or permitting improvement in civic conditions for Jews raises the related issue of change in the Jews themselves. One of the oldest reforming rationales among Christian Germans was the belief that with emancipation Jews would become more modern and less obscurantist, more "German" and less "foreign."[154] Nevertheless, many Bavarian communities expressed the conviction that emancipation would not change the Jew. Belief that Jews would not change was part of the arguments based on Jewish economic practice, foreign nature, or religion,[155] but many petitioners also enunciated it as a general fact. Numerous petitions echoed the phrase "Jews remain Jews."[156] In the same vein, another petition stated, "the Jew is and remains a Jew whether he is baptised or not."[157] History, some argued, proved that where Jews had already been emancipated, they remained evil.[158]

Another way Christian petitioners raised the question of Jewish improvement was to speculate on the results of emancipation. A few merely expressed doubts about the good effects of emancipation on Jews,[159] but most of those making a forecast were decidedly pessimistic. Conditions were bad, a petition from Swabia read; if emancipation occurred, they would be worse.[160] The same point was made by several petitions: if Jews were emancipated, Bavaria would serve Jews;[161] if emancipated, Jews will "have us by the throat";[162] if they are emancipated, we will become slaves;[163] if emancipated, this "refined" people will fill all offices;[164] and if Jews are emancipated, they will dominate.[165] Several petitions stated that the future was not the issue. Bavarians needed immediate emancipation from Jews rather than Jews from Christians.[166] Control and domination of Christians by Jews in general, and not just economically, was a recurring motif in the petitions.[167]

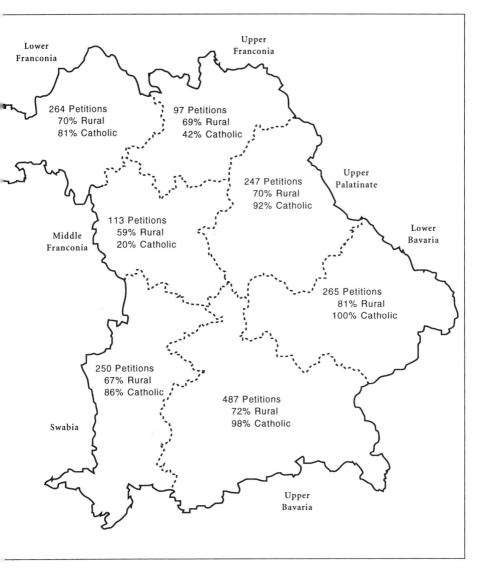

Map 3. Number of Petitions against Jewish Emancipation by Province, with the Percentage Rural and Catholic. (Data from the 1852 census; see table 2.6.)

Residential Factors and the Origins of the Petitions

It remains to be determined whether examination of the origins of the petitions sheds any light on the motivations behind them. The petitions were not equivalent to public opinion on Jewish emancipation but were rather "activist" expressions of opinion. Thus analysis of the types of communities submitting written protests against emancipation may be significant. Three separate questions may be profitably posed. First, did more petitions emanate from communities with no Jewish residents? Second, were more petitions generated in Catholic rather than in Protestant communities? Third, did more petitions come from small, rural communities rather than larger, urban centers? These questions reflect contemporary concern that most petitioners did not know Jews and, conversely, that those Bavarians who did, who lived with them in a community, did not submit petitions. Contemporaries also argued that Catholics led the campaign against emancipation and assumed that city dwellers were better equipped intellectually to compete with Jews.

Analysis of the first two questions is easiest because of the high level of religious segregation in early nineteenth-century Bavaria. Confessional segregation is self-evident in Oberbayern and Niederbayern and is also clear in the case of the Oberpfalz, as shown in table 5.3. Both Protestants and Jews resided almost entirely in the three Franconian provinces and in Schwaben. But even there segregation was a fact of life. On all levels, large and small cities, market towns, and rural districts, it is easy to show numerical dominance of either Catholics or Protestants and rare to find an even division. Thus, in Oberfranken 33 small cities were more than 90 percent Catholic, 45 were more than 90 percent Protestant, and the remaining 10 were predominantly Protestant. In Protestant Mittelfranken 59 of 64 Protestant cities and market towns were more than 90 percent Protestant, and 19 of 27 Catholic municipalities reached the same figure. In Unterfranken 70 of 80 Catholic cities and 15 of 22 Protestant cities were over the 90 percent mark. In Schwaben 27 of 74 Catholic cities and markets were 100 percent Catholic. Despite the lack of religious data for the small communities, it seems clear that most followed in the exclusionary footsteps of all larger entities. The census figures of 1852 show the tendency toward exclusion of other religions increasing as communities became smaller.

As shown in table 5.4, in large cities one finds little significant difference between Catholic and Protestant exclusion of Jews, but among the smaller cities and market towns, only 15 percent of Catholic as compared to 36 percent of Protestant cities contained any resident Jews. In Oberfranken only forty-five rural communities had Jewish residents in a province of nearly one thousand such centers. On this limited basis, it seems reasonable to expect a much smaller percentage of villages with Jewish residents, but it is not clear if, at this lower population level, there would also be a corresponding difference in religious exclusion.[168] In general, Protestant cities and towns appear to have been much more open to Jewish settlement than similar Catholic ones.

The petitioning record of cities containing Jews is clear (see table 5.5). Among independent cities with Jewish residents, no Protestant municipalities submitted petitions against Jewish emancipation, but one, Fürth, supported it. In comparison, eight of nine Catholic cities with resident Jews submitted petitions opposing emancipation: Augsburg submitted several, generally with large numbers of signatures. This must be seen in context. Only one independent city, Ingolstadt, submitted an "official" petition opposing emancipation, that is, one supported by the council members. Conservative Catholic organizations like the Association for Constitutional Monarchy and Religious Freedom operated in Catholic cities, but the political structure did not provide leadership. Communal submission of petitions did not dominate in the bigger cities.

Among the smaller cities and market towns, the record is muddled where Jewish presence is considered but clear where religious composition is at issue (see table 5.6). In most cases, 119 out of 133, petitions came from municipalities where no Jews were resident. This is not surprising in prov-

TABLE 5.3. Urban and Religious Population by Province in 1852

Province	Urban Population	Urban Catholic %	Urban Protestant %	Urban Jews %	% of Jews in Total Population	Urban Jews as a % of All Jews
Upper Bavaria	201,491	95	4	.6	.2	99[a]
Lower Bavaria	105,455	99	2	.0	.0	40[b]
Upper Palatinate	139,821	89	10	.6	.2	97[c]
Upper Franconia	153,930	38	60	1.2	1.1	34
Middle Franconia	215,819	19	78	3.2	2	65
Lower Franconia	175,020	78	19	2.9	2.7	32
Swabia	182,429	77	21	1.3	1.2	36
Palatinate	122,383	35	61	3.4	2.6	27
Bavaria	1,296,348[d]	68	30	1.6	1.1	42[e]

Source: Data from the 1852 census; see source to table 2.6.

[a]Of 1,218 Jews in Upper Bavaria, 1,205 resided in the two cities of Munich and Au.

[b]Four of the ten Jews in the province lived in Passau.

[c]Of 910 Jews in the province, 880 lived in four cities.

[d]The total population of Bavaria east of the Rhine was 3,875,359.

[e]The total Jewish urban population of Bavaria east of the Rhine was 18,315, out of a total Jewish population of 43,427.

inces like Niederbayern, Oberbayern, and the Oberpfalz, because there were so very few Jews resident there. In Schwaben and Mittelfranken, which contained relatively sizable Jewish populations, all petitions against emancipation originated in cities with no Jews, and in Oberfranken only one of eight cities submitting a petition contained a Jewish community. But in Unterfranken, the province with the largest Jewish population, nine of the twenty cities and market towns submitting petitions opposing emancipation contained substantial Jewish communities. Lacking religious data on the small community level, it is impossible at this point to say if this pattern of active Catholic opposition and Protestant apathy would apply there too. The record in Unterfranken (discussed in ch. 6) shows remarkably broad similarity to the pattern in the larger towns and cities.[169]

Whether exposure to Jews on a daily basis mitigated negative stereotypes about them transmitted from earlier ages or other areas cannot be determined in most Bavarian jurisdictions because Jews resided in so few areas. In Unterfranken, where enough Jews lived to make the test applicable,

TABLE 5.4   Where Jews Resided in Bavaria in 1852

Province	Catholic Cities[a] with Jews	Protestant Cities with Jews	Catholic Markets[b] with Jews	Protestant Markets with Jews	Catholic Rural Districts[c] with Jews	Protestant Rural Districts with Jews
Upper Bavaria	2	0	1	0	4	0
Lower Bavaria	1	0	1	0	2	0
Upper Palatinate	1	0	3	3	8[d]	1
Upper Franconia	1	1	8	8	14[e]	5[f]
Middle Franconia	0	5	4	24	2	22
Lower Franconia	2	1	41	16	36	5
Swabia	2	2	7	2	14	1
Bavaria	9	9	65	53	80	34

Source: Data from the 1852 census; see source to table 2.6.
[a]Independent cities only; see table 5.2 n.a.
[b]*Market* as used here includes smaller cities of the second and third class as well as market towns (*Märkte*), regardless of total population; *Market* is used to avoid confusion with independent cities.
[c]Rural districts; usually containing between fifteen and thirty communities not including independent cities. Although the district might be predominantly one confession, segregation was common, and the confession that was in the minority in the district might dominate in isolated communities. Data on religious division on the community level is nonexistent.
[d]Eighty-two percent of Jews lived in Protestant cities and markets located in these Catholic rural districts.
[e]In the fourteen predominantly Catholic rural districts, 4,331 Jews resided.
[f]In the five Protestant rural districts, there were 340 Jews, but 298 lived in one district.

the evidence indicates no hesitation in petitioning against the emancipation of one's neighbors. But it is dubious if Jews and Christians considered each other "neighbors" in any genuine sense. Bavarians in communities with no Jews and wishing to continue to exclude them had a direct reason to petition against the bill; for communities already with resident Jews that issue was moot. Pragmatically, as Zander pointed out, emancipation was a way communities might "lose" their Jews through migration to communities in which no Jews lived. Nonsubmission of a petition should not be automatically interpreted as indicating positive willingness to accept the bill. In addition to possibly reflecting a desire to rid themselves of Jews, not petitioning might

TABLE 5.5.   Petitions Against Emancipation from Independent Cities in 1849–1850

Province	No. of Independent Cities	Catholic Cities		Protestant Cities	
		No.	No. of Petitions	No.	No. of Petitions
Upper Bavaria	2	2	2	0	0
Lower Bavaria	3	3	3	0	0
Upper Palatinate	2	2	2	0	0
Upper Franconia	3	1	1	2	0
Middle Franconia	8	1	1	6	0
Lower Franconia	3	2	1	1	0
Swabia	8	5	2	3	2
Bavaria	29	16	12	12	2

Source: Data from the 1852 census; see source to table 2.6. The number of petitions is based on my analysis of the collection of petitions in the Bayerische Haupsstaatsarchiv, Munich; Kammer der Reichsräthe, 2656–61.

TABLE 5.6.   Petitions Against Emancipation in 1849–1850 from Smaller Cities and Market Towns

Province	No. of Cities	Average Population 1852	Catholic Cities		Protestant Cities	
			No.	No. with Petitions	No.	No. with Petitions
Upper Bavaria	67	1,599	67	29 (44%)	0	0 —
Lower Bavaria	69	1,127	69	22 (32%)	0	0 —
Upper Palatinate	92	1,192	85	28 (33%)	7	0 (0%)
Upper Franconia	88	1,272	39	8 (21%)	49	0 (0%)
Middle Franconia	91	1,154	27	9 (33%)	64	0 (0%)
Lower Franconia	102	1,334	80	17 (21%)	22	3 (14%)
Swabia	78	1,418	74	17 (23%)	4	0 (0%)
Bavaria	587	1,293	441	130 (30%)	146	3 (2%)

Source: Bayerische Haupsstaatsarchiv, Munich; Kammer der Reichsräthe 2656–61; author's computation.

signify a lack of awareness of the issues, political apathy, fear of the government, fear of Jewish retaliation, or simple embarrassment.

There was a much more obvious and substantial connection between religious confession and protest against Jewish emancipation. From the data in tables 5.5, 5.6, and 5.7, it is clear that Catholic areas opposed emancipation much more often than Protestant ones. Among independent cities, 12 of 16 Catholic municipalities submitted petitions, but none of the 12 Protestant ones did. Likewise, among smaller cities and markets, only 3 of 146 Protestant municipalities submitted petitions, while 130 of 441 Catholic ones did so. And 1,574 communities approved petitions against Jewish emancipation in predominantly Catholic rural districts, compared to 63 communities in districts where Protestants were in the majority. Even allowing for a 70 percent Catholic majority in the general population, these numbers show an overwhelming edge in active opposition to Jewish emancipation by Catholic areas. Because more Catholic districts had no resident Jews and the law would allow new residency in those areas, Catholic jurisdictions would have been, statistically and attitudinally, more likely than Protestant communities to fear emancipation.[170]

Turning to the question of a possible urban-rural bias in submission of petitions against emancipation, only a few conclusions seem warranted by the data. Among independent cities, the Catholic-Protestant split, 16 to 13, was only slightly more Protestant than in the general population. And among the smaller cities and market towns, Protestants were slightly underrepresented, using the same comparison to Bavaria as a whole. Thus Protestants appear slightly more urban than Catholics, and urban areas appear somewhat less actively opposed to Jewish emancipation than smaller population cen-

TABLE 5.7.   Petitions Against Emancipation from Rural Districts in 1849–1850

Province	No. Rural Districts	Catholic Rural Districts		Protestant Rural Districts	
		No.	No. Petitions	No.	No. Petitions
Upper Bavaria	38	38	482	0	0
Lower Bavaria	28	28	257	0	0
Upper Palatinate	30	29	239	1	0
Upper Franconia	31	15	96	15	0
Middle Franconia	34[a]	4	84	28	19
Lower Franconia	46	40	205	6	39
Swabia	41[b]	35	231	1	5
Bavaria	248	189	1,594	51	63

Source: Bayerische Haupsstaatsarchiv, Munich; Kammer der Reichsräthe, 2656–61; author's computation.
[a]Five rural districts did not provide data on religion.
[b]No data was available on religious composition in two rural districts.

ters. Nearly half of independent cities (45 percent) submitted petitions against emancipation, but only one was an official stand taken by a city council, and all represented (in numbers of signatories) a much smaller percentage of the local population than at lower levels. But 23 percent of all smaller cities and market towns submitted petitions, and most, unlike the larger cities, were official community statements. So, too, among the rural small communities, about 21 percent submitted petitions, and most were official protests.[171] It seems, especially when one considers the very low average size of the smaller cities and markets (as shown in table 5.6), that the term *urban* can only be applied to the independent cities and that they were much less actively and officially opposed to emancipation than were the "rural" villages, towns, and small cities of Bavaria.

On average we may conclude that the inhabitants of Catholic, rural, small cities and communities were more actively opposed to Jewish emancipation than Protestant, urban Bavarians. Among these the most substantial difference was religious: Catholics far outnumbered, both numerically and proportionately, their Protestant compatriots in actively opposing Jewish emancipation. Bavaria was a predominantly Catholic country and Protestants had long been a minority. In the north of Germany, where Protestants predominated, they were more anti-Semitic than their Catholic brethren. Can we conclude from this that religious minorities tend not to oppose other religious minorities?

In his recent work on the Rhineland, Jonathan Sperber shows that minority status played a significant role in political activity. In the Palatinate, where Protestants predominated and democrats were in control, Catholics were conservative. In the Prussian Rhineland, Catholics predominated numerically, but within a Protestant state in which conservatives were in control; there they tended toward the left. In both cases the economy enabled differences that should not be overlooked. Nevertheless, while religious belief alone cannot be easily used to explain the Catholic-Protestant political differences in the Rhineland, minority status in religion and politics combined can. The popular campaign against Jewish emancipation in 1849–50 demonstrates that Germany was a collection of localities and regions that did not always fit neatly into the nation.[172]

NOTES

1. See ch. 1, n. 1–3.

2. See especially the discussions of petitions in Heinrich Best, *Interessenpolitik und nationale Integration 1848/49: Handelspolitische Konflikte im frühindustriellen Deutschland* (Göttingen, 1980), 291–92, and Klaus Tenfelde and Helmut Trischler,

eds., *Bis vor die Stufen des Throns: Bittschriften und Beschwerden von Bergleuten in Zeitalter der Industrialisierung* (Munich, 1986), 9–13.

3. Only 14 percent were dated January 15–31, and a mere 1.8 percent in February. Only 14.5 percent of the petitions, from 256 communities, could not be securely dated, but many of these undoubtedly also stemmed from late December and early January. See appendix C for four of these petitions; a fifth may be found in Harris, "Public Opinion and the Proposed Emancipation of the Jews in Bavaria in 1849–50," *LBIY* 34 (1989): 67–79. For the weather, see n. 6 below.

4. Best, *Interessenpolitik,* 126, describes petitioning as a form of direct action demanding few qualifications and involving little risk.

5. Assuming the same average as in table 5.1 n. g, 99.3 per petition, that would mean an additional 14,299 signatures, but strictly understood, it would mean much more, because the "whole village" seldom signed any petition. Assuming citizenship to be essentially equal to the number of adult male heads of resident families, the 1852 census gives 994,148 as the number of families in Bavaria. On that basis, further assuming these signatories to be virtually all adult male heads of families (as they normally stated they were), these signatures represent 10.2 percent of that figure. Of course, some communities may never have heard the news about passage of the bill in the lower house.

6. No. 13, Brennberg, RD Falkenstein, Opf, noted that snow made many communities impossible to reach. No. 88, also from this district, arrived separately from the Brennberg petition due to broken communications. No. 91, from five communities in the Opf, noted that two mayors and their seals were missing due to snow and the short time available. The petitions are not numbered in the archive; I have assigned numbers for ease of reference.

7. See petition nos. 131, in RD Günzburg, Schw, 139; Dettendorf, in Aibling, Ob; 163, Hirschenberg, in Miesbach, Ob; 204, from four rural districts in Ob, Opf, and Nb; 537, Mkt. Kösching, in Ingolstadt, Ob.

8. Based on my analysis of selected districts in both data sets; thorough comparison will depend on computer-aided research. The petitions are in the Landtagsarchiv, Munich, J3a and J3b, "Addressen für [and "gegen"] unbedingte Einführung der Reichs Verfassung und der Grundrechte;" see also Gernot Kirzel, *Staat und Kirche im bayerischen Landtag zur Zeit Max II (1848–1864)* (Munich, 1974), 101ff., who apparently used the unknown compiler's original count of petitions. The count given here is my own; the original listed 580 for, 505 against, and did not count communities separately.

9. Dieter Langewiesche, "Die politische Vereinsbewegung in Würzburg und in Unterfranken in den Revolutionsjahren 1848/49," *JfFräL* 37 (1977): 232–33.

10. The democratic role in the petitioning for and against the Basic Rights and Constitution in Bavaria has not been studied; but see my article "Rethinking the Categories of the German Revolution of 1848: The Emergence of Popular Conservatism in Bavaria," *CEH* 25, no. 2 (1993): 123–48, based on these petitions.

11. A file in the Hauptstaatsarchiv, Munich, Kammer der Reichsräthe, 2657, contained seven documents: six are petitions, one is a statement by forty Bavarian rabbis on the role of the Talmud in Jewish life. The three individuals were District

Rabbi S.W. Rosenfeld of Bamberg in Upper Franconia, District Rabbi L. Seligman of Kaiserslautern in the Palatinate, and Heinrich Goldschmidt of Munich. The three communities were Fürth in Middle Franconia in the form of the Bürgerverein zu Fürth, Hürben in Swabia, and Erlangen in Middle Franconia. Dr. A. Eckstein, *Kampf,* 71, 78, and esp. 104, suggests a tactical decision by Bavarian Jews not to submit petitions in 1849–50.

12. On petitioning as active involvement, see Best, *Interessenpolitik,* 128–29, and Charles Tilly, *The Contentious French* (Cambridge, Mass., 1986), 390–93, for a discussion of this activity in France. Rüdiger Moldenauer, "Jewish Petitions to the German National Assembly in Frankfurt 1848/49," *LBIY* 16 (1971): 185–223, notes that only fifteen out of more than eight thousand extant petitions related to Jews, of which five were no longer extant and four were anti-Semitic, (including one from Karlstadt in Lower Franconia.

13. No. 124, from the city of Waldmünchen, Opf.

14. See no. 3A.

15. For example, no. 289, from six communities in RD Neunburg a/W, Opf, stated that the signatures to the petition would show who was in the majority. Nos. 238 and 243, from five and three communities in Mfr and Ufr respectively, estimated five-sixths; no. 386, from two communities in Ufr, said nine-tenths; and no. 509, from two communities in RD Traunstein, Ob, said three-fourths.

16. See especially nos. 110, 166, 213, 265, 297, 329.

17. Developed further below.

18. No. 96, from thirteen communities in RD Eichstädt, Mfr; no. 128, from twenty communities in RD Dettelbach, Ufr; and no. 329, from Lempferding in RD Ebernberg, Ob.

19. No. 286, Eichenhofen & Seifersdorf, RD Parsberg.

20. E.g., no. 384, Mkt. Rosenheim in RD Rosenheim, Ob; esp. no. 353, Burgkundstadt in RD Weismain, Ofr; also no. 448, Asenkofen in RD Rottenburg, Nb.

21. Nos. 104A, 122, 277, 293, 295, 317, 339, 352, 360, 398, 519. No. 317 saw emancipation as more damaging than freedom of movement and the right to subdivide; no. 519 noted concern for the amnesty bill but saw emancipation as far more important.

22. No. 347, ten communities in RDs Arnstorf, Dingolfing and Landau, Nb; no. 397, Oberneukirchen, in RD Mühldorf, Ob.

23. RD Neuburg, a/Donau, Schw.

24. In RD Erding, Ob.

25. No. 137, Eichenbühl, Ufr.

26. Falkenberg, Diepoltskirchen 1 and 2, and Unterhausbach.

27. No. 337, from four communities in RD Zusmarshausen, Schw.

28. No. 504, from two communities in RDs Pfaffenhofen and Schrobenhausen, Ob.

29. No. 478, from five communities in RD Pfaffenhofen, Ob.

30. Nos. 279, Hohendorf (unknown), and 523, three communities in RD Landshut, Ob.

31. No. 350, Martinsbuch in RD Mallersdorf, Nb.

32. Von der Pfordten admitted as much publicly; see ch. 3.

33. Nos. 4, 27, 68, 81, 89, 160, 161, 193, 203, 223, 295, 421, 431, 452, 453, 480, 501, from fifty-six communities.

34. Nos. 22, 81, 89, 144, 146, 201, 223, 234, 248, 309, 316, 399, 412, 421, 422, 448, 452, 470, 501, 513, 534; six overlap with those in n. 33, but the rest are separate and from fifty-four communities.

35. No. 248, Märkte Waldsassen, Mitterteich, and Konnersreuth in RD Waldsassen, Opf.; 309, three communities in RDs Kastl and Parsberg, Opf.; and 412, Unterfinnig in RD Diessen, Ob.

36. Nos. 412, Unterfinnig in RD Diessen, Ob; 421, eight communities in RD Neumarkt, Opf. No. 523, three communities in RD Landshut, Nb, described Frankfurt, where the constitution for Germany was being written, as a "machine of Hell."

37. No. 68, from five communities in RDs Kötzting and Viechtach.

38. Nos. 2, 3, 4, 20, 32, 43, 130, 148, 160, 164, 173, 180, 220, 378, and 424 (Tuntenhausen); no. 32, eight communities in RD Baunach, Ufr; no. 368, three communities in RD Eggenfelden, Nb; no. 220, Kaldorf in RD Greding, Mfr, complained that the three deputies from that region had voted for, against, and abstaining, respectively, negating public sentiment, which was against.

39. No. 216, Waidhaus in RD Bohenstrauss, Opf; no. 251, five communities in RD Prien, Ob.

40. No. 69, Lauterbrunn in RD Wertingen, Schw; no. 374, Hirschau in RD Amberg, Opf.

41. Nos. 203, 540, 534, 507, 104; no. 122 for "cooling," nos. 79, 258, and 518 predicted "Judenverfolgungen" (pogroms), and nos. 13, 175, and 422 were for defense with weapons.

42. No. 121, Untersambach in RD Wiesentheid, Ufr.

43. For "left" see no. 251; for democracy, nos. 20, 343, 332, 146, 18; for social democrats, no. 125; for "Umsturzpartei," nos. 193, 29; for Communists, no. 75; for revolution, no. 442, and no. 338 saw emancipation as a "child of revolution."

44. Landtagsarchiv, see n. 8. It was the rare exception for any community other than a large city to submit differing petitions.

45. Nos. 63, 64, 71, 365, 395, 436, 440, 478, 549.

46. Nos. 68, 150, 178, 490.

47. No. 4, four communities in RD Rottenburg, Nb.

48. No. 342, Ering in RD Simbach, Nb.

49. No. 469, ten communities in RD Regenstauf, Opf.

50. No. 410, three communities in RD Landsberg, Ob.

51. No. 123, four communities in RD Stadtamhof, Opf.

52. Nos. 64, 146, 212, 213, 293, 365, 514, 549.

53. No. 121; see also n. 49.

54. No. 125, Oberroth in RD Dachau, Ob.

55. No. 246, thirty-six communities in RD Ebern, Ufr.

56. No. 230, Tacherting in RD Trostberg, Ob; no. 506, four communities in RD Wertingen, Schw.

57. No. 4; see also n. 55.

58. No. 68, five communities in RDs Kötzting and Viechtach, Nb; no. 490, Egglham in RD Pfarrkirchen, Nb.
59. No. 14, Nittenau, Opf; no. 16, six communities in RDs Forchheim and Bamberg, Ofr.
60. No. 293, from (illegible) in OB.
61. Nos. 27, 264, 359, and, in a variation, 493; nos. 544 and especially 282, which reads: "the demands of the *age* are not what a few rabble-rousers and poor daily papers want but rather what the people want."
62. No. 190, Hirschau in RD Amberg, Opf; Christian beggars were real and are described in Ingeborg Weber-Kellermann, *Landleben,* 395ff., esp. the illustration on 337. No. 47, three communities in RD Straubing, Nb, 94, Kleinsassen and Schockau in RD Hilders, Ufr; no. 284, Hausheim in RD Kastl, Opf, 351, Gützingen in RD Aub, Ufr; no. 374, Hirschau in RD Amberg, Opf (and in app. C); no. 412, Unterfinnig in RD Diessen, Ob. See also the data in ch. 2.
63. No. 374, the city, third class, of Hirschau, Opf; also no. 250, three communities in RD Oberviechtach, Opf.
64. RD Schollkrippen, by four officials in the name of the whole community.
65. There is a great deal of new research on Bavarian Jews and Jewry, noted in the introduction and ch. 2.
66. E.g., no. 147, in RD Kempten; according to the 1852 census there were no Jews resident there.
67. No. 170, RD Pottenstein, where thirty-six Jews were resident in 1852.
68. Nos. 250, 257, 355, 358.
69. No. 199, from three communities in RD Türkheim, Schw, on *Zwischenhandel;* no. 374, Hirschau, RD Amberg, Opf, notes that Jews began first at the gate and then went village-to-village.
70. No. 424, Tuntenhausen in RD Aibling, Ob.
71. No. 440, from three communities in RD Landshut, Nb.
72. No. 374, see also n. 59.
73. No. 199, thirty-three communities in RD Türkheim, Schw, Jewish money was a danger to landowning; another, no. 170, from sixteen communities in RD Pottenstein, Ofr, claimed Jews owned one-third of the land in that rural district.
74. No. 515, in RD Traunstein.
75. No. 79, three communities in RD Königshofen.
76. Nos. 317 (Ofr), 331 (Mfr), 339 (Opf), 393 (Opf), 398 (Nb), 423 (Ob), 427 (Ob), 435 (Nb), 449 (Ob), 463 (Ob), 464 (Ob), 469 (Opf), 485 (Ob), 491 (Ob), 523 (Nb), 551 (Opf).
77. No. 319, three communities in NB; see W. Conze, "Bauer," in O. Brunner et al., eds., *Geschichtliche Grundbegriffe: Historisches Lexikon zur politisch-sozialen Sprache in Deutschland* (Stuttgart, 1972), 423 n. 60.
78. Nos. 68, 127, 131, 142, 165, 188, 190, 250, 257, 301, 331, 358, 440, 492.
79. No. 358, six communities from RD Aub, Ufr; also no. 306, four communities in RD Neumarkt, Opf.
80. Nos. 353, 196; no. 355 stated that a Jew only entered "Ökonomie" (agriculture) to get residency rights; no. 142, in Opf, stated that the community had been

persuaded to accept Jews, who first entered agriculture but quickly became dealers in rye and *Schacher*.

81. No. 214, Neukirchen in RD Burghausen, Ob. The Bible reference is to Genesis 3:19.

82. No. 51, from two communities in RD Herrieden, Mfr.

83. No. 250, four communities in RD Oberviechtach, Opf, "born *Wucher*"; no. 371, four communities in RD Zusmarshausen, Schw and Moosburg, Ob, "*Schacher* by birth"; no. 512, RD Kemnath, Opf, "traders by nature"; and see below. This is discussed at length in Joan Campbell, *Joy in Work*.

84. No. 6.

85. No. 199, also in Schw.

86. No. 413, in RD Schweinfurt, UFr, from Schonungen and Weÿher.

87. The number of petitions excluding Jews from offices do not duplicate religious opposition as such; the percentages are discrete.

88. No. 426, from five communities in RD Neuburg a. d. D., Schw, was an exception when it stated that "Judaism is the greatest enemy of Christianity."

89. No. 42.

90. No. 87.

91. They were not unique; see also no. 193, three communities in RD Wolfrats-hausen, Ob, and no. 506, four communities in RD Wertingen, Schw.

92. See no. 81 in RD Rottenberg, Nb, for "Todfeinde"; nos. 54 (Ufr) 68 (Nb), 72 (Ufr), for "sworn" enemies; nos. 37 (Ob), 42 (Opf), 293 (7), 315 (Mfr), 330 (Nb), 441 (Schw & Nb), 450 (Ob), 465 (Nb), for "born enemies"; nos. 150 (Schw), 452 (Ob), for "will hate us as long as they are Jews."

93. Very few; see nos. 220 (Mfr), 489 (Schw), and, implied, 426 (Schw).

94. No. 27, Mkt. Stamsried in RD Roding, Opf.

95. Also very few, see nos. 386 (Ufr), 444 (Opf), 522 (Ofr).

96. No. 206, from two communities in Rottenburg, Nb, refers to *Pradin Bavaria Sancta*, vol. 2, 313 and 331, vol. 3, 173 and 177. This was one of very few references to printed sources.

97. See nos. 522 (Ofr) and 461, in RD Ottobeuren, Schw, "what God has separated should remain so."

98. I found only fifteen of this type, seven specifying the Talmud.

99. No. 86 from fourteen communities with 423 signatures, including those of officials with their seals.

100. No. 196 (Steinach, Windheim, and Roth) in RD Münnerstadt with 121 signa-tures, including officials and seals, stating literally "mit dem Köpfen der Christen noch zu kegele" [sic]. For a remarkably similar saying, "We must play bowls with rich men's heads," see Eugen Weber, *Peasants*, 253, apparently from the 1848–51 years.

101. No. 384, Flotzheim, RD Monheim, Schw. In his reply to Adler, Zander also accused Jews of using this prayer. See *VBO*, no. 26, 30 Jan. 1850, p.2.

102. No. 238, by the city of Buching (third class) with 146 signatures along with four other communities in the name of the whole community.

103. At least thirty from 131 communities: nos. 58, 73, 76, 132, 149, 152, 167,

197, 203, 225, 234, 254, 256, 295, 334, 362, 370, 385, 437, 454, 455, 484, 499, 503, 506, 510, 518, 540, 541.

104. No. 58 Irlbach, RD Straubing, NB, with fifty-six signatures.

105. No. 197, seven communities in RD Stadtsteinach, OFr, with signatures from three communities while four communities were in the name and wish of all community members, a total of ca. 510 families based on the 1858 census; see Königliches Statistisches Bureau, ed., *Verzeichniss der Gemeinden des Königreichs Bayern mit ihrer Bevölkerung im Dezember 1861, geordnet nach Kreisen, Verwaltungs-Districten und Gerichtssprengeln, unter Beifügung der einschlägigen Rentämter, Forstämter und Baubehorden* (Munich, 1863).

106. No. 87 in RD Kipfenberg.

107. No. 455.

108. See nos. 87, 198, 234, 269, on Jews as bishops and priests; nos. 414 and 461 for the Sabbath. No. 290 asked if the cross should be removed from the Wittelsbach crown.

109. No. 76, "oriental"; no. 79, "asiatic cholera."

110. Nos. 75, 240, 399, and 435 argued that they were foreign because they did not like to work.

111. No. 304, Kammer in RD Traunstein, Ob; no. 375, city of Neumarkt, Opf.

112. Nos. 159 (Ufr), 315 (Mfr), 367 (Ob), 493 (Nb), 518 (Mfr), 551 (Opf).

113. No. 259, four communities in Wolfratshausen, Ob.

114. No. 26, Schweinspaint in RD Monheim, Schw.

115. No. 278, in RD Mitterfels, Nb. in the Bayerischer Wald.

116. No. 38, Schwabhausen and Ramsach in RD Landsberg, Ob.

117. No. 448, two communities in Rottenburg, Nb, Jews were separate from birth; no. 167, four communities in RD Lohr, Ufr, they would always be separate; no. 175, two communities in Marktbreit, Ufr, Jews were so different they could never be absorbed; no. 199, thirty-three communities in RD Türkheim, Schw, that Christians could not become Jews or vice versa; no. 33, two communities in RD Öttingen, Schw, and no. 50, Riedenhausen in RD Aub, Ufr, that Jews were foreigners and would remain so.

118. No. 158 from five communities in RD Weissenburg and Greding, MFr with 157 signatures.

119. No. 386, two communities in RDs Schweinfurt and Hassfurt in Ufr.

120. No. 151 (Ob); also nos. 186, 420, 508, 550.

121. Nos. 165, 182, and 429; but a few wanted to admit no more Jews to Bavaria, nos. 71 and 183, or to limit the increase in the number of Jews, nos. 229 and 351.

122. No. 359, Hollstadt in RD Neustadt a/S in Ufr, noted an instance five years earlier when the community helped a Jewish family emigrate.

123. No. 47, three communities in Straubing, Nb, and no. 148, two communities in RD Feuchtwangen, Mfr.

124. Nos. 4 (Nb), 132 (Ofr), 168 (Ufr), 170 (Ofr), 332 (Schw), 373 (Nb), 394 (Nb), 462 (Ufr), 463 (Ob), 522 (Ofr), 525 (Ob).

125. No. 72.

126. No. 533, the city of Iphofen in RD Markt-Bibart, Mfr.

127. No. 218, two communities in RD Titmoning, Ob.

128. Nos. 8, 13, 22, 167, 394, 428.

129. This was traditional; see Walker, *Home Towns*, 139ff., and Wilhelm Imhof, *Die geschichtliche Entwicklung des Gemeinderechte im rechtsrheinischen Bayern seit dem Jahre 1818* (Munich, 1927), 55ff.

130. No. 374, Hirschau, St. third class, RD Amberg, Opf.

131. See Th. Max Safely, *Let No Man Put Asunder: Control of Marriage in the German Southwest* (Kirksville, Mo., 1984), and Klaus-Jürgen Matz, *Pauperismus und Bevölkerung: Die gesetzlichen Ehebeschränkungen in den süddeutschen Staaten während des 19. Jahrhunderts* (Stuttgart, 1980), 153–74, 221–31. Marriage restrictions were still common in 1849–50.

132. See ch. 3.

133. No. 252.

134. See ch. 3.

135. Nos. 132, 237, 250, and nn. 136–40 below.

136. Especially no. 207, two communities in RD Deggendorf, Nb, and no. 372, Mkt. Kraiburg, RD Mühldorf, Ob; also, generally; nos. 12, 193, 218–19, 234, 265, 307, 323, 385, 483, 494, 506, 508, 533, 538.

137. No. 242, Nussdorf ?, and no. 85, two communities in RD Moosburg, Ob, which accused the ministers of making the change.

138. No. 27, nine communities in Roding, Opf; no. 228, Mkt. Riedenburg in Opf; and no. 454, six communities in RD Straubing, Nb.

139. No. 126, city of Geiselhoring in RD Mallersdorf, Nb.

140. No. 352, two communities in Kaufbeuren, Schw, and no. 550, arnshausen in Euerdorf, Ufr.

141. Nos. 29, 39, 60, 90, 240, 266.

142. No. 478, five communities in Pfaffenhofen, Ob.

143. No. 90, two communities in Neustadt a/S, Ufr; no. 312, Uffing in RD Weilheim, Ob; and no. 347, eleven communities in RDs Arnstorf, Dingolfing, and Landau in Nb.

144. No. 426, five communities in Neuburg a. d. D., Schw.

145. No. 39, four communities in Wasserburg, Ob, and no. 60, Rottershausen in RD Münnerstadt, Ufr.

146. No. 249, two communities in Eschenbach, Opf, and 394, Grossköllnbach in RD Landau, Nb.

147. No. 427, three communities in RD Erding, Ob, and no. 456, Ruhrstorf in RD Griesbach, Nb.

148. No. 93, two communities in RDs Würzburg r./M and Ochsenfurt, Ufr, and no. 439, Frontenhausen in RD Vilsbiburg, Nb.

149. No. 492, Steinbach, Wiesenfelal, and Rohrbach, RD Karlstadt; also no. 138, Hanbach in RD Gemünden, Ufr.

150. No. 493, five communities in RD Osterhofen, NB.

151. No. 481, two communities in Haag, Ob.

152. See n. 110.

153. No. 402, Schwanskirchen in Erding, Ob.

154. See chs. 2 and 3.

155. See n. 117.

156. Nos. 54, 177, 366, 440, 466, 551.

157. No. 343, two communities in RD Landau, Nb; variations were nos. 472, and 508, "The Jew is and remains a Jew with or without emancipation"; no. 451, "who believes the Jew will change?"

158. No. 11, four communities in RD Eggenfelden, Nb, and no. 449, three communities in Traunstein, Ob.

159. No. 23, five communities and the city of Augsburg, unofficially, but with 463 signatures, in Schw; no. 91, five communities in the Opf and Ob.

160. No. 33, two communities in Öttingen, Schw, and no. 317, three communities in RD Ebermannstadt, Ofr.

161. No. 58, Irlbach in Straubing, Nb, and no. 247, Enkering in RD Kipfenberg, Mfr.

162. No. 142, three communities in Bohenstrauss, Opf.

163. No. 164, six communities in Friedberg, Ob. No. 281, three communities in Pfaffenhofen, Ob.

164. No. 376, Eggstädt in RD Trostberg, Ob.

165. No. 24, Heidingsfeld in RD Würzburg l/M, Ufr, and no. 92, City of Rain, Ob.

166. Nos. 49 (Mfr), 50 (Ufr), 151 (Ob), 180 (Ofr).

167. Nos. 18 (Ufr), 20 (Ufr), 24 (Ufr), 27 (Opf), 98 (Ob), 104 (Nb), 246 (Ufr).

168. Guth, *Landgemeinden,* 393.

169. In RD Hilders (Ufr), 69 percent Catholic, eighteen communities supported the Basic Rights and another eighteen opposed Jewish emancipation; the breakdown, based on partial data on religious composition, suggests the former to be Protestants and the latter Catholics.

170. Dietrich Thränhardt, *Wahlen und Politische Strukturen in Bayern 1848–1953: Historisch-soziologische Untersuchungen zum Entstehen und zur Neuerrichtung eines Parteiensystems* (Düsseldorf, 1973), 44–46, writes that in Franconia the political divisions within each confession was the same, but that in general, Catholic Old Bavaria was predominantly conservative, and the new provinces were predominantly leftist.

171. One or two petitions hint at another factor that should be considered in evaluating the number of petitions from rural communities—smallness. The small community of Kallbach in RD Marktheidenfeld, Ufr, reported to the district director that it had not submitted a petition because it was too small and insignificant. Perhaps the very small communities were naturally less politically active. Or perhaps they could not financially afford to be active.

172. See Jonathan Sperber's excellent work *Rhineland Radicals: The Democratic Movement and the Revolution of 1848–1849* (Princeton, N.J., 1991), 438ff., 452, 483ff., and Wolfgang Schwentker, *Konservative Vereine und Revolution in Preussen 1848/49: Die Konstituierung des Konservatismus als Partei* (Düsseldorf, 1988), 320, 340.

Chapter 6

Organization at the Grass Roots:
The Case of Lower Franconia

Study of press involvement and petitioning make clear that support for Jewish emancipation by the administration, by a large majority of the lower house of Parliament, and by most of the newspaper press encountered strong popular opposition. Newspapers covering the campaign against Jewish emancipation, especially left-leaning papers, questioned whether that popular opposition was genuine. The government, too, was deeply interested in the answer to that question. The government's officials in Lower Franconia closely monitored the petition movement there, and their reports enable us to determine the degree of spontaneity in the opposition to Jewish emancipation.

The State Bureaucracy Acts

The Bavarian state wasted no time when collecting information on the response to Jewish emancipation. The Ministry of the Interior sent an order to the eight provincial governors, "under his royal majesty's highest command," the day after the passage of the bill by the lower house on 14 December 1849.[1] The ministry's immediate concern was that passage might stimulate disquiet and violence, especially as the result of local assemblies that might be held during the approaching Christmas holidays. Consequently, the state directed the governors to be alert, to use trustworthy men as sources of information, to take the requisite measures to keep order, and to keep the ministry informed of important events. From the beginning the central government worried about adverse reaction that might become organized opposition and even violent uprising. By doing so it seems clear that the ministers worried about a possible repetition of the upsets that occurred in the spring of 1849 over the rejection of the Basic Rights and the Frankfurt Constitution. Some may have had in mind the anti-Jewish riots of March 1848 or even 1819. A small number of petitions do show evidence of a potentially violent response.[2]

Responding to the ministerial directive, Hohe, the head of the local office of the Ministry of the Interior in Lower Franconia,[3] drafted and sent his own directive to eight of the forty-nine offices under his jurisdiction, a mixture of rural districts, independent cities, and police offices. These eight officials were those whose views he especially trusted in communities with significant numbers of Jewish residents. By 31 December Hohe was able to send to Munich all eight reports and a cover letter in which he agreed with their evaluations. He noted that the bill had caused a "vigorous sensation," adding that though there might be disturbances of public order and isolated acts of hatred, there was nothing to fear in revolutionary terms.[4]

Hohe was especially well-organized and energetic compared wlth the other seven governors in Bavaria. But all responded quickly to the directive from Munich, even if in a much less substantive way. All eight replies to the directive are extant, and that from Lower Franconia is the most complete.[5] About a month later in mid-January, stimulated by newspaper reports that the upper house had received 317 addresses against emancipation, including 61 from Lower Franconia, Hohe drafted and sent out a new directive to all forty-nine lower offices, instructing them to respond to four specific questions "immediately." His new directive asked whether petitions against emancipation had been sent to the upper house from each district and, if so, who had initiated and finalized them? He wished to know whether the communal officials, individual communal members, or both had supported these petitions. Finally, and most surprisingly, he requested a description of each district's "true, not fabricated, sentiment on Jewish emancipation."[6]

Every office in Lower Franconia respondcd to Hohe's notice and answered the four-part questionnaire. Some answers were thin, especially where there was no petition, no opinion, or a lazy official. But most were serious attempts to answer Hohe's queries, and one district director, imitating his superior's methods, requested and received reports from all sixteen communities in his rural district. Taken as a whole, this material represents a remarkably detailed and complete source for the study of public opinion on Jewish emancipation and on Jews. Moreover, the motivation for the investigation derived from concern over the production of petitions and agitation rather than from an attempt either to encourage petitioning or to question the petitions' validity.[7] That such information gathering took place only in Lower Franconia indicates the informational, rather than suppressive, intention of the state.

The request for information from the central state was not unusual. Maximilian II became infamous for his insistence on knowing everything he could about every issue. His cabinet secretary after 1 August 1849, Franz Xavier Pfistermeister, described Maximilian as a "man primarily with a burning curiosity and a broad circle of interests, but also with a rare sense of duty,

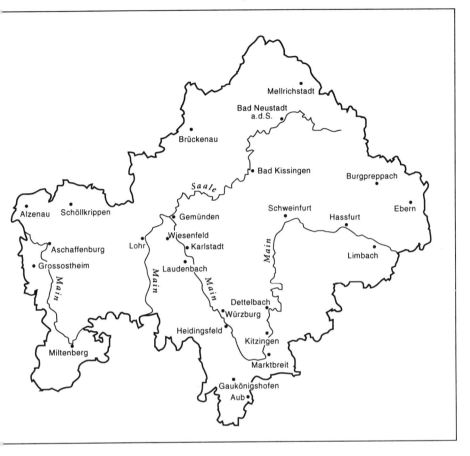

Map 4. Lower Franconia in 1849

incapable of dropping a subject before he had mastered it fully, tireless in questioning and requestioning." His support for scholarship was well known, but Maximilian's use of the governmental bureaucracy to gather information was the real hallmark of his administration. Historians characterize Maximilian as cautious, unproductive, and passive, given to compromise rather than to command. In public he appeared neither dynamic nor attractive, lacking the ability to make either himself or his plans popular.[8]

Whether Maximilian was progressive or conservative is still open to question and subject to debate.[9] One modern analyst argues that his penchant for investigation, though a conservative characteristic, was carried to an extreme.

It is troublesome that the king saw his Ministry of the Interior with its middle and lower offices too much as an intelligence and opinion gathering institution. The complaint [that] the Bavarian government, especially the Ministry of the Interior, did too much governing and too little ruling, a standing complaint in the entire nineteenth century and beyond, finds in such bureaucratic activity a partial explanation.[10]

In the first few months of his reign, Maximilian requested regular reports about the political and economic situation in each province, regular periodic reports on the uplifting of the proletariat, and, from each rural district and city, monthly reports on public opinion, *Volksstimmung*.[11] Thus the decision to ask the bureaucracy for reports on the probable results of Jewish emancipation was a normal occurrence. Its normalcy explains why some officials responded in depth and others did not. Some officials were clearly bothered by the paper shuffling it necessitated, but others—and Hohe stands out in this regard—agreed with Maximilian II's approach. The government correctly predicted that the apparent immanence of Jewish emancipation would cause an outburst of spontaneous popular opinion.

Formation and Expression of Popular Opinion

In its initial directive, the Ministry of the Interior warned that caution was needed because assemblies might be held during the Christmas holidays (see app. B). Hohe's second directive specified concern for the drafting and acceptance of petitions. By specifying observation of both public assemblies and the formulation of petitions, the state showed that it understood well the dynamics of opinion formation in both city and community. The years 1848 and 1849 had been an educational experience in this regard. Assembly and petition were two parts of the same process. Petitions were usually the end product of an assembly—frequently the only product—and in many cases they constituted the original reason for calling the assembly.

The process of formulating petitions was not new in 1849. Its use in one form or another dates to the Middle Ages. Essentially it allowed either an individual subject (later, citizen) or a municipality to plead his or its case in a direct request, not always written, to monarch or lord (later state or Parliament).[12] The revolution of 1848 precipitated a tremendous increase in the frequency and size of public assemblies and in the number of petitions.

Individuals and communities could submit petitions to government on any outstanding issue, but most made the effort only on the most vital questions. Assemblies submitted petitions in droves during the first month of the revolution in March 1848, usually listing demands for reform. Petitions for and against the Basic Rights also appeared in large numbers during the winter of 1849, and there were smaller numbers of petitions in April and June on the more inclusive issue of the Frankfurt Constitution. Dieter Lange-wiesche has provided an excellent picture of the political organizations at work in Lower Franconia in 1848 and 1849.[13] His painstakingly thorough archival research shows clearly that popular political activity in Lower Fran-conia was extremely vigorous and highly democratic. In 1849 the people banded together in associations in unprecedented numbers—by June 283 political associations existed in Lower Franconia alone.[14]

Associations formed spontaneously during the early weeks and months of the revolution and later expanded as people became more politically so-phisticated. Many of these associations were short-lived, spontaneous ex-pressions of opinion rather than well-organized, durable political group-ings.[15] Recent research on early political organizations, whether political "parties" in the modern sense or not, depicts a remarkably similar pattern.[16] The key to the organization of political associations, as in the formulation of petitions, was the assembly.

Volksversammlungen, or "people's assemblies," were little more than groups of interested people, citizens and noncitizens alike, in numbers rang-ing from a few to more than ten thousand (even in Lower Franconia), who met in inns or in the open air, sometimes advertising their existence only by word of mouth. Contemporary descriptions, both written and pictorial, por-tray these meetings as crowds with little formal organization, yet respectable in dress and action.[17] In the smaller communities, the mayor and members of the council were typically among the meetings' chairpersons and speakers. As organizations like the March Association (*Märzverein*) grew, they orga-nized their own assemblies and provided both the chairpersons and many of the speakers from their own ranks. The same was true of the Pius Associa-tions and the Association for Constitutional Monarchy and Religious Free-dom. Petitions to the king, his ministers, and Parliament were a common product of these meetings, and all assemblies seem to have passed some form of resolution as the conclusion of their work. For example, the *Cen-tralmärzverein* in Würzburg called an assembly for 13 April 1849 and adopted a petition in support of the Frankfurt Constitution, which collected 10,700 signatures by 20 May.[18]

In Lower Franconia the records reveal a large number of communities expressing opinions on Jewish emancipation. Since almost all opposed both Jewish emancipation and Parliament, this marks the development of a coun-terrevolutionary or antiliberal phase in local popular politics. Opposition to Jewish emancipation was also opposition to the state. The government per-ceived the petitions opposing emancipation as such, and the language of the petitions leaves little doubt that that was so. The localities saw the bill for Jewish emancipation as an attack on their local rights, especially on their right of residence. By defending local rights, they acted in a democratic, if nonideological, manner. The role of popular democracy had not ended with the April decision of the king of Bavaria to regard the Frankfurt Assembly and Constitution as null.

In Bavaria, most democratic organizations did not oppose Jewish emancipation, and some supported it, but never in the form of a petition.[19] Organized opposition to Jewish emancipation came mainly from two conservative, Catholic groups: the Association for Constitutional Monarchy and Religious Freedom and the Pius Associations, both founded in 1848.[20] Little is known about the extent of either organization or the amount of political power each possessed. The Association for Constitutional Monarchy may have had sixty branch associations and eighty thousand members at its peak in summer 1849, but it began to decline soon after and had dissolved by late 1852 or early 1853. The Pius Associations, founded in Mainz, were often led by Catholic clergy, but they were neither as numerous nor as politically active as their counterparts on the left. Most Pius Associations in Bavaria were in the Palatinate, but perhaps fifty-one branches existed in the rest of Bavaria, and they also suffered rapid decline in summer and fall 1849.[21] The press appears to have greatly exaggerated their numbers. Only twenty-six petitions in all Bavaria came from these organizations directly, although this does not mean that they did not influence community decisions indirectly. Although both of these organizations were present in Lower Franconia, neither submitted a petition there. But their influence may have been strong, judging by governmental reports that indicate a strong and active involvement by clergy, especially Catholics.[22]

The influence of the local priest or pastor derived from the same source as the mayor and local school teacher, even though all three differed from each other substantively in origin, function, and outlook. These three officials possessed authority as mediators: in religion the priest or minister mediated between the people and God and the church, in education the teacher provided a framework for understanding the world outside the village, and in civic affairs the mayor represented the community to other communities and to the state. Interaction among these three constituted a complex dynamic relationship, stemming from tension caused by differences in goals and methods. Though established religion had come under attack during the revolution, this had not always been so, and much pastoral power lived on untouched in the myriad small communities that dotted the Bavarian countryside.[23] It is not entirely clear how far the process of change in communal politics had progressed by 1849.

Many historians have argued that Germany "modernized" in the nineteenth century—that Germany experienced economic growth and industrialization; centralization of the state; enlightenment in educational, intellectual, and religious areas; and population increase and the rise of the large urban city at the expense of traditional family life in the small towns and villages.[24] It is hard to deny that most of these changes occurred, although it is not clear that they were already present in Bavaria in 1849.[25] Even more questionable is the assertion that certain changes, such as increasing illegitimacy or declining religious piety,[26] were symptoms of modernization and not of other factors. Urbanization and industrialization were not yet very advanced.[27]

Critics of the "modernizationists" argue that the theory is wrong—that in the early nineteenth century a changing economy did not hurt the peasant family or community; that weakness in the church predated these events; and that though the state changed, it did not manage to successfully intervene in the social-economic functions of the community.[28] The number of small holdings in Bavaria actually increased in prominence, and the advent of machinery and subsequent industrial change did not occur until the late nineteenth century. Illiteracy rates of 40 to 50 percent still dominated peasant society in Bavaria in the late 1840s. The birthrate, too, was low in Bavaria between 1818 and 1852 (.067/year) compared with the rest of Germany, where only Württemberg was lower.[29] Whether justified in attacking the theory of modernization, the critics make a good case for seeing traditional society as still largely in place in midcentury Bavaria.

Although it is not easy to generalize with assurance, clerics and teachers seem to have begun to move in opposite political directions in Bavaria in the early nineteenth century. Catholic clergy were rarely democratic and more often promonarchical.[30] In Bavaria in 1848 the marked anticlerical attitudes of many democrats frightened Catholic priests, stimulating them into joining active conservative political organizations.[31] Similarly, few Protestant clergy could be called radical.[32] But some teachers played a significant role in the revolution in Bavaria in a wide variety of ways: in assemblies, in writing petitions, in associations, and in the press.[33] Participation of teachers in the revolution is borne out by the strongest evidence possible—the record of Maximilian's tough measures against disloyal teachers in the Palatinate and Lower Franconia, including dismissal, forced retirement, transfer, censure, and denial of promotion.[34]

Less is known about the political activity of mayors in Lower Franconia. The explanation for our limited knowledge may lie in the function of their office.[35] Largely administrators and probably drawn from the wealthier landowning peasantry, the *Vollbauer,* mayors were practical men for whom administration of their community was a job that directly affected their personal position as citizens and as property owners. As head of a council of representatives of the citizens, the *Bevollmächtigten,*[36] the mayors could act only on the basis of consensus. The smaller, rural communities remained remarkably stable during the revolution and acted as internally cohesive units when they bothered to act at all. One reason why about one-third of communal councils did not bother to seek support for their opposition to emancipation from the community at large in the form of signatures was their confidence that they genuinely and accurately reflected (or controlled?) communal consensus on important issues.[37]

Despite the evidence of active expression of communal opinion on political issues, it is risky to label communities as politically left or right, let alone liberal, democratic, or conservative. For example, many Germans perceived the revolution in contradictory terms. Peasants wished freedom from outdated obligations but opposed a republic and remained aloof from nationalism. Artisans wished revival of guild protections, opposed free trade and freedom of occupation, and showed little interest in nationalism. Some of both of these groups supported the revolution in 1848 but gradually either lost interest in it or came to oppose it in 1849 and later. The political sphere grew rapidly during these years, but not in a clear-cut, ideological fashion.[38]

Support for Emancipation

Judged only by the petitions sent to the upper house, very few communities supported Jewish emancipation in Bavaria. In addition to three Jews who sent in their own petitions, only three communities, Fürth, Hürben, and Erlangen, supported the bill. In Fürth, where 16 percent of the population were Jews and 76 percent were Protestant, the Citizens' Association, the mayor, and four members of the executive Committee signed the petition (see app. C, no.1). Fürth was unusual, if not unique, in having decided earlier to admit Jews to residence and full local citizenship. Few other communities of any size had done so.[39] The struggle over Jewish emancipation focused on exactly this issue of whether Jews should be granted full local communal citizenship. Jews, individually or in groups, had the right to petition supporting their own emancipation, and a few did. But petitions customarily came from communities, not individuals, largely excluding Jews from this aspect of the political process. In Hürben the communal executive submitted the petition, but only the three Christian members signed. Jewish members of the councils in Fürth and Hürben declined to sign to avoid charges of self-interest. But all knowledgeable observers knew that Fürth and Hürben supported the bill because so many Jews resided in each. In Erlangen, near Fürth, Jews were a miniscule .3 percent, but Protestants also predominated with more than 87 percent of the 10,910 inhabitants. There is no evidence of Jewish control over their Christian fellow citizens, as Zander argued;[40] rather, these petitions show genuine support for Jewish emancipation.

Evidence of some communal support may be found in the government reports. We should remember that the original directive of 15 December sought information about possible disturbances of the peace resulting from emancipation, and Hohe's directives to his subordinates of 18 December and 15 January also sought information about opposition to emancipation. Point four in Hohe's directive of 15 January, asking about "true, not fabricated," opinion, stimulated some officials to describe support for emancipation in writing their reports. Although no communities in Lower Franconia approved a petition for emancipation, state officials reported that 16 communities supported emancipation.[41] The official in one district, Marktbreit, stated in a bare-bones, two-sentence report that public opinion in his district favored emancipation.[42] Assuming that all 13 communities in Marktbreit supported emancipation, an assumption that would be almost certainly inaccurate, then out of 1,056 communities in all of Lower Franconia, no more than 29 (2.8 percent) were reported as favoring emancipation.[43]

In most cases officials reported that a majority of the general population opposed emancipation, implying the existence of a minority supporting it. The district director in Orb on the Hessian border noted that emancipation had "its defenders and its opponents, whose views only find expression in conversation and elicit no animosity."[44] In Rudenhausen-Wiesentheid, far to the east, the head of the police office noted that, though more citizens opposed than supported emancipation, the greater part of those dependent on the state (presumably officials) and the more insightful favored emancipation because they thought it would improve the Jews morally.[45] The district director in Würzburg left of the Main, where there were more communities favoring emancipation than any district other than Marktbreit, estimated that only the smallest part of the population, perhaps one-ninth, agreed with the decision of the lower house even if the bill were to be seen as "restricted emancipation"—that is, probably, as calling for partial emancipation but retaining the absolute veto and denying Jews the right to hold office.[46] No matter how one counts, it is hard to make a case that more than about 10 to 15 percent of the Lower Franconian population, including Jews, actively supported the emancipation bill.

A relatively small number of officials noted the prevalence of indifference and apathy to Jewish emancipation. Only five districts reported sentiment to be indifferent, nearly always in the briefest of official reports and with laconic wording.[47] These districts only reported that there was "no opposition" to emancipation in their districts, mute testimony, it would seem, to the directives' concern with identifying active opposition rather than active support.[48] Officials in a few areas commented on opinion among the educated. In Kissingen, for example, reports described the majority of the educated as favoring emancipation in principle. But in Schweinfurt the district director noted that "even the more intelligent part of the population, as I have often seen," preferred gradual emancipation, which is to say they opposed equality. And in Amorbach the head of the police office wrote that the greater part of the intelligent class openly opposed emancipation. In a few cases officials expressed frustration at the peoples' poor understanding of the meaning of emancipation.[49] Clearly, Jewish emancipation had captured the attention of the overwhelming majority of the citizens of Lower Franconia, but not their support.

In at least two cases Bavarian citizens successfully resisted moves by their community to approve a petition against emancipation. The first episode occurred in the community of Remlingen in the rural district of Marktheidenfeld.[50] Having learned of a petition against Jewish emancipation from the city of Marktheidenfeld, the mayor assembled the citizens by ringing the *Rathaus* bell three times. He then read the petition to all assembled. No single voice spoke for the Jews, and all favored the petition. In consequence the mayor placed a paper in the communal office for signatures. As the assembly ended, the brothers Seitz and their friends wrote on the paper first, and thereafter no one else would sign. The mayor went on to describe "true" opinion as opposing emancipation, if one judged by the assembly, but added that after the action by the Seitz brothers, it was impossible to separate "true" from "fabricated" opinion.

The mayor appended a copy of the paper on which the Seitz brothers and their friends had written. The brothers and their allies noted the role of the priest and of the local Pius Association in opposing emancipation and then quoted excerpts from the Bible, including Matthew 23:13: "Woe to you Scribes and Pharisees, Hypocrites! Because you shut the Kingdom of Heaven against men. For you yourselves do not gain, nor do you allow those going in to enter." Others noted the parable of the good Samaritan (Luke 10:25–27), the admonition to love your enemies (Matthew 5:44–48), the marriage feast (Matthew 22), and the advice to "Judge not that ye be not judged" (Mark 7). The last entry was appropriately from Luke 6:31: "And as you wish others to do unto you, do you the same to them." In Remlingen embarrassment seems to have prevented the appending of signatures to the petition.

In another case, in Obernburg, the communities of Grossostheim, Obernburg, and Wenigernstadt submitted petitions opposing emancipation. The district director reported that the community officials there were "goodthinking" and that sentiment in the district was opposed to equality. He added that the petitions would have been signed by all the citizenry if draper Bopp, the leader of the local democrats, had not spoken against the petition at the *Rathaus* and in his shop.[51] Thus it is possible to identify a few voices raised, not without some success, against the prevailing mood. But where were the numerous democrats of the previous year? Where were the democrats who organized and joined the bulk of the 283 associations in Lower Franconia?

Some had become apathetic, and some may have submitted petitions against Jewish emancipation.[52]

Because we lack any contemporary explanation of the absence of democratic support for Jewish emancipation, it may be useful to question what it meant to be a democrat in Bavaria and in Unterfranken in 1849–50. Numbers alone do not tell us much, and by winter 1849–50, democrats and democratic organizations may have declined substantially from their peak during the campaign for the Frankfurt Constitution in late spring 1849. Also, modern analysts should not assign a specific content and sophistication in thinking to anyone who chose to be called a democrat. Just as the democrats of Unterfranken in 1849 had proven to be far less radical than the government believed, so, too, democrats may have been more populist and less progressive than expected. Forced to confront a genuinely popular opposition to Jewish emancipation, democratic organizers may have chosen, pragmatically, not to undermine further their already rapidly shrinking political base by supporting a lost cause.[53]

The Opposition to Jewish Emancipation

According to the reports from the forty-nine administrative districts in Lower Franconia, the overwhelming majority of the people in the province opposed emancipation. If one discounts those who were apathetic, disinterested, lacked knowledge of the bill, or took no position, the number of those opposing emancipation must have outnumbered those favoring it by five or six to one. In the course of answering Hohe's question on "true opinion," thirty-five of the districts reported that the majority of people were opposed to Jewish emancipation. The reports indicated that all of the largest cities, Würzburg, Aschaffenburg, Ochsenfurt, and Schweinfurt, opposed emancipation.

Not all of the reporting officials described the status of opinion in cut-and-dried terms, and opposition varied in strength. Five districts were reported as only mildly or marginally opposed to emancipation. In the rural districts of Kitzingen and Miltenberg and the police district of Rudenhausen-Wiesentheid, the reports all used variations of the phrase "more were opposed than for" emancipation. In the rural districts of Ochsenfurt and Euerdorf, the reporting official noted the presence of sentiment for much of the legislation, but not for complete or full emancipation. Too much should not be inferred from these reports, but the wording seems to indicate a milder attitude than elsewhere.

Seventeen rural district directors described opinion as strongly opposed to emancipation. In Gemünden the director described the "entire district" as "very antiemancipation," and in Gerolzhofen the report stated that "no one" in any part of the district would be satisfied if Jews were emancipated. In Karlstadt the district director wrote that emancipation would find no welcome there. The reports called opposition "decisive" in Lohr, Marktheidenfeld, and Rothenfels; "overwhelmingly opposed" in Volkach; and "generally" opposed, especially by the greater part of the intelligent class, in Amorbach. When the reporting official ventured to estimate the opposition in numerical or percentage terms, the results were uniformly negative. In Aschaffenburg the city council[54] wrote that there was no local enmity between Christians and Jews and that the attitude toward emancipation was generally indifferent, but the report stated that if polled, two-thirds would vote against emancipation. The district director in Ebern listed 37 of 42 communities as opposed, in Markheidenfeld 13 of 16 (and here we have each of the local reports to verify the district director's report), and in Volkach 19 of 25. In Rothenfels 3 were indifferent, and all the rest, 14, were decisively opposed. In the districts around Würzburg, opposing sentiment was milder, but in Würzburg to the right of the Main river 12 of 24 opposed emancipation, and only 6 supported it; and in Würzburg to the left of the Main, 6 of 20 opposed the bill and only 2 supported it. Of the 10 remaining rural districts, several submitted reports that indicate indifference or ambiguity.[55] Marktbreit, as noted above, a smaller police district, was the only district described as supporting emancipation.

It is valid to question whether this evidence is reliable. The directive did not require district directors to request reports from the communities and to submit them as proof. The investigative and threatening character of Hohe's directive of 15 January makes the reports especially trustworthy. Emancipation was the government's bill, with the full weight of the state ministers, and apparently the king, behind it. In such a situation, opposition to emancipation, especially in the form of a petition to the upper house, might have been seen as a negative commentary on the stewardship of the district director. In Baunach, for example, the district director, hearing of a petition, pursued it with all the diligence of a prosecuting attorney, requiring testimony from all the suspected communities and from the local teacher who had copied out the petition in a good hand. Irritated at the pressure from above, an official leaked news of the director's behavior, and Zander used it to demonstrate government hostility to the petition campaign. In Ebern, where sentiment strongly opposed emancipation, the district director went to great lengths to assure the state of the loyalty of the communal council in the 1848 revolution. The city council of Ebern, concerned about its relations with the governor, emphasized its loyalty and constancy and expressed the belief, too clearly a hope, that action would not be taken against the city because it submitted a petition, which was their established right. In Heidingsfeld the city fathers expressed their respect for the humane principles of state government and their nonparty outlook before stating that they felt "obliged" to protect their rights with a petition. And in Hofheim the district director found it difficult to determine who had done what because of the intense secrecy surrounding the petition process. The situation was the same in Gemünden, where the mayor misused the communal seal and the organizers of the petition acted in total secrecy, forcing an irritated district director to depend on rumor for his report. In Bischofsheim, in reference to the preparation of a petition in Obernbach, the district director noted that "people point to the district director's circular as disapproval and cease [to organize the petition]."[56]

One of the most telling proofs of the role of the governor's office in the petition campaign exists in the form of a late and amended report from the rural district of Obernburg noting that the communal council of Grossmallstadt had approved a petition opposing emancipation, which the district director was forwarding to the governor for transmission.[57] Hohe drafted his reply, as usual, on the report itself, stating that the royal governor was not disposed to forward the petitions of individuals or of communities and community officials to a higher level, and adding, "Since, however, the royal Bavarian state government has laid a draft law *for* emancipation of the Jews before the Landtag, it will not do what does not lie in the realm of a lower office, that is, to represent an attempt of someone *against* the emancipation to the higher level." The directive of 15 January, Hohe stated, had not been intended to stimulate agitation for or against emancipation, "but rather only to produce knowledge of the factual relationships and the sentiment of the district." Thus the communal council of Grossmallstadt must send its petition on itself.[58] Hohe did not include this petition in the table of petitions submitted that he forwarded to Munich two days later. Despite Hohe's disclaimer, everyone knew the government backed the bill. If this knowledge had any influence, it must have worked to undermine support for opposition among the lower state officials, if not among the general population. Hence these reports probably understated the opposition out of a real or imagined fear of authority.[59]

Evidence of the reliability of the district directors' assessments of opinion and of the essentially democratic nature of its expression may be found throughout the reports in the descriptions of the petition process. The reports contain descriptions of entire communities in five widely scattered districts assembling to hear petitions read and to voice their sentiments for or against Jewish emancipation. This process has already been identified in Remlingen, where the Seitz brothers frustrated the opponents of emancipation, and three other communities in the same district assembled also. In Ebern the city council noted that most of the petitions from that area were similar and might appear fabricated, because they were drafted by the city secretaries. But they had been greeted by loud applause and signed, the report stated. In Werneck the district director reported that where there were petitions, the "assembled communities" had approved them. And in Neustadt on the Saale, five separate communities had met, heard, and signed, "nearly to a man," the petitions. In Heidingsfeld in the rural district of Würzburg left of the Main, the city council discussed and changed one draft, submitting a second to the citizens: led by the mayor and all of the councillors, 267 citizens signed at the *Rathaus* on a Sunday afternoon. Any who did not sign were absent, the report stated, only because of lack of time to attend the assembly.[60]

Because information on the process of approving petitions was not requested, the descriptions occur in reports from only five districts. But assembly prior to signing a petition was clearly a common method, and if serious discussion seldom occurred, it can be explained by the natural reticence of a largely uneducated populace and by the general agreement of these people with what they heard. When offered the opportunity, they applauded and signed in remarkable numbers.

To say that the reports are reliable and that the process was democratic in form does not mean that manipulation and leadership did not exist in Lower Franconia and Bavaria in the campaign against Jewish emancipation in 1849–50. Both were present, although it must be noted at the outset that neither are foreign to the democratic system or to political organizations. The question is not whether organizational activity by individuals and organizations existed but, as the Bavarian state itself wondered, whether their actions perverted the "true" opinions of the people. Were Bavarians who were originally for or indifferent to emancipation seduced into opposition?

Hohe, the head of the royal government in Unterfranken, specifically asked who initiated and prepared the petitions. This appears to constitute one question, but two separate pieces of information were, or could be, at issue: the petition's instigator and its preparer. Hohe's directive also asked whether the petition emanated from communal officials, communal members, or both.[61] Out of confusion, simple laziness, or pragmatism, some reporting officials lumped answers to these questions together. It was not always easy to separate these stages of the process from each other.

State officials in seven rural districts identified Catholic clergy as involved in one form or another in the opposition to Jewish emancipation. In nine additional districts, reports noted "clerical" influence, referred to the "clergy," or used terms like *Pfarrer*, which does not always indicate a Catholic priest. In a province where 80 percent of the population was Catholic, it is probable that many of these references point to involvement in the opposition by Catholic clergy. And it is surely significant that reports never identified Protestant clergy as involved in the agitation against Jewish emancipation. The reports mentioned a Pius Association in only one case, Gemünden, and none noted the presence of the Association for Constitutional

Monarchy and Religious Freedom. A few reports described the clergy as unsuccessful in producing a petition against emancipation. That happened in Remlingen, and another report described the failure of the *Pfarrer* in Goldbach, near Aschaffenburg, to produce a petition. In Schöllkrippe in the rural district of Alzenau, the local *Pfarrer* also failed, after a clash with the local mayor.[62] Still, in many cases the clergy successfully helped to organize petitions against emancipation.

Clergy, Catholic or Protestant, were not the only actors in this drama. Communal officials, usually the mayor acting alone or in association with the town councillors, played a crucial role in the petition process. Some, as in Marktheidenfeld, took it upon themselves to visit other communities to advocate petitions against emancipation. In Gemünden the mayor led the process and even misused the communal seal to do so. Several reports in nine different districts identified communal officials as leading or sharing the leadership of the petition process.[63] But this probably understates the influence and role of the mayors, who were the leading figures in organizing opposition to emancipation.

Some state officials also participated, sometimes very directly, in the campaign against emancipation. For example, in Bischofsheim, Karlstadt, and Marktheidenfeld, a tax official, a finance officer, and a higher tax assessor played active roles. The local count's finance officer, Eckert, prepared and wrote the petition in Bischofsheim. In Wiesenfeld and Steinbach in the rural district of Karlstadt, the finance official led the way, formulating petitions that the community officials then adopted as their own. In Marktheidenfeld the petition came jointly from the mayor and the royal tax assessor, the former communal secretary, Fasel. In Euerdorf, the royal finance officer, Wich, produced the petition, which may have originally come from Anton Ruland, who was a member of the lower house, a priest, and a leader of the opposition to emancipation.[64]

Reports from a handful of districts note the participation of the local teacher in the petition process, but almost always as a copyist. In RD Baunach the communal secretary, Marschall, of Kirchlauter, prepared a good copy of a petition. When questioned, Marschall emphasized that he had not himself done anything else with the petition, had not thought further about the matter, and "would now not do such a thing." But in Dettelbach the communal secretary not only furnished the good copy but circulated it to others in the area.[65] This raises the question whether all secretaries were the local teachers. If they were, the reports understate the participation of teachers, because they single out teachers in only two cases but refer to communal secretaries frequently. In either case, the teachers' task was the mostly prosaic one of presenting the antiemancipation petition in a readable form, with good grammar and in a legible hand.

Some private individuals took a hand in the formulation and spreading of petitions. Freiherr Fuchs was active in Würzburg and in some of the surrounding area. At least three deputies of the lower house, Ruland, Schaeffer, and Hetterich, were active in Euerdorf, Obernburg, and Alzenau.[66] The *Volksbote* editor, Ernst Zander, cooperated with Ruland in Euerdorf. And in Obernburg, the surveyor, Katz, wrote and published the petition, with the permission of the mayor. In Aub the district director stated that action against emancipation came from democrats; even so, he not only named none but went on to describe Catholic clergy as particularly active.[67]

References to "involvement" in the campaign against the emancipation bill by priests, mayors, rent officials, teachers, and other individuals misses the point. The entire experience of "addressing" Parliament was a communal preserve. Though individuals could influence the final result, the community submitted a petition. And in the communities the mayor and the council were the leaders. That was why, in what appears to be about one-third of the cases, only the mayor and council signed the petition, an action in keeping with tradition. Though not entirely new, signature of petitions by the citizenry, especially in a public assembly, was heavily the result of the democratizing effect of 1848. In only two cases, Arnstein and Dettelbach, did anyone attempt to circumvent this established procedure. In both cases participants in district conferences of poor relief officers tried to obtain approval by the mayors present for a collective address. But both attempts miscarried and became the basis for separate consideration by each community.[68]

The reports of the district directors of Lower Franconia portray a system in which the actual organizers or instigators of the petitions, their authors, the mayors and officers of the communities, and the communal members were all part of the same system and knew and accepted their roles. In Karlstadt the district director wrote that the clergy initiated the petitions in Zellingen, Laudenbach, Muhlbach, Karlburg, Rohrbach, Wiesenfeld, and Steinbach, which were then "immediately" adopted by the communal officials, circulated for signature, and submitted to the upper house under the signatures of both the communal officers and the local citizens. But the experience in the rural district of Neustadt a/S showed that the first steps could be reversed. In the community of Hellstadt, the royal *Pfarrer*, Kaiser, wrote and spoke for the petition, but in Wollbach the communal council initiated the petition, submitted it for discussion by the entire community, then requested the *Pfarrer*, named Burger, to complete the draft. In Brendlorenzen the communal council requested the deputy *Pfarrer*, Kempf, to draft a petition that the council then accepted and that the directors of poor relief and the school and church officers of the two communities signed. It was then read to the members at large, who accepted it with great applause. So, too, in Obernburg, in two separate cases, Grossostheim and Wenigernstadt, the petitions came jointly from the communal council and the parish office, were made public, and were signed by many. In Werneck the various parts of the community worked together to produce a petition that nearly everyone supported.[69]

In the rural district of Schweinfurt, the district director listed twelve communities (out of thirty-seven) that submitted petitions against emancipation. He identified the author-instigator of most of the petitions as clerical and noted that the petitions were usually submitted jointly by the communal council and the citizens, in several cases with their names or in the name of all the citizens. As far as distinguishing between "true" and "fabricated" opinion, the director added that it was difficult to do so because of religious fears. "It is easy," he wrote, "to get signatures from an entire community when religion leads and if one hears that Sunday will be replaced by the Sabbath." Despite his obvious distaste for the influence of the Catholic clergy, frequently ultramontane in tendency, the director concluded that most people opposed emancipation, "even among the more intelligent part of the people." He ended his report by advising the governor, "History has already often proven that fabricated opinion can be transformed into genuine opinion."[70]

Popular Justifications for Opposition to Emancipation

Although Hohe's directive of 15 January did not ask the district directors to explain why popular opinion opposed emancipation, twenty-eight provided some explanation, probably assuming that Hohe's request for an estimate of "true" opinion necessitated such an exercise. Many lower-level state officials and even more communal officials clearly described the reasons for opposition to emancipation in their locality. In some cases they explained the reasons given by supporters of a petition, but in many cases the officials intended to explain the motivations of the people in general. The reports of these state officials were usually objective but reflected their position as local residents as well as state officials. Although they were state functionaries, district directors often sympathized with the local population on the issue of Jewish emancipation. Many officials occupying the lowest rungs of the administrative ladder recognized that they would never ascend any higher (contrary to Zander's view noted earlier),[71] and these officials were unquestionably more sensitive to their neighbors' complaints than to talk about "humanity" and "equality." In some cases directly, more commonly indirectly, state officials showed their bias against Jewish emancipation while carrying out the directives issued from above. Others, but probably a minority, thought and felt the same as their superiors.

Officials reported that dislike and fear of the Jewish role in the economy prompted the most widespread and bitter reasons given for popular opposition to the emancipation bill.[72] The reports depicted the people as disliking and even condemning "Jewish" business practices, which they considered to be "shady," "tricky," "dirty," or "unfair." In these reports, Christians appear to have feared Jews because they thought Jews were naturally "better" at commerce, hostile to Christians, and too wealthy. Most of the reports imply or state that Christian perceptions of Jews were accurate reflections of reality.

Judging by the reports, many Christian citizens of Lower Franconia considered *Schacherhandel* a type of commercial dealing or, in more modern terms, a business method.[73] The district directors lumped *Schacherhandel* together with usury (*Wucher*), fraud or swindle (*Betrug*), or fraudulent (*betrügerische*) practices. With the exception of usury, the district directors seldom saw a need to be more specific. They employed this terminology to describe Jewish business. From their standpoint, such practices posed a moral rather than an economic problem. Thus the district director in Ebern, in a lengthy answer to Hohe's request for "true" opinion, explained that Christians did not respect a large part of the Jewish community because of their "fraudulent" commercial practices. He admitted that Jews were becoming artisans and peasants, but he argued that despite police controls, Jews still carried on all possible types of *Schacherhandel*. The mayor's report from Lengfurt in the rural district of Marktheidenfeld stated that Jews engaged in *Schacher* could not reform and would take advantage of emancipation. In Gerolzhofen the district director stated that Jews "never" adopted the form and lifestyle of others.[74]

Some reports repeat the argument that because Jews engaged heavily in trade and commerce rather than agriculture and crafts, largely due to earlier restrictions, and because Christians perceived these activities as damaging to the rest of society, emancipation should be made conditional on Jewish self-improvement. The city council of Würzburg wrote that if Jews "discarded" their "age-old" practices of fraud and *Schacherei*, Christians would repeal restrictions whose retention was seen, in the "popular consciousness," as "absolutely necessary" to Christian welfare. But belief or hope that Jews would improve on their own or, as some "insightful citizens" thought,[75] under the encouragement and stimulation of enacted emancipation, was rare in Lower Franconia in 1849–50.

Fear of Jews appears in the reports in a variety of different, though related, ways. In one of its most basic forms, fear of Jews derived from the widely held Christian belief that Jews were the enemies, even the "natural" enemies, of Christians. In some reports this fear is discernible in comments that if Jews got more freedom through emancipation they would use it to the disadvantage of Christians.[76] In other cases officials explicitly reported the fears of the populace. In Obernburg the district director wrote:

The people see Jewish equality not as a political act of justice, as progress, but rather as favoritism to their enemies and consideration for their disadvantage, as a setback to the material interests of the people to the benefit of a small class of state citizens; [they] see the Jew as he is on a daily basis and as he lives and trades among them, and not as he should become through the new legislation.

The district director's personal sentiment appeared in his conclusion, in which he stated that the law ought to be "strangled at birth," as should have happened to so many of "our March achievements."[77]

Behind much of the fear of Jewish economic dominance lay the conviction that Jews had an advantage over Christians because of their prediliction toward unfair business practices.[78] This perception was especially common in the rural areas that predominated in Lower Franconia and in Bavaria in general. The reports' portrayal of Jews as sly, cunning, and speculative appeared alongside a portrait of the peasant or "countryman" as simple, honest, and not interested in gain for its own sake.[79] The communal council of Ebern commented that no Christian "not spoiled by material interests" wished for Jewish emancipation. In Karlstadt the district director reported that the "simple peasant" came into contact only with the vulgar and dirty Jew, who had the country folk at his mercy.[80]

Some Christians saw Jews as superior to Christian Bavarians in business acumen. Alzenau's district director noted that opposition to emancipation stemmed from fear that if Jews received more freedom they would use "their talent for trade" to the even greater disadvantage of Christians.[81] The Dettelbach report stated that the people feared that after emancipation, "Jews would all settle especially in the prosperous communities [and] by their monetary wealth eventually acquire the better properties, making the less well-off and poor wholly dependent on them." In Karlstadt the district director wrote that the "fact" that "the Christian tradesman cannot prosper at all next to the Jewish" was the historical basis for Jew-hatred among the population of Franconia. In Ebern the district director described reform of the Jews as illusory because of their economic ability. Jews, he wrote, often founded a shop with only 200 or 300 gulden and in a few years had a business worth thousands and lent money at 20 to 30 percent interest.[82]

Officials in several districts reported that the people thought of Jews as wealthy, or in control of capital, and therefore to be feared as dominant in money matters. In Bischofsheim people feared the superiority of Jewish capital, in Hammelburg their "Geldmacht," in Lohr their "financial position," in the city of Würzburg their "overwhelming monetary power"; and in Amorbach the report described the people as openly stating their belief that the gentlemen in Munich who favored emancipation had been bought by the rich

Jews in Frankfurt am Main.[83] In Würzburg the city council saw the retention of the absolute veto as a means of preventing Jewish monetary domination.[84]

The reports show that Jews did not have to be wealthy to be feared in small communities. Some Bavarians in Lower Franconia were especially bothered that two community programs would be shared with Jews upon full Jewish membership in the community: first, administration of the funds each community owned as the basis for support of poor relief and education; and second, the rights of the common lands, essentially wood and pasturage, that many communities still possessed. In both cases the reports make clear a reluctance to admit Jews to the enjoyment of benefits built up over time by Christians.[85] Reports from Arnstein and Karlstadt specifically referred to wood rights, which were very significant in many areas. Wood was especially important to a preindustrial economy, and wood theft was a common crime.[86]

Opposition to emancipation on economic or material grounds, predominant in the attitudes of the residents of Lower Franconia, was not the sole motivation for the rejection of the bill. Among the changes in daily life that equality would bring, in principle, was the right for Jews to hold offices under the same conditions as any Christian. Criticism of this aspect of the law was quite common in the reports, appearing in eleven different district reports and in a few of the communal reports.[87] In several areas the reports described popular opposition to Jewish officials. In the small community of Kallbach in the rural district of Marktheidenfeld, too small in the residents' opinion to send a petition to the upper house, people feared that Jewish officials, true to their religion, would force the Christians to celebrate Sunday on the Sabbath.[88] In the much larger community of Ebern, the city council described Jews as reacting to the immanence of emancipation by "dreaming of the highest state honors" and "outdoing" themselves in putting on bourgeois airs. In direct response, the district director reported, the city organized its petition opposing emancipation.[89]

Reports from other districts directly stated that opposition to Jewish officials began with the principle that no Jew ought to have control over Christians.[90] The city commissioner for Aschaffenburg made this point quite clear:

> However, one cannot think of Jews as civil servants in a Christian state whose basis has been inherited in a way that is so inherently Christian; the idea conflicts with Christian consciousness. How could a Jewish judge accept an oath from a Christian . . . without [causing] irritation? If one allowed the Christian population of the City of Aschaffenburg man-by-man to choose, the great majority would state: "The Jew cannot be a person of authority over us."[91]

In some areas, for example in Gemünden, a similar response was clearly a part of the greater fear of Jews as hostile to Christians and dedicated to their ruin. However, in Bischofsheim the district director wrote that there was no "confessional" tone to the opposition, but that people feared the monetary power of Jews and the collusion of Jews with their fellows if in state service.[92] A general reluctance to admit Jews to state and communal offices, while varying in specific motivation from area to area, provided a firm basis on which to reject full emancipation. In several areas, notably in Würzburg, reports noted that if admission to state office, especially judicial office, along with the absolute veto, were eliminated from the bill, it would permit acceptance of the rest.[93] Thus Jewish office-holding in Bavaria became a shibboleth during the campaign against emancipation in 1849–50.

Religious considerations obviously played a role in the opposition to emancipation. Though it is difficult to separate religious motivation from economic, communal, or bureaucratic considerations, we must discount assertions that religion played no role in the campaign against Jewish emancipation. But there were very few reports of specific fears or opposition to Jews on solely religious grounds.[94] In Weÿhers, the general belief, which, according to the district director, could not be contradicted, was that Jewish religious principles not only did not forbid Jews from taking advantage of a Christian but actually encouraged it. Moreover, the director felt obliged to guarantee that "the genuine, pious (religious) and thoroughly uneducated Jew strongly believed this, and one holds it therefore as a weighty affair to place them [Jews] in political relations in complete equality with Christians." The mayor of Pflochsbach said essentially the same, but more bluntly: "So long as the children of Israel persevere in their Mosaic law, or their Talmud, no citizen or political equality [for them] can be wished by the local inhabitants; better a complete removal of them from Germany to Palestine, their origin."[95]

Residential Factors and Opposition

When Hohe reported to the minister of the interior in Munich on his actions in response to the initial royal directive of 15 December 1849, he wrote that he had contacted certain districts where there were many Jews in residence and others where he especially trusted the officials. Eventually, he decided to query all the districts under his jurisdiction, but his initial action reflects both the physical realities in Bavaria, where Jews and Christians were frequently segregated, and the idea that attitudes were especially important in areas where Jews actually lived. Evidence for that notion may be found in the fact that six different district directors in Lower Franconia volunteered information on the specific question whether opposition was greater or lesser in areas inhabited by Jews, a question never raised by the governor.

In the rural district of Aschaffenburg, the district director noted that Jews lived in five communities. When he asked each of their mayors about conditions there, he was told that no one opposed repealing restrictions on Jewish commerce, but that all opposed allowing Jews to enter state service. In the rural districts of Bischofsheim and Gerolzhofen, the district directors warned about complaints, agitation, and the preparation of petitions in communities where Jews resided and where there were none. In Marktheidenfeld, of twelve communities opposing emancipation, those with Jews (Bütingheim, Erlenbach, Homburg, Remlingen, and Urspringen) took a firm stand. Of the four that did not oppose emancipation, three (two small and prosperous and one poor) had little or no contact with Jews. In the remaining community, Neubrunn, ten Jewish families were resident, leading the district director to believe that the report of its communal council represented only the majority of the council, not of the residents. From Obernburg came the information that the harshest threats against Jews were found in areas where they resided, because Jews placed such heavy burdens on the Christians. And in Schweinfurt the district director, noting that a petition had been prepared in Schonungen, where Jews already resided, concluded that this proved the influence of the local *Pfarrer,* implying that, left to themselves, the residents would not have acted. However, in opposing full emancipation, the citizens of Heidingsfeld cited the presence of a large number of resident Jews as evidence of their knowledge of Jewish life and actions.[96] It is hard not to conclude that the presence of Jewish residents in a community was not a guarantee of acceptance of Jews by Christians.

There is better reason to see urban location as a significant factor influencing petitioning on Jewish emancipation. In two districts, Arnstein and Lohr, the district directors specifically noted that urban communities were more favorably inclined than rural ones to emancipation. In all the rural communities of the two districts, general dissatisfaction with the bill was "loud" and "grew visibly." In the rural district of Lohr the director reported that sentiment in the rural communities was decisively against, but in the small city of Lohr sentiment was more favorable. Likewise, the report from Alzenau described communities near cities as possessing "a more accurate conception" of what emancipation was and approval for it.[97] Even if the sentiment of the residents of cities also opposed emancipation, they were probably less decisively against than their country cousins, which provides some support for a similar conclusion reached in chapter 5.

Consequences

Unlike his earlier directive of 18 December 1849, Hohe's request for information on 15 January did not ask if sentiment against emancipation might induce the use of force. Yet a surprisingly large number of those reporting on the state of "sentiment" predicted agitation and violence if the bill were passed. Such a response has already been noted in the case of Gerolzhofen, and similar sentiments may be found in Hammelburg. Elsewhere the warnings were more specific, even if they differed in form. In Karlstadt the issue was the communal goods and wood rights, which, if lost, "would in any case lead to acts of force against Jews as a result, even if at the same time a political rising is not to be envisioned." The petition in Marktheidenfeld, accepted in four communities, quoted Representative Sepp on the need to use "self-help" to drive out or kill Jews who were sucking the economic blood of Christians. And in Neustadt a/S "a dangerous popular uprising" was to be expected if the bill passed, "which will certainly give vent to pogroms against Jews, as has already occurred [after] the passage of the draft bill by the second [lower] house, since on various occasions the windows in the Synagogue and . . . five Jewish [houses] were broken." In Obernburg the district director noted that one often heard the comment that if emancipation passed, in areas with Jews "one must help himself and a Hepp story [pogrom] approaches." In Amorbach the police official predicted that democrats from nearby Baden and Hessen wanted the bill to pass because they expected it to cause a general uprising that they could join.[98]

Too much should not be made of reports of the possibility of violence. In the upsets over the rejection of the Frankfurt Constitution only months earlier, the Bavarian state had demonstrated a remarkable readiness to believe the worst. That same mentality is apparent in the original action taken by the Ministry of the Interior immediately following the passage of the bill in the lower house in December 1849. Violence was an extreme form of political action and had been notably absent in 1848 and 1849 in most of Germany. The reports that form the basis for analysis of the activity in the petition campaign of 1849–50 in Unterfranken testify rather to a broad-based, complex set of attitudes that, taken together, show adamant refusal to accept the bill passed by their representatives in Munich. Moreover, the reports show that the lower levels of the state bureaucracy sympathized more strongly with the inhabitants of their districts than with their superiors in Würzburg or Munich.

The reports from Lower Franconia contain almost all the same reasons for opposition found in the analysis of the petitions, the press coverage, and the parliamentiary debates, and they reinforce our sense of the separation that existed between the lower and upper levels of Bavarian state and society. Communal councils and assemblies, though democratic in some sense, existed in communities that lived and acted homogeneously. Our sense of the public sphere and of politics as an arena where opposing forces contend appears inaccurate in describing most of communal Bavaria. Resistance to the outside and to interference from above is visible in the antagonism these communities displayed toward Jews, Parliament, and the state. Much of Bavaria resisted and rejected a political arena they commonly identified with Munich. Ultimately, the petition campaign against Jewish emancipation was a political movement, and we must ask what effect it had on the upper house.

NOTES

1. Bayerisches Staatsarchiv Würzburg (BStW), Regierung von Unterfranken, Präsidialakten (Prä), 325, 15 Dec. 1849.

2. See ch. 5 and app. B for the text of the directive of 15 Dec. 1849.

3. Georg Gustav Hohe was evidently acting governor with the title director of the Ministry of the Interior for Unterfranken; the titular governor was Freiherr Friedrich von zu Rhein, appointed 20 June 1849. See Walter Schärl, *Die Zusammensetzung der bayerische Beamtenschaft von 1806 bis 1918* (Kallmünz, Opf., 1955), 119.

4. BStW Prä 325, Reg.-Präs. Hohe to royal Bavarian minister of the interior, 31 Dec. 1849, noting that he had contacted areas where there were many Jews and where he had special confidence in officials. BStW Prä 325, draft and final copy signed by Hohe, 18 Dec. 1849. Letter sent to Würzburg, Aschaffenburg, Schweinfurt, Kitzingen, Karlstadt, Mellrichstadt, Hofheim, and Ochsenfurt.

5. These constitute the file Prä Rep. 0.0-3, 325. Originally sent to Munich, the file was returned after the bill failed in the upper house. The other provinces only submitted letters commenting on conditions.

6. BStW Prä 325, Hohe to all offices, Würzburg, 15 Jan. 1850, requiring responses by the 22nd. See app. B.

7. This is the opposite of the claim made by Eleonore Sterling, *Er ist wie Du*, 176–79, who probably only saw Hohe's report of 31 Dec.

8. M. Doeberl, *Entwicklungsgeschichte*, 171–73, 356, 358.

9. M. Doeberl, *Entwicklungspeschichte*, argued that Maximilian II was good for scholarship but not a strong or successful king; Günther Müller, *König Maximilian II und die soziale Frage* (Munich, 1964), argues the case for Maximilian as socially progressive. Karl Schleunes, *Schooling*, 150, sees Maximilian as conservative, as does Michael Dirrigl, *Maximilian II: König von Bayern 1848–1864*, 2 vols. (Munich, 1984), 1:745–46.

10. Leonhard Lenk; "Revolutionär-Kommunistische Umtriebe," 555–622. There is no good biography. Dirrigl's study, *Maximilian II*, considers only culture.

11. "Public opinion" is not an exact translation of this term; "popular sentiment" is more accurate literally, but public opinion is what was meant. On the occasion of Louis Napoleon's coup, the ministry queried all district directors on its possible affect on Bavaria; see BStA Würzburg, Reg. v. Unterfranken, Präsidialakten, Rep. 0.0.-3, 398, "Die Vorgänge in Frankreich von 2 Dez. 1851, re deren Einfluss auf die öffentliche Stimmung 1851." A similar intent may be seen in an essay contest sponsored by the state on solutions to social problems; see Edward Shorter, "Middle Class Anxiety in the German Revolution of 1848," *Journal of Social History* 2, no. 3 (Spring 1969): 189–215.

12. See R. Moldenauer, "Jewish Petitions," 188–99. More generally see Johann Heinrich Kumpf, *Petitionsrecht und Öffentliche Meinung im Entstehungs Prozess der Paulskirchenverfassung 1848/49* (Frankfurt am Main, 1983), and Diether H. Hoffmann, *Das Petitionsrecht* (Frankfurt am Main, 1959). Those relating to free trade have been used by Heinrich Best, *Interessenpolitik.*

13. Dieter Langewiesche, "Vereinsbewegung," 195–223.

14. Ibid.; see description on p. 217 and the app., pp. 232–33, which lists all 283.

15. Langewiesche, "Vereinsbewegung," 217.

16. See ibid., passim, and also Christoph Klessmann, "Zur Sozialgeschichte der Reichsverfassungskampagne von 1849," *HZ* 218 (1974): 282–337, who was largely only interested in the use of force.

17. Even in radical Mainz Ludwig Bamberger had to exert himself to move the local Citizens Committee to move beyond the compromises of the merchants and businessmen who dominated it. See S. Zucker, *Ludwig Bamberger: German Liberal Politician and Social Critic, 1823–1899* (Pittsburgh, Pa., 1975), 16–17.

18. Langewiesche, "Vereinsbewegung," 224–25.

19. Ibid., 221, 230–31; and see ch. 4 above on Würzburg, for opposition to the campaign.

20. See Jonathan Sperber, *Popular Catholicism in Nineteenth-Century Germany*, (Princeton, N.J., 1985), where he downplays their political role after 1849; Langewiesche, "Vereinsbewegung," 213–14, notes the founding of Pius *Vereine* in November 1848 in Lower Franconia.

21. Anton Doeberl, "Bewegung," 2:68, 9:498–99, 500–503. J. C. Bluntschli, *Denkwürdiges aus Meinem Leben*, 3 vols. (Munich, 1884), vol. 2, *München (1848–1861)*, 109–13, describes his participation in the Association for Constitutional Monarchy; he feared that the Frankfurt Constitution would "revolutionize" Germany, but he also wanted to reform the *Reichsräthe* and opposed use of Bavarian troops in Hesse in 1852 as absolutistic.

22. *Verhandlungen der Kammer der Reichsräthe*, Beilage bd. 3, 1850, Beilage 69, 380–81; Langewiesche, "Vereinsbewegung," 204–5, asserts that Zimmermann was wrong in seeing Catholics as politically active and sees their activity as individual rather than institutional. Catholics were not successful as such at the polls (citing *StAW* 1943/45, no. 9132, 9133). Hermann Greive, *Geschichte des modernen Antisemitismus in Deutschland*, (Darmstadt, 1983), 39–40, states that in Bavaria the ultramontane

Pius *Vereine* and the Association for Constitutional Monarchy and Religious Freedom were active among craft groups in supporting and spreading anti-Semitism. See my article "Rethinking," *CEH* 25, no. 2 (1993): 123–48.

23. See David Sabean's *Power in the Blood: Popular Culture and Village Discourse in Early Modern Germany* (Cambridge, 1984), for descriptions of life in a Württemberg village from the sixteenth to the late eighteenth century, documenting the position of the priest-minister.

24. See Werner K. Blessing, "Zur Analyse politische Mentalität und Ideologie der Unterschichten in 19. Jahrhundert. Aspekte, Methoden und Quellen am bayerischen Beispiel," *ZfbL* 343[3] (1971): 768–816.

25. Most of the analysis in Werner K. Blessing's, "Umwelt und Mentalität im ländlichen Bayern: Eine Skizze zum Alltagswandel im 19. Jahrhundert," *AfS* 19 (1979): 1–42, is drawn from the later nineteenth century.

26. See Fintan Michael Phayer, *Religion und das Gewöhnliche Volk in Bayern in der Zeit von 1750–1850*, (Munich, 1970), 251, who notes piety declining in about 1750, or before modernization.

27. See chs. 2 and 5.

28. W. Robert Lee, "Family," 107–8.

29. Ibid., 98–99, 89. For France, Eugen Weber, a modernizationist, argues in his *Peasants*, passim, that no significant change occurred until the generation prior to 1914, leaving most of the nineteenth century premodern at best.

30. Sperber, *Popular Catholicism*, 50, notes that in the Rhineland, only a small number of mostly young clergy were democratic. See his *Rhineland Radicals*, 438ff., 483ff.

31. Langewiesche, "Vereinsbewegung," 230–31.

32. Friedrich Willhelm Kantzenbach, "Protestantische Pfarrer in Politik und Gesellschaft der bayerischen Vormärzzeit," *ZfbL* 39[1] (1976): 171–200, could only find two or three active in 1848–49.

33. Werner K. Blessing, "Allgemeine Volksbildung," 565. But the author also describes teachers as too poor to buy newspapers, dependent on mayor and priest, fearful of state inspectors, and in general, pious, subordinate, and patriotic (510–13). Also see Schleunes, *Schooling*, 129–31, esp. his notes, for a good discussion.

34. Horst Hesse, "Politisches Verhalten bayerischer Beamter 1848/49," *ZfbL* 42[1] (1979): 127–46, esp. 146; this took place much later, in 1852 and 1853.

35. See Phayer, *Gewöhnliche Volk*, 138ff., for a discussion of the role of the communal mayor. In a broader sense, Walker, *Home Towns*, passim, argues that communities were naturally conservative in a nonideological, apolitical way.

36. Described by Mack Walker, *Home Towns*, 273. Also David Sabean, *Property, Production, and Family in Neckarhausen, 1700–1870* (Cambridge, 1990).

37. See ch. 5.

38. See, e.g., the discussions of the failure of the revolutions in Thomas Nipperdey, *Geschichte*, 663ff., and Hans-Ulrich Wehler, *Gesellschaftsgeschichte*, 2:759ff.

39. Jacob Toury, "Types," 59ff.

40. In the *Volksbote*, no. 336, 10 Feb. 1850, 2, Zander argued that the submission of the Hürben petition for emancipation with no Jewish signatories was an attempt to

make it appear to be Christian when, in reality, the 420 Jews in that city were its "lords and masters." No data is available for 1852; in 1861, the population was 1,168, and if Zander was right that 420 Jews resided there in 1849, they would probably have been about one-third of the total population.

41. BStW Prä 325, reports from Schweinfurt, 22 Jan.; RD Bischohsheim, 21 Jan. 1850; RD Volkach, 20 Jan. 1850; RD Wernecke, 21 Jan. 1850; RD Würzburg (not city), 21 Jan.; RD Würzburg rM, 25 Jan. 1850; the wording of the Schweinfurt report ("since there is no address against and no evidence of opposition, true opinion is in full agreement with the royal state minister") indicates a disingenuous report.

42. Ibid., Police Office, Marktbreit, 16 Jan. 1850; this was a police district, smaller than a rural district but functionally the same.

43. See Hanns H. Hofmann and Hermann Hemmerich, eds., *Unterfranken: Geschichte seiner Verwaltungsstrukturen seit dem Ende des alten Reiches 1814 bis 1980* (Würzburg, 1981), 61–65.

44. BStW Prä 325, RD Orb to governor, 21 Jan. 1850.

45. BStW Prä 325, police office to governor, 21 Jan. 1850.

46. BStW Prä 325, Würzburg RD, left of the Main, to governor, 25 Jan. 1850. The original draft read "1/6th."

47. In the rural districts Baunach, Bruckenau, Kissingen, Mellrichstadt, and Münnerstadt.

48. In the rural districts of Etmann and Rothenbuch and in three of the sixteen communities in RD Marktheidenfeld.

49. E.g., Bischofsheim.

50. BStW Prä 325, mayor of Remlingen to DD Marktheidenfeld, 18 Jan. 1850. This incident made the newspapers; see *NFräZ*, no. 363, 30 Dec., pp. 3–4; but this account claims the mayor did not read the petition and did say the law would give Jews control.

51. BStW Prä 325, Obernburg, 20 Jan. 1850.

52. See the discussion in ch. 5.

53. James F. Harris, "Arms," 133–60.

54. There were two reports from independent cities, one from the city commissioner, the other from the city magistrate.

55. Hassfurt, 6 Feb. 1850, reporting late, added that an address against was sent by a small community, Gresshausen, and that several other communities agreed. Hohe filed it, because it had no affect on the report.

56. Baunach to governor, 24 Jan.; Ebern, DD to gov., 18 Jan. and city council to DD, 17 Jan.; city of Heidingsfeld to DD, Würzburg r/M, 17 Jan.; Hofheim to gov., 20 Jan.; Bischofsheim to gov., 21 Jan.

57. RD to gov., Obernburg, 22 Jan. 1850 (received by the Präsidium, 23 Jan.).

58. Gov. to DD, Obernburg, Würzburg 21 Jan. 1850 (should be 23 Jan.). In the original, Hohe mistakenly named the community Grossostheim.

59. There is corroborating proof for this in the perceptions of the reasons for this legislation (see ch. 5).

60. Marktheidenfeld to gov., 25 Jan.; Ebern, city council to DD, 17 Jan.; Wernecke to gov., 21 Jan; Neustadt a/S to gov., 21 Jan.; Heidingsfeld to DD, 17 Jan.

61. See ch 4.

62. Gemünden to gov., 20 Jan.; Aschaffenburg DD to gov., 19 Jan.; Alzenau DD to gov., 20 Jan.

63. Marktheindenfeld DD to gov., 25 Jan.; Gemünden DD to gov., 20 Jan.

64. In Gemünden a government physician was also involved.

65. Alzenau DD to gov., 20 Jan.; Baunach DD to gov., 24 Jan.; Dettelbach DD to gov., 17 Jan.

66. Several members of the upper house were active in encouraging formulation of petitions, but not in Unterfranken.

67. Euerdorf DD to gov., 20 Jan.; Obernburg DD to gov., 20 Jan.

68. There is no reference to a petition by poor relief officials.

69. Karlstadt DD to gov., Neustadt a/S DD to gov., 21 Jan.; Obernburg DD to gov., 20 Jan; Wernecke DD to gov., 21 Jan.

70. Schweinfurt DD to gov., 22 Jan.

71. Schärl, *Beamtenschaft,* provides the record of state service for all above the level of *Landrichter,* making analysis of that large group difficult. However, judging by the higher levels, only a small percentage of those in lower positions gained promotion. Also, not all of the higher ranks were drawn from the lower ranks. Many entered the upper levels from other states, from the university directly, or from within a ministry. Study of the *Landrichter* level is both lacking and important.

72. Economics played a role in motivation in twenty-one districts, more than half of the thirty-five districts opposing emancipation.

73. Direct reference to *Schacherhandel* exists in seven district reports and three *Gemeinde* reports; individual reference was even more common, appearing in most of the remaining fourteen reports in which economic issues were found.

74. Ebern DD to gov., 18 Jan.; Lengfurt mayor and council to DD, 19 Jan.; Gerolzhofen DD to gov., 16 Jan.

75. Würzburg city magistrate to gov., 12 Jan; Rudenhausen-Wiesentheid police office to gov., 21 Jan.

76. So, e.g., in Alzenau, Aub and Schweinfurt.

77. Obernburg DD to gov., 20 Jan.

78. Thus explicitly in Aub and Lohr, implicitly in most of the reports noted earlier.

79. Can Bavarian peasants have been that different from French peasants? Compare Weber, *Peasants,* passim, who portrays the typical *paysan* as only interested in gain.

80. Ebern city council to DD, 17 Jan.; Karlstadt DD to gov., 20 Jan. See John G. Gagliardo, *From Pariah to Patriot: The Changing Image of the German Peasant 1770–1840* (Lexington, Ky., 1969), who shows that this positive image was only the product of the previous century.

81. Alzenau DD to gov., 20 Jan.; and in Munnerstadt the only opponent of emancipation to speak out was an artisan who feared damage to his business as a consequence of the bill.

82. Dettelbach DD to gov., 17 Jan.; Karlstadt DD to gov., 20 Jan.; Ebern DD to gov., 18 Jan.

83. Bischofsheim DD to gov., 21 Jan.; Hammelburg DD to gov., 19 Jan.; Lohr

DD to gov., 19 Jan.; Würzburg city council to gov., 17 Jan.; Amorbach pol. ofc. to gov., 22 Jan.

84. Würzburg city magistrate to gov., 17 Jan.

85. See especially Heidingsfeld, in the rural district of Würzburg, l/M.

86. Josef Mooser, "Property and Wood Theft: Agrarian Capitalism and Social Conflict in Rural Society, 1800–1850: A Westphalian Case Study," in Robert G. Moeller, ed., *Peasants and Lords in Modern Germany: Recent Studies in Agricultural History* (Boston, 1986): 52–80. Also Günther Franz, "Agrarische Bewegung," 176–77, 176–93.

87. In Würzburg, Arnstein, RD Aschaffenburg, Bischofsheim, the city of Ebern, RDs Euerdorf and Gemünden, the communities of Holzkirchhausen, Marktheidenfeld, and Kallbach in RD Marktheidenfeld, the city of Heidingsfeld in RD Würzburg, and in the police offices of Kreuzwertheim and Rothenfels, including the community of Karbach.

88. Würzburg, Arnstein, Kreuzwerthheim, Rothenfels, and the community of Kallbach in RD Marktheidenfeld.

89. Ebern city council to DD, 17 Jan.; Ebern DD to gov., 18 Jan.

90. In RD Aschaffenburg and the city of Heidingsfeld, RD Würzburg, l/M.

91. Aschaffenburg city commissioner to gov., l9 Jan.

92. Gemünden DD to gov., 20 Jan.; Bischofsheim DD to gov., 21 Jan.

93. Würzburg city council to gov., 17 Jan.

94. Religion was only mentioned, as such, in eight districts.

95. Weÿhers DD to gov., 17 Jan.; mayor of Pflochsbach to pol. ofc. of Rothenfels, l9 Jan.

96. Aschaffenburg DD to gov., l9 Jan.; Bischofsheim DD to gov., 21 Jan.; Gerolzhofen DD to gov., 16 Jan.; Marktheidenfeld DD to gov., 25 Jan.; Obernburg DD to gov., 20 Jan.; Schweinfurt DD to gov., 22 Jan.; Heidingsfeld city council to Würzburg r/M DD, 17 Jan.

97. Arnstein DD to gov., l9 Jan.; Lohr DD to gov., 19 Jan.

98. See responses to first directives of 18 Dec. from Hofheim (27 Dec.) and Ochsenfurt (26 Dec.) predicting agitation and violence; this was not noted in later reports following the directive of 15 Jan.

Chapter 7

Quick Defeat and Slow Progress, 1850–71

By mid-February when the *Reichsräthe* met to discuss the bill for Jewish emancipation, the debate was largely anticlimactic. The press predicted defeat, largely because Count Rechberg, the bill's original floor manager, had fallen ill and had been replaced by, ironically, another Count Montgelas, who was perceived as opposed.[1] True to form, Montgelas reported the committee result to the upper house, recommending rejection of the bill on 3 February 1850. By then other members of this aristocratic assemblage had even taken the trouble to personally encourage the writing and submission of petitions against the bill.[2] But it was not clear how much pressure the government would or could exert to secure a favorable outcome.

In his committee report, Montgelas took the position that though all agreed to the necessity of reforming the laws regarding Jews, equality was out of the question because it would mean that Bavaria would cease to be a Christian state. Here and later Montgelas reiterated his desire that Bavaria not become an "indifferent" or "naked" *Rechtsstaat* in which man-made law would supersede divine. He reasoned that to alter the state in such a fashion was a constitutional change requiring an amendment to the constitution. Responding to the argument, made in the lower house and the press, that because Bavaria had already given Jews the right to vote, hold elective office, and sit on juries, it should not exclude them from other similar and lesser rights, like residence, Montgelas asserted that the earlier (June 1848) grant of privileges did not necessitate further gifts. He cited Freiherr von Thon-Dittmer, then the minister of the interior, who had stated during the 1848 debates that granting some rights did not mean that more would necessarily follow.

Montgelas feared that Jewish emancipation would result in an extraordinary increase in the number of resident Jewish families in Christian communities previously without Jews, although he did not explain how this could occur statistically in a state in which there were not enough Jews to accomplish what he predicted.[3] Montgelas also compared the large numbers of petitions opposing emancipation with the handful in favor. He summarized the petitions as concerned about Jewish officials and the dangerous Jewish economic threat.

Montgelas's committee report was the first substantive evidence that the upper house was not favorably inclined to Jewish emancipation, which could not have surprised anyone. The upper house had long been antiliberal, agreeing to reformist legislation in 1848 only reluctantly and under pressure both from below, through the popular force of democracy, and from above, from an anxious monarch and his pragmatic, moderate ministers. As popular support for reform rapidly ebbed in 1849, the upper house quickly returned to a more conservative stance, placing it in conflict with a government still inclined to push some reformist legislation, even if only to blunt the criticisms of disappointed democrats and liberals. The powerful popular opposition to the bill for Jewish emancipation provided the upper house with a perfect opportunity to reject a key piece of reform legislation with relative impunity under the mantle of the peoples' will. By doing so, that ultraconservative body could reassert its independence both from the liberal lower house and from the moderately conservative royal government.

In contrast to the debates in December in the lower house, the officers and a clear majority of the members of the upper house opposed the government's bill and did not cooperate with the ministers. The committee did not invite ministers, including von der Pfordten, to its deliberations,[4] and Montgelas's report opposing emancipation opened the debates in the *Reichsräthe* on 15 February 1850. But the debates were serious, and outright rejection of the emancipation bill might have been avoided despite the ultimate lopsided defeat. Discussion of the bill occupied all the session on the fifteenth and much of that on the sixteenth of February 1850. These debates were not as lengthy as the debates in December, because most of the arguments and positions were well known by then, and speakers needed less time to make their points. Because the upper house was numerically less than half the size of the lower house, the debates should be regarded as about the same length.

The committee's report began the discussion by recommending rejection, so supporters of emancipation were on the defensive throughout the debates. In addition to all the arguments previously made, both pro and con, the "will of the people" loomed much larger in the upper house because of the petition campaign. Reference to the petitions figured prominently in every major speech by opponents of the bill and made it difficult for supporters to endorse the bill without simultaneously denigrating public opinion. The most important and interesting statement of the strength of the petitions opposing emancipation came from Freiherr von Zu Rhein, the governor of Lower Franconia, who had been nearly invisible during the petition campaign, when Hohe, his deputy, had done the work of that office. Not content with using the petitions to oppose the bill, von Zu Rhein cited information from the reports on activity in Lower Franconia (those that form the basis of chapter 6). He argued that opposition to Jewish emancipation was solidly popular in that province, and he maintained that the government knew it but had not presented to the upper house either that information or other data it had on the social and economic position of Jews.[5] Although von Zu Rhein's speech showed a breach in the governmental front, public opinion was the most important single issue of these debates, and the interpretations of the meaning of the petition campaign best define the opposing political groups in the upper house.

From the start supporters of emancipation in the upper house recognized the strength of the opposition there and its popular base in the country. Joseph Ludwig Graf von Armansperg (1787–1853), the first to speak in favor of the bill, sought new ground on which to fight the legislative battle, suggesting either sending the bill back to committee for revision or, more importantly, amending the bill to apply only to emancipation of Jews in the areas of civil law and procedures. He stated his support for the bill as it stood but also his recognition of and respect for the voice of the people.[6] His approach was obviously pragmatic.

Dr. von Ringelmann, minister of the interior for church and schools, followed von Armansperg in the list of supporters[7] and stated the government's position on the "agitation" that had broken out only after passage in the lower house in December: "The government is not indifferent to the agitation; it cannot be allowed to go unheeded regardless of its source. Nevertheless [the government] has not yet found a reason to see its position of May [1849] as in error." He then reviewed the major arguments against the bill, answering them with essentially the same reasons he had employed in the lower house. Von Ringelmann made two important new points at the end of his lengthy speech: first, that the government was prepared to agree to a modification of the bill relating to the absolute veto over residence based on recognition of the voice of the people; and second, that he interpreted the government's phrase "the necessity of emancipation" as meaning "some form of emancipation," not necessarily "full" emancipation.[8] Even von der Pfordten argued that because everyone appeared to desire some form of improvement in the condition of the Jews, differing only on how much freedom to grant them immediately, the bill should return to committee to be rewritten in a form acceptable to the *Reichsräthe*.[9] Like von Armansperg, the ministers von Ringelmann and von der Pfordten made it clear that the

Bavarian government, faced with the opposition of a majority in the upper house claiming the support of the people in the petition campaign, would take what it could get.

Montgelas was unwilling to compromise, replying to the government's offer of modification of the bill by arguing that it should not be returned to a committee that had already solidly approved rejection. Montgelas's refusal to return the bill to committee had several consequences. Though all agreed that the unamended draft bill from the lower house should somehow be modified, it was still not clear who should modify it and how. Montgelas's position was that because the government had written the bill poorly, it, not the upper house, should now rewrite and resubmit it. In the meantime the bill was on the floor, and Montgelas pushed for a simple vote to accept or reject it.[10] To improve the chances of returning the bill to committee or passing it, von der Pfordten pointed out that if the bill were rejected, the government could not constitutionally submit a new draft until the next regular session of the legislature.[11] As the highest ranking minister in Bavaria, von der Pfordten insisted that a defeated bill could not be resubmitted to the same session and that rejection would therefore mean a delay of perhaps three years. This was obviously a ploy to try to win a vote or two.

Debate late on the fifteenth focused on returning the bill to committee because that appeared to be the easiest path to compromise. Several members spoke in favor of doing so.[12] In the end a proposal by Niethammer, Arnold, and von Armansperg for return to committee was put to a vote and failed narrowly, 18 to 16, in what was clearly the major turning point in the bill's brief life on the floor of the upper house. That defeat ended the debate. Only the floor manager of the committee report, Count Montgelas, and the state ministers could speak again in the session, which continued the following morning at 10 A.M.[13]

On the sixteenth von der Pfordten spoke first and made a strong effort to salvage the bill. In addition to answering points raised by a number of opponents, von der Pfordten again admitted the reality of opposition to Jewish emancipation, adding only that some doubted whether the petitions represented the majority of Bavarians, and insisting that an administration must decide important issues not by petition but by parliamentary discussion and decision.[14] Montgelas responded to von der Pfordten by maintaining that public opinion was also represented in the upper house based on petitions written and submitted to it after the decision by the lower house. He concluded by supporting clarification of the situation for Bavarian Jews through a vote for or against the bill, so that Jews could decide to stay in Bavaria or leave for a land that offered them more rights.[15] By favoring rejection of the bill, Montgelas publicly indicated his desire that Jews leave Bavaria.

In a last ditch attempt to sway some votes, Minister of Justice von

Kleinschrod reiterated the delay of needed reform that would result from resubmission of a revised bill and urged immediate passage.[16] It did no good. The *Reichsräthe* rejected the bill entirely by 29 to 7, defeated von Armansperg's amendment to limit emancipation only to civil law by 24 to 12, and crushed a motion by Niethammer to ask the government to submit a new bill for equality in civil rights by 31 to 5.[17] All three crown princes voted with the majority, and Duke Maximilian of Bavaria, deliberately absent, made his support for rejection plain.[18]

Even at the time it seemed clear to many observers that the rejection of the bill for Jewish emancipation was part of a political struggle between the government and the upper house. The best contemporary analysis of this struggle appeared in the *Augsburger Allgemeine Zeitung,* but it was clear to all.[19] Two days after the vote, von Giech, a moderate member of the *Reichsräthe,* wrote to von der Pfordten. He said nothing about Jewish emancipation, but his warning about the ultramontanes appears to have been influenced by their victory in the case of Jewish emancipation. Based on information from von Armansperg and from his well-connected sister-in-law, Henriette, he warned von der Pfordten that the ultramontanes would no longer tolerate the Protestants, among them of course, von der Pfordten. Referring to the *"Heillose"* position and sentiment of the majority of the upper house, he cautioned that, in the coming amnesty issue, it could mean a change of ministry. The ultramontanes would, he added, find support in the upper house and in public opinion, and the king could not ignore them.[20]

The Catholic-Protestant tensions noted by von Giech and von Armansperg were not new. Religious differences had influenced Bavarian politics at both the electoral and parliamentary levels for years. Like von der Pfordten, von Giech was a Protestant and was in the minority in the upper house both as a Protestant and as a liberal.[21] His leadership of the few supporters of emancipation in the upper house was not propitious considering his background. In the late 1840s he had been highly critical of the conservative minister von Abel and even of Ludwig I. In March 1848 he had personally lobbied Maximilian II in favor of a reform of the upper house. In 1848 he served as the leader of reform by supporting the legislation emanating from the lower house, and he apparently supported a Prussian monarchy in Germany despite his sister-in-law's advice that all Old Bavarians, not merely ultramontanes, opposed it largely on confessional grounds. But by the time he took the latter stand, von Giech had long been alienated from King Maximilian.[22]

Von Giech was well informed on the issue of Jewish emancipation in late 1849 and early 1850, as a result of correspondence with Baron Jakob Hirsch of Gereuth, who had complained to him of the anti-Semitic agitation of the "black party" or Catholics. On the floor of the *Reichsräthe,* von Giech supported emancipation and opposed the notion that Parliament could not give Jews civic equality because Bavaria was a Christian state. Rather than take a dogmatic and subjective view of the state, von Giech argued that the state was an ideal based on the reality of Christian culture. In his view the state was "strong enough to be able to accept foreign elements without thereby losing its essence." Though not a very "democratic" theory, this was far more tolerant than the Catholic, ultramontane, Old Bavarian position.[23]

Because much of the newspaper press had accurately predicted the rejection of Jewish emancipation by the *Reichsräthe,* coverage of its debates differed substantially from coverage of the lower house's deliberations. Roles reversed themselves. The supporters of emancipation were now critical, and the victorious opponents, formerly so raucous, were quiet and restrained. Newspapers provided summaries of the important speeches, but at less length than in the debates in the lower house in December. Newspapers supporting the bill sadly noted the parliamentary attempt by von Armansperg to save the bill by returning it to the committee for modification. Most also totted up who had voted for and against, noting especially the six (out of thirty-eight) who voted yes: Hohenlohe, von Giech, Arnold, Reigersberg, von Armansperg, and Heintz. Several highlighted the absences of Duke Maximilian and Bishop Urban and the votes for rejection by all three royal princes.[24] Other papers noted that because of the bill's complete rejection, it could not be amended by the lower house in the current session but would have to wait until the next full session of Parliament.[25]

Postmortem analyses of the debates and the rejection in the upper house appeared in several newspapers. Zander's *Volksbote* happily wrote that the Christian people who trusted in the upper house had not wasted their efforts using their right of petition. For two years, Zander added self-righteously, the democratic inflammatory press had tirelessly fought the upper house, calling it an enemy of the people, but it, not the lower house, had given the people a voice in this affair.[26] Other papers agreed with Zander's analysis of the role of the upper house, but not so happily.

The *Augsburger Allgemeine Zeitung* argued that the bill itself was not the issue, because it would pass in the next legislative session. The issue was the power of the upper house.[27] Similarly the *Mittelfränkische Zeitung* called the upper house the "Constitutional Institute of the Blind" in its lead article of 24 February. The ministry, it argued, had not acted on the basis of philosophy but had hoped to secure sixty thousand supporters of the state (Jews), and, by rejecting emancipation, the upper house had shoved the Jews rudely back into the opposition.[28] The *Neue Fränkische Zeitung* also was thoroughly disgusted with the upper house, printing several condemnatory poems and articles by Graf von Trockau, who pronounced its death rather prematurely on 21 February, concluding on 24 February with the hope that the lower house would now reform the upper.[29] The *Regensburger Zeitung* warned the "gentlemen" of the upper house of the irritation their decision had caused. They had, it asserted melodramatically and inaccurately, lost public credibility.[30]

Democratic newspapers indulged in self-criticism both during the campaign and in the wake of the rejection. In part this was symptomatic of a more general recognition that times had changed, that the furor and radicalism of 1848 had passed.[31] The change was hard to ignore in the face of new legislation severely restricting the activity and even existence of associations, especially political associations, and the institution of strict new controls on the press.[32] But the self-criticism probed deeper, as evidenced by a poignant article in the *Neue Fränkische Zeitung* on 20 December 1849. The lead article bemoaned the lack of any significant democratic activity and explained the cause very simply: "[The left] found the people in the greatest part of the fatherland not mature enough, logically [and] legally using the parliamentary way, to protect and maintain their rights." It concluded that the solution was to educate the people, because the power struggle was over and the battle of ideas had begun.[33] In a retrospective of 1 January 1850, the paper saw 1849 as the year in which the left reaped the damaging harvest produced by the mob murders of two conservative members of the Frankfurt Parliament, Auerswald and Lichknowsky, on 16 September 1848, and the armistice of Malmø ending the Danish war in the same month.[34]

The *Neue Würzburger Zeitung* took a remarkably similar approach in late February 1850 in a lengthy article entitled "Die Grundlagen." This article maintained that the contraction of the popular base supporting action from very broad to very narrow was natural after all that had happened, because the people were "tired and lifeless" and indifferent about the future. In its opinion, the "biggest fault of the German Volk" was that it was politically fickle, bouncing from extreme favor to extreme indifference, unable to assert itself as sophisticated people should. The new laws restricting political association and the press were deliberate rejections of the revolution, and those who pretended not to hear the thunder deceived only themselves. Rejection of the law for Jewish emancipation was not significant, because its time had come and it would be eventually passed. As for a popular turn to the right, the article weakly and enigmatically concluded, "If an age of petitions should be introduced by those for whom, earlier, this was unacceptable, one must warn against sending petitions against petitions."[35] On the political right, the *Lechbote* predicted that the best result of the petition campaign would be to isolate the leaders of the *Märzvereine,* school teachers and physicians, in the villages.[36]

Criticism of weak royal support for the bill, of an anachronistic upper house, and even of a fickle populace, all true to some extent, avoided the question of popular attitudes toward Jews. Arguing, at least by implication, that Jewish emancipation failed because the revolution failed ignored both the total absence of support for the Jews from the popular left and the amazing outpouring of opposition from the popular right. Political activity in general, and particularly on the left, had receded, but Jewish emancipation was not really a revolutionary issue—it was proposed by a moderate conservative administration after the final failure of the revolution in June 1849. And the repressive laws on association and the press did not appear until the beginning of the debate in the upper house, after the petition campaign was over.

Soon after rejection of the bill, most of the newspapers turned their attention to other matters, and Jewish emancipation largely vanished from the press. But reaction by Bavarian Jews to the rejection was still news. In Munich the Jewish community organized a petition thanking the lower house for its support.[37] Other Jews began to discuss emigration more seriously. The *Regensburger Zeitung*'s Würzburg correspondent reported that wealthy local Jews were preparing to emigrate, commenting that "the money leaves and the usurers stay."[38] The *Allgemeine Zeitung des Judentums* reported from Munich that rich Jewish families there were also preparing to leave and were refusing to buy bonds paying for the conversion from feudalism, which had seriously fallen in value as a result.[39] In Würzburg the *Neue Fränkische Zeitung* published a very bitter article in which a Jew advised other Bavarian Jews to seek self-emancipation through emigration. The unknown author's pessimism stemmed, the author wrote, from the frustration of watching emancipation lose despite the support of the king, the ministers, and more than two-thirds of the lower house, and with the powerful support of the press, excepting only a few vulgar papers of the ultramontanes. When, he asked, would such a favorable constellation of supportive forces recur? Thanking the liberal press, the author urged immediate departure of the Jews.[40]

The author of the article in the *Neue Fränkische Zeitung* did not discuss directly why the bill had been rejected but implied that it was more than merely a "parliamentary" defeat in the upper house; it was a condoning of the stereotypical portrait of Jews presented by Montgelas. Perhaps because it was so obvious, no paper analyzed the depth and breadth of opposition to Jews and Judaism expressed in the petition campaign initiated and encouraged by Zander and the *Volksbote*. Hope for reform of the upper house could not offset the hostility of popular opinion toward Jews. Even if a new emancipation bill passed in the near future, an event that was by no means as predictable as the *Augsburger Allgemeine Zeitung* made it appear, Bavaria could not be seen as desiring Jews to be resident citizens. How could Jews ignore the appearance of posters on the *Theatinerkirche* in Munich proclaiming Maximilian II the king of the Jews?[41] How could Jews ignore Zander's New Year's wish that they should all go to California, find lots of gold and political rights, and thereby emancipate Israel from Bavaria and the reverse, helping both?[42] One week prior to the consideration of emancipation in the upper house, the *Volksbote* published a vicious anti-Semitic brochure that had originally appeared in Vienna, entitled "The Plea of the Christian Slaves to their Jewish Masters for Christian Emancipation." The prestigious *Historisch-politische Blätter für das katholische Deutschland* approvingly reprinted it.[43] Jews could not ignore that the Catholic church, which cared for the spiritual concerns of 70 percent of the Bavarian people, nearly uniformly supported opposition to emancipation. The emigration of Jews from Bavaria in the 1850s and 1860s stemmed in large part from this hostile, anti-Semitic atmosphere that the campaign against Jewish emancipation brought into the open.

Despite the crushing defeat, Maximilian's ministers immediately began to prepare new legislation designed to provide relief from the most obvious of the civil restrictions of the law of 1813 under which Bavarian Jews lived.[44] A draft of a bill to this effect first appeared in the ministerial council on 5 December 1850, presumably as the result of instructions from von der Pfordten or even Maximilian.[45] The draft simply abolished all differences between Jews and Christians in civil law, stating that the laws applied to marriage, property rights, and inheritance. In all these areas, the same civil and procedural laws that governed Christians were to apply to Jews.[46] This simple bill became law after quick and painless acceptance by both houses and signature by Maximilian on 29 June 1851.[47]

The drafting, consideration, and passage of the 1851 law for Jewish equality with Christians in civil law matters was almost lightninglike because the idea of "improvement" had already been accepted by many opponents of full equality. Many legislators opposing the 1849 bill had stated their willingness to accept such changes and, even if they had decided to do so, could not afterwards easily reverse themselves.[48] For most deputies, this was not an area under dispute. In his introduction to the draft, von der Pfordten stated that the government's bill had only failed in the previous legislative session because of issues involving citizenship and residence rights rather than civil law. Since the timeliness of repeal of restrictions in civil areas was still valid and compelling, the government submitted new legislation.[49] The government clearly meant to obtain all the legal reforms it could as quickly, cleanly, and painlessly as possible.

By reverting to the pre-1849 policy of asking for substantially less than full equality, the government stimulated the lower house to revert to its earlier policy of pushing the government to do more than it did. In addition to passing the government's new bill, the lower house requested and the upper agreed that the king submit new draft legislation, as soon as possible, to change the form of the Jewish oath and to repeal the police laws and ordinances relating to Jews, but not to affect prior political laws or the right of residence.[50] Von der Pfordten took the position that the results of these reformed laws should be known before pursuing new legislation. Thus the formal reply to the houses of Parliament reporting the royal approval of the law just passed also stated that the government was not yet clear about the additional requests—that is, about the oath—and "reserved its opinion" on the rest.[51] The documents, discussion, and debates convey the distinct impression that the government, once burned, was now more than twice shy.[52]

Continuing governmental reluctance to try for too much reform too quickly is also apparent in a law passed and approved in early 1852 concerning the sale and subdivision of estates. At first glance this legislation would appear to have nothing to do with Jews, but the reality was quite different. The law punished with a jail sentence and a fine anyone who sold landed estates in smaller parcels or who engaged in such action as a broker or in any commercial way. The historian of the legislative process of emancipation in Bavaria, Schwarz, emphasizes that this law was not directed only against Jews as earlier legislation had been, signifying a "further equalization [of Jews] with Christian citizens."[53] Schwarz was right to note the difference, but he missed the broader significance of the law. Opposition to the subdivision of estates had been a major complaint of the agricultural elements in Bavaria against both the Frankfurt Constitution and the bill for Jewish emancipation.[54] Passage was partially a sign of the success of the conservative right and targeted Jews in all but name. It was not a mark of progress, however much importance one attaches to the phrasing of the law. One may read the law as an attempt to bring similar pressure to bear on those Christians who were adopting "Jewish" business methods.[55]

Following several years (1846–51) of relatively intense activity in the ministries, Parliament, and the press for Jewish emancipation, the decade between 1851 and 1861 showed little legislative concern with Jews. In comparison to the immediate past, what stands out is not only a lack of success in reforming the law of 1813 but a lack of initiative in general. In respect to Jewish emancipation and to political life as a whole, the 1850s resemble the 1820s and 1830s. Into this vacuum stepped a few individuals and communities. Thus Mendel Rosenbaum of Zell wrote several petitions requesting reform.[56] More important than the interests of a few supporters of emancipation and an equally small number of activist opponents[57] was the change in governmental attitude.

The difference in the state's perception of Jews and of revision of the Jew Law of 1813 first appears in a lengthy report on the issue of reform, occasioned by a request by a Jew for residence in Munich over the quota.

Although the request became moot when the applicant, Heinrich Murr, obtained a vacated residence number, the government had already ordered yet another report on Jews in Munich, which was submitted in due course. As always, the city council gave the police director of Munich the task of investigating the issue, although the council also asked the city court for its opinion. The report provided both facts and advice.[58]

After noting that 1,183 Jews, including those with residence permits, lived in Munich, the report stated that only three criminal cases involving Jews had occurred since 1849. The police noted very rare instances of complaints on commercial grounds, with the exception of usury (underlined in pencil by someone then or later), in which Jews accounted annually for about 10 percent of all investigations. Out of 168 Jewish families, 139 pursued the trade that they had used to obtain residency, and 30 had changed to another occupation, usually involving money and commerce. The report stated that Jews tended, although not exclusively, to engage in business and to avoid pursuits with less chance of profit. It also stated that if Jews continued to pursue the trade they had used to obtain residency, they did so only as a sideline. By their "tireless" drive for profit, it concluded, Jews exerted a debilitating influence on Christian tradespeople despite existing restrictions. Its advice to the government was to retain the 1813 restrictions and increase the police action against violations of the law.[59] The government of Upper Bavaria, under Philipp Freiherr von Zu Rhein—the younger brother of Friedrich, the governor of Lower Franconia in 1849–50, and a vocal opponent of emancipation in the upper house—took this advice to heart and advised the king not to revise the law on residence.[60] The cause of Jewish emancipation appeared to have taken a major step backward.

In 1858 von der Pfordten reopened the issue of Jewish emancipation, ostensibly in response to another petition from Mendel Rosenbaum. In a report to the king from the whole cabinet, von der Pfordten made another case for revision of the 1813 law on residence.[61] Jews, his letter states, had to pay the same taxes as Christians and had to serve in the military, but they were restricted in their "most natural" right, the right to have a family. "They appear as a result only as 'tolerated,'" von der Pfordten concluded, "and it must arouse in them a gnawing bitterness against a state law that forbids the most hardworking and talented young man the basis for his own home unless a place is made for him by the death of a coreligionist." The current law allowed arbitrary decisions to deny residency, and the clauses allowing exceptions only made matters worse because they depended on the favor and mood of the community. Revision, he argued, would aid in the moral development of the Jews and improve their relationship with the state and government.

Von der Pfordten separated residence from other restrictions preventing

Jews from engaging in brewing or innkeeping, which he advised retaining, although, he added, if these restrictions did not already exist, he would not advise them. He gave three reasons in his letter for his actions: he believed that in the legislation about Jewish relations a gradual advance was most viable, he saw the few remaining restrictions as no great burden on Jews, and he recognized that they had a certain "grounding in the sentiment of the people." Clearly von der Pfordten had changed his mind fundamentally about which tactics to use to secure Jewish emancipation.

As usual, the king immediately accepted the proposal and instructed the ministry of the interior to formulate a draft law and to investigate potential problems. The result was a lengthy report prepared just over a month later in July 1858 by a ministerial advisor, under the signature, probably, of von Reigersberg, modifying Pfordten's proposal in a significant way.[62] This report demonstrates the ministerial change from von Zwehl to the more conservative von Reigersberg, but it may also indicate the waning of von der Pfordten's power—he submitted his resignation in December 1858, staying on until July 1859 awaiting replacement.[63]

In keeping with the significant differences between the Palatinate, west of the Rhine, and the rest of Bavaria, the ministry of the interior's report separated its analysis and its recommendations on this geographical and administrative border. It noted that in the Pfalz Jews and Christians were essentially equal and that the Napoleonic Decree of 1808 still served a useful purpose by making it difficult for "foreign" Jews from the rest of Bavaria to "flood" into the Palatinate. The reference was to a clause that limited such settlement there to Jews making their living from agriculture only. Because this had worked and there were no complaints about it, the ministry saw no need to make any changes in the existing laws. Concerning Bavaria east of the Rhine, however, the ministry analyzed the law as applied in areas where Jews resided separately from the law's applications in areas where Jews did not yet live. Its review of the operation of the relevant paragraphs of the 1813 law in areas where Jews resided culminated in the conclusion that the law was "originally too narrowly composed and [is] now completely anachronistic."

So far the report echoed von der Pfordten's reasoning in his letter of 10 May. But when the ministerial analyst turned his attention to areas in which no Jews lived, encompassing by far the majority of the communities of Bavaria, he reached a much different conclusion. Noting that the original intention was to make it difficult for Jews to move into commerce, he argued that the exceptions in the 1813 law allowing residence in areas without Jews were mostly for Jews involved in wholesale trade; that is, the overall intention of the law, to protect Christians from Jewish business, was undermined at this point. He concluded that the absolute veto over residence by communities should only allow them to prevent settlement by Jews who intended to pursue retail trade. One can see in this report a support for the needs of the local community that was not in evidence in the government in 1849–50. Moreover, where only a decade earlier those fearing Jews had concentrated on peddling, the discussion had now shifted to small shopkeeping. Jewish peddlers had essentially disappeared, and the ministry had the statistics to prove it. As for the lesser restrictions on beer brewing and innkeeping, the report argued for continuing these for the reasons given by von der Pfordten. Thus the report advised the king to submit a law that allowed for residency rights for Jews in areas where they already resided, but to permit the absolute veto to be used to exclude Jews engaged in retail trades in communities where no Jews resided.

Here the story becomes difficult to follow. In September 1858 Parliament met for the first time since its dismissal in 1856. The leader of the left-wing opposition, Dr. Weis, became second president of the lower house. Anticipating conflict with Weis's election, the king dissolved the chamber on 30 September before its first debates. In a tense situation, von der Pfordten submitted his resignation, but the king did not accept it, probably both out of loyalty to his minister of nine years and because he feared the impact of Cavour's moves to unify Italy and wished to retain a proven diplomat in a potential foreign policy crisis. But in the spring of 1859 the newly elected lower house became even more oppositional and again elected Weis. Additionally Prussia had begun to liberalize its government in 1858. The central European world, not merely Bavaria, appeared to be moving gradually to the left. In response, Maximilian finally accepted von der Pfordten's resignation, replacing him with Karl Freiherr von Schrenck-Notzing.[64]

The parliamentary session that began in 1859 and concluded in 1861 passed a great deal of legislation, much of it progressive, which the king approved. One law passed was a bill to repeal both the residency requirements on Jews and the restrictions on beer brewing and innkeeping of the law of 1813. In favor of simple repeal, the government scrapped both the much more restrictive draft of the ministry of the interior and that of von der Pfordten of 1858, which had not yet been submitted to Parliament. Lacking documents showing a specific motive for this move, it is hard not to see it as a result of the political situation of 1859–61, in much the same way that the bill for full equality had emerged from the political realities of 1848–49. Sponsored by representative Paur, the new bill abolished the two articles of the 1813 edict limiting Jewish right of residency in communities and one part of another article preventing Jews from owning or operating taverns and breweries.[65] Revision of the 1813 law still dominated the agenda.

The third committee provided a report supporting the bill, and the ministry of the interior gave its support, even though it was in the lukewarm form of a statement that the bill would experience no difficulty from the ministers. In light of its own recent position, that was understandable. Only three deputies made critical speeches, two of whom stated that they would vote for the bill anyway. Dr. Ruland, among the most vociferous opponents of the 1849 bill, was alone in opposition.

A strong sense of inevitability permeated the brief speeches of 20 March 1861. They cannot really be called debates, but they provide important insights into the evolving attitudes toward Jews and Judaism in Bavaria. In contrast to 1849, few made any reference to principles, either religious or secular. But experience, whether personal or collective, was ever present. Münch, the committee floor manager who ably introduced the bill, stated the main theme very bluntly: "The Jews of 1861 are totally different than those of 1813." In his opinion, these articles, abolition of which was long overdue, were now causing Jews to emigrate, taking their capital and energy with them. Statistically, Münch argued, the consequences of the 1813 law were clear: in the Palatinate, where they were free, the number of Jews had increased between 1832 and 1846, declining only after 1856; in Bavaria as a whole, the number of Jews had fallen from 60,007 in 1832 to 56,844 in 1851.[66] Münch recognized that these figures included young Jews who went abroad as commercial agents, but practically, these Jews had also emigrated. The number of Jewish families in agriculture, crafts, and normal trade had more than doubled, from 2,419 to 5,280, between 1813 and 1851. Conversely, the number of Jews in peddling and other "Jewish" trades had fallen from 5,243 to 2,230 in the same year. The Christian population had grown 8.6 percent from 1832 to 1852, he noted, but the Jewish population had declined by 5.3 percent. No opponent took issue with these figures.

The mood was certainly different in 1861 than in 1849–50. As representative Paur pointed out, the greatest difference lay in the lack of opposition in the press. Paur's reference was clearly to Zander's *Volksbote,* which was strangely quiet in 1861.[67] Of course, Paur noted, the 1849 legislation was for total equality in contrast to the "more modest measure" of the current bill. In a gesture to the right, he agreed that the 1813 law had done its job—the social condition of the Jewish population had completely changed in forty-seven years. But it had also pushed Jews to emigrate, which imposed on them the great price of never seeing one's relatives again: "These are terrible sacrifices, the more terrible as Jewish family life is very close. I beg you, gentlemen, make an end to these sacrifices!"

The few opponents who spoke out mouthed the same arguments as in 1849, but without force or conviction. Crucial to our understanding of the changes in temper was the absolute refusal of supporters of the bill to lend credence to these old views by replying to them. This is not to say that the deputies feared the opponents or were entirely silent. One deputy after another spoke up to deny any truth to the negative comments made about Jews: they were not troublemakers, they were good citizens, they were honest innkeepers (in the Pfalz where it was legal), and so on. Boyé even raised the question of marriage between Christians and Jews, arguing for its legality. And both Boyé and Römmich criticized the government for excluding Jews from state service as lawyers in practice although that was allowed legally. Some representatives were willing to push the discussion beyond legal equality into the postemancipation arena of debate over social acceptance. Paur, the bill's sponsor, responded warmly to the charge that he had supported the absolute veto on residence in 1849 in a way that illuminates the change twelve years had made: "Yes, I did, and it has left a sour taste." The 1861 bill passed by voice vote in what was near total unanimity.

Too much should not be made of the changed attitude toward Jews in Bavaria as seen in the 1861 discussion and passage of the repeal of residency restrictions. Parliament was not Bavaria and definitely not the countryside, and even those representatives favoring the law knew it. The government did not suggest any further change before Maximilian's death in 1864. In Germany the years after 1864 were Otto von Bismarck's, and the next governmental action vis-à-vis Jews came in the radically changed world of 1866, a world in which Prussia defeated Bavaria in war. Even if southern Germany did not at first join the North German Confederation in which religious freedom was the rule, it saw the handwriting on the wall. Nevertheless, when the Jewish communities of Munich and Bamberg petitioned for full equality with Christians late in 1866,[68] the government replied individually to the specific requests, granting each, but avoiding a sweeping law like the one passed in the North German Reichstag or that which had been defeated in 1850 in Bavaria. The North German law stated simply that all restrictions on Jews making them different from Christians were abolished, and it became effective in Bavaria only in 1871, after incorporation in the Second Empire. The last legal vestiges of the past in Bavaria disappeared finally in 1881, when the *Landtag* abolished the New Year's payment and other petty anachronistic dues on Jews.[69]

One lesson of the conflict of 1849–50 over the bill for emancipation was that Parliament and the people did not agree on the legislation. Emancipation, many had argued, would lead to acceptance of Jews. In his report on sentiment in his district, the *Landrichter* in Hilders had written: "The sentiment of the inhabitants of the local district in reference to Jewish emancipation is excited, naturally so under the influence that has been brought to bear [from the chaplain, Haller]; if the draft law ever becomes actual law, [sentiment toward Jews] ought to become tolerant."[70] Yet once Jews possessed legal rights equal to other Bavarians, conflict with their neighbors shifted to the social, economic, cultural, and political spheres of life. Some of the earliest friction stemmed directly from the legislation. For example, when the hated residency rights ended in 1861 and Jews became citizens of many small communities, the results were not always peaceful.

In 1865 and 1866 in two small rural towns in Lower Franconia, Laudenbach and Wiesenfeld, in the rural district of Karlstadt, anti-Jewish rioting erupted. Research into the causes of that rioting revealed that the issue was Jewish emancipation and opposition by townspeople to the Jews' new rights to wood and other community holdings—much as the local district director of Karlstadt had predicted in 1850.[71] The solution in one of the towns, perhaps both, was a bargain in which Jews surrendered their newly won rights to wood and grazing in return for peace and quiet. The rioting stopped, and it is tempting to argue that both emancipation and the local bargain worked. But before one can make that claim, both the local riots in Unterfranken in 1866 and the statewide campaign against Jewish emancipation in 1849–50 and its aftermath must be seen in context, both in the context of Bavaria and in that of Germany in the nineteenth and twentieth centuries.

NOTES

1. See ch. 4.

2. *Verhandlungen der Kammer der Reichsräthe des Königreichs Bayern vom Jahre 1850,* Dritte Beilage Band, no. 68, 3 Feb. 1850, Munich. Those petitions received that were the consequence of agitation by members of the *Reichsräthe,* nos. 525–52, were filed separately in Akten 2661 and not always counted in the total. Was it because they were seen as tainted?

3. If we assume a population of sixty-thousand Jews of all ages, all of them would have had to move to towns without Jews at about one family per town to provide even one Jewish family per community. This would not be an "extraordinary increase" to most analysts and was, in any event, wildly improbable.

4. As von der Pfordten noted in his remarks; *Verhandlungen,* 15 Feb., 33rd sitting, bd. 5, 117–19.

5. Ibid., 100–117.

6. Ibid., 39–48.

7. Pro and con speakers alternated, ministerial speakers excepted; Rainer Roth, *Politische Bildung in Bayern. Eine historisch-politische Untersuchung der Bemühungen um politische Bildung an den Volksschulen Bayerns in der Zeit der Monarchie. Von Ludwig I. bis zur Gründung des Deutschen Reiches* (Munich, 1974), 185, states that von Ringelmann was responsible for improvement in the Jews' situation.

8. *Verhandlungen,* 15 Feb., 33rd sitting, bd. 5, 73–91; von Heintz, who later spoke in support of the bill, attacked petitions in general, arguing that the "voice" of the Bavarian people could only be found in the lower house, but his position was unique (see pp. 91–100).

9. Ibid., 117–24.

10. Ibid., 124–27, 145–46.

11. Ibid., 117–19, 125–28.

12. Ibid., Graf von Giech, 129–30; von Niethammer, 134–35; von Arnold, 136–42; and von Maurer, 142–44; only von Giech and von Arnold were solid supporters of the bill.

13. Ibid., 146–47.

14. Ibid., 151–65; von der Pfordten appeared especially nettled by von Zu Rhein's comment on the government's lack of data, because, as he said, no one had requested it, and by the use of data from Lower Franconia, which, he also noted, must be seen as "governmental data." In turn, p. 166, von Zu Rhein claimed that the data he cited was not the result of government directive; technically, because he was referring only to the results of Hohe's second directive of 15 Jan., he was correct, but disingenuously so.

15. Ibid., 168–81.

16. Ibid., 185–91.

17. Ibid., 194–98.

18. The *Volksbote* gloried in reporting these facts; see no. 43, 19 Feb., p. 1, Munich, dated 18 Feb.

19. See ch. 4. Also see Eugen Franz, *Von der Pfordten*, 168–69, for poor coverage of von der Pfordten's role in the emancipation in the upper house; interestingly, much of this is based on Prussian diplomatic records, especially the reports of Bockelberg to Schleinitz reflecting the irritations of a Protestant Prussian who, as the author volunteers, was allied to Doenniges, who was married to a Jewess. Franz saw the crisis as a whole as an assertion of individuality by the upper house, as less than a cabinet issue by von der Pfordten, and as a clever ploy by the latter to win support through public opinion.

20. GHA, Nachlass von der Pfordten, 7, 106, von Giech to von der Pfordten, 18 Feb. 1850, Munich. Von Giech was a friend and regular correspondent. His reference to the king seems to imply the latter's hostility to the ultramontanes. A. Eckstein, *Kampf*, 82, writes that Protestant clerics like Dekan Bauer supported emancipation.

21. Heinz Gollwitzer, "Giech," is the only good study of Giech and of the *Reichsräthe* in midcentury. Also see Gernot Kirzel, *Staat und Kirche*.

22. Gollwitzer, "Giech," 146–47, 152.

23. Ibid., 153–54, and *Verhandlungen*, 15 Feb., 33rd sitting, bd. 5, 129–30. Hirsch had worked for emancipation for years; see Eckstein, *Kampf*, 70, 83.

24. *VBö*, no. 40, 15 Feb., München, 14 Feb.; *RZ*, no. 49, 18 Feb., 1, München, 16 Feb.; *BLBo*, no. 53, 18 Feb.; *AZdJ*, no. 10, 4 Mar., 130, München, 15 Feb. noted that von zu Rhein, the governor of Lower Franconia, voted against.

25. *NFräZ*, no. 52, 21 Feb., 166, München, 16 Feb.; *BZ*, no. 50, 19 Feb., 2, München, 16 Feb.

26. *VB*, no. 43, 19 Feb., 1, München, 18 Feb.

27. *RZ*, no. 50, 19 Feb., 1, München, 18 Feb., citing the *AAZ*. The *AAZ*'s prediction was inaccurate.

28. *MFräZ*, no. 55, 24 Feb., 1, "Das konstitutionelle Blinden-Institute," from the *Volksbötin*.

29. *NFräZ*, no. 47, 16 Feb., 1, "Die Kammer der Reichs-Räthe und die Juden-emanzipation"; no. 52, 21 Feb., 1, "Der Reichsräthe unredlicher und unrätlicher Beschluss in der Juden-Emanzipations Frage"; no. 55, 24 Feb., 1, "Die bayerische Reichsräthskammer."

30. *RZ*, no. 58, 27 Feb., 1, München, 24 Feb.

31. See, e.g., the *VB*, no. 6, 6 Jan., 1, München, 5 Jan.

32. The *VB* noted acceptance of the law on associations on 14 Feb., 1, in no. 41, 16, Feb., München, 15 Feb., the day debates on Jewish emancipation opened in the upper house.

33. *NFräZ*, no. 354, 20 Dec., 1, "Was haben die Demokraten gegenwärtig zu thun?" from the Volksbildung Committee of the Märzverein of Franken, probably written by Gätschenberger, also editor of the *NFräZ*.

34. *NFräZ*, no. 1, 1, "Rückblick."

35. *RZ*, no. 56, 25 Feb., 1.

36. *LB*, no. 22, 21 Jan., 1.

37. *RZ*, no. 58, 27 Feb., 1, München, 24 Feb. Actually, according to Eckstein, *Kampf*, 104, the 1850s saw a return to the practice of using addresses to stimulate governmental action.

38. *RZ*, no. 58, 27 Feb., 1, Würzburg, 21 Feb.

39. *AZdJ*, no. 13, 25 Mar., 167, München, 8 Mar. (D.Z.).

40. *NFräZ*, no. 59, 28 Feb., "An die Israeliten Bayerns."

41. *MFräZ*, no. 15, 15 Jan., 1, München, 12 Jan., citing the *Kempter Zeitung;* also see *AZdJ*, no. 7, 11 Feb., 86ff., München, 4 Feb.

42. *VB*, no. 1, 1 Jan., 1, "Der Volksbot' zum neuen Jahr."

43. *VB*, nos. 35–36, 9–10 Feb., and no. 5 Bciwagen, 10 Feb., 1; *Historisch-politische Blätter*, vol. 25, 1850, 1:183—87.

44. Stefan Schwarz, *Juden*, 282–86.

45. The draft made reference to the Anzeigeberichte of 25 Oct. 1850 as one of the pieces of legislation to be submitted to the next Landtag; see BHStA, Staatsrat 3384. Copies also exist in BHStA, MJu, 13390, with four clauses instead of three, but no significant difference. Max gave his internal approval on 15 Feb. 1851, a year to the date after the opening of the discussion that led to rejection in the upper house.

46. Schwarz, *Juden*, 285, provides the full text, which was accepted by the Staatsrat on 19 Feb. 1851.

47. It was signed by Maximilian on 25 Feb. and by both houses on 4 June, and it became law on 29 June 1851.

48. See ch. 5.

49. Staatsrat, 3384, in BHStA Mü; the Ministry of Justice was kept informed of this legislation and apparently sent advice to the minister on its content (see BHStA, MJu, 13390); for instance, it was given the task of carrying out the details of the changes after 29 June. As such, the Ministry of Justice also received correspondence relevant to this issue—e.g., from the merchant, Samuel Schwarz, to MInn., 16 Oct. 1851.

50. Schwarz, *Juden,* 285, citing Beil. 3 in the Protocol of 21 June 1851.

51. BHStA, Staatsrat 3384, dated 21 June 1851, München.

52. The Ministry of the Interior asked the government of Oberbayern in late Jan. 1851 to again ascertain the total number of Jews and the number in trade and in *Schacher,* and to compare the situation of Jews in 1813 and 1821–22 to the present. See SAfOB, RA Fasz. 2090, no. 33875.

53. Schwarz, *Juden,* 286.

54. See ch. 5, on subdivision of estates.

55. See ch. 5, on "Jewish" methods.

56. See Schwarz, *Juden,* 288–91, for Rosenbaum's 1855 petition, the original of which is in GHA, Nachl. Max II, 80/1/249b "Judenangelegenheiten" dated 1 June. But there were also petitions against. See Nachl. Max II 79/3/175, for one dated Schweinfurt 3.8.1856. Understandably, but inaccurately, the family biography of Mendel Rosenbaum elevates his activity to the heroic. See Berthold [Baruch] Strauss, *Rosenbaums,* and Eckstein, *Kampf,* 107–8.

57. One can include in this category an accusation by a citizen of Würzburg that the Maier brothers, Jews, had assembled illegally for political purposes, namely, to raise money to send to Munich to "buy" repeal of the 1813 law. After repeated requests from Munich for an investigation, a report stated that no such assembly had occurred, and the matter was therefore moot. The correspondence is in BStA Würzburg, Präsidial Akten 325.

58. StAOb, RA Fasz. 2090, no. 33875, Munich city magistrate to the royal government of Oberbayern, Munich, 13 Dec. 1853.

59. Schwarz, *Juden,* 287.

60. Schwarz, *Juden,* 288. Walter Schärl, *Beamtenschaft,* 219.

61. GHA, Nachlass Max II, 80/1/249, 1, von der Pfordten to Maximilian, Munich, 10 May 1858. Schwarz did not use this file and hence placed the 1861 law as originating in petitions from the Jewish community of Bamberg in 1860, largely following Eckstein, *Kampf,* 113ff. Despite von der Pfordten's actions and his role in 1849–50, Eckstein, *Kampf,* 111, saw him only as an obstacle to Jewish emancipation.

62. GHA, Nachlass Max II, 80/1/249, 1, MInn to the king, Munich, 18 July 1858. The signature is nearly illegible. The discussion below refers to this document; the advisor was F. Feder.

63. H. Rall, "Entwicklung," 243–45. Little work has been done on Bavarian politics in these years.

64. Ibid., 245–47.

65. *Ver. Kd. Abg.,* 1859/61, Sten. Ber., bd. 1, p. 242, 20 Mar. 1861; Eckstein, *Kampf,* 121–22, cites letters of 22 and 29 Jan. 1861 from Dr. Arnheim, a Jewish member of the lower house, in which he writes that Paur, rather than he, would introduce the bill formulated by the ministry, adding that petitions in support of it would not be amiss.

66. Clearly these totals would be much lower if data for 1861 had been available. The 1861 census, begun in 1858, did not give data by confession. See table 2.1.

67. But Zander had lost none of his combativeness on other issues. See Elmar Roeder, *Zander.*

68. SAfOB, Mü, RA Fasz., 2090, no. 33875, 2 Mar. 1867 forwarding copies of the two petitions to the police director of Munich from the governor of Oberbayern.

69. Schwarz, *Juden*, pp. 293–95. For the New Year's money, see Freiherr von Weissdorf, "Die Verfassungsurkunde des Königreichs Bayern" (n.p., 1905), 181, cited by Schwarz, *Juden*, 295.

70. BStW, Regierung von Unterfranken, Präsidialakten, 325, district director of Hilders to governor, 19 Jan. 1850.

71. I have described this in my article "Bavarians and Jews in Conflict in 1866: Neighbors and Enemies," *LBIY* 32 (1987): 103–17; this book is the result of asking how emancipation could produce such a result. Nearly the same process occurred in Langsdorf in Hessen and is described in Dietmar Preissler, *Frühantisemitismus*, 354ff. In Langsdorf the events took place in 1850 but featured *Katzenmusik* and broken windows, use of the military to restore order, protest by the community, proposal of a compromise by the state, and finally, action by the state to compel the local community to register Jews as residents in 1852.

Chapter 8

Anti-Semitism in Bavaria
in Historical Perspective

From the *Juden Edikt* of 1813 to the defeat of the bill for Jewish emancipation in the *Reichsräthe* in 1850, prejudice against Jews played a powerful role. Even many of those favoring emancipation were critical of Jews they perceived as damaging society. And not all who opposed the emancipation bill were anti-Semites. Because Jews had long been a part of Bavarian society, even when severely restricted by law and custom, any change in either Jewry or the larger society affected the other. Jewish Bavarians lived and moved in the same material and secular landscape as Christian Bavarians, and they confronted the same major changes in state and economy. A number of factors not directly or solely prejudicial to Jews played roles in the struggle over emancipation, but prejudice clearly predominated. It remains to be determined how the obvious hostility displayed toward Jews in the course of Jewish emancipation in Bavaria, especially in the campaign against the bill for equality in 1849–50, relates to the history of anti-Semitism in general and, more particularly, whether it was a part of the emergence and development of "modern" anti-Semitism.

In his widely used general history of anti-Semitism, Jacob Katz does not define anti-Semitism, but refers only to "Prejudice against Jews—anti-Semitism in modern parlance."[1] Katz is representative of most scholars in this regard,[2] but the common disinclination to define the term carefully and precisely originates in the scholarly perception of anti-Semitism as a broad concept, even as an ideology, rather than as only a word like any other. In part, however, reluctance to define the term precisely probably also stems from concern that anti-Semitism may be accurately applied to different historical contexts only if it is defined very simply. Both of these positions have merit.

Reinhard Rürup and Thomas Nipperdey provide the best analysis of anti-Semitism as concept and ideology.[3] Following a thorough etymological and historical discussion of the term *Antisemitismus,* they argue that anti-Semitism, although vague from the beginning, was more than a new form of traditional Jew-hatred. It denoted a secular form of enmity toward Jews and an accompanying ideology.[4] In their eyes anti-Semitism was a reaction against Jewish emancipation in the postemancipation age. But antagonism to Jews alone does not sufficiently explain the ideology: "Sociologically as well as ideologically anti-Semitism is a protest movement against the ideas of 1789, against the liberal state and social order and the accompanying capitalist order." Anti-Semites attacked Jews as the "exposed representatives" of modern development, or of the liberal system. Traditional prejudice against Jews became entangled with the struggle against liberalism in all its forms. Rürup later produced a specific definition of the modern anti-Semite as "one who denies to Jews the capacity for national and cultural structural membership, asserts their cultural, social, religious, and moral inferiority, and sees in the works of Jewry an attack on national and ethnic structures."[5]

Rürup and Nipperdey trace the development of anti-Semitism as a movement with political and cultural projections into daily life from the 1870s to the Nazi era.[6] The Holocaust made anti-Semitism a familiar term, they argue, but diluted its meaning to include all anti-Jewish expressions, tendencies, and movements; the term became a synonym for any unfriendly or hostile position vis-à-vis Jews. The authors conclude by stating that an adequate historical understanding of anti-Semitism depends on use of the narrower, but more complete, pre-Holocaust concept of anti-Semitism as an ideology.[7]

The essential element of Rürup and Nipperdey's approach may be simply stated: modern anti-Semitism, or any other form of hostility toward Jews as a group,[8] existed solely as a part of a specific historical context and can only be fully understood as such. In keeping with their premise that modern anti-Semitism began in the 1870s, the authors only treat the context of the years 1870 to 1945. In this increasingly secular epoch, anti-Semitism was always part of the larger attack on the liberal world. Thus the authors view anti-Semitism as evolving over changing historical periods, a development that raises the possibility of distinct forms of anti-Semitism and evokes concern for proper periodization.

In this short space, analysis of anti-Semitism in the ancient and medieval contexts can only be dealt with superficially. The most obvious linkage between some of the ancient and all of the medieval and modern worlds is that provided by Christianity. Despite interest in this aspect, heightened after the Holocaust, most scholars relegate traditional Christian anti-Judaism to the premodern era, preferring a more secular explanation for less religious times.[9]

Gavin I. Langmuir treats anti-Semitism as an example of the larger historical problem posed by religion, but he hesitates to say that anti-Semitism was inherently Christian, arguing only that Christians prepared the ground for it in the form of xenophobic beliefs about Jews. For Langmuir, chimerical anti-Semitic beliefs emerged in the twelfth century and became socially significant in the thirteenth.[10] Studies of the Reformation indicate that anti-Semitism was already in place, not merely in religious garb, as the term *anti-Judaism* suggests, but in secular form.[11] Because much of it was pre-Christian, the ancient world provides perhaps the best comparison, and it demonstrates strikingly similar modes of anti-Semitism.[12] Though it is inappropriate here to attempt to tie the anti-Semitism of the modern era to the anti-Judaism or anti-Semitism of the ancient and medieval worlds, it is entirely proper to ask how much of that which is considered modern was really new.

Unlike Rürup and Nipperdey, who focus on the content of the concept or ideology of anti-Semitism, others emphasize the type of expression. One of the most carefully crafted analyses of this type is the excellent work on anti-Semitism in Vichy France by Michael Marrus and Robert Paxton.[13] Marrus and Paxton argue that anti-Semites think and act on a gradient, which the authors represent in the form of concentric circles or bands. The outer, largest circle, contains those people with weakly held and relatively mild anti-Jewish feelings. Nearer the center lies the circle of those who, fewer in number, possess an anti-Semitism of greater intensity. At the core are those few possessed of overt, strongly held hatred. This schema reflects the reality of a wide range of anti-Semitic feeling, but it says little about either content or context. The authors are alert to both, noting the emergence of racist ("modern") anti-Semitism in the late nineteenth century, emphasizing the opposition to Jews in the 1930s as part of a broader opposition to immigration in general, and explaining French anti-Semitism in Vichy as the product of native French thinking.[14] But in their schema, the degree of intensity of anti-Semitism is more important than its content.

Similar attempts to explain anti-Semitism by type are found in the work of other scholars on a less formal basis. Richard Levy distinguished between parliamentary and radical anti-Semitism, writing that when "conventional" anti-Semitism was discredited by its political failure before 1914, it "cleared the way for the revolutionary brand practiced by the Nazis." Thus Levy categorized the Hessian anti-Semite Otto Böckel as a populist, anti-Semitic parliamentarian and Theodor Fritsch as an antipolitical anti-Semite and radical. On this basis Levy denies a linkage between the "political" anti-Semitism of men like Otto Böckel in the pre-1914 era and the Nazis but affirms continuity between men like Fritsch and national socialism.[15] Though Levy separates "anti-Semitic sentiment" from "the organization and utilization of that sentiment to some end,"[16] he sees the use of that sentiment by men like Fritsch as new and different.[17]

Other scholars have been sensitive to the vital difference between thinking and acting. In a study of the attitudes of Germans and German Jews toward Eastern European Jews in the pre-1914 period, Jack Wertheimer argues that anti-Semitism, like "any other prejudice," is more than merely a set of "stereotypes." Its history is the story of "actions such as defamation, discrimination, persecution, and annihilation." While others focus on attitudes, Wertheimer prefers to study behavior.[18] However, Fritz Stern takes issue with history that "always" refers to anti-Semitic organization, and he calls instead for more study of "latent" thoughts.[19] A large part of the debate about anti-Semitism in imperial Germany concerns the relative role of ideas and attitudes versus organization and action.

There are some who simplistically see anti-Semitism as a disease.[20] Pathologically similar to judgments of Nazis like Adolf Hitler—or for that matter, of Jews by Nazis—such an analysis may be comforting to one's view of human nature (most people are not ill), but it fails to address the crucial problem of anti-Semitism—that quite normal people, some of them quite intelligent, profess it. A subtle variation on this theme has emerged in Langmuir's argument that the Holocaust was the consequence of "nonrational" thinking. From this he draws the lesson that any inhibition of "rational empirical thinking represses awareness of our common humanity and threatens humanity itself."[21] Criticizing those who deny the comprehensibility of the Holocaust for theological reasons, Amos Funkenstein notes that the annihilation of Jews was a human event, comprehensible on that level, and important for what it teaches us about man rather than about God.[22] When studying anti-Semitism, we are studying man, not God and not diseases.

A number of historians point to the emancipation era as the starting point of modern anti-Semitism. They argue that emancipation radically changed the world by making Jews equal to Christians and that anti-Semitism emerged to attack Jews as equals. Critics of this thesis, not doubting the existence of emancipating legislation, argue that the process itself was slow and partial, and truly complete only in law. Thus Ismar Schorsch cites Wilhelm von Humboldt's famous memorandum of 1809 criticizing limited legal emancipation and urging immediate and complete equality: "A new piece of legislation regarding the Jews which is not quite wise may thereby remove many physical detriments, but it gives rise to the possible danger of creating greater moral drawbacks—by misdirecting public opinion and strengthening old prejudices—than even their present condition presents."[23] Schorsch likewise speculates that the retention of medieval animosity toward Jews in the modern era may stem from the "failure of the state to resolve decisively the ambiguities of Jewish status."[24]

Rürup developed this argument further, noting the great contrast between French emancipation in 1790–91 compared to gradual emancipation in German central Europe.[25] Even 1848 did not bring full emancipation in

Germany, and partial emancipation meant progress based on a parallel affirmation of fundamental Jewish inequality. Also, because emancipated Jews were not fully integrated into society, they had to work toward that end with liberal forces well into the late nineteenth century and attracted all the criticisms of those attacking the liberals.[26] Many people bitterly criticized Jews after 1873 because they perceived them as quintessentially modern and therefore responsible for the crises of modern society.[27] At this point Rürup's argument meshes neatly with other theories, such as those of H. Rosenberg and S. Volkov.

The underlying premise of most of these arguments is that emancipation was beneficial but was either imperfectly legislated or too slow in implementation. A radically different approach is found in the writings of George Mosse, who has maintained that "the basic fact about German history since the eighteenth century has been the failure of the Enlightenment to take root." He notes that in 1918 it was "too late to reestablish the influence of French rationalism over the German mind. . . . that opportunity had been missed with the failure of the revolutions of 1848."[28] This was also the basic message of Mosse's earlier work on the "*völkisch*" ideology and is embedded in most of his essays on German literature.[29] Far from being only an explication of anti-Semitism, Mosse's often brilliant work attempts to deal with all aspects of non-Enlightenment ideas, however vulgar, in Germany. If emancipation represents part of the rationalist urge of the eighteenth century, which element, the *völkisch* or the enlightened, was, at any given point, stronger? In Mosse's view, Hitler used and perverted *völkisch* thought, but he could not have done even that if such thought had not already been significantly present in Germany.

At the opposite extreme from Mosse is Paul L. Rose's assertion that anti-Semitism was essentially a product of revolution. Rose insists not only that modern anti-Semitism was modern in content but that German revolutionaries, including Heinrich Heine and Karl Marx, were responsible for its spread. Anti-Semitism was also antimodern, in keeping with the role of revolution as, in part, a critique of modern society, certainly of modern industrial and capitalist society. When Rose's contentions become generalizations about all revolutionaries and Germans, they clash with the reality of much of the nineteenth century.[30]

The struggle between the forces of enlightenment and tradition in 1813 is difficult to unravel because studies of the attitudes of the various levels of eighteenth-century society toward Jews are scarce. Enlightenment ideas could dominate relatively easily and quickly in an absolutist state that was controlled by a dynastic prince and in which a bureaucracy based on secular education possessed disproportionate influence.[31] Relatively sudden change in the state's attitude toward Jews did not, however, mean an equally broad and deep change in what we must loosely call, for want of a better term, public opinion.

The outpouring of opposition to Jewish emancipation in 1849–50 must have had its roots in an earlier epoch; it did not emerge from a vacuum. Traditional anti-Judaism accounts for only part of the explanation. The major elements of the new, "modern" anti-Semitism trace back to intellectual and popular resistance to the Enlightenment, to disagreement with Dohm's theory of "improvement" of Jews, to bitter disappointment with the 1813 Edict, and to radical critiques of modernity. The years immediately after 1815 produced a sudden outburst of anti-Semitic writings from educated men like Ludolf Holst, Friedrich Rühs, Johann Friedrich Fries, C. H. Pfaff, G. Merkel, Theo. A. Scheuring, and C. F. Schmidt-Phiseldeck.[32] Even Elonore Sterling has focused almost entirely on polemical anti-Semitism in the upper reaches of society. New research on the rise of anti-Semitism in the late eighteenth and early nineteenth centuries is needed to clarify its historical development.

The anti-Semitic riots of 1819, which began in Bavaria but occurred as far north as Hamburg and Kopenhagen, testify to popular antagonism, regardless of whether it stemmed from protest against economic competition or from opposition to reform of the 1813 law.[33] Numerous scholars identify Jewish emancipation as a liberal and radical program plank in the years 1830 to 1848, and liberals, broadly understood, are generally seen as growing in numbers during those years. In many ways 1848 reflects the preparation of these pre-March thinkers, and if liberalism was growing, then emancipation's stock was also rising on a more popular scale. It is not as clear that popular opposition to liberalism, perceived as the political arm of the Enlightenment, also grew. But that was the case in Bavaria.[34]

The public struggle in Bavaria in 1849–50 over the bill for Jewish equality leads to several conclusions that are important to our understanding of the historical development of anti-Semitism. The campaign against Jewish emancipation in the press and especially in the organization of popular opinion through petitions at the grass roots level was anti-Semitic, despite the fact that the term itself had not yet been coined. Most of the justifications for denial of emancipation were criticisms of Jews, Jewry, and Judaism in a conceptual form that, with the sole exception of later "scientific" racial theories, compares exactly to the theories found in the anti-Semitic movements of the 1870s, 1890s, and 1920s. The opponents of emancipation perceived Jews as inherently foreign, unethical, economically damaging to Christians, antagonistic to traditional Bavarian occupations, and anti-Christian both in a religious and secular sense. The charge that Jews would always be Jews, whether converted religiously or acculturated socially, anticipated the later racial theories that added a scientific cachet to what many already firmly believed. An anti-Semitic movement can exist even when the term does not.

Although these anti-Semitic concepts were not the agenda of a particular political party, they were the program of a broad-based, popular, and remarkably well-organized political movement. The role of Zander's *Volksbote,* of the Association for Constitutional Monarchy and Religious Freedom, of the Pius Associations, of parish priests and ministers, of members of the lower and upper houses of Parliament, of some district directors, and of many communal officials makes it impossible to classify the campaign against emancipation as anything but political. The obvious extent of the opposition to emancipation and the near total absence of popular support documents the strength of the movement. Despite the admixture of forces and issues that were not intrinsically anti-Semitic, the unifying concept that tied the opposition together was anti-Semitism. The democratic vehicle of the petition campaign highlights the clear difference between the thinking of the upper levels of society and that of the lower levels. As in later cases, anti-Semites attacked the government, the press, and leftist political leaders and institutions in pursuit of their goals.

The existence of a popular, politically powerful anti-Semitic movement in 1849–50 almost certainly indicates transmission of ideas and attitudes from an even earlier period. With few exceptions, most of the justifications voiced for anti-Semitism in Bavaria in 1849 were traditional. Much the same was true in neighboring Hessen.[35] What was new were the methods used in the organization of forces against the bill for emancipation, including the press and petitions. In light of the relative lack of a public political arena before 1848, it cannot be surprising that this was the first such anti-Semitic political movement in German central Europe. The eruption of this antiemancipation movement owed nothing to economic crisis in the form either of a depression or of a downtrend in a business cycle, unlike in the model most used to explain the antiemancipation movement of the 1870s. Also in contrast to later expressions of anti-Semitism by Protestants in a largely Protestant united Germany after 1870, the movement in 1849–50 was predominantly pushed by Catholics and was most successful in a Catholic state.

The undeniable existence of mass popular opposition to Jewish emancipation using very "modern" terminology and methods in a large area that was predominantly rural and Catholic in late 1849 and early 1850 forces us to reconsider much of what has been written about the earliest emergence of modern anti-Semitism. Much of the problem stems from those scholars who, unlike Schorsch, Rürup, and Mosse, believe that emancipation succeeded, even if only in part and temporarily. The 1850–70 generation has been described as the "calmest phase" of German-Jewish integration, as optimistic even from the Jewish point of view, as part of the modernization process supported by the majority of the urban *Bürgertum,* as demonstrating the full integration of Jews into the Gentile world, and as the period in which Jews succeeded beyond even their own dreams in becoming bourgeois.[36] Nipperdey describes Jewish life as improving substantially in nearly every area during and after 1848; in his words, the riots of spring 1848 were real but were "old fashioned, antiquated, ugly." He denies that the use of Jews as villains in novels like Wilhelm Raabe's *Hungerpastor* or Gustav Freytag's *Soll und Haben* proved the dominance of anti-Semitism: "The thread of continuity is the accomplishment of legal equality, of community." By the late 1860s, he argues, the assimilation of Jews into German society was progressing well, despite some obvious frictions, and the majority of the *bürgerliche* world, including the Jews, agreed.[37]

Evidences of the presence of anti-Semitism as disparate as the 1848 anti-Semitic riots, the attempt by Hermann Wagener to reverse Jewish emancipation in Prussia, the publication of popular novels with anti-Semitic stereotypes of Jews, and the emergence of anti-Semitic literature from the pens of Wilhelm Marr, Richard Wagner, M. A. Niendorf, and Constantin Frantz have been seen by most historians as isolated incidents rather than as indications of a movement.[38] This judgment leads analysts like Katz to label 1850 to 1870 the "incubation" period of the anti-Semitic movement of the 1870s.[39] Perhaps the 1850s and 1860s should be seen as part of a more direct line of development from the prerevolutionary period. Growing irritation at Jewish emancipation seems to have been a national experience, with only Bavaria providing the opportunity for catalysis of sentiment into political action, in the form of opposition to a bill for full emancipation of Jews.

In addition to noting the success of emancipation in midcentury, almost all historians of anti-Semitism in Germany describe it as "emerging," "erupting," or "exploding" in the middle and late 1870s.[40] The use of these words to describe the 1870s focuses not on a particular political event but on the growth of sentiment measured over a number of years. Peter Pulzer stated the basic position when he wrote that modern political anti-Semitism "is different from any earlier, sporadic outbreaks of Jew-baiting. It was brought about by conditions which had not existed before the last third of the nineteenth century; only then was it possible to organize political movements wholly or partially on the basis of anti-Semitism, and to make anti-Semitism part of a coherent set of ideas."[41] More recently Werner Jochmann has written, "Wherever before the *Reichsgründung* anti-Jewish attitudes surfaced or were deliberately used, they had no political significance."[42] Likewise Katz, in his thoughtful study of Richard Wagner's anti-Semitism, wrote, "To be sure, in 1850, the year of the pseudonymous publication of Wagner's *Judaism in Music,* his first expression of hostility toward the Jews, there was no sign of an active, not to speak of an organized, anti-Jewish movement like the one in vogue in the last decades of the nineteenth century."[43]

Perhaps the stark contrast between the "explosion" of anti-Semitism in the 1870s and the "quiet incubation" of the 1850s may be lessened by asserting that the former has been exaggerated and the latter understated. In the 1850s and 1860s politics in general underwent a process of incubation and early growth. All political activity of all ideological colors encountered obstacles in the form of government repression and popular apathy. Political anti-Semitism was no different in this regard from other "radical" sects, such as socialism. Because Jews had been partially emancipated—attested by the gains of 1848 and even those of the 1851 and 1861 legislation in Bavaria—life for many Jews improved in the generation after 1848, leading to a tendency to remember the good much more than the bad. First the economy boomed. Then, during the 1860s, fast-moving national and international events dominated the news and claimed the attentions of most Germans, leaving little room for the growth of sects into movements. The emergence of anti-Semitism on a political basis in Germany after 1870 was a much more gradual affair than is implied by use of words like *eruption*. Wilhelm Marr's famous article using the term *anti-Semitism* appeared only in 1879, after the appearance of many earlier examples of anti-Semitism, some of them his own, in the 1860s and 1870s. With few exceptions, this "explosion" was in the realm of printed polemics of limited circulation. Political anti-Semitism reached its peak much later, in the 1890s, largely in the state of Hesse. Traditional characterizations of the anti-Semitism of both the 1850s and 1870s exaggerate in opposite directions and conceal an underlying continuity.

Looking for causal explanations of the growth of anti-Semitism in the 1870s, historians have naturally sought major events or changes in its immediate past and have found several: the completion of legal emancipation, unification, the "crash" of 1873, and the *Kulturkampf*. It would be foolish to claim that these events, forces, and struggles did not influence and even encourage the development of anti-Semitism. But accepting the fact of an increase in anti-Semitic activity in Germany in the 1870s does not mean we should not distinguish between the causal and catalytic sources of this fact. If modern anti-Semitism existed well before these events occurred, it undermines their causal role and forces us to look elsewhere for the origin of modern anti-Semitism.

The end of Jewish emancipation, dated from 1869 in the North German Confederation and 1871 in Germany as a whole, was part of unification because it was part of the new constitutions. Rürup, who has analyzed the relation between anti-Semitism and emancipation in Baden, argues that modern anti-Semitism is postemancipatory because it sought emancipation from Jews. His argument implies that Jews could only be feared if they were emancipated. In his view, the anti-Jewish actions of the emancipation era merely attacked specific problems—for example, Jewish usury—and not, as in the 1870s, Jews in general as the cause of a bundle of problems.[44] In the latter reasoning, if Jews caused many of society's ills, then "solving" the Jewish problem would help cure society in general. But anti-Semitic references to "the Jew" and "Jews" had dominated the discourse of even small villages in Bavaria a generation earlier.[45] Long before emancipation became fact, opponents accused Jews of causing a wide variety of social and economic problems.

There are two important and closely related variations on the theme of anti-Semitism as postemancipatory, one dealing with equality, the other with visibility. In the first case, Hannah Arendt reasoned that under the legal inequality and restrictions of the preemancipation era, Christians perceived Jews as unequal because of the law, but that emancipation changed that: "The more equal conditions are, the less explanation there is for the differences that actually exist between people; and thus all the more unequal do individuals and groups become." In preemancipation society, Arendt argues brilliantly, Jews could be religious Jews as long as they acculturated in other areas, that is, became German in all but religion. After emancipation the perception of Jews hinged no longer on their adherence to Judaism but on their "Jewishness." This created a vicious problem because, as Arendt puts it, "[formerly] Jews had been able to escape from Judaism into conversion; from Jewishness there was no escape." The "crime" of adhering to Judaism could be punished by restrictions, but the "vice" of Jewishness could "only be exterminated."[46]

In much the same vein, Amos Funkenstein denies that the traditional, orthodox Jew was the target of anti-Semitism. The orthodox Jews faced the older form of anti-Judaism. The emancipated, assimilated Jew who had shed his religion along with his Yiddish, given up such "Jewish" occupations as usury, and abandoned his membership in Jewish society was the target of the new political anti-Semite who sought out and attacked the "Jew in disguise." In Funkenstein's view, and it is fully consonant with the experience of 1849–50, political anti-Semites wanted to reverse emancipation because the Jew was, and remained, despite emancipation and even conversion, a Jew.[47]

Both Arendt's and Funkenstein's arguments gain force if moved back in time to account for such events as those in Bavaria. It is arbitrary and unrealistic to assert that emancipation did not occur until 1870 because full emancipation did not take place until then. Understood as admission to most of the privileges of the Christian world, not as the removal of restrictions for all, emancipation occurred as early as the late eighteenth century for every individual Jew who, through assimilation or acculturation, became German, Christian, or both. That this occurred in a small number of cases is fact; that some perceived it, inaccurately, as true for all Jews does not invalidate the perception. If part of Christian German society saw Jewish emancipation as a reality before its realization in fact, then historians who claim modern anti-Semitism is postemancipatory must extend their search for its origins into the early nineteenth century.

One argument for placing the emergence of modern anti-Semitism after 1870 is that unification was a necessary prerequisite. Historians see unity as both territorial and cultural and normally consider anti-Semitism a negative by-product of the formation of German national identity in the cultural sphere. Thus Shulamit Volkov persuasively argues that anti-Semitism was an important element in the formation of the German self-image after unification, but, like Mosse, who also develops a version of this theory, she writes generally of the nineteenth century, not specifically about the 1870s.[48] This is reasonable because although territorial unity occurred between 1866 and 1871, formation of a national identity started earlier and took longer to fully mature.[49]

In many ways German Jewry reflected this change largely in the form of a strong drive for assimilation. But the reverse was also in evidence. For example, Jehuda Reinharz writes that Jews wished to avoid organizing a Jewish community on a national scale because that would imply a "distinct and common identity [for Jews]."[50] Those other Jews, admittedly few in number, who wanted to be accepted in Germany as a Jewish "nation" or "nationality," saw assimilation, if it were possible, as a denial of their nationhood.[51] Thus Arendt concludes that "the only direct, unadulterated consequence of nineteenth-century anti-Semitic movements was not Nazism but . . . Zionism," the counterideology to an anti-Semitism that denied national status to Jews.[52] Though interesting, this development tells us very little about the origin of modern anti-Semitism.

At least one historian postulates that the unification that occurred in 1866–71 played a specific role in the rise of modern political anti-Semitism. Werner Jochmann writes that German unity irritated many intellectuals, among them a number of conservatives, because of Bismarck's methods, and especially because he formed an alliance with the National Liberal party in 1866–67 to find support for unity. Bismarck's reich was not what they wanted. So, Jochman maintains, they began to collect the dissatisfied, disadvantaged groups and were the leaders of the first anti-Semitic, antiliberal "rallying of the citizens."[53] Jochman is correct that some on the political right were furious with Otto von Bismarck over his role in unification, but they were mostly old-style Conservatives like the aristocratic von Gerlach brothers. Though some Conservatives criticized Bismarck and were anti-Semitic, they did not lead the formation of a new anti-Semitic, antiliberal political group. Jochmann's specific references to anti-Semitic conservative leaders mention by name Adolf Stöcker, Wilhelm Marr, Franz Perrot, and Heinrich von Treitschke. Of these figures only the first came from a traditional conservative background, but he was not at all traditionally conservative in his politics and did not criticize unity. The other three were either former democrats (Marr and Perrot) or liberals (von Treitschke), and the latter only criticized Bismarck before 1866 for seeming not to want to unify Germany. Of these four, the term *intellectual* can only properly be applied to von Treitschke—few traditional conservative leaders can be seen as intellectuals.[54]

Studies of the conservative split in the 1870s show quite clearly that the new Conservative party that emerged in 1876 criticized neither territorial nor cultural unity but some of the policies of the new state, such as free trade, cooperation with the liberals, and the role of the state in the new economy in such events as the railroad scandal of 1872 and the crash of 1873, both of which they perceived as based on the liberal laws of business incorporation passed in 1869.[55] Moreover, these conservatives showed themselves reluctant to support any form of radical or popular anti-Semitism, including, as Jochmann himself notes, that of Stöcker.[56] Jochmann's thesis that conservatives and intellectuals led the organization of an anti-Semitic, antiliberal movement is thus extremely problematic. As a group, intellectuals were not anti-Semitic, antinational, or antiliberal in the 1870s. Conservatives were probably more anti-Semitic than usually acknowledged, but in a traditional, nonpolitical fashion that had little in common with popular anti-Semitism.

Probably the most frequently cited cause of the rise of modern anti-Semitism is Germany's Great Depression of 1873—a theory that owes its existence almost entirely to Hans Rosenberg.[57] In a famous essay of 1943 and a generation later in a book on the effects of the Great Depression of 1873 on social and political life, Rosenberg argued that "the Great Depression not merely *caused* alterations in the political and social framework, it also *conditioned* shifts in social values and political influence and furnished a general background for institutional innovation and changes in policy by setting new limits to political objectives, tactics and strategy."[58] Rosenberg saw the "Slump of 1873–79" as transforming "political parties and ideologies" in general, not merely anti-Semitism in particular. He argued persuasively and cogently that one could not understand the changes in political party relations without knowing the linkages between politics and the changing economic trends.[59]

The structure of Rosenberg's reasoning is clearest in his book, where he spent much time discussing the effects of the economic changes and arguing for the use of economic cycles or "trend periods" as heuristic devices for understanding history.[60] Reduced to its bare bones, his argument is that 1873 began a downtrend in the German economy that lasted until 1896 and that during this period liberalism became discredited as an ideology, protectionism grew in importance, socialists revised the theory of business cycles away from the Marxist view of catastrophy, and modern anti-Semitism emerged.[61] Rosenberg affirmed that the economic trend period caused the effects just noted, anti-Semitism included, producing as evidence a variety of material showing the chronological correlation of the rise of anti-Semitism with the economic downtrend. Until recently all analysts granted that there was a crash and downtrend and that there were political-ideological consequences.[62] Acceptance of these two aspects made it difficult to reject Rosenberg's assertion of a causal connection between the two, and despite his own caveats about avoiding economic reductionism, most have accepted this connection.[63]

By focusing on the crash of 1873, Rosenberg found himself arguing that *a* downtrend in the economy, that of 1873 to 1896, caused certain societal changes, among them the emergence of modern anti-Semitism. Apart from questioning whether such changes were common only to all sharp economic declines, his theory largely ignored the role of the modernization and industrialization of the economy in general.[64] This led Geoff Eley to criticize Rosenberg's theory on the grounds that it is easier to tie the rise in anti-Semitism to the growth of the industrial economy than to a temporary downtrend.[65] In this view, Jews became the targets of anti-Semitism because of their successful role in the "modern" economy, only one part of which was periodic depression. Anti-Semites were not merely searching out scapegoats to blame for economic disaster. They also located in Jews the source of the problems of modern industrial society. Volkov's study of urban master artisans, a group under pressure from a successful new commercial-industrial world throughout the nineteenth century, supplied substantial support for a "modern" anti-Semitism that was essentially antimodern.[66] Economic good times for those riding the crest of the wave of capitalism were hard times for the older, traditional areas of the economy caught in the economic undertow. That was clear in 1849 in Hesse and Bavaria.[67]

Another reason to assert that modern anti-Semitism was a product of the 1870s is the *Kulturkampf* or cultural struggle from about 1872 to 1879, in which the Prussian state, with the active support of Protestant and Jewish liberals and democrats, attacked what they percieved to be the unpatriotic, obscurantist, and politically antiliberal Catholic church. The roots of the conflict were inextricably a part of the older Protestant-Catholic division among Germans, which was so apparent in the religious map of residence in Bavaria in 1849 and in the identification of Prussia as Protestant and of states like Bavaria as Catholic. Among the nonreligious issues involved was the claim that south German Catholics either opposed or did not support the newly unified German state. The ensuing struggle involved Jews because some, as individuals, participated in this criticism of Catholics. When the *Kulturkampf* began to exert real pressure on Catholics, many fought back, and one of the weapons they used against their Jewish critics was anti-

Semitism. It is generally conceded that Catholic anti-Semitism peaked during the *Kulturkampf* as an unfortunate, but understandable, result of attacks by Jewish liberals on Catholics and Catholicism.[68] Historians cite the reluctance of a Catholic political leader like Ludwig Windthorst to indulge in anti-Semitism as evidence that Catholics were less open to its use than Protestants.[69] The increase in Catholic anti-Semitism in the 1870s has been ignored as an explanation of the origins of modern anti-Semitism.

Based on the 1849–50 campaign against Jewish emancipation and on Catholic anti-Semitism during the *Kulturkampf* in the 1870s and 1880s, it is tempting to generalize that German Catholics were about as anti-Semitic as Protestants. But in the 1890s organized anti-Semitic political parties flourished almost exclusively in the Protestant regions north of the river Main.[70] Moreover, political Catholicism in the form of the *Zentrum,* or Center party, demonstrated a remarkable ability to retain its voters despite challenges by the radical right before 1914 and in the emergence of Nazism after the war.[71] In Weimar the Catholic Church in Germany and the leaders of the Center party publicly criticized Nazism.[72] Granted these facts, how can one not see the Catholic position toward Jews in the nineteenth and twentieth centuries as discontinuous?

Using the results of current research, it is possible to clarify the situation, even if the basic problem cannot yet be entirely resolved. The fundamental difficulty is in distinguishing anti-Semitic attitudes from direct political action against Jews. Though there were no anti-Semitic political parties in the south, anti-Semitic attitudes permeated that society not only in 1849–50 but later. David Blackbourn's work on Württemberg describes local Centrists in the 1890s as much more anti-Semitic than their national leaders and the local Center party as rooted in "backwardness" of the type associated with *Mittelstandspolitik* and popular anti-Semitism.[73] In a more recent essay, Blackbourn focuses more directly on anti-Semitism, arguing that it exercised as strong an influence on Catholics as it did on Protestants. He also notes the difficulty in reconstructing how "the raw stuff of popular sentiment" affected political ideology, something that this analysis has attempted to do for Bavaria in 1849–50.[74] Michael Riff has essentially confirmed that what Blackbourn found in Württemberg was also taking place in Baden, where anti-Semitism existed, was growing locally, was no different from the Protestant variety, and was not a single-issue movement. Preissler makes much the same argument for Hessen in 1848.[75]

The task of separating anti-Semitic attitudes from anti-Semitic voting behavior is nowhere more intricate than in Bavaria and Germany in the Weimar years from 1918 to 1933. Superficially, it seems obvious that far fewer Catholics than Protestants voted for the NSDAP and that the Catholic church hierarchy, like Cardinal Faulhaber of Munich, were more critical of

Nazism than were Protestant clerics.[76] But analysts of Weimar Germany tend
to equate political anti-Semitism with Nazism, ignoring that it is a discrete
set of attitudes existing independently of any particular political affiliation.
Thus Catholic voting loyalty to Center candidates has been interpreted as a
sign of resistance to Nazism.[77] If one equates Nazism with anti-Semitism,
then Catholic voters not voting Nazi were not anti-Semitic. Not only is this
reasoning false prima facie,[78] but one must add that many Catholics opposed
Nazism because it directly threatened the established churches, especially the
Catholic church. This anti-Christian anti-Semitism was not present in 1849–
50.[79] One does not have to see Catholic political resistance to Nazism as
criticism of national socialist anti-Semitism. So, too, in 1849–50 in Bavaria,
opposition to Jewish emancipation was not always equivalent to anti-Semitism. As for Catholic attitudes toward Jews in general, the Center party could
hardly be said to be either pro-Jewish or opposed to anti-Semitism.[80]

The Nazi electoral experience in the Franconian provinces, as in Germany, was mixed. Success in Protestant Middle and Upper Franconia was
matched by relative failure in Lower Franconia. The Nazi party was strong
where the Bavarian Peoples' party (BVP) was weak, and the BVP was weak
where there were fewer Catholics. The vulgar Nazi anti-Semite, Julius
Streicher, was successful in Protestant Franconia. He is more than a little
reminiscent of Ernst Zander in his ability to talk to the common man, his use
of invective, his love of scandal, and his talent in innovative use of the press.
But Streicher's power in the party was frequently challenged, and he depended on Hitler for power. In Lower Franconia, where Nazis were weak
before 1933, anti-Semitism grew quickly afterwards, surprisingly so according to a recent study by Robert Gellately. Though anti-Semitism is always
difficult to measure, Gellately shows that the regime's anti-Semitic policies
did not depend solely on force but also relied on active support by people
who "came forward" in the form of denunciations. It is not my intent to try
to prove that popular ideas and attitudes toward Jews from eighty years
before had not changed, but it is surely much harder to show that they did
change. The electoral numbers show the ongoing strength of political Catholicism until 1933, when it removed the ban on membership in the Nazi
party and signed a concordat with the Third Reich.[81]

What emerges from this analysis of the relation of modern anti-Semitism
to postemancipation society, to a newly unified Germany in search of a
self-image, to a changing economy in the form of industrialization and the
depression of 1873, and to the political struggle with Catholics in the *Kulturkampf* is that all were influential, but none solely determined the rise of
anti-Semitism. They were all catalytic agents rather than causal. In each case
one can make a good argument for the continuity of modern anti-Semitism
with the period before 1848 and with the era after 1870. Consideration of the

spread of anti-Semitism after 1870 sharpens our view of its conceptual evolution and of changes in the tactics utilized by its leaders.

The most difficult assertion about the causal origins of modern anti-
Semitism is the contention that the spark that lit the conflagration came from
above, from the educated and the literate, not from the people. The fire, to
continue this analogy, was arson rather than spontaneous combustion. The
question whether modern anti-Semitism was "originally" spontaneous and
popular rather than derivative and created is another by-product of studies
of Nazism. What is supremely important about anti-Semitism in its modern
form is the Holocaust, which, it is widely assumed, would not have occurred
if anti-Semitism had not been the crucial core element in Nazism both at the
polls and in party councils. The search for the origins of anti-Semitism thus
becomes a search for the origins of "national socialist" anti-Semitism.[82]

Organized political anti-Semitism before 1914 was not successful, as
Richard Levy has shown and as most other historians now agree.[83] The peak
of anti-Semitic political activity, measured electorally, occurred in 1896,
when 16 deputies of anti-Semitic political parties sat in a Reichstag with 397
deputies; in 1912 only 2 were left. Levy notes that whether parliamentary
anti-Semitism increased anti-Jewish feeling in Germany is a matter for
conjecture, but he writes that other groups outside Parliament were more
effective in doing so, among them such disparate types as the League of
Agriculturalists, the Pan-German League, and professional anti-Semites,
such as Theodor Fritsch. Levy states that the failure of parliamentary anti-
Semitism left the field open to more radical groups.[84]

At the same time that parliamentary anti-Semitism peaked and then
quickly failed, from about 1893 to 1912, right-wing interest groups and a
small but increasing number of cultural leaders emerged as the carriers of the
stereotypes and ideology of anti-Semitism. The League of Agriculturalists
and the Pan-German League are good examples of the interest groups, and
Paul de Lagarde, Julius Langbehn, and Houston Stewart Chamberlain typify
the cultural leaders.[85] Among the organizations credited with carrying anti-
Semitism forward, anti-Semitic goals were always secondary in importance,
but they became generally validated as a part of the right-wing political
canon. None of this anti-Semitism was really radical or dynamic. Jochmann
has recently explained why this was so: "Anti-Semitism was not a spontaneous movement of disadvantaged social groups that protested against injus-
tices, but rather primarily an instrument of the leadership and educated
classes to uphold and strengthen the standing political order."[86]

There is an unresolved tension in Jochmann's argument. He recognizes
a "push" from "below," asserting that the anti-Semitic petition of 1880–81
demonstrates that areas suffering economic hard times sent in more petitions
than others. How, he asks, did anti-Semites know how to divert the dissatis-

faction of population groups away from the state and onto the Jews? By asking this question, he admits the prior existence of popular dissatisfaction, denying only that the populace itself was capable of making the connection between social-economic problems and Jews. He reasons that because anti-Semitism was present in areas with no Jews, as demonstrated by the petition of 1880–81, anti-Semitic propagandists must have been responsible for attracting support.[87]

Jochmann also argues that the educated and the leaders in Parliament distanced themselves from the raw forms of agitation used by popular anti-Semitic leaders: "Because they wanted to give the population no influence on its own political and economic interests, princes, governments, [and] the socially powerful thwarted all moves that could have set the greater part of the population in movement." In the short period of time needed to call modern anti-Semitism into existence, sometime in the 1870s, a whole series of sorcerer's apprentices recognized that "politicized and excited social groups" were no longer able to be directed and used. Thus Jochmann argues that the antidemocratic thinking of conservative political elites excluded a radical anti-Semitism that might have threatened society in general, not just Jews. But Jochmann asserts that in that short time, "Anti-Semitism had seized and imprinted all levels of society."[88]

The real issue raised by Jochmann's argument, found less clearly stated in other analyses, is how men like Stöcker, von Treitschke, Marr, Glagau, Niendorf, Fritsch, Böckel, Ahlwardt, Liebermann von Sonnenberg, and others could have spread anti-Semitic thinking enough to "imprint" every level of German society in a few years. A few of these men were talented, but most were not. It makes far more sense to conclude that they recognized an existing social discontent with both the economy and with Jews and, contrary to Jochmann's argument, linked one to the other. That is the situation described in chapters 4, 5, and 6, and it would explain the "success" of men like Zander. Otto Böckel's decision to become a political anti-Semite likewise emphasizes his recognition of what he perceived to be the validity of peasant sentiment against Jews.[89] These men became the spokespersons for social groups harboring long-held and deep-seated antagonism toward Jews.

Barely concealed behind Jochmann's assertions lies a more subtle historical question: How much did ideas influence anti-Semitism? Urging the study of bureaucracy as a way of understanding anti-Semitism in France at a later period, Michael Marrus and Robert Paxton write that "historians succumb easily to the temptation to place intellectuals and journalists at the center of their universe—people of the word, who leave traces so readily accessible to research."[90] In this regard Geoffrey Field admits the troublesomeness of evaluating the influence of Houston Stewart Chamberlain on his contemporaries, especially, he writes, because the most successful publicists, like Chamberlain, were "not original thinkers," and thus it is hard to show the effect of his ideas separately from others like him. Lack of originality in one's writing is usually taken to mean derivation of ideas from some earlier thinker, but it can also mean that the ideas derive from popular culture. Field had already written that Chamberlain's writings and their popularity were accurate measures of the strength of anti-Semitism before 1914.[91]

Questioning the use of anti-Semitic ideas and stereotypes brings us back to the power of those ideas and their existence in the German mentality. The essential message of the introduction to G. Mosse's major work on German ideology states this clearly: "It is important to keep in mind that the Nazis found their greatest support among respectable, educated people. Their ideas were eminently respectable in Germany after the First World War, and indeed had been current among large segments of the population even before the war." He wrote even more bluntly: "The *völkisch* movement triumphed in Germany because it had penetrated deeply into the national fabric." Mosse thought his task was to explain how that had happened and to show "that January 1933 was not an accident of history, but was prepared long beforehand." He added that "eventually a majority of the nation was taken in by such self-deception [of exchanging civilized law and attitudes for *völkisch* thought]."[92] Mosse wrote about *völkisch* thought in general, only one large segment of which was anti-Semitic, but the reasoning applies nonetheless.

Trying to explain "why... millions of people respond[ed] to the *völkisch* call," Mosse has shown why the message was attractive, but he has only impressionistically demonstrated the actual process or measured its effect.[93] By examining the penetration of *völkisch* and anti-Semitic ideas in so many normal and respectable areas of German society, Mosse has provided a very convincing impression that millions of Germans had been influenced by such thought. Yet he asserts elsewhere that "German reality and German popular literature had seemed for some people to coincide during the Wilhelmine Reich," by which he meant that *völkisch* thought was not dominant then. With cautious phrasing, he goes on to state that World War I destroyed whatever correspondence had existed; the pre-1914 *völkisch* dreams succumbed to the harsher reality of Weimar, and in that climate the Nazis thrived.[94]

Fundamental to all of Mosse's work and symptomatic of most of the work on anti-Semitism discussed above is the recognition that social and economic conditions contribute to the successful reception of such cultural messages as anti-Semitism. In his chapter "The Jews" in *The Crisis of German Ideology*, Mosse asserts that perceptions of Jews came from older images that had never disappeared,[95] but he strongly implies their diminution. Did received popular stereotypes already exist and provide much of the content of anti-Semitic literature in the early nineteenth century? Of all the elements of "modern" anti-Semitism, only biological racism was lacking in the campaign of 1849–50. Writing for literate, largely urban and bourgeois audiences, not for peasants and artisans, authors like Gustav Freytag presented Jews as *some* may have been and in ways their readers could relate to from their own exposure to the same images, if not to the same reality. Even many Jews did not deny the existence of fellow Jews similar to Veitel Itzig in Freytag's *Debit and Credit,* though they simultaneously denied that such an image accurately reflected the reality of most Jews.[96]

The dominant image of the Jew in Bavaria was complex and negative and was fully in place before the spread of modern anti-Semitism in the 1870s. In this respect the question should be not whether propagandists created modern anti-Semitism but why they recognized and seized on its political usefulness at that point in time. Anti-Semitic writers, especially men like Stöcker and von Treitschke, made the anti-Semitism of the common man intelligible to the educated, not vice versa. Their anti-Semitic activities show the gradual acceptance of anti-Semitism by polite society rather than the injection of those ideas into mass culture by either fanatic zealots or Machiavellian politicians. "Respectable" elements of society were increasingly susceptible to these ideas because of national unity, the temporary success of liberalism, the new industrial economy and the crash of 1873, the threat of the growth of socialism, and the *Kulturkampf.* The historical context of the 1870s favored the growth of modern anti-Semitism, and although those conditions diminished in the years after 1896, they improved radically with World War I and the defeat of 1918.

The most important question about Weimar Germany has been simple and unanimous: How did Hitler and the Nazis emerge as the dominant popular force in 1933? The best answer is a complex and nuanced dialectical combination of the weaknesses of the political structure and the pressures on it from nearly all sides. Hitler and the Nazis did not conquer Weimar at the polls, even with Hitler as chancellor, but became the controlling force as the consequence of presidential appointment and parliamentary approval of dictatorial measures.[97] That should not obscure the fact that Hitler was personally popular, receiving thirteen million votes (36 percent) in a presidential campaign against the incumbent and highly popular conservative general Paul von Hindenburg in 1932, or that the national socialists held more seats than any other party in a Reichstag elected through proportional representation, reflecting 37 percent of the popular vote in the 1932 July elections. One can accurately argue that the National Socialist party was the first to genuinely represent all classes of German society, even if in significantly varying degrees.[98]

Before the Nazis, no other German political party had ever succeeded in attracting as many voters from all classes, and no party had forced a government to recognize its electoral strength and to appoint its leader chancellor. This was true even if we must admit that Weimar was weak, exceptionally so from 1930 to 1933, that the Communists aided the Nazis by attacking Weimar, and that the Nazis shamelessly used scare tactics and intimidation in the elections. Because anti-Semitism played a major role in Nazism, whether it was the most common element or not,[99] one could not vote for Nazis, much less join the party, without either supporting its anti-Semitism or being fully comfortable with those who did.

Why so many millions of Germans voted for an avowedly anti-Semitic party is a complex question involving many more factors than merely anti-Semitism and must be studied in its own historical context. Nevertheless, if Nazi anti-Semitism was essentially the same as that of the pre-1914 era, one can make a case for continuity and can argue that anti-Semitism played a direct causal role in the policies of the Third Reich culminating in the Holocaust.

Concerning continuity, most historians' judgments are simple. Katz states that Nazi anti-Semitism added nothing new ideologically and that Hitler "already contemplated physical annihilation of the Jews" in 1920.[100] Pulzer, too, affirms that the Nazi party's program was unremarkable and "made no contribution to the ideology of the *völkisch* right." He asks: "What, then, was special about the Nazis? To put it bluntly, they had the courage of their convictions."[101] Niewyk writes: "There was nothing new in Nazi anti-Semitism. It simply repeated all the well-known charges."[102] Regardless of their position on other issues, almost all analysts see Hitler's ideas as derivative, especially in the area of anti-Semitism. By asserting the derivative nature of anti-Semitism in the 1920s and in Nazism, these arguments assert, usually by implication, continuity between prewar and postwar anti-Semitism.

An important and sophisticated challenge to the thesis of a direct and continuous link between nineteenth-century and twentieth-century anti-Semitism has been advanced by Volkov.[103] Though she accepts the development of modern anti-Semitism as useful background to the Holocaust, she denies its validity as causal explanation, which she maintains must be sought in the Third Reich.[104] Her argument for this is new because it separates pre-Nazi anti-Semitism from the Nazi version in terms of its mode of expression and aggressiveness rather than in its ideology. The anti-Semitism of the earlier epoch was, she argues, a "written, literary one" that, as in the case of Eugen Dühring, sought to convert through rational persuasion rather than through the emotionalism of charismatic leadership. Hitler, she writes, sensed from the beginning the "basic irrelevance" of rational anti-Semitism to his own version and "set out to surpass its very premises." In Volkov's words, Nazism was a "spoken culture"; "its language was all speech, with no literary dimensions, no privacy, no individuality."[105]

Volkov equates verbal expression of anti-Semitism by Nazis with radicalism. To her, Nazi anti-Semitism was radical because it was verbal instead of written. When Volkov writes that in Nazism verbal aggression was preparation for action rather than a substitute for it, she implicitly identifies pre-Nazi anti-Semitism not only with "written" expression but, more importantly, with peaceful and legal expression as an alternative to action. She writes: "The prose of the prewar anti-Semites was as remote from the marching SS troops as is the normal verbal aggression of small children from the rare assaults of youngsters upon their elders."[106] Volkov's argument is very attractive because it posits a common content in both pre-Nazi and Nazi anti-Semitism, differentiating between the two only in the methods used.

Even if we may question various aspects of Volkov's theses, she nevertheless hits home on a crucial point—the action orientation of Nazi anti-Semitism. "Action" need not narrowly and inevitably mean a Holocaust. Action meant dismantling emancipation, stripping Jews of their citizenship in political terms and of their humanity in social terms. All these actions had already occurred by 1939. Had no Holocaust taken place, history would still regard Nazi anti-Semitism as the most concentrated and organized anti-Jewish activity of the modern world.[107] In reality Nazism demonstrated its capacity for the brutal, cruel, and destructive—there was a Holocaust. To understand the Holocaust, and I agree completely with Amos Funkenstein that the Holocaust was a human event and therefore knowable and comprehensible, we must examine those who did it—the Nazis acting through the Nazi state. When studying this, whether concentrating on individuals like Hitler, Himmler, and Heydrich or on Nazism's party and state structure, we are studying anti-Semitism only as one factor. Nazism produced a policy to implement anti-Semitism, and we know the result as the Holocaust. A variety of forces produced Nazism, among them anti-Semitism.

If we agree that anti-Semitism was essentially the same in 1849–50, the 1870s, and the 1920s, we cannot assert that German society had not changed. The emergence of Germany as a highly industrialized country, the destructive impact of World War I, the revolutions of 1918–19, the hyperinflation of 1922–23, the Great Depression of 1929, and external factors, such as the rise of a communist state in Russia and the weakening of the democratic west of Europe, made the Germany of the 1920s and early 1930s a far different world than that inhabited by the petitioners of 1849–50 in Bavaria. The transmission of traditional anti-Semitic attitudes from generation to generation provided a useful and necessary base on which to enunciate Nazi policy toward Jews. This chapter has argued for the continuity of most of these ideas from the early nineteenth century to the rise of Nazism. Nazi practice is another issue entirely.

Confronted by an uncertain and threatening modernity, some Bavarians opted for an unmodern world. For politically expedient reasons, in 1849–50 the conservative Bavarian state supported modernity in one area, Jewish emancipation, but opposed it in another, the Frankfurt Constitution. Simultaneously, some of the people, mostly democrats, accepted a modern, open political system, but others, mostly conservatives, opposed it. Caught in the middle at a time when democracy had declined drastically in popularity, Jewish emancipation found significant support only from educated elites, both liberal and conservative, failing ultimately in an upper house dominated by obscurantist nobles only too ready to be influenced by conservative popular opinion. The immediate future lay with an open society dominated by educated elites, and both Jewish emancipation and liberal political structures became reality in a relatively brief time. Yet the basis for the rejection of modern politics did not entirely disappear, and in the 1870s and later, that basis waxed in strength when progress caused problems and the liberal political structure weakened.

Regardless of what Nazism stood for before 1933, the Nazi state repudiated, with astonishing speed and thoroughness, all the contextual bases in which modern anti-Semitism had operated since the early nineteenth century. Stated simply, Nazism in practice meant an end to an open society. The list of what vanished almost overnight in the political arena includes a free press, meaningful elections, a parliament with any significant power, and political parties, excepting only a much altered National Socialist German Workers' party. Even the Nazi party learned in 1934 that internal differences of opinion were not possible. The Nazi state was a massive repudiation of political modernity, leaving behind a comparatively meaningless residue of modern technology and science. Whether the Nazi state was postmodern is open to serious question, but there can be no doubt about its fundamental rejection of politics as such. With the struggle between parties and ideas that lies at the heart of modern political life removed, anything was possible. To compare Hitler's applied anti-Semitism to that of his predecessors not only is out of balance in terms of the different amounts of power each possessed but fails to recognize the radically different nature of the state in which Hitler and his lieutenants wielded their power.

The story recounted above shows that the historical context of 1849–50 and of mid nineteenth-century Bavaria in general was not directly linked to the Holocaust. The insights gained by studying the era 1813 to 1871 are used to try to throw critical light on theories that, as Shulamit Volkov puts it, try to explain too much. The events of 1849–50 appear to indicate that events closest to an action have more causal force than events and ideas far removed in time. If we ask whether the leaders of those opposing Jewish emancipation in 1849–50 reflected or created that criticism of Jews we commonly call modern anti-Semitism, we must answer that they merely echoed what was already there. If we ask whether their ideas were more representative of the future than those of the supporters of emancipation, we must be careful about which future we use for comparison, the pre-1914 golden age or the post-1918 crisis atmosphere. If we ask whether modern, political anti-Semitism dates from the 1870s, we must reply that it predated that crisis decade by at least a full generation and that its origins must be sought in an earlier era.

NOTES

1. Katz, *Prejudice to Destruction: Anti-Semitism, 1700–1933,* v. The title is, perhaps, the real definition.

2. Most recently, see the general history by Peter Pulzer, *Jews and the German State: The Political History of a Minority, 1848–1933* (Oxford, 1992), and Bruce F. Pauley, *From Prejudice to Persecution: A History of Austrian Anti-Semitism* (Chapel Hill, N.C., 1992). More specialized studies are no different; see Paula Hyman, *Alsace,* and Hillel Levine, *Economic Origins of Antisemitism: Poland and Its Jews in the Early Modern Period* (New Haven, 1991). But see David A. Gerber, "Anti-Semitism and Jewish Gentile Relations in American Historiography and the American Past," in Gerber, ed., *Anti-Semitism in American History* (Urbana and Chicago, 1986), 3–4, who elaborates a four-point definition, including "speaking ill" of Jews, and notes that people we call anti-Semites "accept at least part of the package [the four points]," even if most do not actively practice anti-Semitism. Also see John G. Gager, *The Origins of Anti-Semitism: Attitudes Toward Judaism in Pagan and Christian Antiquity* (New York and Oxford, 1983), 8, and Gavin Langmuir, "Prolegomena to any Present Analysis of Hostility Against Jews," *Social Science Information* 15 (1976): 689–727.

3. Rürup and Nipperday, "Antisemitismus," in O. Brunner et al., *Geschichtliche Grundbegriffe,* see esp. their bibliographic references.

4. Ibid., 141–42. Religious content was present but secondary.

5. Ibid., 143, and R. Rürup, *Emanzipation,* 116.

6. Ibid., 150ff.

7. Ibid., 152–53.

8. Religious or secular. Historically, religious groups of Jews were also social and communal groups and entities, but groups of Jews defined, e.g., demographically, were also often religious. Significant here is the attitude(s) toward Jews, not toward *a* Jew.

9. There is a growing literature on anti-Semitism in the premodern world. See Heiko A. Oberman, *The Roots of Anti-Semitism in the Age of Renaissance and Reformation,* trans. James I. Porter (Philadelphia, Pa., 1984); Gavin I. Langmuir, "Prolegomena"; and John G. Gager, *Origins.*

10. Gavin I. Langmuir, *History, Religion, and Antisemitism* (Berkeley and Los

Angeles, 1990) and *Toward a Definition of Antisemitism* (Berkeley and Los Angeles, 1990); the latter is largely a collection of his earlier essays, most notably "Prolegomena."

11. Oberman, *Anti-Semitism*, xi.

12. Gager, *Origins*, esp. part 1, "Anti-Semitism and Anti-Judaism: The Modern Debate," pp. 13–34.

13. Marrus and Paxton, *Vichy France and the Jews* (New York, 1983), 33–34; see also Marrus, "The Theory and Practice of Anti-Semitism," *Commentary* 40 (Aug. 1983), 39, for an even clearer and simpler exposition. Both are scholars of repute in French history; see Michael Marrus, *The Politics of Assimilation: French Jewry at the Time of the Dreyfus Affair* (London, 1971).

14. Marrus and Paxton, *Vichy France*, 34ff.

15. Levy, *The Downfall of the Anti-Semitic Political Parties in Imperial Germany* (New Haven and London, 1975), 1–2, 46, 265.

16. Ibid., 6.

17. Ibid., 259.

18. Jack Wertheimer, *Unwelcome Strangers: East European Jews in Imperial Germany* (New York and Oxford, 1987), 4. His book complements that of Steven E. Aschheim, *Brothers and Strangers: The East European Jew in Germany and German Jewish Consciousness, 1800–1933* (Madison, Wis., 1982), which is predominantly a study in ideas.

19. F. Stern, *Gold and Iron: Bismarck, Bleichroeder, and the Building of the German Empire* (New York, 1977), 496, 497n, 498. Similarly, Marrus and Paxton, *Vichy France*, 54. Dietmar Preissler, *Frühantisemitismus*, 357, also distinguishes between latent and "eruptive" anti-Semitism.

20. Marrus, "Theory and Practice," 38 describes it as "the more common view nowadays, repeated endlessly in popular works." Some scholars subscribe to it too; see Helen Fein's introduction to her *The Persisting Question: Sociological Perspectives and Social Contexts of Modern Antisemitism* (Berlin and New York, 1987), xi–xii: "The bacillus survives, but eruptions of the plague on a massive scale seem to have ceased as conditions for its growth are no longer common." Even a scholar like W. Jochmann is not immune from this usage, writing that larger parts of the German population were "infected" by anti-Semitism after 1900, in "Akademische Führungschichten und Judenfeindschaft in Deutschland 1866–1918," in Jochmann, *Gesellschaftskrise and Judenfeindschaft in Deutschland 1870–1945* (Hamburg, 1988), 22.

21. Langmuir, *History*, 368.

22. Amos Funkenstein, "Theological Interpretations of the Holocaust: A Balance," in François Furet, ed., *Unanswered Questions: Nazi Germany and the Genocide of the Jews* (New York, 1989), 302–3.

23. As quoted in Ismar Schorsch, *Jewish Reactions to German Anti-Semitism, 1870–1914* (New York and London, 1972), 209.

24. I. Schorsch, "German Anti-Semitism in the Light of Post-War Historiography," *LBIY* 19 (1974): 270. Arendt and Sorkin illustrate another aspect of this theory because they hold that emancipation worked almost "too well" in producing a Jewish

subculture that was, on average, more successful and bourgeois than the average German. See David Sorkin, *Transformation*.

25. R. Rürup, "Kontinuität und Diskontinuität der 'Judenfrage' im 19. Jahrhundert: Zur Entstehung des modernen Antisemitismus," in Wehler, ed., *Sozialgeschichte Heute: Festschrift für Hans Rosenberg zum 70. Geburtstag* (Göttingen, 1974), 392.

26. Ibid., 393, 396, 398–400; but what is implied here? Would Jews, especially Jews who, as Sorkin argues, had opted for success and rationality have not been liberal anyway?

27. Ibid., 403–8. The use of the year 1873 is deliberate; see p. 220f., below.

28. G. Mosse, *Masses and Man: Nationalist and Fascist Perceptions of Reality* (Detroit, Mich., 1987), 21–22, 49.

29. G. Mosse, *The Crisis of German Ideology: Intellectual Origins of the Third Reich* (New York, 1964).

30. Paul Lawrence Rose, *Antisemitism*, 55, 62–63, 67. And see my review in *AHR* 97, no. 2 (Apr. 1992): 571–72.

31. See the discussion in general in E. Weis, "Begründung," 9–88, but the reforms of Joseph II of Austria or the later Napoleonic reversal of the actions of 1790 are more to the point.

32. Jacob Katz, *Prejudice*, 9–10, 76ff., 92ff., 149, and notes on pages 340–43, 348. All these men authored books highly critical of Jews between 1816 and 1820.

33. See Katz, "Hep-Hep Riots"; *Prejudice*, 92ff.; and Elonore Sterling, "Anti-Jewish Riots."

34. Preissler, *Frühantisemitismus*, 361.

35. Ibid., 365–66, describes pre-1848 anti-Semitism as undefined and lacking a racist component, but very much in existence.

36. Katz, *The Darker Side of Genius: Richard Wagner's Anti-Semitism* (Hanover and London, 1986), 20; F. Stern, *Gold*, 463; Jochmann, "Antisemitismus im deutschen Kaiserreich 1871–1914," in Jochmann, *Gesellschaftskrise*, 30; Katz, *Prejudice*, 3; Sorkin, *Transformation*, esp. 109–11, 173.

37. Thomas Nipperdey, *Geschichte*, 254–55.

38. For Wagener, see Katz, *Prejudice*, 211; for anti-Semitic literature, see G. Mosse, "Literature and Society in Germany," in G. Mosse, *Masses*, 21–51; for Marr see Moshe Zimmermann, *Wilhelm Marr: The Patriarch of Antisemitism* (New York and Oxford, 1986), 38–40, 47–48; for Niendorf, see James F. Harris, "Franz Perrot: A Study in the Development of the German Lower Middle Class Social and Political Thought in the 1870s," in Ekkehard Teja Wilke, ed., *Studies in Modern European History and Culture*, vol. 2 (1976): 73–106; for C. Frantz, see Katz, *Prejudice*, 195–97.

39. Katz, *Prejudice*, 245ff.; note, again, the use of terms implying that anti-Semitism is a disease.

40. Only E. Sterling argues that modern political anti-Semitism may be found in the early nineteenth century, and only R. Rürup partially agrees. Even historians with very different views of anti-Semitism agree on the 1870s as the starting point. Nipperdey, *Geschichte*, 815n, acknowledges the richness of Sterling's material but states that it is "distorted in proportional terms," that is, that it does not adequately reflect

the reality, which was generally favorable to Jews. Most simply ignore the earlier period. Paul Lawrence Rose, *Antisemitism,* is an exception.

41. Peter Pulzer, *The Rise of Political Anti-Semitism in Germany and Austria* (New York and London, 1964; 2nd ed., Cambridge, Mass., 1988), vii.

42. Werner Jochmann, "Antisemitismus," 33, and "Akademische," 15.

43. Katz, *Darker Side,* 3. Here, too, Rose, *Antisemitism,* 362ff., disagrees and places Wagner's anti-Semitism earlier. My interest here is Katz's claim about the absence of a popular, political anti-Semitic movement.

44. Rürup, "Kontinuität," 404–5.

45. More work is needed to trace this discourse to the pre-1848 era.

46. Arendt, *Antisemitism* (New York, 1968), 54, 56–57, 59–60, 86–87.

47. Amos Funkenstein, "Interpretations," 290ff.

48. Shulamit Volkov, "The Written Word and the Spoken Word: On the Gap Between Pre-1914 and Nazi Anti-Semitism," in Furet, *Unanswered Questions,* 41; F. Stern, *Gold,* 498–99, varies the argument slightly, writing that with unity Germans wanted genuine unity and saw Jews as antinational. Mosse, *Crisis,* passim, discusses this in depth, but as much before as after 1870.

49. Harold James, *A German Identity: Germany 1770–1990* (London, 1989).

50. Jehuda Reinharz, *Fatherland or Promised Land: The Dilemma of the German Jew, 1893–1914* (Ann Arbor, Mich., 1975), 10–11.

51. Stephen M. Poppel, *Zionism in Germany, 1897–1933: The Shaping of a Jewish Identity* (Philadelphia, Pa., 1977), 3, 12, 167.

52. Arendt, *Antisemitism,* xi, written for the 1967 edition; see Rürup's definition above.

53. Jochmann, "Antisemitismus," 35.

54. Ibid., 46.

55. James Retallack, "Anti-Semitism, Conservative Propaganda, and Regional Politics in Late Nineteenth Century Germany," *German Studies Review* 11, no. 3 (Oct. 1988): passim, esp. 379–81.

56. Jochmann, "Antisemitismus," 50, and "Akademische," 28; Retallack, "Anti-Semitism," 395ff.

57. E.g., F. Stern, *Gold,* 498–99, who, after noting the claim about the 1873 crash, adds that there were other factors, such as unity, resistance to modernization, and the *Kulturkampf;* more typical, if also more extreme, is Geoffrey G. Field, *Evangelist of Race: The Germanic Vision of Houston Stewart Chamberlain* (New York, 1981), 264, who writes, "Little needs to be added to his [Rosenberg's] penetrating and persuasive analyses."

58. Rosenberg, "Political and Social Consequences of the Great Depression of 1873–1896 in Central Europe," *Economic History Review* 13 (1943), 73.

59. Ibid., 61, 64.

60. Rosenberg, *Grosse Depression und Bismarckzeit: Wirtschaftsablauf, Gesellschaft und Politik in Mitteleuropa* (Berlin, 1967), 1–21.

61. These are developed in ch. 3, in which Rosenberg devotes thirty pages to anti-Semitism and the same number to the other three effects combined.

62. For a critical approach, see S. B. Saul, *The Myth of the Great Depression, 1873–1896* (London, 1972), admittedly based on England.

63. See the excellent discussion and survey of literature in Geoff Eley, "Hans Rosenberg and the Great Depression of 1873–96: Politics and Economics in Recent German Historiography, 1960–80," in Eley, *From Unification to Nazism: Reinterpreting the German Past* (Boston, 1986), 28–50.

64. Rosenberg, *Grosse*, 89, 91, 93, 96.

65. See Eley's introduction to his essay in *From Unification*, 23–24, 36–37, for a clear statement of his own beliefs; see also 35–36.

66. Shulamit Volkov, *The Rise of Popular Anti-Modernism in Germany: The Urban Master Artisans, 1873–1896* (Princeton, N.J., 1978).

67. Preissler, *Frühantisemitismus*, 358–59.

68. Margaret Lavinia Anderson and Kenneth L. Barkin, "The Myth of the Puttkamer Purge and the Reality of the Kulturkampf: Some Reflections on the Historiography of Imperial Germany," *JMH* 54, no. 4 (1982): 647–86; Blackbourn, "Catholics, the Centre Party and Anti-Semitism," in Blackbourn, *Populists and Patricians: Essays in Modern German History* (Boston, 1987), 173. The other side of the coin was, of course, the argument that Protestants were more anti-Semitic, which may be found in works on Conservatives in 1892 and after (see James Retallack, *Notables of the Right: The Conservative Party and Political Mobility in Germany, 1876–1918* (London, 1988); for the greater development of anti-Semitism in the north of Germany in the 1870–90 era, see Pulzer, *Rise*, 243, and Uriel Tal, *Christians and Jews in Germany: Religion, Politics, and Ideology in the Second Reich, 1870–1914*, trans. Noah Jacobs (Ithaca, N.Y., 1975), 89–90—on the role of liberal Protestant theologians as anti-Semitic based on their view of Judaism as obsolete.

69. Margart L. Anderson, *Windthorst: A Political Biography* (Oxford, 1981), 251–61; Blackbourn, "Catholics," 170; Jochmann, "Akademische," 24.

70. See Levy, *Downfall*, passim.

71. Blackbourn, "Catholics," 169; Thomas Childers, *The Nazi Voter: The Social Foundations of Fascism in Germany, 1919–1933,* (Chapel Hill, N.C., and London, 1983).

72. Ian Kershaw, *Popular Opinion and Political Dissent in the Third Reich: Bavaria 1933–1945* (Oxford, 1983).

73. Blackbourn, *Class, Religion and Local Politics in Wilhelmine Germany: The Center Party in Württemberg before 1914* (New Haven, 1980), 105–6, 233ff., and passim.

74. Blackbourn, "Catholics," 168–87, esp. 170–71, 177.

75. Michael A. Riff, "The Government of Baden against Antisemitism: Political Expediency or Principle," *LBIY* 32 (1987): 119–34. Preissler, *Frühantisemitismus*, 302–4, 316–17, notes that the anti-Semitism was almost entirely secular in content.

76. At least before 1933; this is best described in Kershaw, *Popular Opinion*, 189ff.; for the voting record see Childers, *Nazi Voter*, 112ff., 188ff., 258ff.

77. Blackbourn, "Catholics," 169.

78. It is also false in measuring Catholic anti-Semitism if we are to judge from the analyses of Childers and Kershaw in nn. 69–70 above. In Bavaria as late as the November 1932 elections, the Nazis obtained only 30.5 percent of the vote compared to 33 percent in Germany, but, more significantly, only 19 percent in solidly Catholic Lower Bavaria in contrast to 42 percent in Protestant Middle Franconia; see Dietrich Thränhardt, *Wahlen*, 136, table 24.

79. Esp. Kershaw, *Popular Opinion*, 185–223, who devotes an entire chapter to this theme. See Uriel Tal, *Christians and Jews*, for anti-Christian anti-Semitism.

80. Blackbourn, "Catholics," 182–84. For continuity to 1848, see his "The Politics of Demagogy in Imperial Germany," in Blackbourn, *Populists and Patricians*, 219, 225, 239. Also see Childers, *Nazi Voter*, 112–18; Kershaw, *Popular Opinion*, 246–57, 358–72; Hermann Greive, *Theologie und Ideologie: Katholizismus und Judenthum in Deutschland und Österreich 1918–1935* (Cologne, 1967), 95ff., 222–26. See Pulzer, *Jews*, 291–323, for an interesting study of Jewish voting for the Center and SPD in 1930–33.

81. See Kershaw, *Popular Opinion*, 17–29, for the electoral and religious makeup of Bavaria in the 1920s. On Streicher, see Randall L. Bytwerk, *Julius Streicher: The Man Who Persuaded a Nation to Hate Jews* (New York, 1983), 24–30, but, as the subtitle ought to indicate, this work is not the last word on Streicher; see Robert Gellately, *The Gestapo and German Society: Enforcing Racial Policy, 1933–1945* (Oxford, 1990), 89–90, for the surprise of 1933; for popular denunciations, see 259–60, and passim. Gellately's view of the background of anti-Semitism in Lower Franconia moves from 1819 to the aftermath of World War I, in one page, pp. 87–88; despite the title, most of this important study is based on materials from Würzburg and Lower Franconia.

82. The best discussion of this is in S. Volkov, "Written," 33ff.; Zimmermann, *Marr*, vii, writes simply that there would be few biographies of nineteenth-century anti-Semites if Hitler had not existed.

83. Richard Levy, *Downfall*, 2, 259, and passim.

84. Ibid., 259–61.

85. Hans-Jürgen Puhle, *Agrarische Interessenpolitik und preussischer Konservatismus im wilhelminischen Reich (1893–1914): Ein Beitrag zur Analyse des Nationalismus in Deutschland am Beispiel des Bundes der Landwirte und der Deutsch-Konservativen Partei* (Hanover, 1967); Puhle, *Von der Agrarkrise zum Präfaschismus: Thesen zum Stellenwert der agrarischen Interessenverbände des 19. Jahrhunderts* (Wiesbaden, 1972); G. Eley, *Reshaping the German Right: Radical Nationalism and Political Change after Bismarck* (New Haven, 1980); James Retallack, *Notables;* and Roger Chickering, *We Men Who Feel Most German: A Cultural Study of the Pan-German League 1886–1914* (Boston, 1984). Also, more generally, Fritz Stern, *The Politics of Cultural Despair* (Berkeley, 1961), who is representative of this genre.

86. Jochmann, "Akademische," 19.

87. Ibid., 19–26; only about nine thousand signatures came from Bavaria, but about ten times as many had signed petitions against emancipation in 1849–50. Had so many changed their minds? Or was signature collection in 1880–81 dependent on

a variety of factors not mentioned here? There is still no study of that petition. Jochmann's sole evidence of the role of anti-Semitic leadership is a request from Hans von Bülow to Wilhelm Marr for copies of a "hate" piece; see p. 21. Almost all the documentation for his article is from the Marr Nachlass only.

88. Ibid., 27–28.

89. Levy, *Downfall*, 43ff.

90. Marrus and Paxton, *Vichy France*, 54.

91. Geoffrey Field, *Evangelist*, 5, 10–11. This is the best study of an individual anti-Semite in nineteenth-century Germany.

92. G. Mosse, *Crisis*, 1, 8–9.

93. Ibid., 317.

94. G. Mosse, "What Germans Really Read," in G. Mosse, *Masses*, 52–68.

95. G. Mosse, *Crisis*, 127.

96. Stanley Zucker, "Ludwig Bamberger and the Rise of Anti-Semitism in Germany, 1848–1893," *CEH* 3, no. 4 (Dec. 1970): 332–52.

97. If the Center party had joined the SPD in opposing the Enabling Act, it would have failed for lack of the 60 percent majority required of all constitutional changes. Hitler might still have established a dictatorship, but he would not have had the apparent approval of Parliament.

98. Childers, *Nazi Voter*, 196–97, 208ff., 268–69.

99. Donald Niewyk, *The Jews in Weimar Germany* (Baton Rouge, La., 1980), 78–81, argues that anti-Semitism did not bring the party new converts and that it played only a limited role in Nazi success; see esp. 80 n. 141. Also Sarah Ann Gordon, *Hitler, Germans, and the "Jewish Question"* (Princeton, N.J., 1984), 310ff.

100. Katz, *Prejudice*, 315–16; his book ends in 1933 according to the title, but it contains almost nothing on the 1920s.

101. Pulzer, *Rise*, 324–25; he, too, provides only an epilogue for all of 1914–38.

102. Niewyk, *Jews*, 53.

103. Volkov, "Written," 33–36.

104. Ibid., 36–37.

105. Ibid., 50–52.

106. Ibid., 52.

107. Karl Schleunes, *The Twisted Road to Auschwitz: Nazi Policy Toward German Jews, 1933–1939* (Urbana, Chicago, and London, 1970), provides the best picture of the policies of the Third Reich toward Jews.

Appendixes

The Jewish Decree of 1813

Edict Concerning the Conditions of Members
of the Jewish Religion in the Kingdom of Bavaria

To grant to the members of the Jewish religion in Our Kingdom a uniform constitution in keeping with the welfare of the state, We have, after taking advice from our privy councillors, resolved and herewith determined as follows:

Art. 1

Only those Jewish coreligionists who have legally received the right of residence[1] in Our states [sic] can acquire the civic rights and privileges set forth in this Edict.

Art. 2

Registration in the Jewish Lists[2] to be opened in our police offices[3] is a prerequisite for the enjoyment of such rights and privileges.

Art. 3

For that purpose, all Jews presently in Our Kingdom must report within three months of the publication of this Edict at the police office of their place of residence stating their class,[4] age, family size, and livelihood and present the original of their letters of protection, concessions, or other residence permits.

Art. 4

The police office shall check the residence documentation against Our earlier Edicts and Declarations of 31 December 1806 (*Regierungsblatt* 1807: p. 189), of 19 March 1807 (*Regierungsblatt:* p. 476), and of 28 July 1808 (*Regierungsblatt:* p. 1835) and, if found valid, shall require of [each] Jew a declaration

1. whether he will accept a family name if he does not have one yet, and, [if he does], which [name], and

2. whether he will take the oath of loyalty as stated in the Constitution in art. 1, par. 8.

From Stefan Schwarz, *Die Juden in Bayern im Wandel der Zeiten* (Munich and Vienna, 1963), 341–48. Schwarz also provides the variations in draft form.

Art. 5

Jews are not permitted to choose as their future family names the names of well-known families or those that are frequently used. Those Jews, however, who conduct a commercial business under their former name are at liberty to retain the latter in the future, together with their new name.

Art. 6

The police office shall submit the declarations thus given to the General Commissariat, which will decide whether the Jew is suitable for inclusion in the [Jewish] roll.

Art. 7

If the General Commissariat finds the Jew eligible for inclusion in the roll, [the Jew] must swear the oath of loyalty prescribed above on the Bible, whereupon his admission to the roll occurs, and he will receive an excerpt [of this] for his own legitimation, [and this] will replace for him and his descendents the previous letters of protection.

Art. 8

The roll must contain the old and the new names of Jewish families and shall be deposited with the General Commissariat. Each of the lower police offices shall receive a relevant excerpt thereof.

Art. 9

The Jew is required to use the new name registered in the roll in all of his dealings.

Art. 10

Those Jews who, within three months, either
1. do not submit their document of admittance, or refuse
2. to accept a family name, or
3. to take the oath of loyalty,
shall be treated henceforth simply as foreign Jews.

Art. 11

Any immigration and settlement of foreign Jews in the kingdom is strictly prohibited.

Art. 12

The number of Jewish families in communities where they presently reside ought, as a rule, not be increased, but should, on the contrary, be gradually diminished if it is too large.[5]

Art. 13

Settlement in excess in communities where Jews already live, or settlement in areas where there are as yet no Jews, can be permitted only by the highest authority[6] and will be allowed by the latter only under the following conditions:

1. for establishing factories and large commercial enterprises;
2. by adoption of a regular craft, if they hold the title of master craftsman;
3. if they purchase enough land for their own cultivation so that a family can support itself well by agriculture without trading on the side.

Hence, the purchase of an insignificant piece of property or of a house without farming or plying a craft, the establishment of an ordinary depot or stall, and engaging in other, even if legitimate, trades gives the Jew no right to reside either in the area where he is staying beyond the locally determined number [in the roll] or in any other place.

Art. 14

Even in the case of continued residence of accepted families, no permission will henceforth be granted for marriages based on barter,[7] even if the number of accepted families would not thereby be increased; rather, a Jew seeking marriage must, in addition to proving that he will not exceed the permitted number, additionally prove that he is engaged, exclusive of bartering, in a regular, legally sanctioned trade and is able to support himself and his family from it.

Art. 15

To divert the Jews from their traditional occupations, as inadequate as they are harmful to the general welfare, and to open to them every source of employment appropriate to their present condition, they shall be admitted, pursuant to the regulations stated below, to any and all civil livelihoods, such as agriculture, crafts, the operation of factories, manufacturing, and regular commerce, and the currently existing barter trade [*Schacherhandel*] will be gradually, but as quickly as possible, eliminated.

Art. 16

Jews shall therefore be permitted to acquire full ownership and utilization (*dominium plenum et utile*) of houses, agricultural land, and other landed real estate, and may use this property in any way allowed by law. However, acquisition and possession of separate direct ownership (*dominium directum*) of land, the utilization of which belongs to others, as well as seignorial rights in general, remain strictly prohibited to Jews. A Jew is nevertheless allowed to have appropriate direct ownership of land whose utilization is in his own hands and to acquire the full ownership of his land.

Houses and landed real estate that Jews intend to acquire not for their own dwelling and cultivation but for resale can be acquired only through public auctions or *jure delendi* in bankruptcy cases.

Permission of the highest authority is required for the purchase of houses, even for one's own habitation, in the capital.[8]

Art. 17

Jews may have their land worked by Jewish or Christian labor; the use of foreign Jews, however, is not permitted. Leasing of agricultural land is permitted to [Jews]; subleasing is prohibited.

244   *The People Speak!*

Art. 18

The conduct of any manufacturing, fabrication, occupations, and crafts, whether guild or nonguild, (breweries, saloons, and inns excluded) is permitted to Jews as to Christians so long as there is no obstacle to the settlement of the former. Guild trades may be plied by them only if they are proper members of the guild. There must, however, be no Jewish guilds proper; rather, Jews able to practice a trade or craft competently and provided with personal concessions, or also with acquired material collateral, may be admitted into existing guilds. Jews accepted by a master craftsman as apprentices and as journeymen shall be, like Christian apprentices, matriculated, hired out, released, and provided with indentures by the guilds.

Jews will be allowed to offer special rewards for Christian master craftsmen who accept Jewish children. It is understood that any Jew, once he has obtained master status, may, in turn, accept and maintain Christian and Jewish apprentices and journeymen.

Art. 19

Likewise, Jews shall be admitted to normal exchange, wholesale, and retail trade with regular bookkeeping (which, nevertheless, must be done only in the German language), provided they have documented the sufficient capital, good conduct, and professional ability prescribed by the laws and have obtained a regular real or personal trading concession according to generally valid principles.

Art. 20

All peddling, hawking, and bartering shall henceforth be completely forbidden, and grant of residence on this basis shall remain strictly prohibited. Only those Jewish heads of family already resident on this basis who are presently unable to subsist in any other way ought to be allowed to continue such activity until they have acquired a regular trade, for which purpose the police offices will show every cooperation. Peddling is subject to special police regulations.

Art. 21

All Jewish corporations still existing in the kingdom are to be dissolved, the corporation employees dismissed, and the corporation debts in each district that, until now, formed each corporation, will be distributed, with complete guarantees to the creditors. The dissolution shall be effective within six months after publication of this Edict, and the General Commissariat in whose districts such corporations exist are instructed to file with the Ministry of the Interior within three months after this publication a detailed assessment of the implementation of the dissolution in the case of each corporation in particular and a complete projection of the apportionment of the debts.

Art. 22

The Jews living in the various parts of the kingdom, whether they support themselves from regular civil trades or continue to depend on irregular commercial activity, do not form separate Jewish communities but, in community affairs, join the Christian inhabitants of the area with whom they will form only *one* community. They share with the other inhabitants the rights and obligations of the community, with the exception that Jews engaged in irregular commercial activity have no right to use and no share in the community lands of the places where they live (unless they have prior rights to these, which will continue to be respected). Jews engaged in agriculture or in regularly concessioned trades, however, enjoy with regard to community lands the full rights of community members.

Art. 23

All Jewish coreligionists in the kingdom are assured complete freedom of worship. They enjoy all the rights granted to private church societies by the Edict of 24 March 1809 in chapter 2 of the second section (*Reg. Bl.* 1809 St. 11, p. 904, etc.), unless they have been modified or more specifically defined in the present Edict.

Art. 24

Where more than fifty Jewish families live in a given district defined by the territorial division of the state, Jews are permitted to establish a congregation of their own, and in areas where there is a police office, they may have a synagogue, a rabbi, and their own cemetery.

Art. 25

Where they do not form a congregation, they are restricted to private worship at home, and all secret gatherings under the pretext of religious services are forbidden to them pursuant to art. 36 of chapter 1, section 1 of the Edict of 23 March 1809 (*Reg. Bl.* 1809 St. 11, p. 899). Where there is a synagogue, no one other than the rabbi or an authorized substitute is allowed to perform religious functions.

Art. 26

The local rabbi and substitutes are nominated by the members of the congregation, examined by the General District Commissariat, and, according to the circumstances, either confirmed or rejected. Those confirmed cannot be dismissed without the consent of the General Commissariat.

Art. 27

A Jew nominated as rabbi or as substitute must
a) be registered as a royal subject in the roll,
b) have command of the German language and in general have a scholarly education,
c) be without the blemish of usury or of fraudulent bankruptcy and otherwise lead a good and moral life.

Art. 28

Upon confirmation, the rabbi must swear a solemn oath that he will at all times duly obey the laws of the realm, will teach or say nothing against these same, will, if he learns of something contrary to them, faithfully report it to the authorities, and will refrain from any connections whatsoever with foreign powers.

Art. 29

The regulations contained in the three preceeding articles apply also to rabbis currently in office.

Art. 30

The sphere of activity of rabbis is exclusively restricted to the performance of ecclesiastic duties, and any exercise of jurisdiction, in whatever form it may be expressed, as well as any interference by the rabbis and by the Parnassim[9] in civil and communal affairs is forbidden with penalty of heavy fines and imprisonment, in certain cases even dismissal, the futility of such action being self-evident. Hence, Jews, like other subjects, shall take legal action before our judicial authorities, and all the laws of Our Kingdom apply equally to them, unless there are exceptions pertaining to Jews.

Art. 31

Jewish church property is at the exclusive disposal of the Jewish cult. It will be administered in the individual congregations by the rabbi and two elected members of the congregation.

Art. 32

Jewish children of both sexes, like those of Our other subjects, are under obligation to attend public schools in the cities and in rural areas and will receive, with the exception of religious teaching, equal instruction with them, subject to the existing regulations governing schools and education; they are allowed to enter all higher institutions of learning.

Art. 33

Jews are permitted to establish their own schools if they provide properly educated and examined teachers, who are royal subjects and are assured a salary of at least fl 300.[10] The [teachers] are bound by the general curriculum. The hiring of private tutors is determined by the general regulations.

Art. 34

Permission to study Jewish theology shall be granted to no Jewish youth before he has obtained from a public school of the kingdom a valid certificate of his sufficient preparatory knowledge.

The Jews living in Our Realm will gratefully perceive in these regulations a demonstration of Our concern extending to the welfare of all Our subjects, because all of the police offices will have to work strenuously so that this ordinance may be fully implemented, for which reason we have had this brought to public attention through the official gazette.

Munich, 10 June 1813
Max Joseph
Graf Montgelas
by supreme royal command
The General Secretary
F. Kobell.

NOTES

1. *Indigenat.*

2. *Judenmatrikel,* or, in later usage, simply *Matrikel.*

3. Usually *Landgerichte;* in some smaller cases, literally "police offices."

4. Literally *Stand;* the meaning connotes more than mere occupation.

5. "Too large" meant when the number of Jews was greater than the the number present in 1813.

6. The monarchy through the Ministry of the Interior.

7. That is, when the husband's livelihood was barter. The original was *Schacher-handel.* "Barter" is used here for sake of brevity; *Schacherhandel* meant petty dealing of all kinds, not only barter.

8. Munich.

9. Influential elders of the community.

10. Fl is the abbreviation for gulden or florin, the currency in use in Bavaria.

Appendix B

The Directive of 15 December 1849

Kingdom of Bavaria
State Ministry of the Interior

The Royal Provincial Governors know of the decision made in the House of Deputies on the 14th of the Month [December, 1849] regarding the political equality, both state and communal, of Jewish believers.

Because of the multifarious aspects of this situation, it is certainly conceivable that, perhaps as a result of this decision, a sentiment might arise here and there that could be exploited by the enemies of public order for their own purposes and could be used thereby to cause dissatisfaction and upset; the leisure of the approaching holidays would provide a ready-made and welcome opportunity to hold assemblies.

It appears necessary that the Royal Provincial Governors devote special watchfulness to this situation and, through carefully considered confidential relations with responsible men, put themselves in position to acquire information on this matter as rapidly as possible, to take necessary measures, and to notify the undersigned state ministry of important developments.

Eppeln	Munich, the 15th of Dec. 1849
Gen-Sec of the	by the highest command of
Min. & Min-Rath	His Royal Majesty

From BStA Würzburg, Präsidialakten, Rep. O. O. -3, 325.

Appendix C

Selected Petitions

No. 1

Most Honorable Chamber
of Councillors of Bavaria!

Much to our distress, we have learned that the Most Honorable Chamber is receiving many petitions that oppose the emancipation of the Jews, already passed in the second chamber, and [that] seek to bring about rejection of that decision by the Most Honorable Chamber of Councillors.

Though we are not at all concerned that such illegal agitation might influence the Most Honorable Chamber, we feel bound to give assurance, from our local standpoint, that definitely the greater part of the Bavarian people not only regard the emancipation of the Jews from the point of view of humanity and of human rights as an act of justice due to God, as behooves a Christian state, but recognize it as basically effective in connection with the improvement of the Jews and the promotion of public welfare.

We sign, most respectfully,
Erlangen, February 1850
One thousand signatures attached

[The phrase "with 40 enclosures, in the original" (containing the signatures) appeared on the cover sheet.]

From BHStA Munich, Kammer der Reichsräte: no. 1, 2557 [numbering error; file should be numbered 2657]; no. 2, 2658; nos. 3 and 4, 2660.

No. 2

Most Honorable Chamber of Councillors!

Painfully and with great displeasure, we have learned of the disgrace threatening the entire Christian population of the country, in that the Jews, an alien nation by origin and religion, by customs and mores, are to receive civic and political rights completely equal to those of the Bavarian people.

Until now we had thought it impossible that a majority of the Chamber of Deputies would agree to such a decision, even if the Jews made every effort to achieve their emancipation.

More than any other region, the people of Lower Franconia surely had the most legitimate reason to expect, instead of having the Hebrews granted *greater,* indeed completely *equal* rights, exactly the *opposite,* namely, energetic protection against the excessive abuses that these people have already notoriously made of the rights granted to them *earlier.* We expect protection and more effective laws against Jewish swindling, against their fraud and usury, against the systematic exploitation of townspeople and countrymen, who, quite commonly, after an initially small debt to the Jews, soon find themselves so ensnared that they can no longer avoid ruin. But, instead of such expected protection *against* Jews, the Christian people are, conversely, to be totally delivered to Jewish oppression and exploitation through the grant of completely equal rights to that nation. After so many families have already been reduced to beggary by them, so many bloody tears extracted because of them, we are to see them henceforth even as our *judges,* are to open to them all *ministerial* and *government offices,* are to allow Jewish *rent officials* to harass the people and to play into the hands of their fellow tribesmen, and *we,* the Christians, are to bow before their ilk! They are to be allowed to meddle in all of our communal affairs, indeed even have a say in our Church and endowment matters! Such rights are to be granted to an alien people that is hostile to Christians everywhere, that to this day harbours the same hate toward our religion with which it once nailed the Saviour to the Cross!

With indignation we have learned that ninety-one members of the Chamber of Deputies have voted in favor of it; but we still have a high Chamber of *Councillors* and it is to *that body* that we hereby direct the trustful and fervent plea that it

reject the entire Emancipation law and pressure the
government to submit a different, wholly new bill by which
the rights of the Christian people will be fully
safeguarded, to whit, that

1. no Jew be allowed to settle or to marry in a community unless two-thirds of all community members have given their voluntary consent in open communal assembly;

2. no Jew be admitted to a judicial or revenue office, lest we have to humble ourselves before the Jews, swear the Christian oath before the Jews, and be exposed to quite novel financial speculations; also, lest our courts be peopled by Jewish trainees and secretaries, which would play into the hands of their nation in the most outrageous way;

3. that no Jew be admitted to ministerial or higher administrative positions, or, in general, such offices as require some trust, lest the people be betrayed and sold out;

4. that no Jew be given a voice in matters of Christian Church administration, endowments, etc.;

5. that the Jews be prohibited, entirely and under threat of severe penalty, from engaging in haggling and peddling, because, in addition to the shameful importunity of such trading, these not only encourage fraud but draw the countryman into the claws of the Jews, from which he can seldom extricate himself.

With the most humble plea that the honorable Chamber give due attention to this remonstration and reject a law that so grievously infringes on the rights of the Christian population, we remain most respectfully

the honorable Chamber of Councillors'
most obedient servants

Hilders, 10 January 1850

[Here follows 83 signatures, each numbered, at the end of which the following appears:]

Signing to confirm the authenticity of the above signatures, and unanimously joining the request expressed in this declaration,

The Administration of the Market Community
  Hohmann, Mayor
  Handyert, Community Treasurer
  Hohmann, Catholic Parish Priest

[There are five more names without titles, presumably the communal Bevollmächtigten or councilmembers.]

No. 3

Hirschau 18 December 1849

Most Honorable Chamber of Councillors!

According to public gazettes, the fateful bill concerning Jewish emancipation has already been passed in the Second Chamber of Estates,[1] and that, as we are fully aware, by very perfidious means.

We, the obedient undersigned, were already greatly agitated at the very first word of that bill, and we hastened to make our sentiments known to the Second

Chamber of Deputies; however, the haste with which they chose virtually to smuggle in the new law prevented our petition from reaching the House before the unfortunate vote on the 14th of this month. Therefore we have no other alternative but to place our hopes on the First Chamber, on the T. T. Councillors,[2] and so we take the liberty of laying our convictions and experiences before these gentlemen in the following manner, but with profoundest respect.

Although as Christians we have the duty to extend our love also to our Israelite brethren and intend to exercise that duty to its full extent, we find ourselves nevertheless compelled by the equally sacred duty of self-preservation to protest most energetically against the emancipation of the Jews.

First of all, we consider the proposal to grant equality absurd because in many of the main circumstances of civil life, for example, in the observance of religious holidays, in marriages, and so on, they [Jews] can under no conditions ever be part of our community. Money and temporal possessions here change from one family to another mostly through marriages; since this change can never occur between Jews and Christians, the Jews can easily take from us Christians all money and every possession, that is, exploit us, but we Christians can never get it back from them through intermarriage.

If only a few Jewish families settle here, all small shops, tanneries, hardware stores, and so on, which, as things stand, provide their proprietors with nothing but the scantiest of livelihoods, will in no time at all be superseded and completely crushed by these [Jews] such that at least twelve local families will be reduced to beggary, and our poor relief fund, already in utter extremity, will be fully exhausted within one year.

The Jews come into possession in the shortest possible time of all cash money by getting involved in every business; they rapidly become the only possessors of money, and their Christian neighbors become their debtors.

We can speak from experience. For many years a Jew by the name of *Luber* from Hüttenbach, has managed, despite many protestations of the local tradespeople, to secure his residence; and how that man plies his haggling trade! He lurks constantly at the gates of our town and tries to make some deal with anyone entering; he forever makes the rounds of the pubs and private homes, solely to press his wares on people; if a spendthrift housewife, a faithless servant, a son in need of ready money, or such a daughter wants to get hold of money quickly, one pays a visit to the Jew and gets from him what is wanted, to be sure at a very sad extra charge. If business is not good in town, he takes a pack full of goods and goes with it into the surrounding villages, where he keeps pressing the local inhabitants until finally a deal is made; and he takes anything, even stolen goods, in place of payment, knowing how to resell everything through his connections; thus any influx of business from outside is cut off from the local tradespeople, because these will, can, and ought not slink about in the countryside and in town, but rather earn their living by work and the pursuit of agriculture.

Now, if a single Jew, who does not even have the right of settlement here, is already so detrimental to our town and countryside within a radius of many miles, what a scourge and what a canker will several Jews be here, when they, no longer curbed by any law, can settle anywhere and can everywhere ply the same sordid trade.

What has happened to us here is going to happen throughout the Oberpfalz, a province neglected by nature but traditionally devoted with flawless loyalty to its ruling house, even in these most turbulent recent times. To tell the truth, if the hardworking and industrious citizen is deprived by Jewish emancipation of the last remnants of his prosperity, there will soon no longer be the possibility, even with the best intention, of paying taxes and dues, and it would not be at all surprising if the traditional loyalty weakened even in this province. What is certain is that Jewish emancipation will significantly contribute to the growth of the *Proletariat,* but to the extent in which the latter increases, the risk of upheaval and revolution will become more ominous.

Finally, we, the undersigned, declare our complete disapproval of any and all steps so far taken by whichever side in favor of Jewish emancipation and expect from the solid wisdom of the honorable First Chamber that it will categorically deny its consent to the decision of the Second Chamber for Jewish emancipation of the 14th of this month, a decision tantamount to an act of treason, and will not accept it even with modifications of one kind or another; for if this sorry monstrosity touches our national soil with even one foot, it will soon know how to make its full impact felt without undue trouble.

We remain with due and profoundest respect
the most honorable Chamber of Councillors'
most obedient township of Hirschau

[Here follow the signatures,[3] with *Stand,* at the end of which the following appears:]

Confirming the authenticity of the above signatures
Hirschau 20th December 1849
The Municipal Council [with city seal]

No. 4

Most Honorable Chamber of Councillors!

For the last time we approach with absolute trust and profoundest respect to protest in a few words earnestly and solemnly against the disgraceful decision of the Chamber of Deputies in regard to Jewish emancipation.

We have read a great deal for and against this decision that is so degrading to the dear fatherland; the democrats have involved us in political life and made us read and evaluate what our deputies, the representatives in Munich, say and do for or against our welfare; only we discover that they have either lost their sound Christian common sense or have been bribed by Jewish money or possessed by the worst spirits of the age.

We are rightfully indignant about that and declare those deputies who have spoken and acted, secretly or publicly, for unconditional Jewish emancipation to be faithless and characterless men, suborned traitors of the fatherland and of Christ.

We have every reason to see the proposed emancipation of the Jews as the greatest calamity, as the most glaring injustice ever to have befallen or yet to befall our Christian Bavaria. Anti-Christian iconoclasts have already caused havoc in our region; what then Jewish usurers will do against whom we will receive no protection from the venal, profligate, and Godless bureaucracy! We do not wish to dwell on this issue, it has already been fully expounded in the admirable speeches of the conservative Christian deputies; but we would like to remark additionally that if unconditional Jewish emancipation is implemented everywhere, then our trust, our respect, and our obedience toward such a pro-Jewish government [will be] shaken to the core, we will have to consider ourselves victims and slaves of Jewish agitators, and we can no longer guarantee that we will be able, in times of danger, to obey an authority that rewards our traditional loyalty and self-sacrificing devotion with such dismal ingratitude and cynical ruthlessness.

If 500,000 tongues of gallant traditional Bavarians do not yet dare to voice this now, should the insolent party of literati, lawyers, and bureaucrats embitter the good people toward their king by implementing unconditional emancipation of the Jews—a treasonable surrender of the Christians to the Jews—then they [traditional Bavarians] will act for the sake of natural self-preservation by means of the Germanic law of the stronger, with trickery and force.

We therefore ask and implore the most honorable Chamber of Councillors, mindful of its former patriotic loyalty, love of the people, and moral strength, to avert, now while there is still time, a new immanent revolution that might either drive the Jewish vampires and their henchmen from the country or utterly annihilate them, by forcefully rejecting the disgraceful decision of the majority of deputies, and by forcing the royal cabinet to withdraw this present bill and produce one that, on the one hand, will compel the Jews to engage in agricultural and industrial labor and, on the other hand, will fully protect the Christians from Jewish trickery and power. Only then shall we be able to look with happy confidence to the future, to be prepared for even the greatest sacrifices for our dear fatherland, to persevere in unblemished loyalty, to exclaim in most grateful joy:

Long live our most gracious King and Lord
Maximilian II!

Long live the honor, the strength, and the dignity of our most honorable Chamber of Councillors!

We remain with profoundest respect
Altmühldorf the 6th of January 1850

In the name and on the behalf of the whole parish and rural community.

Jos. J. Erlacher, D.D.
Catholic Parish Priest   [with the seal of the community]

[There follows the signature of the Mayor and four others, presumably the council-members.]

NOTES

1. Parliament had been based on estates or orders of society from 1818 to summer 1848, but thereafter it was a parliament elected on a fairly democratic suffrage. This was an obsolete reference.
2. Evidently "T[itulis] T[itulatis]," or "with all titles due."
3. Occupational Distribution of Signatories

Occupation/Stand	*No.*	*%*
All craft masters	29	23.0
All other artisans	63	51.0
Commercial	4	3.0
Brewery owner	1	0.8
Factory owner	1	0.8
Factory workers	2	1.6
Officials	2	1.6
Farmers	7	5.7
No entry	7	5.7
Unknown/illegible	6	4.6
Title of nobility	1	0.8
Draper's widow	1	0.8
Total	124	100

Sources

Archival Materials

Geheimes Hausarchiv, Munich:
Nachlass Maximilian II, 80/1/249b, "Judenangelegenheiten."
———, 79/3/175, "Gesetz-Entwurf die staatsbürgerliche (politischen) und bürger-
lichen Rechte der israelitischen Glaubensgenossen betreffend."
———, 82/4/354 M.
Nachlass v. d. Pfordten, K. 76 L.5 No. 34/34, 2 (First Ministry): 25, 1 and 28, 1;
7 (Letters): 93, 106, 109, 110, 144; 7 (Misc.): 125.
Hauptstaatsarchiv, Munich:
Ministry of Commerce, 8679, 8680.
Ministry of Finance, 63876 (Riots of 1820).
Ministry of the Interior, 44393, 44482, 44248, 44249, 44988, 46130.
Ministry of Justice, 13389, 13390.
Staatsrat, 3381, 3384.
Upper House of Parliament (Kammer der Reichsräte), 2656–61.
Staatsarchiv Oberbayern:
Regierungs Abgabe, 2272, No. 2272, No. 40811.
———, 2090, No. 33875, Die Verhältnisse der israelitischen Glaubensgenossen,
Emanzipation.
———, 2090, No. 33866, Hausirhandel von Juden.
———, 2093, No. 33910, Juden Matrikel 1846.
———, 40540, No. 2255, four volumes on peddling.
Staatsarchiv Würzburg:
Rep. 0.0.–6, (Regierungsabgabe), Stadt-Commisariates Würzburg 2084, Landes-
polizei.
———, Kammer des Innern, Unterfranken 312, 1883.
———, Kammer des Innern, Unterfranken 316, Allgemeine Landespolizei, 1866.
———, Kammer des Innern, Unterfranken, 329, Allgemeine Landespolizei;
Ordnung, Ruhe, u. Sicherheit . . . Generalia.
Rep. 0.2.1.0.–12, Landratsamt Karlstadt, 4248, Rückständige Kultusbeiträge der
Wolf Braunold in Wiesenfeld.

————, Landratsamt Karlstadt, 4919, Verhältnisse in der israelitischen Kultusgemeinde in Laudenbach, 1862–1901.
Landratsamt Marktheidenfeld, 4474, Acten den königlichen Landgericht Marktheidenfeld; Allgemeine Volksstimmung.
Landtagsarchiv, Munich:
    Karton 867, 3 Ausschuss, J 3-A, J 3-B, "Addressen für und gegen unbedingte Einführung der Reichs Verfassung und der Grundrechte," 13 Landtag, 1849.
Staatsbibliothek, Munich, Handschriftenabteilung:
    Nachlässe, Karl von Abel, Ignaz von Döllinger, Johann Nepomuk Sepp.

Newspapers and Periodicals

Allgemeine Zeitung des Judentums. Magdeburg. Weekly. Ed. Dr. Ludwig Philippson.
Augsburger Allgemeine Zeitung. Daily. Ed. Dr. Gustav Kolb, Dr. A. J. Altenhöfer, Dr. C. A. Mebold.
Augsburger Tagblatt. Augsburg. Daily. Ed. Fr. Gräf.
Augsburger Postzeitung. Augsburg. Daily. Ed. Ludwig Schönchen.
Bamberger Zeitung. Bamberg. Daily. Ed. J. M. Reindl.
Der Bayerische Landbote. Munich. Daily. Ed. Geor. Franz.
Bayerische Landbötin. Munich. Daily. Ed. J. B. Allfeld.
Der Eilbote. Landau in der Pfalz. Twice weekly. Ed. Karl Georges.
Gradaus mein deutsches Volk. Munich. Daily. Ed. A. O. Agathon (earlier, Vecchioni).
Historisch-politische Blätter für das katholische Deutschland. Munich. Twice yearly. Ed. G. Phillips and G. Görres.
Der Lechbote. Augsburg. Daily. Ed. J. Schmidbauer.
Mittelfränkische Zeitung für Recht, Freiheit und Vaterland. Nürnberg. Daily. Ed. Friedrich Tünnerl.
Neue Fränkische Zeitung. Würzburg. Daily. Ed. St. Gätschenberger.
Neueste Nachrichten, aus der Gebiete der Politik. Munich. Daily. Ed. K. Schurick.
Regensburger Zeitung. Regensburg. Daily. Ed. Fried. Heinr. Neubauer.
Sinai: Ein Wochenblatt für die religiösen und bürgerlichen Angelegenheiten Israels. Bayreuth. Weekly. Ed. Dr. Joseph Aub, rabbi in Bayreuth, 1846–47.
Die Synagoge: Eine jüdisch-religiöse Zeitschrift; zur Belehrung und Erbauung für Israeliten. Munich. Ed. Dr. L. Adler, rabbi in Kissingen, 1837–39. (Vol. 1 was published in Würzburg.)
Der Volksbote für den Bürger und Landmann. Munich. Daily exc. Mon. and days following major holidays. Ed. Ernst Zander.
Die Volksbötin. Munich. Daily. Ed. M. C. Bertram.
Würzburger Stadt- und Landbote. Würzburg. Daily. Ed. unknown.

Parliamentary Debates

Bavaria. Landtag. *Kammer der Abgeordneten: Verhandlungen 1819–1917/18.* Munich, 1819 et seq.

Bavaria. Landtag. *Verhandlungen der Kammer der Reichsräthe des Königreichs Bayern vom Jahre 1849*, Munich, 1850.

Bavaria. Landtag. *Verhandlungen der Kammer der Reichsräthe des Königreichs Bayern vom Jahre 1850*, Bd. 5, Munich 1850.

Bavaria. Landtag. *Vollständiges alphabetisches Reportorium über die Verhandlung der Stände des Königreichs Bayerns im Jahre 1819* (Munich, 1821).

Statistical Sources

"Bevölkerung des Königreichs Bayern nach Alter und Geschlecht, Familienverhältnissen, Religionsbekenntnissen, Erwerbsarten und Ständen, dann Zahl und Bestimmung der Gebäude, auf Grund der Aufnahme vom Dezember 1852." Bound with *Beiträge zur Statistik des Königreichs Bayern*. Munich, 1850.

Königliches Statistisches Bureau, ed. *Verzeichniss der Gemeinden des Königreichs Bayern mit ihrer Bevölkerung im Dezember 1861, geordnet nach Kreisen, Verwaltungs-Districten und Gerichtssprengeln, unter Beifügung der einschlägigen Rentämter, Forstämter und Baubehörden*. Munich, 1863.

Place Names

Reichspostzentralamt, ed. *Ortsbuch von Bayern*. Neuwied, 1932.

Biographical Sources

Bosl, Karl, ed. *Bosls Bayerische Biographie. 8,000 Persönlichkeiten aus 15 Jahrhunderten*. Regensburg, 1983.

Schärl, Walter. *Die Zusammensetzung der bayerischen Beamtenschaft von 1806 bis 1918*. Kallmünz, Opf., 1955.

Contemporary Sources

Adler, Dr. [Lazarus]. *Die bürgerliche Stellung der Juden in Bayern: Ein Memorandum, der hohen Kammer der Abgeordneten eherbietigst vorgelegt*. Munich, 1846. Pp. 3–23.

Aub, Rabbi Dr. Hirsch. *Rede bey der Einweihungs-Feyer der Synagoge in München am 21 April 1826*. Munich, 1826. Pp. 3–20.

Aub, Rabbi Dr. Hirsch. *Was Maximilian II. uns war: Predigt bei dem in der Synagoge zu München am 24. März 1864 stattgefundene Trauergottesdienste für den höchstseligen Königen Maximilian II*. Munich, 1864. Pp. 3–16.

Von M. in W. *Das Judenthum und die Emancipation der Juden oder Gleichstellung derselben in allen staatsbürgerlichen Rechten mit den Christen in Jeder Beziehung*. Würzburg, 1849.

Statuten des Unterstützungs-Vereins für israelitische Ackerbau -und Handwerks-Lehrlinge in Bayern. Munich, 1841.

Welfauh, F. *Was erwartet das Volk, Was erwartet Deutschland von Bayerns Ständen?* Munich, 1848.

Published Diaries, Papers, and Memoirs

Bismarck, Otto von. *Die Gesammelte Werke.* Bd. 10, *Fürst Bismarcks gesammelte Reden.* Berlin, 1894.

Bluntschli, Johann Caspar. *Denkwürdiges aus Meinem Leben,* 3 vols. Munich, 1884.

Conrads, Norbert, and Günter Richter, eds. *Denkwürdige Jahre 1848–1851.* Cologne and Vienna, 1978.

Diwald, Helmut, ed. *Von der Revolution zum Norddeutschen Bund. Politik und Ideengut der preussischen Hochkonservativen 1848-1866. Aus dem Nachlass von Ernst Ludwig von Gerlach. Erster Teil: Tagebuch 1848–1866. Zweiter Teil: Briefe, Denkschriften, Aufzeichnungen.* Göttingen, 1970.

Huber, E. R., ed. *Dokumente zur deutschen Verfassungsgeschichte.* Vol. 1: *Deutsche Verfassungsdokumente 1803–1850.* Stuttgart, 1961.

Laubmann, Georg, and Michael Doeberl, eds. *Denkwürdigkeiten des Grafen Maximilian Joseph v. Montgelas über die innere Staatsverwaltung Bayerns (1799–1817).* Munich, 1908.

Richarz, Monika, ed. *Jüdisches Leben in Deutschland: Selbstzeugnisse zur Sozialgeschichte 1780–1871.* New York, 1976.

Trost, Ludwig, and Friedrich Leist, eds. *König Maximilian II von Bayern und Schelling: Briefwechsel.* Stuttgart, 1890.

Bibliography

Adam, Uwe Dietrich. *Judenpolitik im Dritten Reich*. Düsseldorf, 1972.

Albrecht, Dieter, et al., eds. *Festschrift für Max Spindler*. Munich, 1969.

Allaire, Max. *Die periodische Presse in Bayern: Eine statistische Untersuchung*. Zweibrücken, 1913.

Anderson, Margaret Lavinia. *Windthorst: A Political Biography*. Oxford, 1981.

Anderson, Margaret Lavinia, and Kenneth L. Barkin. "The Myth of the Puttkamer Purge and the Reality of the Kulturkampf: Some Reflections on the Historiography of Imperial Germany." *JMH* 54, no. 4 (1982): 647–86.

Angermann, Erich. *Robert von Mohl, 1799–1875: Leben und Werk eines altliberalen Staatsgelehrten*. Neuwied, 1962.

Arendt, Hannah. *Antisemitism*. New York, 1968.

Aschheim, Steven E. *Brothers and Strangers: The East European Jew in Germany and German Jewish Consciousness, 1800–1933*. Madison, Wis., 1982.

Bacharach, Walter Zwi. "Das Bild des Juden in katholischen Predigten des 19. Jahrhunderts." In Treml et al., *Geschichte*, 313–19.

Barkai, Avraham. "The German Jews at the Start of Industrialization: Structural Change and Mobility 1835–1860." In W. E. Mosse et al., *Revolution*, 123–49.

———. "German-Jewish Migrations in the Nineteenth Century, 1830–1910." *LBIY* 30 (1985): 301–18.

Barkin, Kenneth D. "1878–1879. The Second Founding of the Reich: A Perspective." *GSR* 10, no. 2 (May 1987): 219–35.

Baron, Salo W. "The Impact of the Revolution of 1848 on Jewish Emancipation." *JSS* (July 1949): 195–248.

Behnen, Michael. "Probleme des Frühantisemitismus in Deutschland (1815 bis 1848)." *BfdL* 112 (1976): 244–79.

Bender, Heinz. *Der Kampf um die Judenemanzipation in Deutschland im Spiegel der Flugschriften 1815–1820*. Jena, 1939.

Berding, Helmut. "Judenemanzipation im Rheinbund." In E. Weis, *Reformen*, 269–86.

———. *Moderner Antisemitismus in Deutschland*. Frankfurt am Main, 1986.

Best, Heinrich. *Interessenpolitik und nationale Integration 1848/49: Handelspolitische Konflikte im frühindustriellen Deutschland*. Göttingen, 1980.

———. "Struktur und Wandel kollektiven politischen Handelns: Die handelspolitische Petitionsbewegung 1848/49." In Volkmann and Bergmann, 169–97.

Bieber, Hans-Joachim. "Anti-Semitism as a Reflection of Social, Economic and Political Tension in Germany: 1880–1933." In Bronsen, *Jews and Germans*, 33–77.

Blackbourn, David. "Catholics, the Centre Party and Anti-Semitism." In Blackbourn, *Populists and Patricians*, 168–87.

———. *Class, Religion and Local Politics in Wilhelmine Germany: The Center Party in Württemberg before 1914*. New Haven, 1980.

———. "The Politics of Demagogy in Imperial Germany." In Blackbourn, *Populists and Patricians*, 217–45.

———. *Populists and Patricians: Essays in Modern German History*. Boston, 1987.

Blackbourn, David, and Geoff Eley. *The Peculiarities of German History: Bourgeois Society and Politics in Nineteenth-Century Germany*. Oxford and New York, 1984.

Blessing, Werner K. "Allgemeine Volksbildung und politische Indoktrination im bayerischen Vormärz: Das Leitbild des Volksschullehrers als mentales Herrschaftsinstrument." *ZfbL* 37² (1974): 479–568.

———. "Umwelt und Mentalität im ländlichen Bayern: Eine Skizze zum Alltagswandel im 19. Jahrhundert." *AfS* 19 (1979): 1–42.

———. "Zur Analyse politischer Mentalität und Ideologie der Unterschichten im 19. Jahrhundert: Aspekte, Methoden und Quellen am bayerischen Beispiel." *ZfbL* 34³ (1971): 768–816.

Bölling, Rainer. *Sozialgeschichte der deutschen Lehrer: Ein Überblick vom 1800 bis zur Gegenwart*. Göttingen, 1979.

Bosl, Karl. *Die Geschichte der Repräsentation in Bayern*. Munich, 1974.

———, ed. *Der moderne Parlamentarismus und seine Grundlagen in der ständischen Repräsentation*. Berlin, 1977.

———, ed. *Oberpfalz und Oberpfälzer, Geschichte einer Region: Gesammelte Aufsätze*. Ed. Konrad Ackermann and Erich Lassleben. Kallmünz, 1978.

Bosse, Friedrich. *Die Verbreitung der Juden im Deutschen Reiche auf Grundlage der Volkszählung vom 1. Dezember 1880*. Berlin, 1885.

Brakelmann, Günter, Martin Greschat, and Werner Jochmann, eds. *Protestantismus und Politik: Werk und Wirkung Adolf Stoeckers*. Hamburg, 1982.

Brandt, Harm-Hinrich. *Hundert Jahre Kitzinger Synagoge: Zur Geschichte des Judenthums in Mainfranken*. Würzburg, 1984.

———, ed. *Zwischen Schutzherrschaft und Emanzipation: Studien zur Geschichte der mainfränkischen Juden im 19. Jahrhundert*. Mainfränkische Studien, vol. 39. Würzburg, 1987.

Breuer, Mordechai. *Jüdische Orthodoxie im Deutschen Reich 1871–1918: Sozialgeschichte einer religiösen Minderheit*. Frankfurt am Main, 1986.

Bronsen, David, ed. *Jews and Germans from 1860 to 1933: The Problematic Symbiosis*. Heidelberg, 1979.

Broszat, Martin, E. Fröhlich, and F. Wiesemann, eds. *Bayern in der NS-Zeit*. 6 vols. Munich and Vienna, 1977–83.

Brunner, Johann. "Die bayerische Postzeitungsliste von 1848." *ZfbL* 3 (1930): 481–85.

Brunner, O., et al., eds. *Geschichtliche Grundbegriffe: Historisches Lexikon zur politisch-sozialen Sprache in Deutschland.* Stuttgart, 1972.

Bytwerk, Randall L. *Julius Streicher: The Man Who Persuaded a Nation to Hate Jews.* New York, 1983.

Cahnman, Werner J. "Friedrich Wilhelm Schelling über die Judenemancipation." *ZfbL* 37² (1974): 614–23.

———. "Village and Small-Town Jews in Germany: A Typological Study." *LBIY* 19 (London, 1974): 107–30.

Campbell, Joan. *Joy in Work, German Work: The National Debate, 1800–1945.* Princeton, N.J., 1989.

Caplan, Jane. "Postmodernism, Poststructuralism, and Deconstruction: Notes for Historians." *CEH* 226, nos. 3–4 (Sept.-Dec. 1989): 260–78.

Caron, Vicki. *Between France and Germany: The Jews of Alsace-Lorraine, 1871–1918.* Stanford, Calif., 1988.

Caron, Vicki, and Paula Hyman. "The Failed Alliance: Jewish-Catholic Relations in Alsace-Lorraine, 1871–1914." *LBIY* 26 (1981): 3–19.

Chickering, Roger. *We Men Who Feel Most German: A Cultural Study of the Pan-German League 1886–1914.* Boston, 1984.

Childers, Thomas. *The Nazi Voter: The Social Foundations of Fascism in Germany, 1919–1933.* Chapel Hill, N.C., and London, 1983.

Clement, Horst. *Das bayerische Gemeindeedikt vom 17 Mai 1818.* Kassel, 1934.

Cobet, Christoph. *Der Wortschatz des Antisemitismus in der Bismarckzeit.* Munich, 1973.

Conze, Werner. "Bauer." In O. Brunner et al., *Geschichtliche Grundbegriffe,* 407–39.

Conzemius, Victor. "Ignaz von Döllinger und Edmund Jörg: Analyse einer Freundschaft und ihres Zerfalls." In Albrecht, *Festschrift,* 743–65.

Dahrendorf, Ralf. *Society and Democracy in Germany.* London, 1968.

Dawidowicz, Lucy. *The Holocaust and the Historians.* Cambridge, Mass., 1981.

———. *The War Against the Jews.* New York, 1975.

Daxelmüller, Christoph. "Fränkische Dorfsynagogen." *Volkskunst* 4 (Nov. 1981): 234–41.

———. *Jüdische Kultur in Franken.* Würzburg, 1988.

———. "Jüdisches Alltagsleben im 19. und 20. Jahrhundert am Beispiel Unterfrankens." In Treml et al., *Geschichte,* 287–98.

Deneke, Bernward, et al., eds. *Siehe der Stein schreit aus der Mauer: Geschichte und Kultur der Juden in Bayern.* Nuremberg, 1988.

Dickinson, John K. *German and Jew.* Chicago, 1967.

Dirrigl, Michael. *Maximilian II: König von Bayern 1848–1864.* 2 vols. Munich, 1984.

Doeberl, Anton. "Die katholische Bewegung in Bayern in den Jahren 1848 und 1849." *Historisch-politische Blätter für das katholische Deutschland* 170 (1922), hefte 1:7–17, 2:65–70, 4:211–22, 5:249–59, 8:429–45, 9:494–503.

Doeberl, Michael. *Entwicklungsgeschichte Bayerns.* Vol. 3, *Vom Regierungsantritt König Ludwigs I. bis zum Tode König Ludwigs II. Mit Einem Ausblick auf die*

Innere Entwicklung Bayerns unter dem Prinzregenten Luitpold. Ed. Max Spindler. Munich, 1931.

Domansky, Elisabeth. *Die jüdische Gemeinde: Beiträge zur Geschichte Iserlohns.* Iserlohn, 1970.

Domarus, Max. *Bürgermeister Behr: Ein Kämpfer für den Rechtsstaat.* Würzburg, 1971.

Doney, John Christopher. "The Catholic Enlightenment and Popular Education in the Prince Bishopric of Würzburg, 1765–95." *CEH* 21, no. 1 (Mar. 1988): 3–30.

Dubnov, Simon. *History of the Jews.* Vol. 5, *From the Congress of Vienna to the Emergence of Hitler.* Trans. Moshe Spiegel. S. Brunswick, New York, and London, 1973.

Eckstein, Dr. A[dolf]. *Der Kampf der Juden um ihre Emanzipation in Bayern.* Fürth in Bayern, 1905.

Eichmeyer, Jens Peter. *Anfänge liberaler Parteibildung (1847 bis 1854).* Ph.D. diss., University of Göttingen, 1968.

Eichstädt, Volkmar. *Bibliographie zur Geschichte der Judenfrage.* Bd. 1: *1750–1848.* Hamburg, 1938.

Eley, Geoffrey. *From Unification to Nazism: Reinterpreting the German Past.* Boston, 1986.

———. "Hans Rosenberg and the Great Depression of 1873–1896: Politics and Economics in Recent German Historiography, 1960–80." In Eley, *From Unification,* 28–50.

———. "Labor History, Social History, *Alltagsgeschichte:* Experience, Culture, and the Politics of the Everyday—a New Direction for German Social History." *JMH* 61, no. 2 (June 1989): 297–343.

———. *Reshaping the German Right: Radical Nationalism and Political Change after Bismarck.* New Haven, 1980.

Engelbert, Hermann. *Statistik des Judenthums im Deutschen Reiche ausschliesslich Preussens und in der Schweiz.* Frankfurt am Main, 1875.

Engelsing, Rolf. *Analphabetentum und Lektüre: Zur Sozialgeschichte des Lesens in Deutschland zwischen feudaler und industrieller Gesellschaft.* Stuttgart, 1973.

———. "Zur politischen Bildung der deutschen Unterschichten 1789–1863." *HZ* 206 (1968): 337–69.

Epstein, Klaus. *The Genesis of German Conservatism.* Princeton, N.J., 1966.

Erb, Rainer, and Werner Bergmann. *Die Nachtseite der Judenemanzipation: Der Widerstand gegen die Integration der Juden in Deutschland 1780–1860.* Berlin, 1989.

Evans, Richard J., and W. R. Lee, eds. *The German Family: Essays on the Social History of the Family in Nineteenth- and Twentieth-Century Germany.* Totowa, N.J., 1981.

Fehn, Hans. "Das Land Bayern und seine Bevölkerung seit 1800." *HbG,* 4^2: 647–707.

Fein, Helen, ed. *The Persisting Question: Sociological Perspectives and Social Contexts of Modern Antisemitism.* Berlin and New York, 1987.

Feistle, Karl. *Geschichte der Augsburger Postzeitung von 1838–1871: Ein Beitrag zur*

Geschichte der katholischen Presse. Munich, 1951, Ph.D. diss., University of Munich, 1951.

Fenske, Hans. "Politischer und sozialer Protest in Süddeutschland nach 1830." In Reinalter, 143–201.

Field, Geoffrey. *Evangelist of Race: The Germanic Vision of Houston Stewart Chamberlain.* New York, 1981.

Fischer, Heinz-Dietrich. *Handbuch der politischen Presse in Deutschland 1480–1980.* Düsseldorf, 1981.

Flade, Roland. *Juden in Würzburg 1918–1933.* Würzburg, 1985.

———. "Juden und Christen in ländlichen Gemeinden Unterfrankens im 19. Jahrhundert, dargestellt anhand von Selbstzeugnissen aus jüdischer Feder." In *Jüdische Landgemeinden in Franken,* 43–46.

———. "Ländliches Judentum in Unterfranken im 20. Jahrhundert." In *Jüdische Landgemeinden in Franken,* 47–50.

Franz, Eugen. *Ludwig Freiherr von der Pfordten,* Munich, 1938.

Franz, Günther. "Die agrarische Bewegung im Jahr 1848." *ZAA* 7 (1959): 176–92.

Fried, Pankraz. "Die Sozialentwicklung im Bauerntum und Landvolk." *HbG* 4², 751–80.

Friedrich, J. *Ignaz von Döllinger: Sein Leben auf Grund seines schriftlichen Nachlasses.* 3 vols. Munich, 1901.

Funkenstein, Amos. "Theological Interpretations of the Holocaust: A Balance." In Furet, *Unanswered Questions,* 275–303.

Furet, François, ed. *Unanswered Questions: Nazi Germany and the Genocide of the Jews.* New York, 1989.

Gager, John G. *The Origins of Anti-Semitism: Attitudes Toward Judaism in Pagan and Christian Antiquity.* New York and Oxford, 1983.

Gagliardo, John G. *From Pariah to Patriot: The Changing Image of the German Peasant 1770–1840.* Lexington, Ky., 1969.

Gailus, Manfred. "Soziale Protestbewegungen in Deutschland 1847–1849." In Volkmann and Bergmann, *Sozialer Protest,* 76–106.

———. "Zur Politisierung des Landbevölkerung in der Märzbewegung von 1848." In Steinbach, *Modernisierungsprozess,* 88–113.

Gall, Lothar. *Bismarck: The White Revolutionary.* 2 vols. Trans. J. A. Underwood. London, 1986.

Gebhardt, Hartwig. *Revolution und liberale Bewegung: Die nationale Organisation der konstitutionellen Partei in Deutschland, 1848/49.* Bremen, 1974.

Gellately, Robert. *The Gestapo and German Society: Enforcing Racial Policy, 1933–1945.* Oxford, 1990.

Gerber, David A. "Anti-Semitism and Jewish-Gentile Relations in American Historiography and the American Past." In Gerber, *Anti-Semitism,* 3–54.

———, ed. *Anti-Semitism in American History.* Urbana and Chicago, 1986.

Glashauser, Gabriele. *Das Entstehen der politischen Parteien in Bayern 1848.* Ph.D. diss., University of Munich, 1944.

Gleibs, Yvonne. *Juden im kulturellen und wissenschaftlichen Leben Münchens in der Zweiten Hälfte des 19. Jahrhunderts.* Munich, 1981.

Goldstein, Alice. "Aspects of Change in a Nineteenth-Century German Village." *Journal of Family History* (Summer 1984): 145–57.

——. "Some Demographic Characteristics of Village Jews in Germany: Non-nenweier, 1800–1931." In Ritterband, *Modern Jewish Fertility*, 112–43.

——. "The Urbanization of Jews in Baden, Germany, 1825–1925." *Papers in Jewish Demography 1981*, 71–86.

Gollwitzer, Heinz. "Graf [Franz Friedrich] Carl Giech 1795–1863: Eine Studie zur politischen Geschichte des fränkischen Protestantismus in Bayern." *ZfbL* 24 (1961): 102–62.

——. *Ludwig I. von Bayern: Königtum im Vormärz. Eine politische Biographie*. Munich, 1986.

Gordon, Sarah Ann. *Hitler, Germans, and the "Jewish Question."* Princeton, N.J., 1984.

Gotthelf, Jakob. *Historisch-dogmatische Darstellung der rechtlichen Stellung der Juden in Bayern*. Munich, 1851.

Grab, Walter, ed. "The German Way of Jewish Emancipation." *The Australian Journal of Politics and History* 30, no. 2 (1984): 224–35.

——. *Jüdische Integration und Indentität in Deutschland und Österreich 1848–1918*. Tel Aviv, 1984.

Greive, Hermann. *Geschichte des modernen Antisemitismus in Deutschland*. Darmstadt, 1983.

——. *Theologie und Ideologie: Katholizismus und Judentum in Deutschland und Österreich 1918–1935*. Cologne, 1967.

Guth, Klaus, et al., eds. *Jüdische Landgemeinden in Oberfranken (1800–1942): Ein historisch-topographisches Handbuch*. Vol. 1. Bamberg, 1988.

Habermas, Jürgen. *The Structural Transformation of the Public Sphere: An Inquiry into a Category of Bourgeois Society*. Trans. Thomas Burger. Cambridge, Mass., 1989.

Hamerow, Theodore S. "Guilt, Redemption, and Writing German History." *AHR* 88, no. 1 (Feb. 1983): 53–72.

Harris, James F. "Arms and the People: The Bürgerwehr of Lower Franconia in 1848 and 1849." In Larry Eugene Jones and Konrad Jarausch, eds., *In Search of a Liberal Germany: Studies in the History of German Liberalism from 1789 to the Present* (New York, Oxford, Munich, 1990), 133–60.

——. "The Authorship of Political Tracts in Post-1848 Germany." *German Studies Review* 10, no. 3 (Oct. 1987): 413–41.

——. "Bavarians and Jews in Conflict in 1866: Neighbors and Enemies." *LBIY* 32 (1987): 103–17.

——. "Franz Perrot: A Study in the Development of the German Lower Middle Class Social and Political Thought in the 1870s." In Ekkehard-Teja Wilke, ed., *Studies in Modern European History and Culture*, vol. 2 (1976): 73–106.

——. "Public Opinion and the Proposed Emancipation of the Jews in Bavaria in 1849–50." *LBIY* 34 (1989): 67–79.

——. "Rethinking the Categories of the German Revolution of 1848: The Emergence of Popular Conservatism in Bavaria." *CEH* 25, no.2 (1992): 123–48.

————. Review of Paul Lawrence Rose, *Revolutionary Antisemitism in Germany from Kant to Wagner* (Princeton, 1990). In *AHR* 97, no. 2, (April, 1992): 571–72.

Hartmannsgruber, Friedrich. *Die bayerische Patriotenpartei 1868–1887*. Munich, 1986.

Hauff, Ludwig. *Leben und Wirken Maximilian II, König von Bayern: Ein Volksbuch*. Munich, 1864.

Häusler, Wolfgang. "Judenfeindliche Strömmungen im deutschen Vormärz." In Treml et al., 299–312.

Heinen, Ernst. "Antisemitische Strömmungen im politischen Katholizismus während des Kulturkampfes." In Heinen, ed., *Geschichte*, 259–99.

————. *Geschichte in der Gegenwart: Festschrift für Kurt Kluxen zu seinem 60. Geburtstag*. Paderborn, 1972.

Heintz, Eckard. *Der Beamtenabgeordnete im bayerischen Landtag. Eine politiologische Studie über die Stellung des Beamtentums in der parlamentarischen Entwicklung Deutschlands*. Munich, 1966.

Hertzberg, Arthur. *The French Enlightenment and the Jews*. New York and London, 1968.

Herzig, Arno. *Judentum und Emanzipation in Westfalen*. Münster, 1973.

Hesse, Horst. "Politisches Verhalten bayerischer Beamter 1848/49." *ZfbL* 42^1 (1979): 127–46.

————. *Die sogenannte Sozialaesetzgebung Bayerns. Ende der sechziger Jahre des 19. Jahrhunderts: Ein Beitrag zur Strukturanalyse der bürgerlichen Gesellschaft*. Munich, 1971.

Higham, John. "Social Discrimination Against Jews in America, 1830–1930." *Publications of the American Jewish Historical Society* 47, no. 1 (Sept. 1957): 1–33.

Hobsbawm, Eric. *Captain Swing*. New York, 1968.

————. *Primitive Rebels: Studies in Archaic Forms of Social Movement in the Nineteenth and Twentieth Centuries*. Manchester, 1971.

Hofmann, Hanns H. *Historischer Atlas von Bayern: Teil Frankens*. Munich, 1960.

Hofmann, Hans H. and Hermann Hemmerich, eds. *Unterfranken: Geschichte seiner Verwaltungsstrukturen seit dem Ende des alten Reiches 1814 bis 1980*. Würzburg, 1981.

Hoffmann, Diether H. *Das Petitionsrecht*. Frankfurt am Main, 1959.

Hoffmann, Hermann. "Die Würzburger Judenverfolgungen von 1349." *Mainfränkisches Jahrbuch für Geschichte und Kunst* 5 (1953): 91–114.

Hoffmann, Kurt. "Sturm und Drang in der politischen Presse Bayerns 1848 bis 1850." *ZfbL* 3 (1930): 205–66.

Huber, E. R., ed. *Dokumente zur deutschen verfassungsgeschichte*. Vol. 1: *Deutsche verfassungsdokumente 1803–1850*. Stuttgart, 1961.

Hsia, R. Po-Chia. *The Myth of Ritual Murder: Jews and Magic in Reformation Germany*. New Haven and London, 1988.

Hyman, Paula E. *The Emancipation of the Jews of Alsace: Acculturation and Tradition in the Nineteenth Century*. New Haven, 1991.

————. "The History of European Jewry: Recent Trends in the Literature." *JMH* 54, no. 2 (June 1982): 303–19.

Imhof, Wilhelm. *Die geschichtliche Entwicklung des Gemeinderechts im rechtsrhein-ischen Bayern seit dem Jahre 1818.* Munich, 1927.

Israel, Jonathan I. "Central European Jewry during the Thirty Years' War." *CEH* 16 (Mar. 1983): 3–30.

Jäckel, Eberhard. *Hitlers Weltanschauung: Entwurf einer Herrschaft.* 2d. ed. Stuttgart, 1981.

James, Harold. *A German Identity: Germany 1770–1990.* London, 1989.

Jeggele, Utz. *Judendörfer in Württemberg.* Tübingen, 1969.

Jochmann, Werner. "Akademische Führungsschichten und Judenfeindschaft in Deutschland 1866–1918." In Jochmann, *Gesellschaftskrise,* 13–29.

———. "Antisemitismus im deutschen Kaiserreich 1871–1914." In Jochmann, *Ge-sellschaftskrise,* 30–98. Originally in W. E. Mosse and Arnold Paucker, eds., *Juden im Wilhelminischen Deutschland: Ein Sammelband* (Tübingen, 1976), 389–477.

———. *Gesellschaftskrise und Judenfeindschaft in Deutschland 1870–1945.* Ham-burg, 1988.

Jüdische Landgemeinden in Franken: Beiträge zu Kultur und Geschichte einer Min-derheit. Bayreuth, 1987.

Kantzenbach, Friedrich Wilhelm. "Protestantische Pfarrer in Politik und Gesellschaft der bayerischen Vormärzzeit." *ZfbL* 39[1] (1976): 171–200.

Kaplan, Steven Laurence. "Long-Run Lamentations: Braudel on France." *JMH* 63, no. 2 (June 1991): 341–61.

Katz, Jacob. *The Darker Side of Genius: Richard Wagner's Anti-Semitism.* Hanover, N.H., and London, 1986.

———. *From Prejudice to Destruction: Anti-Semitism, 1700–1933.* Cambridge, Mass., 1980.

———. "The Hep-Hep Riots in Germany in 1819: The Historical Background." *Zion* 38 (1973): 62–115, in Hebrew.

———. "The Term 'Jewish Emancipation': Its Origin and Historical Impact." In Alexander Altmann, ed., *Studies in Nineteenth-Century Jewish Intellectual History* (Cambridge, Mass., 1964): 1–25.

———. *Out of the Ghetto: The Social Background of Jewish Emancipation 1770–1870.* Cambridge, 1973.

Kershaw, Ian. "Antisemitismus und Volksmeinung: Reaktionen auf die Judenver-folgung." In Broszat, Fröhlich, and Wiesemann, *Bayern,* 2-A: 281–348.

———. "The Persecution of the Jews and German Popular Opinion in the Third Reich." *LBIY* 26 (1981): 261–89.

———. *Popular Opinion and Political Dissent in the Third Reich: Bavaria 1933–1945.* Oxford, 1983.

Kilian, Hendrikje. "Die Anfänge der Emanzipation am Beispiel der Münchener jüdis-chen Gemeinde." In Treml et al., *Geschichte,* 267–75.

Kirzel, Gernot. *Staat und Kirche im bayerischen Landtag zur Zeit Max II (1848–1864).* Munich, 1974.

Klessmann, Christoph. "Zur Sozialgeschichte der Reichsverfassungskampagne von 1849." *HZ* 218 (1974): 282–337.

Knodel, John. "Malthus Amiss: Marriage Restrictions in 19th Century Germany." *Social Science* 47, no. 1 (Winter 1972): 40–45.

Knoll, Simon. *Predigten auf alle Sonn- und Festtage des katholischen Kirchenjahres für Stadt und Land.* Vol. 1. Schaffhausen, 1862.

Kober, Adolf. "Emancipation's Impact on the Education and Vocational Training of German Jewry." *JSS* 16 (1954): 151–76.

———. "Jews in the Revolution of 1848 in Germany." *JSS* (Apr. 1948): 135–64.

Kobler, Franz. *Napoleon and the Jews.* New York, 1976.

Kopp, August. *Die Dorfjuden in der Nordpfalz: Dargestellt an der Geschichte der jüdischen Gemeinde Alsenz ab 1655.* Meisenhain am Glan, 1968.

Koselleck, Reinhard. *Preussen zwischen Reform und Revolution: Allgemeines Landrecht, Verwaltung und soziale Bewegung von 1791 bis 1848.* 1967. Reprint. Stuttgart, 1975.

Krug, Gisela. "Die Juden in Mainfranken zu Beginn des 19. Jahrhunderts: Statistische Untersuchungen zu ihrer sozialen und wirtschaftlichen Situation." In Brandt, *Zwischen Schutzherrschaft,* 19–137.

Krzywinski, Ulrike. "Jüdische Landgemeinden in Oberfranken (1800–1942): Ergebnisse des DFG-Projektes 'Judendörfer in Oberfranken.'" In Treml et al., *Geschichte,* 219–23.

Kulka, Otto Dov. "Major Trends and Tendencies in German Historiography on National Socialism and the 'Jewish Question' (1924–1984)." *LBIY* 30 (1985): 215–42.

Kulka, Otto Dov, and Paul R. Mendes-Flohr, eds. *Judaism and Christianity under the Impact of National Socialism.* Jerusalem, 1987.

Kumpf, Johann Heinrich. *Petitionsrecht und öffentliche Meinung im Entstehungsprozess der Paulskirchenverfassung 1848/49.* Frankfurt am Main, 1983.

Kuppelmayr, Lothar. "Die Tageszeitungen in Bayern (1849–1972)." *HbG* 4²: 1146–73.

Langewiesche, Dieter. "Die deutsche Revolution." *AFS* 21 (1981): 459–87.

———. "Die politische Vereinsbewegung in Würzburg und in Unterfranken in den Revolutionsjahren 1848/49." *JFräLG* 37 (1977): 195–233.

Langmuir, Gavin I. *History, Religion, and Antisemitism.* Berkeley and Los Angeles, 1990.

———. "Prolegomena to any Present Analysis of Hostility Against Jews." *Social Science Information* 15 (1976): 689–727.

———. *Toward a Definition of Antisemitism.* Berkeley and Los Angeles, 1990.

Lee, W. Robert. "Family and 'Modernisation': The Peasant Family and Social Change in Nineteenth-Century Bavaria." In Evans and Lee, *German Family,* 84–119.

———. *Population Growth, Economic Development, and Social Change in Bavaria, 1750–1850.* New York, 1977.

Lempfrid, Wilhelm. "Der bayerische Landtag 1831 und die öffentliche Meinung." *ZfbL* 24 (1961): 1–101.

Lenk, Leonhard. "Die Bauern im Bayerische Landtag 1819–1970." In *Bauernschaft u. Bauernstand 1500–1970: Büdinger Vorträge 1971–72* (Limburg, 1975): 245–64.

————. "Revolutionär-Kommunistische Umtriebe im Königreich Bayern: Ein Beitrag zur Entwicklung von Staat und Gesellschaft 1848–1864." *ZfbL* 28$^{1/2}$ (1965): 555–622.

Lestschinsky, Jakob. *Das wirtschaftliche Schicksal des deutschen Judentums: Aufstieg, Wandlung, Krise, Ausblicke.* Berlin, 1932.

Leuckart von Weissdorf, Hans Freiherr, ed. *Die Verfassungsurkunde des Königreichs Bayern und die auf die Verfassung bezüglichen sonstigen Gesetze.* Ansbach, 1905.

Levine, Hillel. *Economic Origins of Antisemitism: Poland and Its Jews in the Early Modern Period.* New Haven, 1991.

Levy, Richard. *The Downfall of the Anti-Semitic Political Parties in Imperial Germany.* New Haven and London, 1975.

Liebeschütz, Hans, and Arnold Paucker, eds. *Das Judentum in der deutschen Umwelt 1800–1850: Studien zur Frühgeschichte der Emanzipation.* Tübingen, 1977.

Low, Alfred D. *Jews in the Eyes of the Germans: From the Enlightenment to Imperial Germany.* Philadelphia, Pa., 1979.

Lowenstein, Steven M. "Jewish Residential Concentration in Post-Emancipation Germany." *LBIY* 28 (1983): 471–95.

————. "The Pace of Modernization of German Jewry in the Nineteenth Century." *LBIY* 21 (1976): 41–56.

————. "The Rural Community and the Urbanization of German Jewry." *CEH* 13, no. 3 (Sept. 1980): 218–36.

————. "Voluntary and Involuntary Limitation of Fertility in Nineteenth-Century Bavarian Jewry." In Ritterband, *Modern Jewish Fertility,* 94–111.

————. "The Yiddish Written Word in Nineteenth-Century Germany." *LBIY* 25 (1979): 179–92.

McCagg, William O., Jr. *A History of Habsburg Jews, 1670–1918.* Bloomington, Ind., 1989.

Marrus, Michael. *The Holocaust in History.* Hanover, N.H., and London, 1987.

————. *The Politics of Assimilation: A Study of the French Jewish Community at the Time of the Dreyfus Affair.* Oxford, 1971.

————. "The Theory and Practice of Anti-Semitism." *Commentary* 40 (Aug. 1983), 38–42.

Marrus, Michael R., and Robert O. Paxton. *Vichy France and the Jews.* New York, 1983.

Martin, Bernd, and Ernst Schulin, eds. *Die Juden als Minderheit in der Geschichte.* Munich, 1981.

Massing, Paul W. *Rehearsal for Destruction: A Study of Political Anti-Semitism in Imperial Germany.* New York, 1949.

Matz, Klaus-Jürgen. *Pauperismus und Bevölkerung: Die gesetzlichen Ehebeschränkungen in den süddeutschen Staaten während des 19. Jahrhunderts.* Stuttgart, 1980.

Merkl, Peter. *Political Violence under the Swastika: 581 Early Nazis.* Princeton, N.J., 1975.

Michel, Thomas. *Die Juden in Gaukönigshofen/Unterfranken (1550–1942).* Wiesbaden, 1988.

Mistele, Karl. "Volkskundliche Aspekte traditioneller Judenfeindschaft." In Treml et al., *Geschichte,* 321–26.

Moeller, Robert G., ed. *Peasants and Lords in Modern Germany: Recent Studies in Agricultural History.* Boston, 1986.

Moldenauer, R[üdiger]. "Jewish Petitions to the German National Assembly in Frankfurt 1848/49." *LBIY* 16 (1971): 188–99.

Möller, Horst. "Aufklärung, Judenemanzipation." In *Jahrbuch des Instituts für deutsche Geschichte,* vol. 3, *Deutsche Aufklärung und Judenemanzipation,* 19–53. Tel Aviv, 1980.

Mommsen, Hans, ed. *Herrschaftsalltag im Dritten Reich: Studien und Texte.* Düsseldorf, 1988.

Mooser, Josef. "Property and Wood Theft: Agrarian Capitalism and Social Conflict in Rural Society, 1800–1850: A Westphalian Case Study." In Moeller, *Peasants,* 52–80.

Morgenstern, Friedrich. "Hardenberg and the Emancipation of Franconian Jewry." *JSS* 15 (1953): 253–74.

Mosse, George L. *The Crisis of German Ideology: Intellectual Origins of the Third Reich.* New York, 1964.

———. "Literature and Society in Germany." In G. Mosse, *Masses,* 21–51.

———. *Masses and Man: Nationalist and Fascist Perceptions of Reality.* Detroit, Mich., 1987.

———. "What Germans Really Read." In G. Mosse, *Masses,* 52–68.

Mosse, Werner E., Arnold Paucker, and Reinhard Rürup, eds. *Revolution and Evolution: 1848 in German-Jewish History.* Tübingen, 1981.

———. "The Revolution of 1848: Jewish Emancipation in Germany and Its Limits." In W. E. Mosse et al., *Revolution,* 389–401.

Müller, Arnd. *Geschichte der Juden in Nürnberg, 1146–1945.* Nürnberg, 1968.

Müller, Günther. *König Maximilian II und die soziale Frage.* Munich, 1964.

Muller, Jerry Z. "Communism, Anti-Semitism and the Jews." *Commentary* (Aug. 1988): 28–39.

———. "German Historians at War." *Commentary* 87 (May 1989): 33–41.

Niewyk, Donald. *The Jews in Weimar Germany.* Baton Rouge, La., 1980.

Nipperdey, Thomas. *Deutsche Geschichte 1800–1866: Bürgerwelt und starker Staat.* Munich, 1983.

———. "Verein als soziale Struktur im späten 18. und frühen 19. Jahrhundert." In *Geschichtswissenschaft und Vereinswesen im 19. Jahrhundert* (Göttingen, 1972): 1–44.

Nipperdey, Thomas, and R. Rürup. "Antisemitismus." In O. Brunner et al., *Geschichtliche Grundbegriffe,* 129–53.

Noelle-Neumann, Elizabeth. *Spiral of Silence: Public Opinion—Our Social Skin.* Chicago and London, 1984.

Oberman, Heiko A. *The Roots of Anti-Semitism in the Age of Renaissance and Reformation.* Trans. James I. Porter. Philadelphia, Pa., 1984.

Ophir, Baruch Z., and Falk Wiesemann, eds. *Die jüdischen Gemeinden in Bayern 1918–1945: Geschichte und Zerstörung.* Munich and Vienna, 1979.

Ophir, Baruch Z., et al., eds. *Pinkas Hakehillot: Encyclopedia of Jewish Communities from their Foundation till after the Holocaust. Germany—Bavaria.* Jerusalem, 1972.

Ostadel, Hubert. *Die Kammer der Reichsräthe in Bayern von 1819 bis 1848: Ein Beitrag zur Geschichte des Frühparlamentarismus.* Munich, 1968.

Paschen, Joachim. *Demokratische Vereine und preussischer Staat: Entwicklung und Unterdrückung der demokratischen Bewegung während der Revolution von 1848/49.* Munich and Vienna, 1977.

Pauley, Bruce F. *From Prejudice to Persecution: A History of Anti-Semitism.* Chapel Hill, N.C., 1992.

Pauer, Max. "Dr. Anton Ruland." *Mainfränkisches Jahrbuch für Geschichte und Kunst* 12 (1960): 305–11.

Peal, David. "Antisemitism by Other Means? The Rural Cooperative Movement in Late Nineteenth-Century Germany." *LBIY* 32 (1987): 135–53.

Pfundtner, Fritz. *Die Münchener politische Presse im Revolutionsjahre 1848.* Würzburg-Aumühle, 1939.

Phayer, Fintan Michael. "Lower-class Morality: The Case of Bavaria." *Journal of Social History* (Fall 1974): 79–95.

———. *Religion und das Gewöhnliche Volk in Bayern in der Zeit von 1750–1850.* Munich, 1970.

Poppel, Stephen M. *Zionism in Germany, 1897–1933: The Shaping of a Jewish Identity.* Philadelphia, Pa., 1977.

Preissler, Dietmar. *Frühantisemitismus in der Freien Stadt Frankfurt und im Grossherzogtum Hessen (1810 bis 1860).* Heidelberg, 1989.

Prestel, Claudia. *Jüdisches Schul- und Erziehungswesen in Bayern 1804–1933.* Göttingen, 1989.

Prinz, Arthur. *Juden im Deutschen Wirtschaftsleben: Soziale und wirtschaftliche Struktur im Wandel 1850–1914.* Tübingen, 1984.

Puhle, Hans-Jürgen. *Agrarische Interessenpolitik und preussischer Konservatismus im wilhelminischen Reich (1893–1914): Ein Beitrag zur Analyse des Nationalismus in Deutschland am Beispiel des Bundes der Landwirte und der Deutsch-Konservativen Partei.* Hanover, 1967.

———. *Von der Agrarkrise zum Präfaschismus: Thesen zum Stellenwert der agrarischen Interessenverbände des 19. Jahrhunderts.* Wiesbaden, 1972.

Püls, Detlev, ed. *Wahrnehmungsformen und Protestverhalten: Studien zur Lage der Unterschichten im 18. und 19. Jahrhundert.* Frankfurt am Main, 1979.

Pulzer, Peter G. J. *Jews and the German State: The Political History of a Minority, 1848–1933.* Oxford, 1992.

———. *The Rise of Political Anti-Semitism in Germany and Austria.* New York and London, 1964. 2d ed. Cambridge, Mass., 1988.

Rall, H. "Die politische Entwicklung von 1848 bis zur Reichsgründung 1871." *HbG* 4¹: 224–82.

Reinalter, Helmut, ed. *Demokratische und soziale Protestbewegungen in Mitteleuropa 1815–1848/49.* Frankfurt am Main, 1986.

Reinharz, Jehuda. *Fatherland or Promised Land: The Dilemma of the German Jew, 1893–1914.* Ann Arbor, Mich., 1975.

Remlein, Karl-Thomas. "Der Bayerische Landtag und die Judenemanzipation nach der Revolution." In Brandt, *Zwischen Schutzherrschaft,* 139–208.

Renda, Gerhard. "Fürth, das 'bayerische Jerusalem.'" In Treml et al., *Geschichte,* 225–36.

Retallack, James. "Anti-Semitism, Conservative Propaganda, and Regional Politics in Late Nineteenth Century Germany." *German Studies Review* 11, no. 3 (Oct. 1988): 377–403.

———. *Notables of the Right: The Conservative Party and Political Mobility in Germany, 1876–1918.* London, 1988.

Richarz, Monika, ed. "Emancipation and Continuity: German Jews in the Rural Economy." In W. E. Mosse et al., *Revolution,* 95–115.

———. "Jewish Social Mobility in Germany during the Time of Emancipation (1790–1871)." *LBIY* 20 (1975): 69–77.

Riff, Michael A. "The Government of Baden against Antisemitism: Political Expediency or Principle." *LBIY* 32 (1987): 119–34.

Ritterband, Paul, ed. *Modern Jewish Fertility.* Leiden, 1981.

Roeder, Elmar. *Der Konservative Journalist Ernst Zander und die politischen Kämpfe seines "Volksboten."* Munich, 1971.

Rose, Paul Lawrence. *Revolutionary Antisemitism in Germany: From Kant to Wagner.* Princeton, N.J., 1990.

Rosenberg, Hans. *Grosse Depression und Bismarckzeit: Wirtschaftsablauf, Gesellschaft und Politik in Mitteleuropa.* Berlin, 1967.

———. "Political and Social Consequences of the Great Depression of 1873–1896 in Central Europe." *Economic History Review* 13 (1943): 58–73.

Rosenfeld, Mosche N. "Jüdischer Buchdruck am Beispiel der Sulzbacher Druckerei." In Treml et al., *Geschichte,* 237–44.

Roth, Hans-Georg. "Entstehungsgeschichte des Bayerischen Senats: Tradition und Kontinuität des Bayerischen Zweikammersystems." *ZfbL* 40 (1977): 231–44.

Roth, Rainer A. "Historische Entwicklung und politische Bedeutung des Exekutivorgans in Bayern: Vom Herzoglichen Rat zur Staatsregierung des Freistaats Bayern." *ZfbL* 40 (1977): 191–230.

———. *Politische Bildung in Bayern: Eine historisch-Politische Untersuchung der Bemühungen um Politische Bildung an den Volksschulen Bayerns in der Zeit der Monarchie. Von Ludwig I. bis zur Gründung des Deutschen Reiches.* Munich, 1974.

Rude, George. *The Crowd in History.* New York, 1964.

———. *The Crowd in the French Revolution.* Oxford, 1959.

Rupieper, Hermann-Josef. "Die Sozialstruktur der Trägerschichten der Revolution von 1848/49 am Beispiel Sachsen." In H. Kaelble et al., eds., *Probleme der Modernisierung in Deutschland: Sozialhistorische Studien zum 19. und 20. Jahrhundert,* 80–109. Opladen, 1978.

Rürup, Reinhard. "Emancipation and Crisis: The 'Jewish Question' in Germany 1850–1890." *LBIY* 20 (1975): 13–25.

————. *Emanzipation und Antisemitismus: Studien zur "Judenfrage" der bürgerlichen Gesellschaft.* Göttingen, 1975.

————. "The European Revolutions of 1848 and Jewish Emancipation." In W. E. Mosse et al., *Revolution,* 1–53.

————. "German Liberalism and the Emancipation of the Jews." *LBIY* 20 (1975): 59–68.

————. "Kontinuität und Diskontinuität der 'Judenfrage' im 19. Jahrhundert: Zur Entstehung des modernen Antisemitismus." In Wehler, *Sozialgeschichte Heute,* 388–415.

Rürup, Reinhard, and T. Nipperdey. "Antisemitismus." In 0. Brunner et al., *Geschichtliche Grundbegriffe,* 129–53.

Sabean, David Warren. "The Communal Basis of Pre-1800 Peasant Uprisings in Western Europe." *Comparative Politics* 8, no. 3 (1976): 355–64.

————. *Power in the Blood: Popular Culture and Village Discourse in Early Modern Germany.* Cambridge, 1984.

————. *Property, Production, and Family in Neckarhausen, 1700–1870.* Cambridge, 1990.

Safely, Thomas Max. *Let No Man Put Asunder: Control of Marriage in the German Southwest.* Kirksville, Mo., 1984.

Sammons, Jeffrey L. *Wilhelm Raabe: The Fiction of the Alternative Community.* Princeton, N.J., 1987.

Saul, S. B. *The Myth of the Great Depression, 1873–1896.* London, 1972.

Scherg, Leonhard. "Homburg—Das Schicksal einer Jüdischen Kultusgemeinde auf den Land während des 19. und 20. Jahrhunderts." *Mainfränkisches Jahrbuch für Geschichte und Kunst* 35 (1983): 135–51.

Scheuner, Ulrich. "Volkssouveränität und Theorie der parlamentarische Vertretung: Zur Theorie der Volksvertretung in Deutschland 1815–1848." In Bosl, *Parlamentarismus,* 297–340.

Schleunes, Karl. *Schooling and Society: The Politics of Education in Prussia and Bavaria 1750–1900.* Oxford, New York, and Munich, 1989.

————. *The Twisted Road to Auschwitz: Nazi Policy Toward German Jews, 1933–1939.* Urbana, Chicago, and London, 1970.

Schmelz, Usiel 0. "Die demographische Entwicklung der Juden in Deutschland von der Mitte des 19. Jahrhunderts bis 1933." *Zeitschrift für Bevölkerungswissenschaft* 8, no. 1 (1982): 31–72.

Schmid, Anton. "Gemeinschafts- und Gemeinderechte im altbayerisch-schwäbischen Gebiet." *ZfbL* 4 (1931): 367–98.

Scholem, Gersom. "Noch Einmal: das deutsch-jüdische Gespräch." In *Judaica,* 3 vols. (Frankfurt am Main, 1970), 2:17.

————. "On the Social Psychology of the Jews in Germany: 1900–1933." In Bronson, 9–32.

Schönhoven, Klaus. "Der politische Katholizismus in Bayern unter der NS-Herrschaft 1933–1945." In Broszat, Fröhlich, and Wiesemann, *Bayern,* 5:541–646.

Schorsch, Emil. "The Rural Jew: Observations on the Paper of Werner J. Cahnman." *LBIY* 19 (1974): 131–33.

Schorsch, Ismar. "German Anti-Semitism in the Light of Post-War Historiography." *LBIY* 19 (1974): 257–71.

———. *Jewish Reactions to German Anti-Semitism, 1870–1914.* New York and London, 1972.

Schubert, Ernst. *Arme Leute: Bettler und Gauner im Franken des 18. Jahrhunderts.* Neustadt an der Aisch, 1983.

Schulte, Wilhelm. *Volk und Staat: Westfalen im Vormärz und in der Revolution 1848/49.* Regensburg and Münster, 1954.

Schwarz, Stefan. *Die Juden in Bayern im Wandel der Zeiten.* Munich and Vienna, 1963.

Schwentker, Wolfgang. *Konservative Vereine und Revolution in Preussen 1848/49: Die Konstituierung des Konservatismus als Partei.* Düsseldorf, 1988.

Seitz, Max. "Die Februar- und Märzunruhen in München 1848." *Oberbayerisches Archiv für vaterländische Geschichte* 78 (1953): 1–104.

Sepp, Dr. Johann Nepomuk. *Ein Bild seines Lebens nach seinen eigenen Aufzeich-nungen: Xenium zum hundtertsten Geburtstag (7 August 1916), 1 Teil. Von der Geburt bis zum Abschluss der öffentlichen Tätigkeit.* Regensburg, 1916.

Sheehan, James J. *German History: 1770–1866.* Oxford, 1989.

Shorter, Edward. *The Making of the Modern Family.* New York, 1975.

———. "Middle Class Anxiety in the German Revolution of 1848." *Journal of Social History* 2, no. 3 (Spring 1969): 189–215.

Siemann, Wolfram, ed. *Der 'Polizeiverein' deutscher Staaten: Eine Dokumentation zur Überwachung der Öffentlichkeit nach der Revolution von 1848/49.* Tübingen, 1983.

———. "Soziale Protestbewegungen in der deutschen Revolution von 1848/49." In Reinalter, *Protestbewegungen,* 305–26.

Silbergleit, Heinrich. *Die Bevölkerungs- und Berufsverhältnisse der Juden im Deutschen Reich.* Berlin, 1930.

Sorkin, David. *The Transformation of German Jewry, 1780–1840.* New York, 1987.

Sperber, Jonathan. *Popular Catholicism in Nineteenth-Century Germany.* Princeton, N.J., 1985.

———. *Rhineland Radicals: The Democratic Movement and the Revolution of 1848–1849.* Princeton, N.J., 1991.

Spindler, Max. "Die Konservative Periode 1832–1847." *HbG* 4[1]: 175–210.

———. "Die Regierungszeit Ludwigs I (1825–1848)." *HbG* 4[1]: 89–223.

———, ed. *Briefwechsel zwischen Ludwig I. von Bayern und Eduard von Schenk, 1823–1841.* Munich, 1930.

———, ed. *Handbuch der bayerischen Geschichte.* Vol. 4[1-2] *Das neue Bayern 1800–1970.* Munich, 1974.

Stegmann, Dirk. *Die Erben Bismarcks: Parteien und Verbände in der Spätphase des Wilhelminischen Deutschlands. Sammlungspolitik 1897–1918.* Cologne and Berlin, 1970.

Steinbach, Peter, ed. *Probleme politischen Partizipation in Modernisierungsprozess.* Stuttgart, 1982.

Sterling, Elonore 0. "Anti-Jewish Riots in Germany in 1819: A Displacement of Social Protest." *Historia Judaica* 12 (Oct. 1950): 105–42.

———. *Er ist wie Du: Aus der Frühgeschichte des Antisemitismus in Deutschland (1815–1850)*. Munich, 1956.

———. "Jewish Reactions to Jew-Hatred in the First Half of the Nineteenth Century." *LBIY* 3 (1958): 103–21.

———. *Judenhass: Die Anfänge des politischen Antisemitismus in Deutschland (1815–1850)*. Frankfurt am Main, 1969.

Stern, Carola, and Heinrich A. Winkler, eds. *Wendepunkte deutscher Geschichte*. Frankfurt am Main, 1979.

Stern, Fritz. "The Burden of Success: Reflections on German Jewry." In Stern, *Dreams*, 97–114.

———. *Dreams and Delusions: The Drama of German History*. New York, 1987.

———. *Gold and Iron: Bismarck, Bleichroeder, and the Building of the German Empire*. New York, 1977.

———. "The Integration of Jews in Nineteenth-Century Germany: Comments on the Papers of Lamar Cecil, Reinhard Rürup and Monika Richarz." *LBIY* 20 (1975): 79–83.

———. *The Politics of Cultural Despair*. Berkeley, 1961.

Stern, Menahem, ed. *Greek and Latin Authors on Jews and Judaism*. Vol. 2, *From Tacitus to Simplicius*. Jerusalem, 1980.

Stern, Wilhelm. "Die Juden in Unterfranken während der ersten Hälfte des 19. Jahrhunderts." *ZGJD* 6 (1935): 229–38.

Stern-Taeubler, Selma. "Der Literarische Kampf um die Emanzipation in den Jahren 1816–1820 und seine ideologischen und soziologischen Voraussetzungen." *Hebrew Union College Annual* 23, part 2 (1950–51): 171–96. KTAV reprint. New York, 1968.

Strauss, Berthold [Baruch]. *The Rosenbaums of Zell: A Study of a Family*. London, 1962.

Tal, Uriel. *Christians and Jews in Germany: Religion, Politics, and Ideology in the Second Reich, 1870–1914*. Trans. Noah Jacobs. Ithaca, N.Y., 1975.

Tannenbaum, William Zvi. "From Community to Citizenship: The Jews of Rural Franconia, 1801–1862." Ph.D. diss., Stanford University, June 1989.

Tenfelde, Klaus, and Helmut Trischler, eds. *Bis vor die Stufen des Throns: Bittschriften und Beschwerden von Bergleuten im Zeitalter der Industrialisierung*. Munich, 1986.

Thieme, Karl, ed. *Judenfeindschaft: Darstellungen und Analysen*. Frankfurt am Main, 1963.

Thränhardt, Dietrich. *Wahlen und politische Strukturen in Bayern 1848–1953: Historisch-soziologische Untersuchungen zum Entstehen und zur Neurrichtung eines Parteiensystems*. Düsseldorf, 1973.

Tilly, Charles. *The Contentious French*. Cambridge, Mass., 1986.

Toury, Jacob. "Der Eintritt der Juden ins deutsche Bürgertum." In Liebeschütz and Paucker, *Das Judentum*, 139–242.

————. *Der Eintritt der Juden ins Deutsche Bürgertum: Eine Dokumentation.* Tel Aviv, 1972.

————. "Jewish Manual Labour and Emigration: Records from Some Bavarian Districts (1830–1857)." *LBIY* 14 (1971): 45–62.

————. *Die politischen Orientierungen der Juden in Deutschland: Von Jena bis Weimar.* Tübingen, 1966.

————. "Die Revoution von 1848 als innerjüdischer Wendepunkt." In Liebeschütz and Paucker, *Das Judentum,* 359–76.

————. *Soziale und Politische Geschichte der Juden in Deutschland 1847–1871: Zwischen Revolution, Reaktion und Emanzipation.* Düsseldorf, 1977.

————. "Types of Jewish Municipal Rights in German Townships: The Problem of Local Emancipation." *LBIY* 22 (1977): 55–80.

Treitschke, Heinrich von. *Deutsche Geschichte im Neunzehnten Jahrhundert.* 5 vols. Leipzig, 1927.

Treml, Manfred. "Von der 'Judenmission' zur 'Bürgerlichen Verbesserung': Zur Vorgeschichte und Frühphase der Judenemanzipation in Bayern." In Treml et al., *Geschichte,* 247–65.

Treml, Manfred, Josepf Kirmeier, and Evamaria Brockhoff, eds. *Geschichte und Kultur der Juden in Bayern.* Munich, 1988.

Valentin, Veit. *Geschichte der deutschen Revolution von 1848–49.* Berlin, 1930–31. Reprint. Aalen, 1968.

Volkert, Wilhelm. "Die Juden im Fürstentum Pfalz-Neuburg." *ZfbL* 26³ (1963): 560–605.

Volkmann, Heinrich, and Jürgen Bergmann, eds. *Sozialer Protest: Studien zu traditioneller Resistenz und kollektiver Gewalt in Deutschland vom Vormärz bis zur Reichsgründung.* Opladen, 1984.

Volkov, Shulamit. "Antisemitism as a Cultural Code: Reflections on the History and Historiography of Antisemitism in Imperial Germany." *LBIY* 23 (1978): 25–46.

————. "Kontinuität und Diskontinuität im deutschen Antisemitismus 1878–1945." *Vierteljahrsheft für Zeitgeschichte* 33 (1985): 221–43.

————. *The Rise of Popular Anti-Modernism in Germany: The Urban Master Artisans, 1873–1896.* Princeton, N.J., 1978.

————. "The Written Word and the Spoken Word: On the Gap Between Pre-1914 and Nazi Anti-Semitism." In Furet, *Unanswered Questions,* 33–53.

Walker, Mack. *German Home Towns: Community, State, and General Estate 1648–1871.* Ithaca and London, 1971.

Wassermann, Rudolf. "Die Entwicklung der jüdischen Bevölkerung in Bayern im 19. Jahrhundert." *Zeitschrift für Demographie und Statistik der Juden* 1, no. 11 (Nov. 1905): 11–13.

Weber, Eugen. *Peasants into Frenchmen: The Modernization of Rural France, 1870–1914,* Stanford, Calif., 1976.

Weber-Kellermann, Ingeborg. *Landleben im 19. Jahrhundert.* Munich, 1987.

Wehler, Hans-Ulrich, ed. *Deutsche Gesellschaftsgeschichte.* Vol. 2, *Von der Reformära bis zur industriellen und politischen 'Deutschen Doppelrevolution,' 1815–1845/49.* Munich, 1987.

————. *Sozialgeschichte Heute: Festschrift für Hans Rosenberg zum 70. Geburtstag.* Göttingen, 1974.

Weill, Georges. "French Jewish Historiography: 1789–1870." In Frances Malino and Bernard Wasserstein, eds., *The Jews in Modern France*, 313–27. Hanover and London, 1985.

Weis, Eberhard. "Die Begründung des modernen bayerischen Staates unter König Max I (1799–1825)." *HbG* 4^1: 1–88.

————. *Montgelas, 1759–1799: Zwischen Revolution und Reform.* Munich, 1971.

————. ed., with Elisabeth Müller-Luckner. *Reformen im rheinbündischen Deutschland.* Munich, 1984.

Wertheimer, Jack. *Unwelcome Strangers: East European Jews in Imperial Germany.* New York and Oxford, 1987.

Wiesemann, Falk. *Bibliographie zur Geschichte der Juden in Bayern.* Munich and New York, 1989.

————. "Fränkische Dorfsynagogen." *Volkskunst. Zeitschrift für volkstümliche Sachkultur* 4 (Nov. 1981): 234–41.

————. "Rabbiner und jüdische Lehrer in Bayern während der ersten Hälfte des 19. Jahrhunderts: Staat-Reform-Orthodoxie." In Treml et al., *Geschichte*, 277–86.

————. *Die Vorgeschichte der nationalsozialistischen Machtübernahme in Bayern 1932–1933.* Berlin, 1975.

Winkler, Heinrich A. "1866 und 1878: Der Machtverzicht des Bürgertums." In C. Stern and H. A. Winkler, *Wendepunkte*, 37–60.

Wirtz, Rainer. "Die Begriffsverwirrung der Bauern im Odenwald 1848: Odenwälder 'Excesse' und die Sinsheimer 'republikanische Schilderhebung.'" In Püls, *Wahrnehmungsformen*, 81–104.

Zimmermann, Moshe. "Two Generations in the History of German Antisemitism: The Letters of Theodor Fritsch to Wilhelm Marr." *LBIY* 23 (1978): 89–99.

————. *Wilhelm Marr: The Patriarch of Antisemitism.* New York and Oxford, 1986.

Zittel, Bernhard. "Die Volksstimmung im Dritten Reich im Spiegel der Geheimberichte des Regierungs-präsidenten von Ober- und Mittelfranken." *Jahrbuch für Fränkische Landesforschung* 34/35 (1975): 1059–1078.

Zmarzlik, Hans-Günter. "Antisemitismus im Deutschen Kaiserreich 1871–1918." In Martin and Schulin, 249–70.

Zorn, Wolfgang. "Die sozialentwicklung der nicht-agrarischen Welt (1806–1970)." *HbG* 4^1: 846–82.

————. "Die wirtschaftliche Struktur Bayerns um 1820." In Albrecht et al., *Festschrift*, 611–31.

Zucker, Stanley. "Ludwig Bamberger and the Rise of Anti-Semitism in Germany, 1848–1893" *CEH* 3, no. 4 (Dec. 1970): 332–52.

————. *Ludwig Bamberger: German Liberal Politician and Social Critic, 1823–1899.* Pittsburgh, Pa. 1975.

Index

DATE DUE

SEP 1 8 1995	X		
AUG 2 3 1995			